MW00650945

Introduction to Criminalistics

Introduction to Criminalistics

The Foundation of Forensic Science

Barry A. J. Fisher
Los Angeles County Sheriff's Department
Los Angeles, California

William J. Tilstone
Forensic Science Solutions International
Auchterarder, Scotland, U.K.

Catherine Woytowicz
Department of Chemistry
The George Washington University
Washington, DC

AMSTERDAM • BOSTON • HEIDELBERG • LONDON
NEW YORK • OXFORD • PARIS • SAN DIEGO
SAN FRANCISCO • SINGAPORE • SYDNEY • TOKYO
Academic press is an imprint of Elsevier

Cover Credits:

Crime scene at water edge: Courtesy Barry Fisher, Los Angeles County Sheriff's Crime Laboratory

Fire: Stockxpert (Figure 9.1); Bullet: Courtesy Barry Fisher, Los Angeles County Sheriff's Crime Laboratory; Ecstasy tablets: Courtesy DEA (http://www.usdoj.gov/dea/images_ecstasy.html)

Golf ball: Courtesy of BVDA INTERNATIONAL (http://www.bvda.com/EN/sect1/en_1_6c.html); Wool: Modified from http://en.wikipedia.org/wiki/Image:ESEM_color_wool.jpg; Shoe print in snow: Stockxpert

Elsevier Academic Press
30 Corporate Drive, Suite 400, Burlington, MA 01803, USA
525 B Street, Suite 1900, San Diego, California 92101-4495, USA
84 Theobald's Road, London WC1X 8RR, UK

This book is printed on acid-free paper. ♾

Library of Congress Cataloging-in-Publication Data
Fisher, Barry A. J.
   Introduction to criminalistics: the foundation of forensic science / Barry A. J. Fisher,
   Catherine Woytowicz, William J. Tillstone.
      p. cm.
   Includes index.
   ISBN 978-0-12-088591-6 (hardcover : alk. paper) 1. Forensic sciences.
2. Criminal investigation.   I. Woytowicz, Catherine.   II. Title.
   HV8073.F488 2009
   363.25--dc22

                                                                                    2008040347

British Library Cataloguing in Publication Data
A catalogue record for this book is available from the British Library

ISBN 13: 978-0-12-088591-6

For all information on all Elsevier Academic Press publications
visit our Web site at www.elsevierdirect.com

Printed in China

09 10 9 8 7 6 5 4 3 2 1

Working together to grow libraries in developing countries

www.elsevier.com | www.bookaid.org | www.sabre.org

ELSEVIER   BOOK AID International   Sabre Foundation

To our families and to those whose daily use of science in the quest for justice identifies the guilty, protects the innocent, and benefits the victims.

Contents

vii

Contents

viii

Foreword

The landscape of forensic science education has changed dramatically in the past decade. We have experienced an evolution from a field directed primarily at educating Criminal Justice majors to an era of growing numbers of programs directed at science majors. *The Technical Working Group on Education and Training* (TWGED) was established in the United States by the National Institute of Justice to formulate recommended standards for forensic science education. As a follow-up to TWGED, the American Academy of Forensic Sciences established *The Forensic Science Education Programs Accreditation Commission* (FEPAC), which now accredits bachelor's and master's degree programs in the United States.

The most widely used and readily available introductory textbook over the past thirty years has targeted criminal justice majors. The growing popularity of forensic science programs for scientists has created a demand for textbooks that introduce forensic science to freshman and sophomore science majors. Barry Fisher, Catherine Woytowicz, and William Tilstone have pooled their many years of experience as forensic scientists and laboratory administrators to write an outstanding entry text that targets science majors. *Introduction to Criminalistics* has several important features that will make it enjoyable for both students and professors. Many of the chapters have a section titled "Central Questions" that introduces the student to the current status of a particular type of evidence. Each chapter contains a concise chapter summary, a problem set, and a glossary that will help the student identify the most important points. Numerous well-chosen case studies stir interest in the topics and separate boxes address interesting and important details. The format is efficient with little unnecessary verbiage, making it much easier than in most texts to identify salient material.

It is important that teachers have textbooks that are commensurate with their teaching styles and the knowledge base of their students. *Introduction to Criminalistics* is a welcome addition for introducing this exciting field to prospective forensic scientists.

Charles "Chris" Tindall
Professor, Department of Chemistry
Metropolitan State College of Denver

Preface

The story of the book began with a chance meeting between two of us, Barry Fisher and Catherine Woytowicz, in the hallways of the American Chemical Society. Barry was attending a meeting of the Council of Scientific Society Presidents in Washington, DC, and Catherine was serving as the ACS's Science Policy Fellow. Over subsequent coffee meeting conversations the two former colleagues (Catherine having worked for Barry at the Los Angeles County Sheriff's Crime Laboratory) reached an agreement to pursue this book. It was realized that translating the concept to reality needed more resources, and Bill Tilstone, a long-standing professional colleague and friend of Barry, was roped into the project.

So why another forensic science textbook? As teachers, case-workers, and managers in forensic science, we were united and motivated by the vision that our combined expertise could give something extra to the growing number of students with an interest in the subject.

Forensic science is a very diverse and complex subject. The book is organized pretty much along the lines of a conventional full-service crime laboratory, but there are other applications of science to legal or regulatory matters. Examples include DNA testing to explore family history, toxicology testing to ensure that the outcomes of horse races are not prejudiced by administration of drugs, analysis of air and water to ensure that manufacturing plants are disposing of toxic wastes safely, and the gathering of intelligence to identify and circumvent terrorist attacks.

The testing is likewise varied. Matching patterns, a skill we learn at a very young age, is important to many aspects of criminalistics from identifying a fingerprint to crime scene reconstruction. Observation and documentation are key. At the other end of the complexity spectrum, rapid and effective transfer of Nobel Prize-winning technologies has been vital in the application of DNA to identify who left blood or semen or sweat at a crime scene.

We hope that you enjoy studying criminalistics and that this book will help make the subject clear and interesting. Good luck if you choose to make a career of it!

Barry A. J. Fisher
William J. Tilstone
Catherine Woytowicz

SECTION I
Introduction, Field and Laboratory

From top left, clockwise: Protection of the scene is vital, and often law enforcement officers and crime scene technicians will seal off access using crime scene tape with a message such as "Police Line Do Not Cross." The scene of a violent crime will often contain shed blood. Evidence collected at the scene is packaged in a way that will prevent loss or contamination and reveal unrecorded attempts to access it: Red or blue "evidence tape" that is impossible to peel away without damaging it is often used. Sometimes physical objects with an obvious evidential value are found; this handgun can be tested for fingerprints and DNA to attempt to identify the shooter, and bullets and cartridge cases from fired ammunition can be compared to those in the NIBIN database to see if the weapon has a history of criminal use. Fingerprints, whether obvious ones in blood as shown here or latents developed using a variety of techniques, have been the mainstay of scene evidence used to identify perpetrators for more than 100 years. Image from Stockxpert.

CHAPTER 1
Forensic Science: Scope and Perspective

WHAT IS FORENSIC SCIENCE?

Forensic has several meanings, one of which pertains to courts of judicature. However, Webster includes "relating to or dealing with the application of scientific knowledge to legal problems" in its more modern definition. The application can be in one or more of many specific fields of study or branch of specialized knowledge such as science, technology, medicine, or other area of knowledge used to assist courts to resolve disputes, whether criminal, civil, or administrative. The term used in the book title is **criminalistics**, which is the application of forensic science to criminal matters. The term *criminology* is sometimes inaccurately used as a synonym for criminalistics but refers to the social science study of crime and criminal behavior, whereas criminalistics is the application of science to the solution of crimes.

Physical Evidence

In practice, "the application of science to the solution of crimes" is the examination of **physical evidence** in the field or the crime laboratory. Physical evidence consists of tangible articles such as hairs, fibers, latent fingerprints, and biological material. The strength of criminalistics lies in the reliability and objectivity of the scientific testing. The objectivity is a distinguishing feature of physical evidence from testimonial evidence such as written statements or the spoken word from the victims or witnesses.

Some evidence will be absolute, in that the examination reveals direct information about its identity and therefore its role in the crime being examined. Examples include Documents (Chapter 5); Drugs and Toxicology (Chapters 8 and 10); Explosives and Accelerants (Chapter 9); and Digital Evidence (Appendix B). Many times, however, samples removed from the crime scene are tested to produce evidence of association between people and places or objects, between different objects, or between people and other people. Examples include Tool Mark and Impression Evidence (Chapter 2); Firearms (Chapter 3); Fingerprints (Chapter 4);

Physical Evidence (Chapter 6); Hair and Fiber (Chapter 7); Biology (Chapter 11); DNA (Chapter 12); and Personal Effects (Appendix A).

> ## BOX 1.1 LOCARD'S EXCHANGE PRINCIPLE
>
> The principle underlying the value of testing associative evidence is that every time someone enters an environment, something is added to and removed from it. This concept has become known as **Locard's exchange principle**, named after the French criminalist Dr. Edmond Locard, who wrote several treatises in the 1920s postulating that microscopic examination of clothing and other physical evidence could reveal information about the history of the wearer. However, he never actually enunciated the principle, and its value is tempered by factors such as loss of transferred materials, contamination, and the extent to which the material is common throughout the environment of interest. Locard and others have called physical evidence the "silent witness," and it can provide valuable information as to the circumstances of a crime.

INCEPTIVE EVIDENCE

Physical evidence may be a vital element in proving there was a crime, as in the case of identification of drugs in dealing or possession offenses, and the identification of accelerant in arson. Evidence used to show whether or not a crime has been committed is known as **inceptive evidence**. Inceptive evidence seldom also contains identification or associative evidence information.

4

FIGURE 1.1
Types of evidence.
Clockwise from top:
Identity evidence,
fingerprint kit used to
dust surfaces to visualize
latent fingerprints.
Inceptive evidence,
seized blocks of cocaine
providing evidence of
drug dealing. Associative
evidence, photograph
of vehicle involved in
a hit-and-run collision
showing damage to
headlamp, paintwork,
and windshield, all of
which could be sources
of trace evidence
transferred to the victim.
Cocaine blocks, U.S.
federal government,
DEA. Fingerprint kit,
image from Stockxpert.
Vehicle image, courtesy
of Foster and Freeman.

IDENTIFICATION EVIDENCE

Physical evidence may help identify someone, as with fingerprints and DNA testing and databases. It is generally accepted that fingerprints (Chapter 4) and DNA profiles (Chapter 12) are sufficiently close to unique to provide compelling evidence of identity. However, it is important to be aware that the only absolute conclusion that can be drawn from physical evidence is that of non-identity, when the testing excludes a putative source as the origin of the physical artifact. Firearms (Chapter 3) and questioned documents (Chapter 5) are particular forms of **identification evidence** where the objective of the testing is to identify the weapon that fired a bullet or the person or machine responsible for creation of a document.

ASSOCIATIVE AND CORROBORATIVE EVIDENCE

As described previously, a common reason for testing physical evidence is to explore whether or not people and objects have been in contact with each other. The strength of this **associative evidence** depends on several things, including the circumstances of the case and how unique the material is that has been transferred. In the absence of an exclusion, physical evidence falls into the category of **corroborative evidence** providing support to testimonial or other physical evidence. Consider the situation where a rape victim nominates a man as her assailant. A DNA match between semen on a swab from the victim and the DNA of the suspect is a powerful corroboration indeed, but before the introduction of DNA, blood groups identified from tests on these samples might have matched but also have been found in 50% of the population — not very compelling yet not a result that refutes the testimonial evidence of the victim. And even the DNA evidence has its limitations: It proves intercourse between the two; however, intercourse is a crime only when there is no consent, and DNA is silent in that regard.

THE CRIME SCENE

Everything that happens at the crime laboratory concerning the scientific examination of physical evidence begins with the criminal act — at the crime scene. The crime scene therefore is the start of any forensic science investigation. Crime scenes may be indoors or outdoors. They may be expansive or quite small. In the case of a violent crime, the assailant's body is also a crime scene.

Evidence is collected by any number of different personnel, depending on the nature of the crime. In less serious crimes, the first officer to arrive at the scene may collect evidence. In more serious or complex crime scene investigations, specialized personnel such as crime scene investigators and sometimes forensic scientists may be used. It generally depends on the resources of the investigating agency.

Scene Processing

Processing the scene follows a fairly consistent methodology. The scene must be well documented and the location of evidence recorded. This is done by

No evidence of contact is not evidence of no contact. Physical evidence such as fibers, soil, gunshot residues, paint, and glass fragments all can be transferred on contact — but they all redistribute on, and are lost from, the recipient surface. Depending on the nature of the materials and the elapsed time since contact, little or no transferred traces may be detected. Finding no transferred materials must not be taken as disproving contact. Exclusions can be based only on finding something that could not have originated from the nominated source.

5

> ## BOX 1.2 THE CRIME SCENE
>
> The essential elements of successful crime scene investigation are
> - Protection of the scene against contamination, degradation, and loss of evidence
> - **Documentation** of the scene to ensure the integrity of identification of samples and the place where they were found
> - Systematic searching to ensure identification and collection of relevant evidence
> - Appropriate collection, packaging, and labeling of evidence
>
> In some cases with outside scenes, special steps will need to be taken to ensure one or more of the requirements is met. For example, it may be necessary to erect a tent to protect a scene from rain and wind, or physical marks such as tire tracks in snow may need to be given priority before the integrity of the mark is lost.

FIGURE 1.2
Documenting and collecting evidence from the scene. A crime scene officer from the Los Angeles County Sheriff's Department identifying the locations of firearms evidence at an outdoor scene and collecting handgun for subsequent laboratory investigation. Image courtesy of LACS Crime Laboratory.

a variety of procedures: crime scene sketches, photography, videography, and, more recently, using laser-computer-assisted surveying devices. The point of this effort is to capture how the scene appeared after the crime was committed in hopes of reconstructing it, i.e, figuring out what happened and noting the location of physical evidence present at the scene.

Large scenes may be searched using one of several orderly approaches. Two common patterns are

- Spirals working outward from a focal point
- Lanes in which the scene is divided into lateral or lengthwise segments

A smaller outdoor scene or an indoor scene such as a house can be methodically searched by areas or rooms, starting from the perimeter access point.

Vehicles can be searched on-site at the scene or transported to a garage or workshop. In the latter case, it may be advisable to conduct a preliminary search of the outside of the vehicle before removing it to the workshop so that evidence is not lost during the transportation process. On the other hand, a thorough search of a vehicle can involve methodical dismantling of the body-work, for example, in locating concealed drugs.

Generally, the most fragile evidence is collected first. Thus, photographs are taken before anything is moved. Fingerprints are often collected next, as they may be accidently destroyed. Next, small and even microscopic items of evidence are collected. The process may take a few hours to, in some cases, several days, depending on the nature of the scene. Sometimes time is of the essence, such as in a rain shower or when the scene is on

FIGURE 1.3
Crime scene investigators recording a crime scene by video. The video is being taken at some distance from the scene to set the physical placement context, and the officers will move closer for the next clip. The tree and the "School Children" sign (the scene is in the UK) identify the location of the filming. Note the protective clothing worn by the crime scene technicians even at a distance from the actual scene. Image from http://commons. wikimedia.org/wiki/ Image:ForensicsScene. jpg#file.

a busy highway or intersection. Experience, flexibility, and the nature of each case dictate how one may proceed. Each case has the possibility of being totally different from anything anyone has ever seen. Above all, cooperation and team-work are key.

Preservation of Evidence

Crime scene personnel need to be aware of the potential that they possess to contaminate the scene. Protective clothing such as Tyvek paper suits (see Figure 1.3), mouth masks, hair nets, latex or nitrile gloves, sleeve protectors, and shoe covers are essential when examining a scene where biological or trace evidence may be collected. Aids such as an alternate light source (see Chapter 6, "Physical Evidence") or fingerprint collection kits may need to be deployed.

Entry and egress points need to be controlled to prevent damage to marks (Chapter 2) or introduction of misleading marks from investigator footwear or vehicles.

Collected evidence must be packaged correctly. Biological samples should be collected dry, or if that is not possible, placed in paper bags; in order to prevent development of molding, they must never be placed in plastic bags. Weapons require special care to prevent accidental discharge of firearms or damage to or from knives.

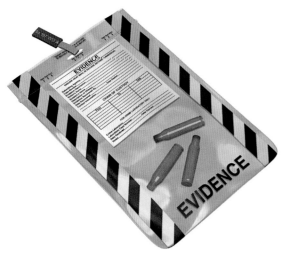

Drug laboratories are highly specialized scenes with many hazards including reaction chemicals, highly potent drug products, and even deliberate placement of booby traps.

Evidence such as clothing must be placed in packages that are completely sealed in a manner that prevents loss or contamination of contents, and the packages must be labeled with a unique identification that is recorded in the scene log. Seals should be made with material that will show when an attempt to tamper with the closure has been made. In the case of larger items, evidence areas can be protected by taping paper over the area of interest. Smaller trace materials can be removed by taping, vacuuming through a filter, or scraping (Chapter 6).

FIGURE 1.4
Evidence bag. This bag is made from strong plastic and is very suitable for nonbiological materials. In this case it is obvious that the evidence consists of cartridge cases. However, note the space on the label for chain of custody information as well as that for identification. The bag will be sealed with tamper-evident tape. Image from Stockxpert.

8

Chain of Custody

Every item removed from the scene and taken to the laboratory must be identified in a way that guarantees its integrity. It must have a unique marking that can be used to identify its history from collection to disposal.

PROVISION OF FORENSIC SERVICES

Crime Laboratory Services

Crime laboratory services are delivered in a wide variety of ways. The American model varies from state to state and is different from most other systems throughout the world. The United States maintains a federal delivery system and a state–local system, each with differing yet occasionally overlapping jurisdictions. Most of the crimes are committed within state jurisdictions. Federal violations are typically interstate crimes and federal crimes, for example, counterfeiting and smuggling. Federal investigators and their forensic science laboratories, such as the FBI and the Drug Enforcement Administration, investigate these crimes while local jurisdictions rely on state or local crime laboratories in the majority of criminal investigations.

FIGURE 1.5
The FBI laboratory building at Quantico, VA. Opened in April 2003, the FBI laboratory provides a wide range of analytical and investigative services, including all the topics described in the individual chapters in this book. Image published by the U.S. federal government (FBI).

State and municipal forensic science services are provided for in different ways depending on the region of the country. Most forensic science or crime laboratories are under the jurisdiction of police or sheriff's departments. Some come under prosecutor's offices, and others are part of medical examiner or coroner offices. A few states have forensic science departments that are not directly affiliated with police or prosecutorial offices. Most crime laboratories provide services at no charge.

Crime laboratories vary in the range of services that they provide. Most of the medium to larger size facilities offer "full service" operations. These are essentially the tests described in this book, namely:

- Tool marks and pattern evidence (Chapter 2), often provided as part of the firearms section (Chapter 3) and sometimes provided by law enforcement personnel not part of the crime laboratory
- Fingerprints (Chapter 4), and as with tool marks, sometimes provided by law enforcement personnel not part of the crime laboratory
- Documents (Chapter 5), one area that has seen a decline in its presence in public laboratories in recent times but that has an active private sector presence, especially for civil work
- Physical evidence (Chapter 6) and hair and fibers (Chapter 7), often combined into "trace evidence" but an area that has changed from dominating associative evidence to become less significant with the almost explosive growth of DNA
- Controlled substances (Chapter 8)
- Arson and explosives (Chapter 9), often described as "chemical trace" and sometimes combined with the paint and glass work of the physical evidence section
- Toxicology (Chapter 10), often restricted to alcohol and mainly found in the very largest crime laboratories and medical examiner–coroner facilities
- Biology (Chapter 11) and DNA (Chapter 12), with biology being mainly pre-DNA screening; DNA is also the area of criminalistics that has the greatest volume of delivery from the private sector, but mainly in the form of analysis of reference samples for DNA databasing
- Digital evidence (Appendix B)

Specialist areas such as terrorist and civilian bomb scene analysis are conducted mainly by federal units, including the Bureau of Alcohol, Tobacco, and Firearms; other specialist techniques such as bloodstain pattern analysis are found mainly in larger crime scene units attached to law enforcement rather than crime laboratory sections.

Death Investigation

Death investigation is under the purview of the medical examiner or coroner's office, which has the responsibility to determine the manner and mode of death. That task is the responsibility of the forensic pathologist.

Some medical examiner and coroner offices are large enough to maintain postmortem forensic toxicology services to examine tissue for the presence of drugs. Alternatively, that service may be performed by the crime lab or private laboratories.

QUALITY ASSURANCE AND PROFESSIONAL ISSUES

It should be obvious that the test results and conclusion of forensic science work are important to the outcome of police investigations. Appalling things can happen if mistakes are made in the lab. The wrong person has been sent to prison and in some instances executed because of improper work. It is no stretch of the imagination to suggest that if an innocent person is convicted, the guilty may continue to commit crimes. The consequences are significant, and the public has an interest in first-rate forensic science work being done in criminal investigations.

How can the criminal justice system and the public be assured of quality forensic science? Consider hospitals as a benchmark. It is doubtful that anyone would deliberately go to a nonaccredited hospital for a medical procedure. Similarly, patients would be averse to using non-board-certified physicians to perform surgeries. Forensic science laboratories and practitioners should be viewed in the same fashion.

Accreditation

In August 2004, the American Bar Association adopted the following resolution (which is part of a larger series of recommendations) on forensic evidence:

> The American Bar Association urges federal, state, local and territorial governments to reduce the risk of convicting the innocent, while increasing the likelihood of convicting the guilty, by adopting the following principles: Crime laboratories and medical examiner offices should be accredited, examiners should be certified, and procedures should be standardized and published to ensure the validity, reliability, and timely analysis of forensic evidence.

Accreditation, **certification**, and **proficiency testing** are the corner stones to an effective quality assurance program in a forensic science laboratory. While no program can guarantee a process to be totally error free, a well run quality assurance program lessens the chances for errors to occur. In the United States, quality assurance programs are largely voluntary. A few states require their public crime laboratories to be accredited.

There are two accreditation programs for crime labs in existence today in the United States, both based around ISO 17025. The American Society of Crime Laboratory Directors/Laboratory Accreditation Board (ASCLD/LAB) program is the oldest specialist crime laboratory accreditation program in the world. A more recent accreditation program for forensic science based on an internationally accepted standard for the competency of testing laboratories was introduced in 1999 by Forensic Quality Services, and a similar program is now also offered by ASCLD/LAB. Programs for toxicology laboratories and for medical examiners are offered by the American Board of Forensic Toxicology and the National Association of Medical Examiners, respectively.

Certification

In contrast to accreditation, which is focused on the overall quality system implemented by the laboratory, certification deals with credentialing individual practitioners and demonstrating competency in various forensic disciplines. Certification of forensic scientists, like accreditation of crime laboratories, is largely a voluntary program. Some forensic science laboratories use certification as a means to evaluate competency to promote practitioners from entry-level positions to journeyman-level positions

The American Board of Criminalistics (ABC) defines certification as

> a voluntary process of peer review by which a practitioner is recognized as having attained the professional qualifications necessary to practice in one or more disciplines of criminalistics

ABC has earned wide acceptance in the forensic science community in forensic chemistry, forensic biology, and criminalistics-related areas.

Other organizations that offer certifications in related fields are the International Association for Identification (IAI) and the American Board of Forensic Toxicology (ABFT). The ABC, IAI, ABFT, and other credentialing bodies are well regarded in the forensic science community, and practitioners who work toward these certifications often show great promise in the forensic field. However, not all certifying bodies have shown the same degree of professionalism. The American Academy of Forensic Sciences (AAFS) established the American Specialties Accreditation Board as an independent body to accredit certifying bodies.

Proficiency Testing

If laboratory accreditation and individual certification are essential elements to quality in forensic science, proficiency testing helps to demonstrate that labs and examiners maintain a level of competency in their field. Proficiency tests are manufactured, made-to-look-like-evidence tests. They are available for purchase from external vendors, can be produced by other forensic labs, or prepared by the forensic lab.

There are a few different types of proficiency tests that forensic labs use: blind, declared, and re-examination tests. Blind samples are tests that are made to appear like casework and are created so that examiners do not know they are being tested. Outwardly, blind tests look like any other case.

Blind proficiency tests lend themselves to high-volume cases such as drug and toxicology casework. They are easily prepared and simple to introduce into the lab as casework. Blind proficiency

FIGURE 1.6
The Forensic Specialties Accreditation Board. The FSAB is an initiative of the American Academy of Forensic Sciences to ensure oversight of the quality of certification programs. The program provides a way for forensic science organizations and the community as a whole to assess, recognize, and monitor organizations or professional boards that certify individual forensic scientists or other forensic specialists. Courtesy FSAB.

11

tests do present some difficulties as tests for evidence in major crime cases. Often, labs have backlogs in their major crime cases, that is, homicides, rapes, and assaults. As a consequence, the way in which crime labs prioritize such cases is to triage them. The most serious cases, cases with court dates, high profile cases, and so on, are given priority and examined first. Often, examiners contact detectives to decide what work needs to be done on a given case or if the case is still active. For blind proficiency testing to work, detectives, and in some cases, prosecutors, have to "play along" and convince the examiner that the examination is really needed.

In addition to having detectives and prosecutors participate in keeping a blind proficiency test program "blind," another issue concerns types of evidence placed into state or national databases. Part of the DNA testing protocol involves entering results into CODIS, the national DNA database. Naturally, these samples need to be "flagged" and the results removed at some point.

While some who are unfamiliar with case management or forensic lab operations suggest that blind proficiency testing is a viable solution to enhanced laboratory performance, others recognize that these practices are often difficult to manage and cause undue burdens on already over burdened forensic laboratories.

SUMMARY

Forensic science is the application of scientific knowledge to legal problems. Criminalistics is the application of forensic science to criminal matters.

Physical evidence consists of tangible materials. The strength of criminalistics lies in the reliability and objectivity of the scientific testing.

Evidence may include documents, drugs, biological fluids, tool marks, fingerprints, firearms, DNA, or even personal effects.

Locard's exchange principle posits that every time someone enters an environment, something is added to and removed from it.

Inceptive evidence is used to show whether or not a crime has been committed. Identification evidence is sufficiently close to unique to provide compelling evidence of identity. Corroborative evidence supports testimonial or other physical evidence.

The absence of evidence is not the evidence of absence.

The crime scene is the start of any forensic science investigation. Evidence may be collected by different personnel under different circumstances; however, the steps to processing a crime scene are generally the same:

- Secure the scene against contamination, degradation, and loss of evidence
- Document the scene
- Search the scene and collect relevant evidence
- Package, label, transport the evidence to the lab

Documentation captures the scene after the crime was committed—noting the location of physical evidence present—so that a reconstruction may be attempted. Methods of documentation include sketches, photography, videography, or laser-sighted computer-assisted surveying devices.

Large crime scenes may require **pattern searches**. Two common methods are spirals working outward from a focal point and "lanes" in which the scene is divided into lateral or lengthwise segments.

Collected evidence must be collected and packaged correctly. For example, wet biological samples should be placed in paper bags and firearms must be secured to prevent accidental discharge. Trace materials can be removed by taping, vacuuming through a filter, or scraping.

Every item removed from the scene and taken to the laboratory must be identified in a way that guarantees its integrity.

Crime laboratories vary in the range of services that they provide. Processing may include:

- Tool marks and pattern evidence
- Firearms
- Fingerprints
- Documents
- Physical evidence (paint, glass, etc.)
- Hair and fibers
- Controlled substances
- Arson and explosives
- Toxicology
- Biological samples and DNA
- Digital evidence

Accreditation, certification, and proficiency testing are the corner stones to an effective quality assurance program in a forensic science laboratory.

13

PROBLEMS

1. Give the word or phrase for the following definitions:
   a. the application of scientific knowledge to legal problems
   b. the application of forensic science to criminal matters.
   c. evidence used to show whether or not a crime has been committed.
   d. evidence consisting of tangible materials.
   e. evidence supporting testimonial or other physical evidence.
   f. a process which ensures the quality of a laboratory or facility.
2. Explain Locard's exchange principle.
3. Describe the steps to processing a crime scene.
4. Describe several methods of documentation.
5. Describe two common methods of searching.
6. Describe the process of removing evidence from a crime scene.
7. Name seven types of evidence.
8. Describe the uses of accreditation, certification, and proficiency testing.

GLOSSARY

Accreditation ensures the quality of a laboratory or facility.

Certification ensures the quality of a forensic examiner.

Criminalistics the application of forensic science to criminal matters.

Documentation sketches, photography, videography, or laser-sighted computer-assisted surveying to capture the scene after a crime was committed—noting the location of physical evidence present so that a reconstruction may be attempted.

Forensic science the application of scientific knowledge to legal problems.

Identification evidence evidence sufficiently close to unique to provide compelling evidence of identity.

Inceptive evidence evidence used to show whether or not a crime has been committed.

Locard's exchange principle every time someone enters an environment, something is added to and removed from it.

Pattern searches methods to search large crime scenes.

Physical evidence tangible materials; physical evidence may include documents, drugs, biological fluids, tool marks, fingerprints, firearms, DNA, or personal effects.

Proficiency testing evidence manufactured to look like a real case to test forensic examiners' abilities.

SECTION II
Pattern Evidence

Examples of pattern evidence. Clockwise from top: Marks in cheese made by damaged slices; hold-up note compared to torn-off papers; tire tracks in snow; technician lifting sole impression from shoe. Cheese and hold-up note original work of author; tire track from Stockxpert; footprint courtesy of Los Angeles County Sheriff's crime laboratory.

CHAPTER 2

Introduction to Pattern Evidence: Tool Marks and Impressions

Case Study

The Wood-Chipper Homicide

Helle Crafts lived with her husband Richard and three children near Newtown, Connecticut. But all was not well with the Crafts, despite their glamorous life: She was an attractive blond Danish-born flight attendant, and he was a pilot. Helle believed that Richard was cheating on her and hired a private investigator to check it out. The investigator, Keith Mayo, became concerned at a cessation of contact with his client and called the Newtown police on December 1, 1986, to report that Helle had disappeared and he feared she might have been murdered by her husband. The police investigated and were informed by Richard that he had not seen his wife since November 19, when she left to visit her sister. At first the police were not overly concerned, but that changed as their interviews produced evidence of Richard's infidelity. When he agreed to take, and passed, a lie detector test, they were inclined to treat the matter as a missing person case.

Further inquiries revealed inconsistencies in Richard's accounts of events around the time of Helle's disappearance. The police and Keith Mayo began to dig deeper, almost literally in Mayo's case, as he searched through the city garbage dump to recover pieces of carpet from the Crafts's home that Richard said he had discarded because of a kerosene spill. Mayo did find the carpet, but the hoped-for blood traces were not found. What did happen was that the interest of the media in the case was raised, and the

state attorney-general had the investigation transferred to the state police.

They began by examining Richard's financial records and found two items of interest: a credit card purchase of a large-capacity freezer and a payment of $900 for machinery rental. Why did he need an industrial-size freezer, and what was the rental for? Police were granted a search warrant for the Crafts's home and went there on Christmas Day, 1986, accompanied by Dr. Henry Lee. Richard and the children were vacationing in Florida at the time. Traces of blood were found at several locations and on discarded towels.

The case that Richard had murdered Helle was building, even without the body. But the credit card records resulted in a significant and gruesome lead: The rental item was a large wood chipper, which Richard had collected from the rental depot on November 19. Things were falling into place. There was a record of a utility worker seeing a wood chipper being used in the midst of a snowstorm that day. The worker was interviewed and took police to the scene where they found not just piles of wood chippings but papers with Helle's name, blond hairs, bone fragments, pieces of cloth, and various unidentified materials. Everything was collected, cataloged, and taken to the state crime laboratory for examination. The chipper was found at the rental store and taken to the crime laboratory; a search of the lake near the site produced a chain saw with its serial number filed off; other fragmented human remains were uncovered.

Piecing the elements together, police postulated that Richard had beaten Helle to death in their bedroom and then moved the body to the industrial freezer. He next used the chain saw to cut up the body into smaller pieces, which were stored in the freezer before being put through the chipper. He had intended that the fragments spray into the lake, but many fell out on dry land to be discovered during the police search.

It was a compelling story that fit the known circumstances. Richard Crafts was charged and the trial set. To complete the case, it was necessary to link the physical evidence to the tools — the chain saw and the chipper — and so to Richard Crafts. Dr. Lee was able to show that the various fragments of bone, teeth, and human tissue had all been made by the chipper. He also showed that the chain saw not only had traces of teeth, blond hair, and human tissues, but also had fibers that could have come from the carpet in the Crafts's bedroom. The laboratory was able to restore the serial number of the chainsaw and trace its purchase to Richard Crafts.

Eventually, almost 3 years from the date of Helle's disappearance, Richard Crafts was convicted of her murder.

INTRODUCTION

One of the most important techniques used by the forensic scientist is observation. This skill is applied in two different ways: the search of a scene or an item in the laboratory to identify objects or features that may yield significant evidence on further testing; and a major category of evidence that we can loosely describe as pattern evidence. The basic principle underpinning pattern evidence is that physical objects can leave impressions on other materials, and examination of the impressions or marks can be used to draw conclusions as to whether or not the mark was made by the object of interest. Hence, without minimizing its importance, one of the ways criminalists process evidence is actually by using a skill you learned in kindergarten: pattern matching. Some examples are given in Table 2.1 and the introductory illustration. However, forensic examiners must do it at a much more exacting level.

CENTRAL QUESTIONS

- What are the class characteristics imparted by the object or process that made the mark?
- What are the individual characteristics imparted by the object or process that made the mark?
- Can the individual object be identified from pattern evidence?

We cannot answer/we are researching:

- When was the mark made?
- Can we use computers to capture three-dimensional images of marks and make it more likely that we will find individual characteristics?
- Can we develop a statistically rigorous model proving that complex, randomly generated patterns are unique?

Table 2.1	Some Examples of Pattern-Matching Evidence	
Source	Mark or Impression	Application
Vehicle tires	Tracks on a roadway, soil, snow	Place a specific vehicle at a scene. Identify a vehicle from make of tire and vehicle track width and wheel base dimensions.
Tools	Impression on object made by the tool, or where the tool was applied	Link pry bar to door or window at scene of break-in.
Footwear	Impressions in soil, marks in blood, marks on hard surface	Place footwear at location.
Firearms	Tool mark striations on fired ammunition, impression marks from firing mechanism	Associate bullets and cartridge cases with specific weapon. See Chapter 3, "Firearms."
Fingerprints	Ridge patterns left on objects	Identify person who touched the surface bearing the print. See Chapter 4, "Fingerprints."
Jigsaw fit of broken or torn objects	Glass and paint fragments, torn paper, adhesive tape	Associate recovered glass or paint fragment with scene (window at break-in or vehicle at hit-run). Match paper or adhesive tape to source. See Chapter 6, "Physical Evidence."

CLASS AND INDIVIDUAL CHARACTERISTICS

Physical evidence is described with increasing detail by class characteristics and individual characteristics. **Class characteristics** are identifying traits shared by a group of similar objects. **Individual characteristics** are identifying traits that are unique to a specific object and distinguish it from other members of its class. For example, consider a dozen pairs of shoes of the same size from a single run by the same manufacturer. Initially, each pair has the same shape, the same laces, and the same tread pattern on its sole. However, once the shoes are worn for a while by different individuals—say, members of a football team—differences in the wear patterns emerge. A punter might scuff the toes of the shoes while kicking, but a receiver might grind on the heels while cornering.

In the laboratory, criminalists examine individual and class characteristics from evidence. Individual characteristics—whether macroscopic or microscopic—become the basis for points of comparison between the evidence item and

Even the manufacturing process can deposit information on "new" shoes. A specific machine may leave microscopic marks or defects allowing its manufacture to be traced back to it versus another production line.

a known or an exemplar. For pattern-matching evidence, the examiner is looking for unique features that will help in identifying an unknown. In other cases, such as a roughly torn piece of tape, the examiner might try to see if the evidence from one side matches up with the other (a positive and a negative). By observing these points of comparison and using their training and knowledge, criminalists form conclusions about the evidence called "opinions."

The basic principles are illustrated in Figures 2.1 through 2.4, which show how the tread of a trainer-type shoe can contain class and individualizing marks, leaving a negative impression in a soft surface such as soil and a positive imprint on a solid surface.

The conclusions reached by examiners usually involve three levels of distinction: identification, inconclusive, and exclusion. **Identification** means that the criminalist has sufficient data to say—on the basis of the pattern comparisons—that the pattern from the evidence can be ascribed to a specific person or object. A ruling of *inconclusive* is appropriate when there was not enough data to identify or exclude a person or object. Finally,

FIGURE 2.1
The sole of a worn Rockport-brand trainer shoe. The sole pattern is unique to this brand and model, but the pattern is an example of class characteristics since it does not individualize the shoe. Original photograph by author.

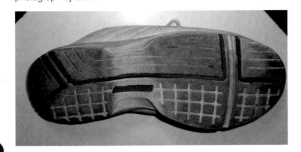

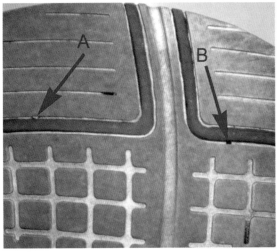

FIGURE 2.2
Close-up of part of the sole of the same shoe.
The effects of wear are obvious but of a general nature. There are two small stones trapped in the tread (shown by the arrows), and these could provide individualization. However, they are not permanent, it is not possible to say when they were trapped, and they are too small to be seen clearly in impressions from the shoe. Original photograph by author.

FIGURE 2.3
Pattern evidence left from dust on the sole of the shoe in Figure 2.2 when pushed against a door to force it open. Note that not all tread features are seen, as the mark is only of the high points of the tread pattern. There is sufficient detail to use the class characteristics to conclude that the print could have been made by a Rockport shoe, but nothing to permit individualization. Original photograph by author.

FIGURE 2.4
Impression left in soft soil by the Rockport shoe (Figure 2.2). As with the imprint shown in Figure 2.3, there is sufficient detail to use the class characteristics to conclude that the print could have been made by a Rockport shoe but nothing to permit individualization. Original photograph by author.

when a criminalist finds differences in the known and the evidence, he or she may say it is **excluded**.

TOOL MARKS

Strictly speaking, a **tool mark** is an artifact left from using a tool on a material. The mark may be an impression, a scrape, or even a cut through an object. Tool mark examiners study evidence for class characteristics to identify the type of tool used. When possible, they also look for individual characteristics that could result in the identification of the specific tool used.

Mark Evidence

Marks may be two-dimensional or three-dimensional. They may be positive or negative.

A positive two-dimensional impression is like the mark made by a rubber stamp or a fingerprint. Ink is coated onto the stamp or finger and deposited when the inked surface touches a paper. (It is the process by which your mother figured out who tracked mud into the house.) A negative two-dimensional impression would be created if you stepped on a freshly waxed floor and lifted some of the wax away with your shoe. Stepping off would leave a dull impression of your sole in the shine of the floor (see Figures 2.3 and 2.4). Some evidence may be both positive and negative, such as comparing a torn tape to the roll it came from.

In a sense, a negative tool mark happens when the object a tool is used on affects the tool itself. For example, the pattern of a screw pressed into the jaw of a pair of pliers. This happens when the object is harder or less compressible than the material of the tool.

Most three-dimensional tool marks are positive impressions but can be caused by different actions. **Compression** marks are made when a tool is pressed into a softer material. Stepping into wet cement or biting into an apple leaves a compression mark. **Sliding** a tool across a surface produces a scrape. Deep compression combined with sliding produces **cutting**.

Collection and Preservation of Mark Evidence

As with most physical objects that will be submitted as evidence, the place to start when collecting and preserving tool marks and impressions is photography. Afterward, depending on the type of evidence, its location, and its portability, the mark may be taken to the laboratory for further analysis, lifted (like a fingerprint), or cast.

PHOTOGRAPHY OF MARKS

Contextual photographs must be taken to locate the impression in the crime scene. This is usually followed by a series of close-up photos that illustrate the details of the evidence. At least one picture is usually taken at 90 ° to the impression. In low-contrast situations such as mud or snow, a series of angled pictures or the use of angled lighting may be taken. Figure 2.5 shows a nice, clear print well captured by photography. The contrast of snow impressions can also be enhanced with colored sprays (paint or dye) or with Snow Print Wax, used for casting snow impressions. When using a color spray, the examiner must take care not to damage the impression. All photographs should include an appropriate scale.

22

FIGURE 2.5
Impression mark made by shoe in snow. Image from Stockxpert.

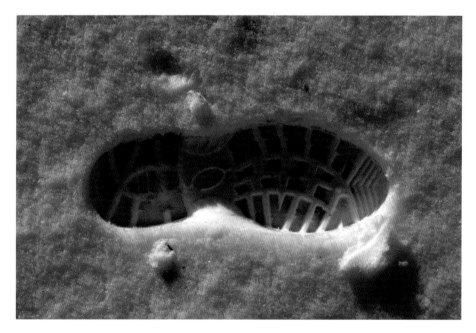

CASTING

When shoe or tire marks are left in soft material, like mud, the impressions must be photographed and cast. Impressions left in rocky, sandy, or otherwise coarse soil are difficult to cast and will not contain the fine detail that may be needed for individualization.

Casting is done after photography to provide a complementary 3-D image. While plaster may still have occasional use, commercial materials like DieCast and Dental Stone are easier to prepare, faster to set, and better able to capture fine details. Casting materials are mixed and then poured into the impression. Premixing is important to avoid damaging the impression. Once dry, the model of the tool, tire, or shoe can be removed and taken back to the laboratory for further study.

Figures 2.6 through 2.9 show the preservation of a shoe impression mark in snow using Snow Print Wax and casting with Dental Stone. The first step is spraying with Snow Print Wax, which highlights the impression and solidifies on contact with the cold snow (Figure 2.6). Next, Dental Stone impression material is mixed in a plastic bag and gently poured into the impression (Figure 2.7). Identification information, such as date and a unique evidence number, is carefully scratched into the surface of the casting (Figure 2.8). Finally, after the Dental Stone is cool and hard, the cast impression is removed (Figure 2.9). Note that the red color from the Snow Print Wax makes it easier to see detail in the impression than would be the case with the gray-white natural color of the Dental Stone.

FIGURE 2.6
Stabilizing and delineating the impression by spraying with Snow Print Wax. Courtesy of Forensic Source © 2008.

23

LIFTING TWO-DIMENSIONAL PRINTS

Prints made of dust or dirt, whether positive or negative, can be lifted similarly to fingerprints. Lifting the print allows a "real," life-sized image to be transported to the laboratory for further testing. The lift medium must cover the entirety of the print or impression, and care must be taken not to disturb fine dust while

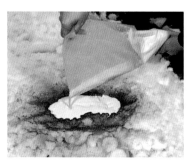

FIGURE 2.7
Mixing the Dental Stone and carefully pouring into the Snow Print Wax–protected impression. Courtesy of Forensic Source © 2008.

FIGURE 2.8
Scratching in identifying information. Courtesy of Forensic Source © 2008.

FIGURE 2.9
Removing the cast. Courtesy of Forensic Source © 2008.

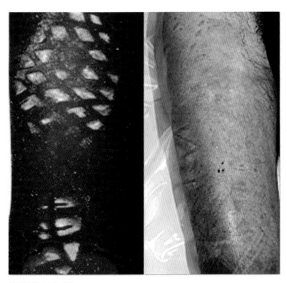

FIGURE 2.10
Barely visible dust print of shoe sole pattern on skin (right) and same print after lifting using an electrostatic device. From T. Adair and M. Dobersen, *Journal of Forensic Identification*, Vol. 56, Issue 3, by permission of the publisher.

The static electric charge attracts dust to the plate the way your hair is attracted to a charged balloon.

lifting. Adhesive lift media work best on dry prints from nonporous surfaces. Gelatin lift media work on both wet and dry prints and both porous and nonporous surfaces. Both adhesive and gelatin lift media come in a variety of colors and sizes. Tacky prints can sometimes be enhanced with colored fingerprint powders before lifting.

Electrostatic lifting devices can pull dry, dusty impressions from porous and nonporous surfaces. A sheet of plastic film is pressed against the impression, connected to electrodes, and charged. As the charge develops on the film, dust is attracted to it. This technique works well in situations where there is very little contrast between the dust print and the surface or when the impression is on a highly colored or patterned surface. Because the lift film carries a residual charge, it should be carefully preserved against a background to avoid contamination or damage. The method works even in difficult situations such as recovery of prints on skin (Figure 2.10).

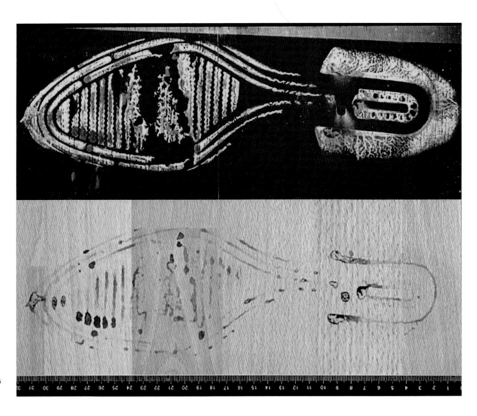

FIGURE 2.11
Bloody footprint on hardwood floor (bottom) and same print viewed in UV light after treating with Acid Yellow stain and lifting with a gel medium (top). Note the increase in print detail, especially at the heel region. Courtesy of BVDA INTERNATIONAL.

ENHANCING MARKS

The electrostatic lift shown in Figure 2.10 not only recovered and protected the mark but also produced a much enhanced image. The same applies to faint or almost invisible footwear prints left by someone who has stepped in blood. Treating the mark with one of the many chemicals that can be used to detect even invisible traces of blood (see Chapter 11, "Forensic Biology") will often result in a clear image of the footwear pattern (Figure 2.11).

COMPARISON OF PATTERN EVIDENCE

Features of the Possible Source Object

When the investigator recovers evidence in the form of a mark, the possible source object must be examined carefully for its class and individual characteristics. In the case of a tool mark, if a toolbox is recovered, it might contain several implements with the same size blade. Class characteristics might limit the search to chisels and screwdrivers. Then examination of individual wear patterns could help identify the actual "perpetrator." There has to be point-for-point correspondence between the tool and the tool mark to be considered a match.

Once a potential match is found, the examiner might be tempted to fit the shoe into the shoe print or the tool into the tool mark, but no trained investigator would ever do that. First, even if the shoe and shoe print or tool and tool mark match, tiny individual characteristics that gave the evidence value could be damaged by such contact. In court, testifying that the tool was fitted into the tool mark could give rise to accusations of evidence tampering or manufacturing. Further, trace evidence (described in Chapter 6) embedded in the tool mark or tool could be **transferred** or lost.

If fitting the tool into the tool mark is forbidden, how can an investigator be sure that the tool is the right one? The answer involves an attempt to duplicate the tool mark. For some impressions, scrapings, and cuttings made with objects like screwdrivers or chisels, lead is used to capture the marks. For shoes and tires, impressionable foams or casting agents can be used. These **exemplars** can then be compared to the evidence and the results documented. The best thing to do is a direct comparison of photographs, lifts, or casts of the evidence mark with the same record of the suspected source.

Tools

Macroscopically, tool mark examiners may compare the jaws of pliers for class characteristics such as width, depth, and surface "grip" pattern. They will also look for defects, wear, and damage that might affect an impression. Within a scrape or cut, the examiner can sometimes find **striations**, lines made by surface imperfections on the edge of a tool. Some of these imperfections are manufacturing artifacts. Others are the result of using the tool. Because it is very unlikely that manufacturing and wear could produce identical defects in a tool's surface, striations in a scrape or cut can help identify the tool used. Tiny imperfections in the surface of the tool are examined side by side with the tool mark under a comparison microscope. If there are sufficient points of comparison, the examiner may have a match.

Shoe Print and Tire Databases

Shoe prints are treated similarly to fingerprints in terms of databases. One commercially available suite of databases is Foster & Freeman's Shoeprint Image Capture and Retrieval (SICAR) system. The pattern of the sole of a shoe is scanned or imaged and then encoded with descriptors for each feature of the tread pattern. The SICAR program searches the recovered mark against footprint (SoleMate) and tire print (TreadMate) databases (see Figure 2.12).

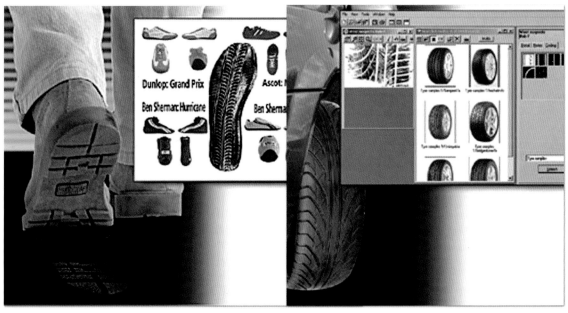

26

FIGURE 2.12
SoleMate and TreadMate databases. Courtesy of Foster & Freeman.

The information is recorded into three databases. A crime database stores shoe prints recovered from crime scenes, a suspect database that holds information on suspects' shoes, and a reference collection of sole prints from several manufacturers. Searching the databases may link a suspect to a crime scene or link together shoe prints from several crime scenes. Potential matches are displayed for the investigator's comparison.

OTHER PATTERN EVIDENCE
Vehicle Identification

Tire impressions can tell a lot about the vehicle that left them. Single tire impressions can place a vehicle at a crime scene. Multiple impressions can tell even more. Tracks will show the direction a vehicle was facing, which way it went, and whether the driver was in a hurry. Measurement of the *wheelbase*—the distance between the front and rear wheels—and the *track width*—the distance separating the front two tires—can narrow the number of makes and models of possible vehicles. If marks from the original tires are found, this will further narrow the range of possibilities.

Fabric Impressions

Fabric impressions can be imprints of fabric in a softer material like mud, or fractured patterns impressed on other materials such as a pattern of unusual weave stamped in blood on another surface. They are often fragile and should be well documented with photography before any attempt to collect them is made. Fabric impressions may contain embedded fibers that must be processed (we will discuss fibers in Chapter 6).

Bite Marks

Bite marks can be used as evidence, though their quality varies widely with the material in which the bite is registered. Gum, cheese, and fruit have provided excellent records. With living victims, due to the skin's elasticity and the body's ability to heal itself, bite marks can be more problematic. Bite marks must be photographed as soon as possible. They can also be swabbed for saliva and epithelial cells to give to DNA analysts. In deceased victims, the bite mark may be removed and preserved as a tissue sample; however, even with careful preservation, the bite mark can degrade with time. An impression is taken of the suspect's teeth and inspected by a forensic odontologist for specific relationships between the teeth.

27

As defense and prosecuting attorneys become more rigorous in the standard required of pattern evidence, the acceptability of bite marks is lessening. One of the most infamous examples is the Chamberlain, or dingo baby, case from Australia.

Case Study

The Dingo Baby and Bite Marks

Lindy and Michael Chamberlain were enjoying a family vacation camping near the famous Australian landmark of Ayer's Rock. On the night of August 17, 1980, Lindy Chamberlain cried out from the tent that a dingo (a wild Australian dog) had taken her baby Azaria from her bed. The disappearance was investigated and Lindy convicted of the murder of Azaria, whose body was never found. There were many doubts about the evidence that those representing the Chamberlains pursued through many years of trial and retrial, and finally a high-level judicial inquiry. Part of the evidence at the trial was forensic odontology. Damage to various items of the child's bedding was examined, and the odontologist concluded that the marks were made by scissors and could not have been made by the teeth of a dog. However, the judicial inquiry heard that the action of canine incisors could well have caused the damage and the confident assertion of the odontologist at trial was not dependable. The bite mark evidence, along with several other aspects of the original forensic testing, was declared unreliable and the conviction overturned.

SUMMARY

The basic principle underpinning pattern evidence is that physical objects can leave impressions on other materials, and examination of the impressions or marks can be used to draw conclusions as to whether or not the mark was made by the object of interest.

For pattern-matching evidence, the examiner is looking for unique features that will help in identifying an unknown. Class characteristics are identifying traits shared by a group of similar objects. Individual characteristics are identifying traits that are unique to a specific object and distinguish it from other members of its class. Criminalists form conclusions about the evidence, called "opinions."

The conclusions reached by examiners usually involve three levels of distinction: identification, inconclusive, and exclusion.

Marks may be two-dimensional or three-dimensional. They may be positive or negative. Most three-dimensional tool marks are positive impressions, but they can be caused by different actions. Compression marks are made when a tool is pressed into a softer material. A negative tool mark happens when the object is harder or less compressible than the material of the tool.

A tool should never be fitted into the tool mark to verify attribution, but, under certain circumstances, an attempt to duplicate the tool mark may be undertaken.

Tire impressions can place a vehicle at a crime scene, show the direction it was facing, and show which way it departed.

Contextual photographs must be taken to locate the impression in the crime scene. This is usually followed by a series of close-up photos that illustrate the details of the evidence. At least one picture is usually taken at 90° to the impression. Casting is done after photography to provide a complementary 3-D image.

Lifting the print allows a "real," life-sized image to be transported to the laboratory for further testing. Both adhesive and gelatin lift media come in a variety of colors and sizes.

Electrostatic lifting devices can pull dry, dusty impressions from porous and nonporous surfaces.

Tiny imperfections in the surface of the tool are examined side by side with the tool mark under a comparison microscope. If there are sufficient points of comparison, the examiner may have a match.

There are searchable databases for tire prints, shoe treads, and other manufactured goods.

PROBLEMS

1. Give the word or phrase for the following definitions:
   a. leaving evidence behind or moving evidence from one surface to another by contact
   b. an impression caused by a tool coming into contact with a softer object
   c. a known sample

2. Describe class characteristics for shoe or tire prints.
3. Describe individual characteristics for shoe or tire prints.
4. Categorize the following as individual or class characteristics:
   a. a chip in the cutting surface of a chisel
   b. the shoe print of a new, women's size 9 Manolo Blanik left pump
   c. a tire puncture that has been patched
5. Describe the use of the following tests and techniques:
   a. casting
   b. tool mark duplication
   c. comparison microscopy
6. What information can be used for individualization?
7. Should a tool ever be fitted to a tool mark to verify they match, and why or why not?
8. What should be done with a shoe print made of fine dust particles?
9. When should a tool mark be duplicated for evidentiary purposes?
10. What databases exist for pattern evidence?

GLOSSARY

Class characteristic an identifying feature that puts an item in a group.

Compression a mark made by pressing a tool into a softer material.

Cutting a combination of compression and sliding with a tool that severs the material.

Exclusion no match between a tool mark and a tool suspected of producing it; a term used to indicate a lack of association between evidence or a suspect and a crime scene.

Exemplar a known sample.

Identification a match between a tool mark and the tool that produced it; a match between evidence and a crime scene.

Individual characteristic an identifying feature that distinguishes a member of a class. For example, a worn shoe will exhibit a wear pattern unique when compared to all other shoes of the same manufacturer.

Sliding a tool mark made by scraping a tool across a surface, making tiny lines.

Striations lines made by scraping or sliding a tool across a surface.

Tool mark any impression, cut, gouge, or abrasion caused by a tool coming into contact with another object.

Transfer leaving evidence behind or moving evidence from one surface to another by contact.

29

From top left, clockwise:

- Bullets being examined in firearms comparison microscope. The instrument is essentially two microscopes joined by a bridge. Bullets are mounted in the left and right sample holders and the images viewed in a split screen to compare land and groove patterns and individual striations imparted on the bullet from the barrel (see also Figure 3.6).
- Rounds of ammunition, including shotgun shells and bullets.
- A Glock 30 pistol at the moment of firing. Note the discharge of gases from the muzzle—these contain materials that can be detected as organic and inorganic firearms discharge residues.
- Part of the handgun reference collection held by Los Angeles County Sheriff's Crime Laboratory.

Comparison microscope and handgun collection courtesy LA County Sheriff's Crime Laboratory through Barry Fisher. Ammunition from Stockxpert; firing image from http://everystockphoto.s3.amazonaws.com/glock_glock30_firingrange_1394456_o.jpg

CHAPTER 3

Firearms

The DC Snipers

It is 6:30 PM on Tuesday, October 2, 2002. James Martin of Silver Spring, Maryland, is shot and killed in the car park of the Shoppers Food Warehouse grocery store in Wheaton. There are no obvious suspects or motives, but apart from that, the incident is treated by police as an uncomplicated homicide. Things change rapidly, when the following day sees five people shot and killed in the DC Beltway area. The first victim is 39-year-old Sonny Buchanan, shot dead at 7:41 AM while mowing grass at the Fitzgerald Auto Mall in Rockville, Montgomery County, Maryland. Less than an hour later, Premkumar Walekar is shot dead while pumping gas into his taxi in Aspen Hill, also in Montgomery County. Within 30 minutes, Sarah Ramos becomes the third victim of the day, shot and killed while sitting on a bench, reading a book, in the Leisure World Shopping Center in Aspen Hill. At 9:58 AM Lori Ann Lewis-Rivera is the last victim of the morning, killed at a gas station in Kensington, Maryland. However, Lori Ann is not the last victim for the day: Pascal Charlot is shot at 9:15 PM when walking on Georgia Avenue in Washington, DC, and dies shortly thereafter.

October 4 and October 7 see two more shootings. Fortunately, both victims survive. They are Caroline Seawell, shot in the parking lot of a Michael's craft store at Spotsylvania Mall in Spotsylvania County, Virginia, and Iran Brown, shot as he arrives at Benjamin Tasker Middle School in Bowie, Prince George's County, Maryland.

The shootings continue, with fatalities on October 9 (Dean Meyers at a gas station in Prince William County, Virginial); October 11 (Kenneth Bridges at a gas station just off I-95 in Spotsylvania County, Virginia); October 14 (Linda Franklin outside a Home Depot store in Fairfax County, Virginia); October 19 (Jeffrey Hopper in a parking lot near the Ponderosa steak house in Ashland, Virginia); and October 22 (Conrad Johnson while outside his bus in Aspen Hill, Maryland).

Johnson was the last victim, as the perpetrators were found and arrested on October 24. However, during the investigation two earlier fatal shootings were identified: Paul LaRuffa, shot and killed on the night of September 5 while locking up his pizza shop in Clinton, Prince George's County; and Claudine Parker, shot and killed on September 21 during a robbery at the liquor store in Montgomery, Alabama, where she worked.

The preceding brief chronology needs no elaboration to describe the fear that resulted from the attacks, which became known as the DC sniper case. The eventual identification and apprehension of the perpetrators, John Allen Muhammad and his young associate, John Lee Malvo, owe as much to public vigilance and the eventual successful application of basic law enforcement investigation as to anything. However, there are several places were physical forensic science made important contributions to building the case against Muhammad and Malvo.

Identification of Weapon

Eyewitness accounts were varied, but the nature of the shootings and witness statements pointed to a high-powered rifle. The timing of the October 3 shootings, the absence of ammunition cases at any of the scenes, and the reasonable degree of marksmanship all indicated that the shots were fired from a vehicle by someone with a degree of training or experience. Examination of the class characteristics of bullets recovered from the bodies confirmed that it was a .223-caliber weapon such as a Bushmaster XM-15, which is a civilian equivalent of the military M-16. (See Figure 3.1.)

Associative Evidence

Laboratory examination of individual characteristics of bullets fired from the sniper weapon showed that the same gun had been used in the DC Beltway shootings. These characteristics also provided an additional link to suspect John Allen Muhammad, as they matched projectile fragments recovered from a tree stump in a home he had rented in Tacoma, Washington. Tests showed that a different gun had been used in the Alabama shooting.

Link to Malvo and the Shooting of Claudine Parker in Alabama

Although firearms examination did not provide any associative evidence between the DC and Alabama shootings, other forensic science testing did. Once investigators were aware of the likely link, they looked again at the crime scene evidence from the Montgomery, Alabama, liquor store. A fingerprint on a piece of paper was identified as being from John Lee Malvo.

FIGURE 3.1
The Bushmaster XM-15 rifle. The weapon used by the DC snipers was a stolen Bushmaster XM-15 semi-automatic rifle. From Leanora Brun-Conti, from FBI/NFSTC Trace Evidence Symposium, http://projects.nfstc.org/trace/

FIREARMS

The main work of the firearms examiner is essentially tool mark comparisons of **cartridge** cases and projectiles to associate them with specific weapons. However, firearms examiners are more than just experts in **firearms identification** and examination of ammunition. They can help determine the distance and angle from which a weapon was fired or tell whether a weapon could be fired at all. They also rebuild weapons, recover serial numbers, and reconstruct bullets. Chemists in the laboratory also analyze gunshot residue.

When a firearm is discharged, the firing pin strikes a cartridge, igniting gunpowder inside it and propelling the bullet down the gun barrel toward the muzzle. The process marks the bullet and cartridge. The bullet emerges from the weapon bearing the negative impression of the rifling and imperfections within the barrel. If the markings on a bullet from a crime scene are matched to markings on a bullet test fired from a suspect weapon, the gun can be linked to the crime.

CENTRAL QUESTIONS

- What are the class characteristics of firearms?
- What are the individual characteristics imparted by firing a weapon?
- Who shot?
- What was the distance of the shot?

We cannot answer/we are researching:

- When was a weapon discharged?

Classification of Types of Firearms

Firearms are characterized by how they may be used. Handguns are designed to be held in and operated with one hand. They include revolvers, pistols, semiautomatic handguns, and machine pistols. Long guns, like rifles and shotguns, are sometimes called "shoulder guns" because the user must stabilize the firing position. Larger guns and weapons mounted on vehicles, tanks, ships, and aircraft include machine guns. Finally, guns larger than .50 caliber may be called cannons.

ACTION

Firearms may also be characterized by their **action**, the mechanism by which the weapon loads, fires, or removes cartridges. Examples include single-action revolvers, in which the trigger functions solely to cause the hammer to strike the ammunition, double-action revolvers, in which the trigger also cocks the hammer ready for the next firing, and bolt, pump, lever, semiautomatic, and automatic rifles and handguns. (See Figure 3.2.)

BARRELS

The barrel of a firearm plays an important role in how a bullet emerges from a weapon. Longer barrels impart greater accuracy. Features imparted on the barrel during its manufacture are important in the work of the firearms examiner associating fired ammunition with a gun.

Rifling

Rifling is designed to spin the projectile as it is expelled from a weapon, thereby giving it a straighter trajectory. Most firearms have rifling, a series of helical lands and **grooves**, down their barrels like the seam on a tube of crescent rolls. **Lands** are the high portions of the barrel between two grooves. The diameter of the barrel is called the **caliber**. Measured across opposite lands, the caliber of a weapon

FIGURE 3.2

Glock 30 handgun (left) and its five main component part groups (right). The slide (A) is forced back by recoil after each shot. The action ejects the spent casing, loads the next round, and readies the spring-loaded firing pin. The barrel (B) is cold hammer-forged to an octagonal profile with a right-hand twist. It is covered by the slide in the assembled gun. The recoil spring (C) is the driving force for the semi-automatic ammunition extraction, ejection, and loading process by collecting and transferring the recoil energy produced when a round of ammunition is fired. The frame (D) is manufactured from a high-strength polymer, based on nylon. This extensive use of polymer led to the Glock being dubbed as a "plastic" gun of questionable strength and rumored to be able to pass through metal detectors unseen. Both are untrue: The frame has proven to be very durable and the extensive use of metal in the weapon means that even the sub-compact model 30 is readily detected by screening devices. The magazine (E) carries 10 rounds of .45 caliber ammunition (shown at F). From http://commons.wikimedia.org/wiki/Image:Glock_30-JH01.jpg and http://commons.wikimedia.org/wiki/Image:Glock_30-JH02.jpg

is given in millimeters (e.g., 9 mm) or hundredths of an inch (e.g., 0.38 in, often just 38). It may differ slightly from the original **bore** of the barrel due to the rifling process used. The left hand side of Figure 3.3 is the inside of a gun barrel showing rifling and the right hand side of the figure shows the land and groove impressions imparted by the rifling onto fired bullets.

Weapons of any caliber can be produced with rifling that spirals to the left or the right and containing any number of lands and grooves. Manufacturers use different rifling systems for different products, but within a single product—for example, Heckler and Koch 9 mm automatic pistols—all of the rifling is the

The idea behind rifling is the same idea behind a quarterback spinning a long pass. The spinning keeps the football from tumbling off from the aim of the trajectory.

FIGURE 3.3

Barrel rifling. A is a photograph of the barrel of a .35 caliber Remington showing rifling with a right hand twist. B and C are two bullets showing the land and groove impressions imparted by barrel rifling, B shows impressions from a barrel with a left hand twist and C those from one with a right hand twist. Barrel rifling from http://en.wikipedia.org/wiki/Image:Marlin_35_rem_2.jpg The bullets are courtesy of Jack Dillon.

same. This provides an important class characteristic for firearms examiners. A projectile marked with right-spiraling markings could not be produced from a gun with left-spiraling rifling. A bullet marked with five lands could not have been fired from a gun barrel with six. A database of manufacturers' specifications called the General Rifling Characteristics File is maintained by the FBI.

Rifling Processes. Once a tube has been bored from a steel rod, a variety of methods can be used to create rifling for the barrel of a firearm. Mechanically, a rifling pattern can be cut into the inner surface of a barrel using a broach cutter, formed around a button, or pressed around a mandrel. Alternatively, the lands and grooves can be etched into the barrel using electrochemical methods. The main methods are shown in Figure 3.4.

Broach Rifling. Broach rifling uses a hardened steel rod with several evenly spaced cutting rings. Each successive cutting ring is slightly larger in size until the last one, which determines the groove depth. Gaps between the cutting rings account for the lands. The rod is twisted as it is pulled through the barrel, and this forms the spiral to the rifling pattern.

Button Rifling. Button rifling, more commonly used today, is accomplished by forcing a hardened steel plug down an unrifled barrel. With either a broach or

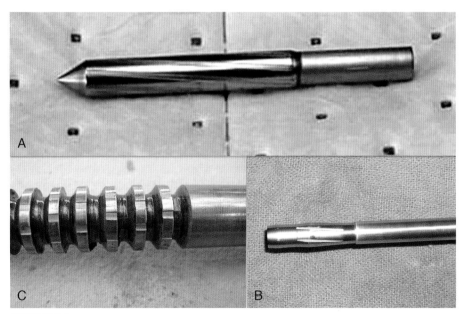

FIGURE 3.4
Methods used to create rifling in gun barrels. A, mandrel, in which the barrel is hammer forged against the steel rifling template; B, button ritling, in which the hardened steel plug is forced through the barrel; C, broach rifling, in which the hardened steel rod with its cutting rings is pulled through the barrel with a twisting motion. A, Figure courtesy of Professor James Higley, Purdue University Calumet; B, Image courtesy Lilja Precision Rifle Barrels Inc, www.riflebarrels.com; C, Image from http://commons.wikimedia.org/wiki/Image:Raeumnadel-erste_Zahnreihen.JPG

button rifling process, the direction of rotation and the speed give rise to the direction of rotation and pitch of the rifling within the barrel.

Mandrel Rifling. Mandrel or hammer rifling is a newer technique commonly used by Glock. A hardened steel mandrel bearing the rifling pattern is inserted into a barrel blank. The barrel is then hammered or machine-compressed against the mandrel such that the inner surface takes on the shape of the template. Hammer forging produces polygonal rifling patterns with less distinct transitions between lands and grooves, making it difficult to measure the individual rifling elements.

Electrochemical Rifling. Electrochemical rifling is an etching process by which the metal of the barrel is eaten away to create grooves in the barrel. An electrochemical cell is created in a solution of electrolytes using the barrel as the positive terminal (anode) and a metal bar containing the rifling pattern as the negative terminal (cathode). When an electric current is applied, the resulting redox reaction creates grooves in the barrel by dissolving minute amounts of metal.

Examination of Weapons and Ammunition

The work of the firearms examiner to associate spent ammunition with a possible source depends on the presence of tool marks imparted during the manufacture of the weapon, which in turn are imparted on the ammunition when the gun is fired. These fall into two categories: striated action marks and impressed action marks. **Striated action marks** are fine lines imparted onto a bullet as it is forced through the gun barrel. **Impressed action marks** are left on the cartridge case by the mechanisms involved in loading, firing, and removing the ammunition from the gun. Impressed action marks may also bear **striations** caused by tool mark defects imparted on the action mechanism during manufacture.

STRIATED ACTION MARKS

The manufacturing processes used to make rifle gun barrels leave striations on the lands and grooves. Striations are microscopic tool marks created during the process of drilling the tube of a gun barrel and during its rifling. When a projectile is fired, the soft, hot lead expands into the lands and grooves. Whether produced by a tiny imperfection in the cutting tool, a defect in the metal of the barrel tube that chips away, or a turning that scrapes along the inside of the barrel producing a scratch, these tiny lines mark the bullet with characteristics individual to a particular firearm. Figure 3.5 is a photograph of a fired bullet showing striations on the lands and grooves.

IMPRESSED ACTION MARKS

Discharging a weapon produces more than just rifling marks. Impressions made by the firing pin, breechface, extractor, ejector, or other machined surfaces all may provide valuable clues for identification if they can be duplicated. As with striated action marks, impressed action marks are individual rather than class marks.

36

FIGURE 3.5
Marks on fired bullets. Photograph of a fired bullet. The photograph was taken using a firearms examination microscope and the lands, grooves, and fine rifling striations are clearly visible. From Los Angeles County Sheriff's Crime Laboratory, courtesy Barry Fisher.

Firing Pin Impressions

As discussed earlier in the chapter, when the trigger is pulled, the firing pin strikes the primer, igniting the powder. Depending on the weapon, firing pins may hit the center (center fire) or the rim (rim fire) of the cartridge case. The force of the impact stamps the image of any surface imperfections on the nose of the firing pin into the metal of the primer or rim of the cartridge case. It may be possible to recover a firing pin impression if the part is broken, fails to strike the primer of a cartridge with sufficient force for it to discharge the projectile, or misses the primer entirely. (See Figure 3.6.)

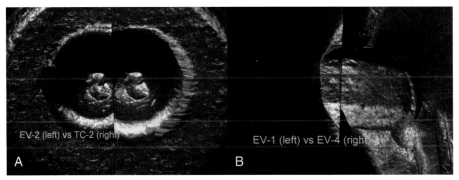

EV-2 (left) vs TC-2 (right)

A

EV-1 (left) vs EV-4 (right)

B

FIGURE 3.6
Centerfire and rimfire firing pin impressions. A and B are photographs of firing pin impressions taken using a firearms examination microscope. A shows side-by-side images from two cartridge cases from a shooting scene where the weapon used a centerfire mechanism and B shows the marks from a .22 rimfire gun. (Note: the green lettering is an annotation of the evidence by the examiner.) From Los Angeles County Sheriff's Crime Laboratory, courtesy Barry Fisher.

FIGURE 3.7
Breech marks. Photograph of breech face tool mark impressions, taken using a firearms examination microscope. The side-by-side images are of two cartridge cases from a shooting scene, each showing the scratch-like marks imparted on the case. The firing pin impressions can also be seen. From Los Angeles County Sheriff's Crime Laboratory, courtesy Barry Fisher.

Breech Marks

In physics, every action has an equal and opposite reaction. The force that pushes the projectile toward the muzzle of a weapon pushes the firearm toward the shooter, an action commonly called *recoil*. As the cartridge case is pushed backward, it strikes the breech face. The recoil marks the primer or the cartridge case with the negative impression of any superficial defects from the breech face. **Breech marks** may be seen as a group of parallel lines, a circular pattern, or a stippled pattern. (See Figure 3.7.)

Ejector and Extractor Marks

Modern firearms use mechanical operations to remove the cases from spent ammunition. The mechanical operation will leave impression

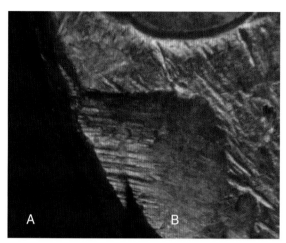

FIGURE 3.8
Extractor marks. Photograph of extractor mechanism tool mark impressions, taken using a firearms examination microscope. The side-by-side images are of two cartridge cases from a shooting scene. From Los Angeles County Sheriff's Crime Laboratory, courtesy Barry Fisher.

38

FIGURE 3.9
Composition of ammunition. A round of ammunition consists of 5 main parts: 1, the bullet or projectile; 2, the case; 3, the propellant which is an explosive that fires the bullet when it is ignited; 4, the rim which usually is marked with the manufacturer's headstamp; and 5, the primer, a percussion-sensitive chemical in a cap in the rim and which ignites the propellant. From http://en.wikipedia.org/wiki/Image:Bullet.svg

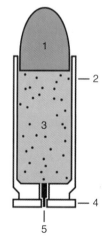

A cartridge without a bullet is called a *blank*.

marks. Ejector marks may appear as striations or impressions that are imparted as the cartridge is ejected from the firearm after discharge. Striations may be induced by hand chambering and then ejecting a live cartridge, but impressions from the **ejector** apparatus are often indicative of the weapon's firing.

The **extractor** is a dog-leg-shaped part that removes a cartridge or cartridge case from the chamber of a firearm. In an automatic weapon, as the slide moves backward, the extractor catches the cartridge case and ejects it from the chamber. If an extractor marks the cartridge case, the striations would be found both if the weapon was fired or if a round was hand-chambered and extracted without firing. (See Figure 3.8.)

Ammunition

A bullet is the projectile discharged from a firearm. Bullets usually come in a **cartridge,** a case containing the bullet with a primer and gunpowder to propel it from the weapon. **Shells**, like those used in shotguns, contain explosives to help propel the projectile.

As Figure 3.9 shows, a cartridge contains the following:

- A projectile, the bullet
- The primer, to ignite the propellant
- The propellant, usually gunpowder
- The rim, the bottom of the cartridge
- A casing formed over the components to hold them together

Bullets contain a variety of metals. Usually, they are molded from lead, a soft, pliable metal. To harden the bullet, it might be jacketed with another metal such as steel or copper. However, steel-jacketed bullets are coated with copper, a softer metal, so that the harder metal does not scratch the rifling.

Jacketing a bullet can increase its man-stopping power. A hollow-point bullet has a small hole drilled into its nose, causing the projectile to tear into a sharp-edged flower shape when fired. The less penetrating, less lethal "dum dum" round is another type of expanding bullet. On impact, the lead cracks its hard metal shell and bows out in a mushroom shape (see Figures 3.10 and 3.14).

BULLET COMPARISONS

Although it would allow the rifling to be seen, it would be impractical to saw a gun barrel in half to match the striations to a recovered bullet—not to mention the fact it would destroy a portion of the evidence. Instead, exemplars are created by test-firing bullets from the weapon. Early recovery traps used wads of cotton, but even this soft material could cause damage to the bullets. Today, test firings are made into a tank of water. The water in the tank slows the bullet down, "catching" the projectile with all the striations and rifling marks intact. Upon recovery, the bullet can be inspected for class characteristics and then compared for individualizing characteristics. Figure 3.11 shows side-by-side images of striations in two bullets fired from the same gun (left) and from two different guns of the same type (right).

FIGURE 3.10
9 mm hollow-point ammunition. A round of 9 mm hollow-point ammunition. From http://en.wikipedia.org/wiki/Image:Hollow_point. JPG

For crowd control, nonlethal technologies involving plastic bullets, rubber bullets, and beanbags have been built into cartridges.

Hunting paranormal creatures? Silver is a very soft metal that would foul the barrel of a gun and spread greatly on impact, so the fictional werewolf hunter's silver bullet is not a practical proposition.

Striations on evidence and exemplars are examined using a comparison microscope. Once the bullets are properly mounted on their rotating stages, the investigator chooses a well-defined feature in one bullet and looks for it in the other. If a common land or groove is found, the examiner looks to ensure that the tiny striations are also identical. Then both of the bullets are rotated together to look for other points of correspondence. Through-the-lens photography allows the images to be captured on film or video.

Invention of the comparison microscope for examination of bullets and cartridge cases is generally attributed to Calvin Goddard, one of the early greats in the field of forensic firearms examination. In fact, the instrument probably was invented by his colleague Phillip Gravelle, but it was certainly Goddard who pioneered its use.

Goddard earned a deserved reputation for his work but probably is remembered for his follow-up investigations in the St. Valentine's Day Massacre.

Automatic weapons, high-caliber weapons, and high-power weapons may have to be test-fired under special conditions at outdoor ranges, because a water tank does not provide enough stopping power for the projectiles.

FIGURE 3.11
Matching and non-matching striations on fired bullets. Photograph of recovered bullets viewed through a firearms examination microscope.
A shows side-by-side images of two bullets recovered from the same gun. B shows side-by-side images of two bullets recovered from
different examples of the same type of gun. From Los Angeles County Sheriff's Crime Laboratory, courtesy Barry Fisher.

The St. Valentine's Day Massacre

40

On Valentine's Day 1928, members of Al Capone's gang gunned down seven members of the rival Moran gang in broad daylight in northside Chicago. There was an outcry for law enforcement to solve the crime and bring a time of rampant lawlessness to a close. Unfortunately, rumors abounded, including implications of police involvement in the murders. The rumors were based on the ruse used by the Capone gang members—they dressed up as police officers—and the weapon used—the "Tommy gun." However, authorities did respond quickly and arrests were made.

Calvin Goddard was engaged to conduct an examination of the firearms evidence. Goddard used microscopy of the scene and test-fired ammunition to show that the killers had used a 12-gauge shotgun and two Thompson submachine guns. He further tested all the Thompson submachine guns used by the police and showed that none of them was involved in the killings. In contrast, he found positive matches to guns later found in the home of one of the suspects. (See Figure 3.12.)

Like any mechanical process, firing a weapon creates wear that can slowly change the look of the fine striations. As a consequence, it may be more difficult to decide whether bullets fired at different times do or do not come from the same gun.

An important consequence of Goddard's work in the case is that funding was provided for him to establish in 1929 the Scientific Crime Detection Laboratory at Northwestern University. This is credited as being the first independent crime laboratory in the United States, although August Vollmer undoubtedly had been responsible for instituting several laboratory-based investigations in U. C. Berkeley and in Los Angeles in the period 1910 to 1923.

The Slug in the Wall: The Reality of Deformed Bullets

Unlike projectiles fired into the controlled environment of a recovery tank, or cartridge cases, bullets recovered from crime scenes are often damaged on

FIGURE 3.12
The "Tommy gun." A popular weapon with gangs in the prohibition era, the Thompson submachine gun was the first successful rapid fire gun available to civilian and military users. The first models were introduced in 1921 and the model shown here is the M1928, introduced in 1928. From http://commons.wikimedia.org/wiki/Image:Submachine_gun_M1928_Thompson.jpg

impact—even with a body. In some cases, the bullet may flatten or appear to "rip." Examiners still make every attempt to draw as much information as possible from these projectiles. Despite the considerable damage that can occur, recovered bullets can show sufficient detail to permit microscopic comparison of striations. Figure 3.13 shows bullets that are deformed, whether by design (left image, hollow-point) or as a result of impact on a hard surface (right image).

Shotguns

Shotguns are different from rifled firearms. For shotguns, the barrel diameter is called **gauge**. Like with wires and needles, gauge numbers for shotguns go down as the size of the bore goes up. That means the bore of a 16-gauge shotgun is smaller than that of a 12-gauge. The reason for this oddity is a historical one. Gauge has nothing to do with shot size but comes from the number of solid spheres of a diameter equal to bore of the barrel that could be made from a

 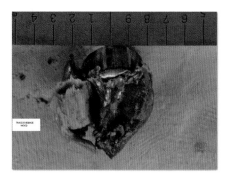

FIGURE 3.13
Deformed bullets. The image on the left is a hollow-point bullet showing the intended mushrooming deformation on impact. The image on the right is a regular bullet that was deformed following passage through wood; note that there is a fragment of wood trapped in the deformed bullet that could be examined for trace evidence. Note also that the lands and grooves can still be seen in both images. Left image (mushroomed hollow-point), from http://commons.wikimedia.org/wiki/Image:.38_Special_mushrooming_side_view.jpg; Right image courtesy Ronnie Freels.

FIGURE 3.14
Shotgun shell. Shotgun shells share some features with regular ammunition, including the presence of a cap and primer, and propellant. However, the bullet is replaced by shot, separated from the propellant by a wad, and the round is contained in a plastic case. Older shells had paper cases. The case is crimped shut at the top to contain the charge of shot. From http://commons.wikimedia.org/wiki/Image:Cartridge.gif

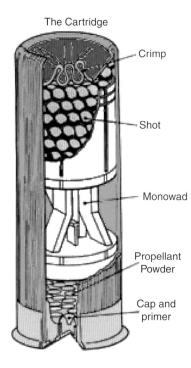

The Cartridge

Crimp

Shot

Monowad

Propellant Powder

Cap and primer

pound of lead. Hence, the popular 12-gauge shotgun has an inside diameter equal to that of a sphere made from ½ of a pound of lead. (See Figure 3.14.)

Shotgun ammunition differs too. Just the name refers to the fact that shotgun shells are not like bullets. Rather than firing a single projectile, a shotgun disperses a number of balls or pellets, called **shot**, packaged together in a shell. Depending on the size of the balls, it is referred to as *birdshot* (diameter smaller than 0.20 inches or 5 mm) and *buckshot* (diameters from about 0.24–0.36 inches). Finally, shotgun barrels have smooth bore, so the shot is not marked with striations. Instead, examiners use the size and weight of recovered shot to identify the type of shell fired. Association with a specific weapon depends on examination of the spent cartridge cases. Shotgun barrels have a constriction, called the **choke**, near the muzzle to control shot dispersion.

Some hunters use the rule of thumb that birdshot pellets can be measured into the cartridge by weight and poured in, while buckshot pellets must be carefully placed in a specific arrangement within a shell to make the shot fit.

The one gauge oddity is the .410 caliber shotgun, whose barrel diameter really is 0.410 inches (that would be about 67 gauge). This caliber "weapon" was intended for skeet shooting, though some people do hunt with it.

Automated Firearm Identification Systems

THE NATIONAL INTEGRATED BALLISTIC INFORMATION NETWORK (NIBIN)

The National Integrated Ballistic Information Network (NIBIN) is a database of fired cartridge casing and bullet images. Photomicrographs of bullets and cartridge casings are scanned or recorded directly to the system. The network can compare evidentiary images with those from regional and national databases. Potential matches are then verified by a firearms examiner.

THE INTEGRATED BALLISTIC IDENTIFICATION SYSTEM (IBIS)

Before NIBIN, the FBI and the ATF each had an automated search system. The FBI's program, DRUGFIRE, emphasized cartridge images. The ATF system, called the Integrated Ballistic Identification System (IBIS), had one database for bullets (Bulletproof) and one for cartridges (Brasscatcher). NIBIN incorporates IBIS technology, microscopes, and data recording and mining. NIBIN has pages for success stories, including a continually updated "Hit of the Week." Figure 3.15 shows an IBIS workstation and Figure 3.16 is a screen capture of images processed by it.

REFERENCE COLLECTIONS

States like New York and Maryland require new guns to have sample casings and bullets submitted to a reference collection. Such databases are not backdoor

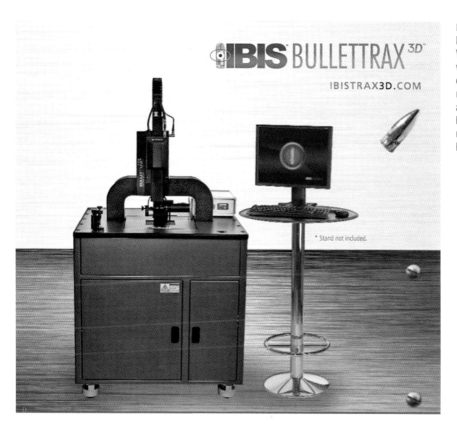

FIGURE 3.15
IBIS Bullettrax 3d Workstation. The workstation consists of a sample holder, microscope, computer, and display. Reproduced by permission of FTI, manufacturers of the IBIS unit.

43

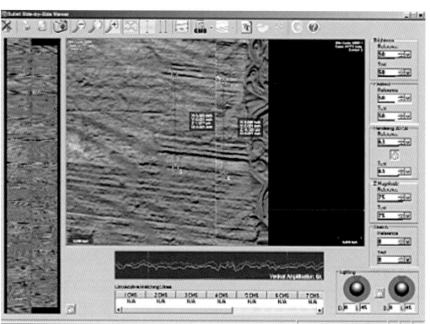

FIGURE 3.16
Bullettrax screenshot. Screenshot from Bullettrax showing side-by-side images of bullets. Reproduced by permission of FTI, manufacturers of the IBIS unit.

gun registrations. They contain no information about the gun owner but merely serve as a registry for ballistic samples.

Bullet Holes

Examination of bullet holes in clothing and entrance and exit wounds to the body can provide information that can assist in reconstruction of the shooting. For example, it may be possible to determine which direction the bullet was traveling. Physical examination together with chemical testing can provide information about how far away from the target the gun was when fired.

ENTRANCE HOLES

Bullet entrance holes typically have even margins. The diameter of the entrance mark is not an accurate measure of the caliber of the bullet. Because fabric can stretch, most noncontact entrance holes are slightly smaller than the bullet that created them. Entrance holes may exhibit *bullet wipe residue,* a darkened ring around margins of the hole literally made by lead wiped from the bullet as it passed. Bullet holes in bloodstained clothing will become distorted and smaller as the blood dries. Figure 3.17 shows the circular hole and surrounding **stippling** from discharge residues on white cotton from a bullet fired at 8 inches from a Colt. 38. Compare with the entry hole in Figure 3.18 of an angled entry wound.

Bullets approaching at an angle leave elongated entrance marks with even margins. If there are several holes in a garment, aligning them may give information about the position of the body when the shot was fired.

Fragment Entrance Holes

A bullet that strikes a hard surface before the target can fragment or expand. The intermediate impact slows the bullet. The entrance holes of fragments or expanded bullets have irregular margins and may be difficult to distinguish from exit holes. Because the bullet has passed through another object, there likely will not be any bullet wipe. However, minute portions of the object that the bullet struck may be embedded in its final target.

Exit Holes

Exit holes have irregular margins and are largely free from bullet wipe residue. Exit holes may be larger in diameter than the entrance hole or diameter of the bullet. When the bullet exits material, it may be frayed outward. This is especially true when expanding bullets are used or if the bullet fragments. Figure 3.18 shows the elongated entry hole and the characteristic star-shaped exit hole from a close-range shot to the head.

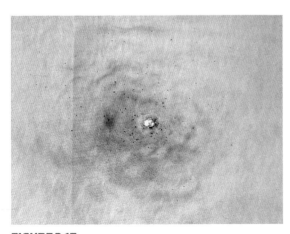

FIGURE 3.17
Bullet hole and discharge pattern. The hole and discharge pattern resulting from firing a bullet from a .38 Colt straight into white cotton at a distance of 8 inches. Courtesy Ronnie Freels.

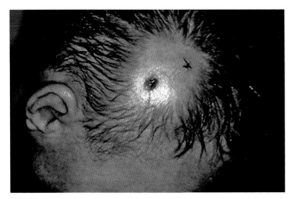

FIGURE 3.18
Entry and exit wounds from close-range shot to the head. Note the elongated entry hole with dark residue staining around it, and the typical star-shaped exit wound. Courtesy Dr. Edward C. Klatt.

FIGURE 3.19
Muzzle discharge. The photograph shows the muzzle discharge from a Glock 30 at the moment of firing. From http://www.everystockphoto.com/photo.php?imageId=1394460

Gunshot Residues

The gases that propel a bullet out of a firearm also expel gunshot residues (GSR) when the bullet exits the weapon. Primers, gunpowder, and even microscopic bits of metal are emitted in a cone-shaped pattern that begins at the muzzle. Gunshot residues also may be emitted from the gap between the barrel and cylinder in a revolver.

The distance that residue travels varies with the firearm and type of gunpowder used. Handguns with short barrels do not expel residues as far as rifles with longer barrels. Flake, tubular, and irregularly shaped gunpowder will not travel as far as ball powder because it encounters more drag. As the distance between muzzle and target increases, gunshot residue patterns become broader and less concentrated with materials.

COMPONENTS OF GUNSHOT RESIDUE (GSR)

Gunshot residue is normally a combination of unburned and partially burned gunpowder (nitrates), soot (carbon black) from completely burned gunpowder, and lead, but it may contain detectable traces of other materials such as antimony and barium from primers. Because lead is toxic, many manufacturers are reducing the content of lead in their products. Some ammunition, like that used for hunting in wetlands, is nearly lead free.

Gunpowder

Modern smokeless gunpowder and black powder contain nitrate compounds. Black powder is a mixture of potassium nitrate, charcoal, and sulfur. The smoke in this powder comes from the charcoal component.

Single-based gunpowder usually contains nitrocellulose (cellulose hexanitrate). These powders are "smoke free" but still leave deposits. Double-based

Firearms must be kept clean. The amount of residue emitted from a gun varies from shot to shot even with the same type of cartridge. Repetitive firing can slowly increase the amount of residue because of fouling in the barrel.

powder is a mixture of nitrocellulose and nitroglycerin (glyceral trinitrate). Triple-based powders may contain nitroguanidine in addition to a double-based mixture.

Nitrates. Nitrates are the oxidizing material in black powder. Potassium nitrate can be mined as a mineral or created by chemical processes. Even though the powder is burned in the firing process, nitrate deposits will be found in GSR.

Lead. Lead residues can be lead styphnate from the primer or minute amounts of lead vapor and particulates from the melting of the bullet during firing. Particulate lead, tiny balls of metal, will travel farther than vaporous lead. However, the dense lead vapor can "raft" on gunpowder particles and travel to the target.

Antimony and Barium. Some primers contain barium nitrate and antimony sulfide, though newer primer formulations avoid these metals and lead.

DETECTING GSR

Evidence may be inspected for GSR stippling with the unaided eye and with a microscope. One place to start is near a bullet hole. After looking for visible traces of GSR, chemical tests for nitrates and lead are applied. Collection and analysis of metal particle residues is covered later.

Chemical Tests

Griess Test for Nitrites. The **Griess test**, or (Dillon's) modified Griess test, is a color test that detects nitrite residues. The results of this test can help firearms examiners with **distance determination**. A test paper, essentially a type of photographic paper desensitized to light, is sprayed with Griess reagent (sulfanilic acid and α-naphthol) and heated while pressed against the area suspected of having GSR, which was sprayed with dilute acetic acid (vinegar solution). The resulting reaction produces an orange azo dye. (See Figure 3.20.)

Triple-based powders are used by the military and are not widely seen among game or target shooters.

Nitrocellulose is the flash paper used by magicians to burn a sheet leaving "nothing." It was used in film by the movie industry but was replaced, as the hot bulbs of movie projectors could cause the film to flash over in the same way.

46

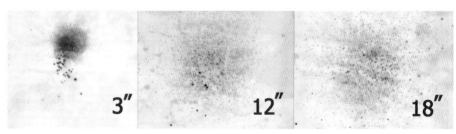

FIGURE 3.20
Firearms discharge residues. Discharge residues from a gun fired at 3, 12, and 18 inches away from the target. The residues are detected by the Griess test for nitrite produced by the propellant. Images from LA County Sheriff's Crime Laboratory, courtesy Barry Fisher.

Sodium Rhodizonate Test for Lead. Evidence is sprayed with yellow-orange sodium rhodizonate solution. The salt reacts with lead to form a bright pink complex. This color test is confirmed by application of diluted hydrochloric acid. A color change from pink to blue indicates lead deposited. Figure 3.21 is the same material as shown in Figure 3.17 but developed with sodium rhodizonate reagent to detect lead residues.

Gunshot Residue Distance Standards

Because gunshot residue varies, firearms examiners create distance standards to attempt to duplicate the evidence and bracket the muzzle-to-target distance. Using the same weapon and ammunition, the examiner fires test shots into squares of white cloth called *witness panels*. Tests are made at distances from contact to about 4 feet in small increments.

The witness panels are then processed like evidence. The results of the Griess and **sodium rhodizonate tests** are used to estimate the muzzle-to-target distance. The witness panel at the minimum firing distance (closest position likely) will show more concentrated residue with less dispersion than the evidence. At maximum firing distance, the witness panel will show a lighter, more dispersed pattern of residues.

Gunshot Residue Rule of Thumb

If the firearm is not recovered or if it has been rendered incapable of generating distance standards, there are some indicators of firing distance seen in gunshot evidence. As the weapon is brought closer to the target, the residue concentrations increase but the size of the pattern decreases. Though the size of the residue plume may vary, the range that is most interesting is less than 4 feet.

> Color tests detect the presence or absence of a chemical but may not give an indication of its quantity. These are sometimes referred to as *presumptive tests*. Chemical tests must be applied in a certain order. The Griess test is performed first because it does not interfere with tests for lead residues. We will learn more about the order of testing in the fingerprints chapter (Chapter 4).

> At shorter distances, handguns may deposit greater concentrations of gunshot residues than rifles.

47

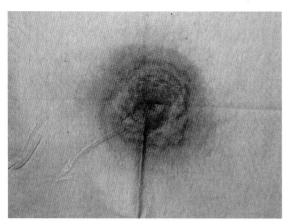

FIGURE 3.21
Lead in firearms discharge residues. Discharge residues contain lead from primer and traces of lead deposited in the barrel when lead bullets are fired. This can be detected by the rhodizonate test, as shown in this figure. This is the same material as shown in Figure 3.17. Image courtesy Ronnie Freels.

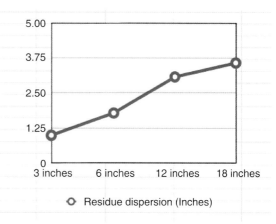

Residue dispersion (Inches)

FIGURE 3.22
Distance determination. The muzzle discharge dissipates with distance. The width of residue patterns from the Griess or rhodizonate test can be used to give an indication of firing distance. This chart is constructed from the data shown in Figure 3.20. Created by author.

Contact or Near Contact

Contact or near-contact gunshots deposit a dark ring of GSR around the margins of the entry hole. Heat from the shot may melt synthetic fibers or scorch natural ones. The blast may even carry fibers and GSR deep into the wound.

Close Range (2–12")

Close-range gunshots leave the entrance hole marked with GSR that is visible to the unaided eye.

Intermediate Range (12–24")

The GSR pattern from an intermediate-range gunshot may not be easily seen with the eye. Such evidence should be processed by microscopic examination.

The absence of evidence is not the evidence of absence. When no GSR is found around a bullet hole, it may mean the weapon was fired at such a distance that the residues could not reach the target, the bullet passed through an object on the way to the target, or the residues were removed by mechanical means (brushing or washing).

Moderate Range (24–48")

Detecting GSR at this range can be difficult. The deposit depends upon the caliber, barrel length, and powder type used in the ammunition.

At longer distances, only a trace of GSR may be found. Such trace levels can arise from handling a weapon or being near one that was discharged.

PRIMER RESIDUE ON THE HANDS: WHO IS THE SHOOTER?

As mentioned earlier, primers are formulated with lead styphnate, barium nitrate, and antimony sulfide. Other compounds containing elements such as aluminum, sulfur, and tin may also be present. When a gun is fired, blowback from the primer is deposited on the back of the firing hand. It can then be transferred elsewhere by movement, and, as with GSR, traces of primer residue may wind up on a person who handles a weapon or is standing nearby when it is discharged. Primer residue can be washed away or mechanically disturbed (brushing or scrubbing), so it is advisable to take samples from a potential shooter's hands or "bag" them to recover the evidence.

If present, primer residue is lifted from the hands with adhesive tape or an *adhesive chuck*, a holder specific to the microscope, that is searched with a scanning electron microscope (SEM) equipped with an energy-dispersive X-ray (EDX) analysis array. Once very time consuming for the examiner, laboratories now employ automated SEM–EDX systems that permit unattended scans for the characteristic particles formed when the discharge gases condense.

This testing provides information about the morphology and composition of the particles. The X-rays are employed to provide the energy-dispersive pattern and, thereby, the elemental composition of the particles in terms of lead, barium, antimony, and others.

The morphology of the microscopic particles and their elemental composition provide identification that the material is residue from a gunshot and not environmental contamination (see Figure 3.23). Before the advent of automated

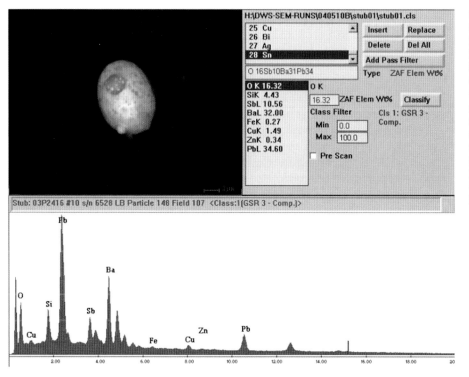

FIGURE 3.23
SEM image of gunshot residue particle, and its X-ray spectrum. Screen shot from SEM showing a GSR particle (top left) and its X-ray energy spectrum (in red at bottom). The particle size and shape together with the lead, antimony, and barium composition is characteristic of a GSR. Courtesy of Ronnie Freels and Bob Poole.

scanning stages in SEMs equipped with EDX analyzers, evidence of firing a gun was obtained from analysis of washings from the hands of the suspected shooter.

Atomic absorption (AA) spectrophotometry was the most common technique used to detect the presence of barium and antimony. A sample is vaporized to its constituent elements using a flame or electrical heating element. A hollow cathode lamp, specific for the element to be tested, is beamed through the elemental vapor. The extent to which the excited atoms absorb the radiant light is measured by a detector array and can be used to calculate the concentration of the element in the sample.

Serial Number Restoration

Serial numbers are used to identify everything from cars to firearms to computers. On metal components, the serial number is usually stamped in during manufacturing. In plastics and other items, the identification mark might be molded or etched into the surface.

FILLING THE SERIAL NUMBER

Serial numbers may be recovered by drawing material deep into the remainder of the markings. On nonmetal objects, contrast media may work. Alternatively, a tiny metal particle can be drawn into crevices using a magnet from the reverse side.

49

BOX 3.1 GSR TEST SPECIFICITY

The specificity of tests to prove the presence of various chemicals in firearms discharge residues has been questioned for several decades. Attempts were made to improve the specificity of identification of discharge residues by improving the specificity of the analytical technique, but the issue has always been to prove that the chemical detected came from discharge residue and not another source.

For example, the "paraffin test" for nitrates, first introduced into the United States in 1933, is rarely used anymore. Melted paraffin wax was applied to the hand, cooled, and then peeled away. The wax sample was sprayed or swabbed with diphenylamine, now considered a carcinogen, yielding a blue color if nitrates were present. Unfortunately, the test could not distinguish GSR nitrates from nitrates of other sources.

As far as metallic residue from primer is concerned, attempts were made to get round the issue of specificity of source by measuring the relative concentrations of detected metals and using more accurate techniques such as neutron activation analysis (NAA) and inductively coupled plasma mass spectrometry (ICP-MS). However, there is general agreement today that chemical testing alone can be regarded only as presumptive.

RAISING THE SERIAL NUMBER

Sometimes, for metal surfaces, the metal around the serial number can be eaten away with an acid solution. Because the metal directly under the number was hardened when stamped, it resists etching, and the softer, unstamped metal will be eaten away, causing the serial number to rise up.

SUMMARY

Rifling, a series of helical lands and grooves running down the barrel of a firearm, is an important class characteristic. Rifling spins the projectile, giving it a straighter trajectory.

Striations are microscopic tool marks created during the process of drilling the tube of a gun barrel and during its rifling. When a bullet is fired, the soft, hot lead expands into the lands and grooves and is marked with these tiny lines individual to a particular firearm.

Impressed action marks include those made by the firing pin, breech face, extractor, ejector, or other machined surfaces.

Bullets usually come in a cartridge, a case containing the bullet with a primer and gunpowder to propel it from the weapon. Bullets are examined using a comparison microscope. The investigator chooses a well-defined feature in one bullet and looks for it in the other. Then the bullets are rotated together to look for points of correspondence.

The gases that propel a bullet out of a firearm also expel gunshot residues (GSR) when the bullet exits the weapon. Primers, gunpowder, and even microscopic bits of metal are emitted in a cone-shaped pattern that begins at the muzzle. The distance that residue travels varies with the firearm and type of gunpowder used.

Gunshot residue is normally a combination of unburned and partially burned gunpowder, soot (carbon black) from completely burned gunpowder, and lead, but it may contain detectable traces of other materials. The Griess test is a color test that detects nitrite residues. The sodium rhodizonate test identifies lead.

Because gunshot residue varies, firearms examiners create distance standards to attempt to duplicate the evidence and bracket the muzzle-to-target distance. Using the same weapon and ammunition, the examiner fires test shots into squares of white cloth called *witness panels*. The results of the Griess and sodium rhodizonate tests are used to estimate the muzzle-to-target distance.

PROBLEMS

1. Give the word or phrase for the following definitions:
   a. the diameter of a gun barrel measured between opposing lands
   b. the diameter of a shotgun barrel
   c. spiraling grooves running the length of the barrel of a weapon
   d. a pattern of gunpowder residue deposited on an object shot at close range
   e. the raised portion between the grooves in a rifled bore
   f. a target used in determining firing distance
2. Categorize the following as individual or class characteristics:
   a. six grooves, right-twist rifling
   b. the mark made by a firing pin
3. Describe the use of the following tests and techniques:
   a. Griess test
   b. sodium rhodizonate test
   c. atomic absorption spectroscopy
   d. comparison microscopy
   e. scanning electron microscopy
   f. gunshot residue distance standards
4. Which of the following can be used for individualization?
   a. recovered bullets
   b. recovered shotgun shot
   c. recovered cartridge casings
   d. rifling in a recovered weapon
   e. firing pin marks from a recovered weapon
5. Describe the difference between the barrel of a rifle and that of a shotgun.
6. Describe the variance of GSR deposits with distance from contact to 4 feet.
7. How can a firearms examiner approximate firing distance?
8. What elements are present in gunshot residue?
9. What elements are present in primer residue?
10. Describe a method for restoration of a serial number.

GLOSSARY

Action the mechanism by which the weapon loads, fires, or removes cartridges.

Bore the interior of a firearm barrel.

Breachface the part of the breechblock which is against the head of the cartridge case or shotshell during firing.

Breechblock the rear part of a firearm barrel.

Caliber the diameter of the barrel of a rifled firearm measured across opposing lands; caliber may have units in hundredths of an inch or millimeters.

Cartridge a case containing the bullet with a primer and gunpowder to propel it from the weapon.

Choke an interior constriction placed at or near the muzzle end of a shotgun's barrel for the purpose of controlling shot dispersion.

Distance determination the process of determining the distance between the firearm and a target, usually based on the distribution of powder patterns or the spread of a shot pattern.

Ejector the mechanism in a firearm that throws the cartridge or fired case from the firearm.

Extractor the mechanism in a firearm by which a cartridge of a fired case is withdrawn from the chamber.

Firearms identification a discipline mainly concerned with determining whether a bullet or cartridge was fired by a particular weapon. Not to be confused with *ballistics*, which is the study of a projectile in motion.

Gauge size designation of a shotgun, originally the number of lead balls with the same diameter as the barrel that would make a pound. For example, a 12-gauge shotgun would have a bore diameter of a lead ball $1/12$ pound in weight. The only exception is the .410 shotgun, in which bore size is 0.41 inch.

Griess test a chemical test for nitrites from gunshot residue.

Grooves the cut or low-lying portions between the lands in a rifled bore.

GSR Gunshot Residues, the total residues resulting from the discharge of a firearm. GSR includes gunpowder and primer residues, plus metallic residues from projectiles, fouling, etc.

Impressed striation marks marks left on the cartridge case by the mechanisms involved in loading and removing the ammunition from the gun.

Lands the raised portion between the grooves in a rifled bore.

Rifling the spiral grooves that are formed in the bore of a firearm barrel that are designed to import spin to the projectile when it is fired.

Shells shotgun ammunition, the equivalent of a cartridge.

Shot balls or pellets packaged in a shotgun shell.

Sodium rhodizonate test a chemical test for lead, used to locate gunshot residue.

Stippling a pattern of dots; in a gunshot case, this can be a pattern of primer and gunpowder residue left on the shooter or a person or object shot at close range.

Striated action marks striations on the lands and grooves that are transferred to a bullet as it is forced through the barrel.

Striations microscopic tool marks.

Friction ridge evidence. Fingerprints are the impressions left by the friction ridge skin at the tips of fingers. Similar marks are made by friction ridge skin at other sites on the hands, and on feet. These marks are a special example of the general category of impression evidence, that includes footwear and tire tracks. The figure shows, clockwise from the left: shoe prints, footprints, fingerprint, hand print, fingerprint, print of whole finger. From Stockxpert.

CHAPTER 4
Fingerprints

Clarence Hiller

Late one September night, Clarence was awakened by his wife, who had heard noises from downstairs. Unfortunately for Clarence, the noises had been caused by an armed burglar who shot and killed him. The police found four fingerprints at the scene that matched those of a convicted vfelon that they had on record. The suspect eventually was tried and convicted.

This is an almost everyday story in detective fiction and in fact, of how fingerprints can give a positive identification of a suspect leading to his arrest and trial. This was no ordinary case, however. Clarence was Clarence Hiller, the year was 1910, and the trial and subsequent appeal of the suspect, Thomas Jennings, established the admissibility of the fingerprint evidence in U.S. courts. The Illinois Supreme Court found that "there is a scientific basis for the system of fingerprint identification, and that the courts are justified in admitting this class of evidence; that this method of identification is in such general and common use that the courts cannot refuse to take judicial cognizance of it." Fingerprint evidence remains today as the forensic science gold standard for personal identification, despite more than a century of challenge and despite the advances in DNA evidence.

CENTRAL QUESTIONS

What can be answered:

- Do the fingerprints belong to the individual in question?

We cannot answer the following:

- When were the fingerprints deposited?

We are learning or researching the following:

- What is the race/gender/age of the person who deposited the fingerprints?
- Obtaining DNA from fingerprints.

FINGERPRINTS AND IDENTITY: A BRIEF HISTORY

Fingerprints have imparted a sense of identity for hundreds of years. In ancient China, fingerprints were used to seal documents, and at around the end of the eighteenth century, the English naturalist Thomas Bewick identified his engravings with "his mark" — his fingerprint. The systematic use of fingerprints as a means of identification is more recent, with the following significant timeline:

1858: William Herschel required recipients in Bengal, India, to "sign" for their pensions by leaving their fingerprint.

1880: The first-recorded suggestion that fingerprints could be used to identify someone was made in a letter to Nature by the Scottish physician, Dr. Henry Faulds.

1891: Argentine criminalist Dr. Juan Vucetich began to devise a way to group fingerprints. Confronted with a growing data management problem, he developed a classification system capable of sorting prints efficiently. The framework of his early classification system is still in operation in many Spanish-speaking countries.

1892: Francis Galton set out three principles of fingerprints that formed the basis of a classification system still in use today. In *Finger Prints*, the first book on the subject, Galton suggested that fingerprints were unique to the individual, unchanging throughout one's lifetime, and contained sufficient detail to create a classification system by assigning fingerprints to three patterns: loops, whorls, and arches. An ethical scientist, he noted that his system lacked the ability to identify heredity, race, or gender. (Even today, such information cannot be determined from a fingerprint alone.)

1897: Sir Edward Richard Henry created a classification system that is the basis of the one used in the U.S. today. Building on Galton's work, Henry published a treatise on **dactyloscopy** in 1900.

1902: First systematic use of fingerprints in the U.S. was conducted by the New York City Civil Service Commission, to avoid fraud in tests.

1904: Fingerprint records used in Leavenworth Federal Penitentiary.

1918: Edmund Locard proposed that if 12 points are the same in two fingerprints, then they are from the same person.

1924: Congress established the Identification Division of the FBI.

THE ANATOMY OF A FINGERPRINT

Fingerprints can be regarded as a special category of mark evidence. The main difference is that the marks are created in skin and therefore offer a means of personal identification. Skin is the largest organ of the body. It provides our first line of defense to infection and the mechanism for our sense of touch. Friction skin provides grip to the hands and feet. In fact, the same friction skin ridges that allow you to hold an object (say, the lid of a cookie jar) may tell a criminalist that you touched it.

Looking at the tip of your finger, you will see a pattern of ridges and grooves. The pattern seen on the epidermis, the outermost layer of skin, is generated by a layer of cells that lie below it. These cells are the **dermal papillae**. They form a layer between the outer skin and the inner skin, or dermis. Though they grow as we mature, the patterns created by the dermal papillae do not change. Hence, our fingerprints do not become more (or less!) complex over our lives.

Deep in the dermis are the mechanical works of the skin: nerves, capillaries, and sweat glands. Sweat travels up ducts from the dermis to emerge through tiny pores in the cells of the skin ridge. When an object is touched, the fingers work like a self-inking stamp pad.

Figure 4.1 illustrates how the dermal papillae produce the characteristic patterns of friction ridge skin.

You do not always leave fingerprints. People with very dry skin may not make fingerprints when they pick up an object. The same is true for someone who recently washed and dried his or her hands.

FINGERPRINTS AS EVIDENCE OF IDENTITY

Taken together, the principles that Galton outlined in his 1900 text are the reason why fingerprints may be used as evidence in court. We will explore each in turn.

Fingerprints Are Unique

So far, no two fingerprints have been found to be the same. If fingerprints were found to be coincidentally the same, there would be no way to use them to identify individuals. In his early work, Galton calculated there might be 64 billion different fingerprints. More recently, mathematicians have considered that there may be no limit to the number of possible fingerprints. Due to the large number of features present in a fingerprint, the probability for the existence of two identical impressions is extremely small.

Fingerprints Do Not Change over Your Lifetime

Fingerprints do not grow or lessen in complexity as we mature. However, wounds that disturb the dermal papillae will form scars that manifest in the epidermis. Suspects have cut into their fingertips and burned them with heat or chemicals. However, the results are often less than successful. The irony is that any scar formed would in itself become a distinguishing mark identifying the individual.

There are snowflakes that are alike! Snowflake patterns are dictated by the hydrogen bonding of water molecules. While there are millions of combinations, obeying the rules for combining water molecules sets a chance for snowflakes to be the same. For fingerprints, there is no such rule to limit pattern formation, suggesting there may be an infinite number.

57

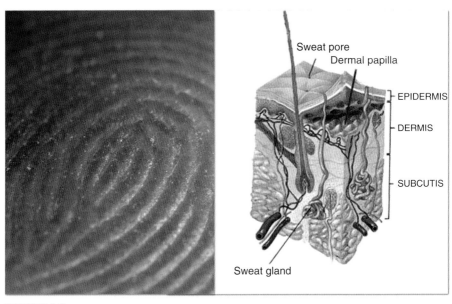

FIGURE 4.1
Skin and fingerprints. Left: a close up of the dermal ridges on a finger pad. Right: two-dimensional diagram through the full thickness of skin showing the features of significance in forming dermal ridge patterns and fingerprints. These are the dermal papillae (identified by blue typescript and shown by the blue arrow) and the sweat glands and sweat pores that secrete the substances that form the fingerprint when the skins comes in contact with a surface. The papillae are the features responsible for the formation of the friction skin patterns. Finger pad from Stockxpert; skin modified by author from http://en.wikipedia.org/wiki/Image:Skin.jpg

When a person is not adequately hydrated or has very dry skin, his or her fingerprints may exhibit lines that look like long vertical cracks. These are striation marks. Because their pattern changes with the water content of the skin, striations are not part of the classification system, but they can be a descriptive of an individual.

Fingerprints Have Sufficient Detail to Allow Them to Be Classified Systematically

All fingerprints can be divided into three classes on the basis of their general pattern: loops, whorls, and arches. From 60 to 65% of the population has loops, 30 to 35% has whorls, and about 5% has arches (see Figure 4.2).

FINGERPRINT CLASSIFICATION

Fingerprint records are classified and stored by systems that depend on the three fundamental characteristics described previously. Each of the three pattern types has distinguishing focal points, which are the basis for all 10-finger classification systems presently in use. Systematic classification is aided by other features in the print. **Deltas** are triangular formations, or a dividing of the ridges, and are found between loops. Loops have a defined center, the **core**, which provides a reference point.

Loop

The **loop** pattern is the most common in fingerprints. Occurring in 60 to 65% of fingerprint patterns, loops are concentric hairpin ridges that enter and exit from the same side of the pattern and contain two distinct focal points: the core and

WHORL

In a whorl pattern, the ridges are usually circular.

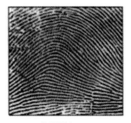

ARCH

In an arch pattern the ridges enter from one side, make a rise in the center, and exit generally on the opposite side.

LOOP

In a loop pattern, the ridges enter from either side, re-curve, and pass out or tend to pass out the same side they entered.

FIGURE 4.2
Whorls (W), Arches (A), and Loops (L) are the three basic ridge patterns used to describe fingerprint morphology. The ridges are usually circular in whorls, enter from one side then rise in the center and exit on the opposite side in an arch, and enter from one side and curve back to exit on the same side in loops. From www.fbi.gov/hq/cjisd/takingfps.html

a delta. The **ulnar loop**, which tilts toward the ulna bone, or little finger, is the most common. **Radial loops**, tilting toward the radius bone or index finger, are less common and most often found on the index finger. Deltas can be seen at the bottom left of the highlighted area in the whorl and the loop in Figure 4.2

Whorl

Found in about 30% of fingerprint patterns, the **whorl** is a rounded or circularly shaped pattern containing two or more deltas. Whorls are divided into plain, **central pocket loop**, **double loop**, and **accidental** types. Plain whorls and a central pocket loop have at least one ridge that makes a complete circuit. To tell the difference between them, an imaginary line is drawn between the two deltas. If the line touches any of the spiral ridges, the pattern is called a **plain whorl**. If not, the pattern is a central pocket loop. Double loop patterns must contain two separate loops, each with a distinct core in the same fingerprint. Finally, accidental patterns are a broad, catchall class containing combinations of patterns or patterns that do not fit into any other categories. (See Figure 4.3.)

Arch

The arch pattern has no delta or core and occurs only in about 5% of fingerprint patterns. In a **plain arch**, the ridge pattern rises in the middle but does not form a loop. In a **tented arch**, the center rises sharply in the middle but still does not form a loop.

The FBI Fingerprint Classification System

The FBI database contains more than 47 million records and is the largest in the world. The physical records in the **FBI classification system** are called *10-print cards*

FIGURE 4.3
As well as the plain whorl pattern shown in Figure 4.2, whorls can be present as central pocket, double loop, or accidental sub-classes. The central pocket and double loop characteristics are obvious from Figure 4.3. The accidental is more complex and is defined as consisting of a combination of two different types of patterns with the exception of the plain arch, with two or more deltas, or a pattern which possesses some of the requirements for two or more different types or a pattern which conforms to none of the definitions. Image from www.fbi.gov/hq/cjisd/ident.pdf

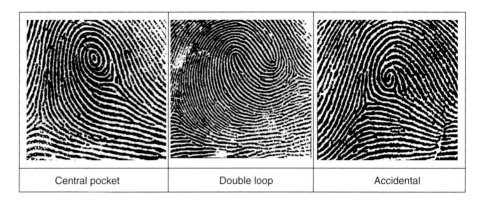

| Central pocket | Double loop | Accidental |

because they contain inked images of each finger. These are the marks labeled "**Rolled Impressions**" in Figure 4.4 and are—as the name implies—obtained by rolling each inked finger individually over the card. The rolling ensures that all ridge detail is captured. The "**Plain Impressions**" at the bottom of the card are taken by pressing all fingers directly onto the card and are used as a quality control check of the sequence of rolled prints.

The primary classification comes from the Henry system. It is called the *primary* classification because it is the first step in the FBI classification system. Ridge patterns from all 10 fingers are used to divide fingerprints into classes. To find the primary classification, the ridge patterns of fingerprints are converted into letters and numbers, and the scores are paired in a fraction as follows:

$$\frac{\text{R. Index R. Ring L. Thumb L. Middle L. Little} + 1}{\text{R. Thumb R. Middle R. Little L. Index L. Ring} + 1}$$

The basis for the determination of the primary classification is the presence or absence of the whorl pattern. Arch and loop patterns are given values of zero. Whorl patterns have different values depending on where they occur. In the first pair, the value of the whorl pattern is 16, and it decreases by a factor of 2 for each pair. The reason for adding 1 to the sum of values in the numerator and denominator is to avoid a zero classification and avoid dividing by zero.

Rolled Impressions →

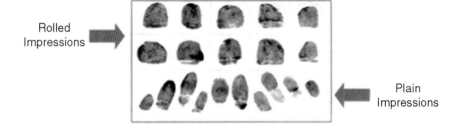

← Plain Impressions

FIGURE 4.4
A 10-print record card. From www.fbi.gov/hq/cjisd/takingfps.html

| 0 | 0 | 0 | 0 | 0 | arches or loops |
| 16 | 8 | 4 | 2 | 1 | whorls |

R. Index R. Ring L. Thumb L. Middle L. Little + 1

R. Thumb R. Middle R. Little L. Index L. Ring + 1

LIMITATIONS OF THE PRIMARY CLASSIFICATION

Using the primary classification, fingerprints can be grouped into 1024 categories. For example, if no whorls occur, the primary is 1/1. About 25% of people fall into this primary classification. Hence, even the FBI system can identify not an individual but rather a group of likely suspects.

Because they depend on complete prints from all 10 fingers, the Henry and FBI classification systems best serve cases where a full set of fingerprints is collected for comparison. Most crime scenes do not afford the investigator that luxury.

FINGERPRINTS AND IDENTIFICATION

Although loops, whorls, and arches, together with deltas and cores, provide an effective method for classification of fingerprints, they do not contain sufficient unique detail to permit identification of the person who left a print at the scene of a crime. Identification depends on the finer detail contained in ridge patterns. The broad categories described by Galton are described as general ridge flow and pattern features, or level 1 detail. Level 1 detail may be used for exclusion but, as we saw earlier with the primary classifications in the FBI database, it cannot provide identification. The next level of detail— level 2—found in minutiae does permit individualization and is discussed in the next section. There is a further degree of detail—level 3—but we will focus on the widely used information present at level 2, leaving level 3 for more advanced study.

Minutiae

Despite their pattern, all fingerprint types have many distinguishing characteristics in their ridge details, collectively termed **minutiae**. These fine details are the basis for individualization from a fingerprint lift. Examples of minutiae include **ridge endings** (where a ridge terminates), **bifurcations** (the branching of one ridge into two), and **islands** (short ridges; sometimes the island is extremely small and is classed as a *dot*). Minutiae are mapped by scanning a recovered print into a computer and then analyzing the resulting image. A single rolled print may have as many as 100 individual points, the number depending on the location of the print, there being more in the region near a delta. (See Figure 4.5.)

61

1   2   3   4

FIGURE 4.5

Latent print identification does not depend on the macro characteristics shown in Figures 4.2, 4.3, and 4.4, but uses the spatial location of specific features called minutiae. Examples include: Enclosures (1); ridge endings (2); islands, shown here as a point but could be a short length of ridge (3); and ridge bifurcation (4). Original drawings by author.

COMPARING MINUTIAE

Comparison of minutiae—sometimes referred to as *Galton points*—is the accepted method for identification of latent prints. The basis of the comparison lies in the relative spacial orientation of the minutiae, sometimes assisted by reference to a fixed point such as a delta. A typical "map" is shown in Figure 4.6.

Many examiners in the U.S. now follow the so-called **ACE-V method** for identification: analysis, comparison, evaluation, and verification. *Analysis* consists of the objective qualitative and quantitative assessment of level 1, level 2, and (in some cases) level 3 details to determine their proportion, interrelationship, and value to individualize. *Comparison* is the objective examination of the attributes observed during analysis in order to determine agreement or discrepancies between two friction ridge impressions. *Evaluation* is the cyclical procedure of comparison between two friction ridge impressions to effect a decision, that is: made by the same friction skin, not made by the same friction skin, or insufficient detail to form a conclusive decision. *Verification* is the independent analysis, comparison, and evaluation by a second qualified examiner of the friction ridge impressions. Evaluation is a subjective step, and that is why the verification process is so important.

FIGURE 4.6

Images are scanned, either manually by an examiner or electronically, and minutiae are identified and recorded. The figure shows some of the minutiae present in the whorl from Figure 4.2. Note that the arrows are used to identify some of the minutiae in the print but this is not a complete mapping. Annotated image based on http://en.wikipedia.org/wiki/Fingerprint

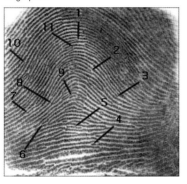

With poor-quality images, sometimes the data must be enhanced before a comparison can be attempted. Enhancing an image often requires an adjustment of the contrast. The process uses filters similar to those found in commercial digital photography software. A low-pass filter decreases contrast, while a high-pass filter increases it. Filters and algorithms with different selectivity are used to increase the contrast of a fingerprint from a colored or patterned background. A similar process can be applied to deconvolute overlapping prints. It is important that any process used only enhances the quality of the data and does not result in qualitative changes. Finally, examiners are increasingly turning to computers to assist with the task of comparing minutiae. Ridge detail data can be scanned in from the image of a latent print or analyzed from a digital photograph. Once digitized, information from the latent image can be compared to known information on file.

BOX 4.1 HOW MANY POINTS?

There is no standard for, nor do experts agree on, the number of minutiae required for two fingerprints to be considered the same. Ninety years ago Locard suggested 12 points, and most jurisdictions subsequently established rules requiring somewhere between 12 and 16 points, although some required as few as 8. However, in 1973 the International Association for Identification (IAI) published a report that concluded, "No valid basis exists at this time for requiring that a predetermined minimum number of friction ridge characteristics must be present in two impressions in order to establish positive identification." An international conference in June 1995 came to the same conclusion.

METHODS OF DETECTING FINGERPRINTS

Natural fingerprints transferred to articles at a crime scene arise from deposits of secretions from eccrine sweat glands, or from secondary residues from sebaceous or apocrine glands picked up on the fingers by touching surfaces such as the nose and that are then left in the fingerprint. Other sources include prints left in blood or imprints from greasy materials such as lubricants that might have been used in a rape.

Processing the crime scene or evidence items for fingerprints starts with a search for **visible prints**. They might be rendered in dirt, blood, or grease and found on hard or soft, porous or nonporous surfaces. On very soft surfaces like wax, clay, or paint, the criminalist may find **plastic prints**, an actual impression of the friction skin ridges. Plastic prints are almost like castings of fingerprints. Both of these types of fingerprints can be seen with the unaided eye.

After completing the search for visible (or patent) prints, the examiner will look for **latent prints,** or those that are not readily visible. There are many procedures available for development of latent prints, and the choice depends on several factors. In all cases—visible and developed latent prints—it is essential to record the evidence by photography and to process the items in a manner that preserves the integrity of the print.

To find a latent print, the examiner will select an appropriate method based on properties of the surface being examined, such as whether it is hard or soft, porous or nonporous, absorbent or nonabsorbent. Porous surfaces generally will preserve the print because it penetrates into the material, but they can present problems to some of the reagents used, as they too soak into the substrate. In contrast, nonporous surfaces such as glass require careful handling to prevent the latent print from smearing or being wiped off. The techniques applied will proceed from the least destructive method. Generally, the order of application is the use of lights, dusting, chemical staining or developing, and lifting/preserving.

63

The Mickelberg Finger

The importance of the integrity of recording and development of latent prints is illustrated by the case of Ray Mickelberg and his brothers.

Because latent prints are a physical deposit, it is theoretically possible to lift a print from one solid object and transfer it to another. The transfer could also be made from a facsimile of the original finger. The Perth (Australia) mint was hit by a sting operation in 1982. Two men made a series of small purchases of gold bullion, and, having established credibility, bought $650,000 (Australian) of bullion with a check that then bounced. Police arrested and charged three brothers, Peter, Ray, and Brian Mickelberg. The brothers were tried and convicted in 1983 on evidence that included a partial print recovered from the check that was a match to Ray.

The Mickelbergs protested their innocence, claiming that the fingerprint was a plant. During the investigation, the police had raided the brothers' apartment and found a bucket of silicone rubber casts of the hand and fingers of Ray. The brothers claimed that the police had then used one of the finger casts to plant the partial print by coating it with sebaceous secretions from the nose and rolling it over the check. There were several appeals, and points concerning the fingerprint were never completely resolved. One of the issues was whether the photographs of the latent print images were positives or negatives. If the partial print on the check had been planted as alleged, then the developed print would have been a negative of a natural print because the sweat secretions on the cast would be on the surface of the ridges rather than in the valleys, as is the case with natural prints. The records of the print processing could have been better, opening the door to several challenges. There were also disagreements as to whether the pattern of a print rolled from a firm object such as the cast would look the same as a rolled print from much a softer finger. None of the several appeals succeeded.

An interesting postscript to the cases was written 20 years after the trial when one of the officers involved admitted that the confessions produced in evidence were false. The Mickelbergs were freed, but no judgment was made regarding the prints.

We will consider the main techniques in the order that they are generally applied and then review some of the recommended protocols for approaching the development of latent prints.

Lights

Using light to visualize and record a print photographically is a nondestructive technique that does not interfere with the application of subsequent visualization methods. Using fiber-optic cables, light can even be made to bend around corners for a better look. There are several systems available, but the underlying principle of most is to use high-energy beams of ultraviolet (UV) light in the 400 to 200 nm wavelength range to locate prints on nonabsorbent surfaces. UV light is invisible to the naked eye but interacts with organic chemicals to cause fluorescence, resulting in the emission of light in the visible spectrum. The interaction can be with components of sweat or with chemicals applied to the surface. Natural fingerprints detected in this way are then photographed or further developed and preserved.

BOX 4.2   SEEING CLEARLY

Not all latent print detection systems use UV light and fluorescence. Some rely on reflected UV or visible wavelength light into a visible form, and some depend on visible region light inducing infrared luminescence. As well as enhancing the print, selective use of light sources can minimize interference from background sources. Figure 4.7 shows the dramatic enhancement obtained by using reflected light of 530 nm.

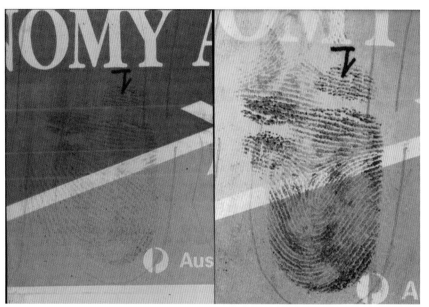

FIGURE 4.7
The differentiation between a latent print image and background can sometimes be enhanced by viewing reflected light at selected wavelengths. In this case, reflected light at the 530 nm wavelength markedly increases the clarity of the latent print image. Courtesy Rofin Australia.

65

LASERS

There was considerable interest in using lasers as the light source, but due to their cost and advances in chemical techniques, lasers have largely been replaced by alternative light sources. The differences between the two light sources are narrowing as lasers become less costly and more portable on the one hand and alternate light sources become more powerful on the other. (See Figure 4.8.)

ALTERNATIVE LIGHT SOURCES

Alternative light source (ALS) is the term generally used to describe a portable, high-intensity light source, such as halogen and xenon or indium arc lamps. These powerful light sources can be tuned to a particular wavelength using filters. Tuning the wavelength modulates the contrast of the print from its surface.

FIGURE 4.8
There are many light sources available for examination of evidence at the scene or in the laboratory. The figure shows the Rofin Polilight 7000 (left) intended for use in the laboratory, and the Poliray (right) intended for use as a handheld screening device at the scene. Courtesy Rofin Australia.

> **BOX 4.3   OTHER USES OF ALS**
>
> Lasers and ALS units have many uses in forensic science apart from latent print development. They are widely used at crime scenes to search for body fluids and can be used when examining inks or obliterated writings in questioned document cases. They have become more useful as the power of the units has increased, and crime scene and laboratory personnel must always be careful to wear protective eye coverings.

Dusting

Dusting powders consist of an adhesive and a contrast agent or colorant. When dusting for fingerprints, contrast is key. Dark powders, such as pulverized charcoal, are applied to light-colored surfaces and vice versa. The dusting agent is gently applied with a brush and either adheres to or reacts with components in the fingerprint, giving definition to the ridge pattern.

Use of hydragyrum, composed of one part mercury and two parts chalk by weight, was discontinued in 1967 because mercury vapor and dust are health hazards.

Many common powders are formulated with metals. Aluminum agents are generally adherents, while silver salts may be used to actually react with the print. Despite their toxicity and expense, these powders offer great stability. On rough surfaces, or to avoid smudging the print with a bristled brush, a criminalist can employ magnetic-sensitive powder using a *magna brush*, a magnetic wand.

Newer powders are formulated with a variety of fluorescent and phosphorescent dyes. Once these agents bind to a print, they can be illuminated and photographed under various light sources. These powders give good contrast for prints on uneven or multicolored surfaces but often need to be used in controlled conditions, making them poor choices in the field. Examples of dyes include crystal violet, acridine orange and yellow, Nile blue, and rhodamine B. (See Figure 4.9.)

Developers and Stains

IODINE

The oldest chemical technique in the book is the use of **iodine**. Fuming iodine is an excellent method for finding fingerprints on paper and cloth. Iodine reacts with fatty acids and moisture, visualizing a latent print with a yellow-to-brown color within a few seconds. However, because iodine sublimates so easily, developed prints will fade. The visualized prints must be immediately photographed or fixed.

FIGURE 4.9
Various techniques are used to develop latent prints, often depending on the color and nature of the substrate. Clockwise from top left: Camel hair brushes used to apply powders and light print developed on dark background by applying silver powder; magnetic brush and print on golf ball developed using magnetic gray powder formulated for use on plastic surfaces; fluorescent powder and print developed on multicolored background by application of the powder. Images courtesy BVDA America Inc.

Fixing the prints, like fixing a photograph, requires one more chemical step. The simplest method is treatment with a starch solution, which results in a long-lasting, blue-tinted print. On fine porous surfaces, such as facial tissue or tissue paper, 7,8-benzoflavone is used as the fixative.

More durable surfaces can be rubbed with silver foil or dusted with silver powder. Iodine adsorbed on the fingerprint residue will react with silver atoms to give a yellow salt, silver iodide. This salt eventually oxidizes in air and light to silver oxide, turning the print black.

NINHYDRIN

Ninhydrin has surpassed iodine as the most popular chemical method for processing latent fingerprints on porous, absorbent surfaces like paper, cardboard, and wood. Because amino acids do not react with the cellulose in paper or wood, the technique can be used on old prints. Ninhydrin reacts with amino acids in sweat, coloring the print purple (Ruhemann's purple). The color develops slowly and may take several hours to fully react. To increase their contrast, nonfluorescent Ruhemann's purple prints may be treated with metal salts to form photoluminescent complexes that reflect well when illuminated with laser light. Similar to ninhydrin but more sensitive, 1,8-diazafluoren-9-one (DFO) reacts with the amino acids and can be used to visualize fingerprints on paper using a tunable light source.

CYANOACRYLATE

Also called the "fuming Superglue technique," **cyanoacrylate** is used for processing latent prints on paper, plastic, and skin. Cyanoacrylate undergoes base-catalyzed polymerization. The polymer binds with sweat to visualize a latent print in a flat, white color over a few hours. To improve the visibility and contrast, the white prints can be dusted with fluorescein or crystal violet dye or a rhodamine-based magnetic powder and then photographed using an appropriate light source. The technique is so successful that small handheld devices have been created to allow the criminalist to work on prints in place at the scene. (See Figure 4.10.)

PHYSICAL DEVELOPER

When ninhydrin does not work, chemists often turn to **Physical Developer** (PD), an excellent reagent for paper and wood surfaces. PD reacts with oils, and, as such, it can be used on wet paper or paper that has been washed. Unfortunately, PD is a destructive method. Because it destroys any trace proteins, it must be used last. Further, the reagent solution is both difficult to prepare and unstable once made.

The formulation contains an aqueous solution of silver ions (silver nitrate), a buffered iron redox reaction, and a detergent. The detergent prevents the premature deposition of silver ions. Silver reacts with the print to produce a black image. Silver nitrate can be used on its own to develop prints on surfaces such as paper. The development of the latent print is caused by the reaction between the silver and chloride ions in sweat in the latent print. The silver chloride is light sensitive and turns black on exposure to light.

Iodine is a dark purple crystal that vaporizes to a purple gas. Like naphthalene (moth crystals), it turns into a gas at room temperature and pressure without going through the liquid phase. The process, called *sublimation*, is accelerated by heating.

68

SMALL PARTICLE REAGENT

A small particle reagent is a suspension of small particles of molybdenum disulfide that adheres physically to fatty substances in the latent print. It is notable for being resistant to water and can even work under water.

VACUUM METAL DEPOSITION

Vacuum metal deposition is a mechanical recovery method that works on the principle that fingerprint contamination hinders the deposition of a metallic film following evaporation under vacuum. This extremely sensitive technique for fingerprint detection on a variety of surfaces can be used in conjunction with cyanoacrylate fuming. (See Figure 4.11.)

FIGURE 4.10
Superglue fuming cabinet. A portable enclosed hood that can be used for Superglue fuming of smaller articles at a scene or in the laboratory.

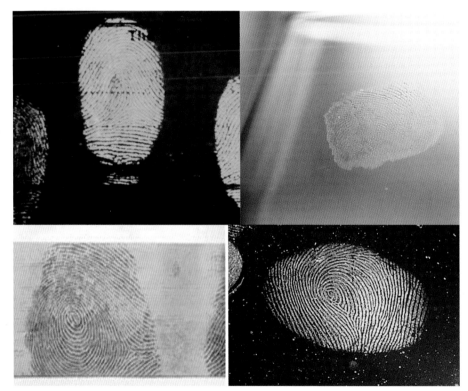

FIGURE 4.11
Chemical treatment of latent prints. Various chemical treatments are employed to enhance latent prints. Clockwise from top left: fluorescence; cyanoacrylate (Superglue) fuming; Sticky side powder; gel lifts. Sticky side powder is a reagent designed for the development of latent prints on the glue ("sticky") side of adhesive tapes. The gel lift image is a greasy print recovered from glass by using a gel lifter, and is include because this simple physical process is more effective than chemical treatment in this situation. Fluorescent print courtesy Rofin Australia; cyanoacrylate image from Stockxpert; Sticky side powder and gel lift prints courtesy BVDA America Inc.

BLOODSTAINS

Contact between bloody fingers and objects often results in deposition of a patent fingerprint. However, latent prints deposited by bloodstained fingers where there is insufficient blood for a patent image can be developed using reagents that stain proteins or those that react with the heme in blood and that are used as screening reagents in forensic biology. The general protein stains include amido black, coomassie blue, and Hungarian red. Heme reactants include leucomalachite green and luminol. All these reagents, other than luminol, produce a color that can be seen by the naked eye and recorded by conventional photography. Luminol, which is by far the most sensitive, produces a short-lived fluorescence that needs a darkened environment to see and special photography. Luminol is also toxic and must be used with care. Latent print examiners must always remember that blood itself can carry lethal pathogens such as HIV and hepatitis C and should treat every blood scene as potentially infective.

TAPES

Adhesive tapes, such as those used to bind and gag victims, present a challenge to the examiner because of their surface nature—usually one shiny nonporous surface and the other porous and sticky. Reagents that work with tapes include gentian violet, Sticky Side powder, and titanium dioxide. Gentian violet reacts with fatty substances in the sebaceous secretions, and the other two physically fill the print.

70

Selection of Reagent for Development of Latent Prints

There are dozens, if not hundreds, of reagents available for development of latent prints. In many cases the choice reflects the personal experience and preference of the examiner. However, the more commonly used reagents can be classified according to the surface on which they are best suited for use. Table 4.1 is based on the recommendations of the FBI for reagent selection. See also Figure 4.11.

Table 4.1	Some Reagents for Development of Latent Prints on Different Types of Surfaces	
Substrate	**Reagent**	**Reaction**
Porous or nonporous	Powders	Physical adherence to moisture and lipids. Includes metallic powders and luminescent dye-tagged powders. Very wide range available; select to give optimum contrast with substrate.
	Iodine	Physical process, fumes react with sebaceous secretions.

(Continued)

Table 4.1	Some Reagents for Development of Latent Prints on Different Types of Surfaces—cont'd	
Substrate	**Reagent**	**Reaction**
Porous	DFO	Chemical reaction with amino acids.
	Ninhydrin	Chemical reaction with amino acids.
	Physical Developer (silver nitrate)	Chemical reaction with lipids. Works on previously wet materials.
Nonporous	Cyanoacrylate fuming	Chemical reaction, polymerization of latent print residues. White deposit, which can be enhanced with fluorescent dyes and viewing under UV light.
	Small particle reagent	Physical process, adheres to sebaceous secretions. Can be used on wet surfaces and is one of the few reagents that will work after print has been treated with cyanoacrylate.
	Vacuum metal deposition	Metal is deposited on fatty components of latent residues. Works on plastic and is good for use on older prints.
	Sudan black	Chemical reaction with fatty components. Good for use on greasy prints.
Bloodstained	Amido black	Reacts with serum proteins. Effective on plastics and cotton. React with serum proteins.
	Coomassie blue, crystal violet, Hungarian red, leucomalachite green, luminol	React with heme.
Reagents for use on tapes	Gentian violet	Reacts with skin cells and lipids. Use on light-colored adhesive tape.
	Sticky Side powder	Physical process. Use on light-colored tape.
	Titanium dioxide	Use on plastic, electrical, and duct tape — both sides.

71

Preservation of Developed Prints

The two most common ways to preserve fingerprint evidence are photography and lifting the print. As a first step in preservation, fingerprint evidence is usually photographed. The crime scene photographer will take an image of the print where it was discovered, a context photograph, and several close-up images. Depending on how the print was visualized, the photography might be done under an alternate light source.

If the print is on an object that is too big to be used in court or impossible to remove from the crime scene, the criminalist may "lift" it using tape. When removed, an image of the developed print will strip away with the tape. The image then can be attached to a piece of cardboard and easily transported to the courtroom or elsewhere. Today there are also commercial lift kits where the tape and backings—in a variety of colors—are combined. (See Figure 4.12.)

DATABASES OF FINGERPRINTS

Automated Fingerprint Identification System (AFIS)

As fingerprint collections have continued to grow, manual searches of card files have been greatly augmented by computer searches. Automated fingerprint identification systems (AFISs) can encode or search even for single, partial prints with high speed and throughput.

Recovered prints are scanned. Then the resulting digitized images are mapped for ridge details such as terminations, bifurcations, and islands. The maps are stored as geometric patterns in large databases. When a new print is recovered, a search algorithm can look through the database for prints that are similar to the exemplar and provide an estimate of the correlation. The recovered print and the print from the database then can be examined side by side.

Like any system, AFIS has limitations. Poor-quality prints or poorly scanned prints may not show enough correlation to generate a hit. Worse, until recently

When interpreting fingerprint evidence, you must remember that the absence of evidence is not the evidence of absence, and that a fingerprint is a physical object with few or no intrinsic characteristics that can tell when it was deposited.

72

  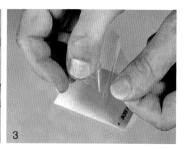

FIGURE 4.12
Lifting fingerprints. How fingerprints are lifted from the scene and prepared for comparison in the laboratory. 1: the adhesive-backed lifting tape is prepared; 2: the tape is applied to the developed print and the powder adheres to it; 3: the transferred print is protected with a transparent film and is ready for analysis. Courtesy BVDA America Inc.

there was little interoperability between jurisdictions. The National Institute of Standards and Technology (NIST) created a data template that allowed for freer exchange of fingerprint information.

Integrated Automated Fingerprint Identification System (IAFIS)

In 1999, the FBI and its Criminal Justice Information Services (CJIS) Division launched the Integrated Automated Fingerprint Identification System (IAFIS), a national fingerprint and criminal history database. This represented a great breakthrough of interoperability. With more than 47 million entries in its criminal profile register, IAFIS is now the largest biometric data bank in the world. (See Figure 4.13.)

The fingerprints and corresponding criminal histories, as well as queries to the database, are submitted by law enforcement agencies of all levels: municipality, county, state, or federal. Because the submissions and queries are electronic, there is never a delay to starting a search or making a new set of data available. In some cases, information can even be exchanged with the field. The database can also be used for civilian purposes such as for pre-employment background investigations.

Computer searches should not substitute for printing known suspects. Further, computers do not determine identification or testify in court. A trained examiner must render that opinion after comparing the presence and location of minutiae.

FIGURE 4.13
Examiner at CJIS IAFIS station. From www.fbi. gov/hq/cjisd/iafis.html

73

FINGERPRINTS AND COLD CASES

The advances in technology for latent print identification and in data storage and automated comparisons have meant that fingerprints are one of the most powerful tools in the current wave of interest in reopening old, unsolved cases—cold cases.

Case Study

George Akopian—A Successful Cold Case

As an illustration, the Los Angeles police cold case detectives solved a decades' old homicide, bringing bittersweet closure to the victim's family and the investigators themselves.

During the evening hours of March 18, 1973, George Akopian, 54, of Tarzana, was home with his wife when he was shot and killed by a man who had answered Akopian's advertisement to sell a stamp collection. Akopian was heard arguing with the suspect just prior to the shooting. The suspect shot Akopian once in the chest, killing him.

The case lingered unsolved until 2005, when cold case detectives Rick Jackson and Richard Bengston reopened the investigation. They discovered that a fingerprint had been lifted from original evidence recovered at the scene, but it had never been matched to a suspect. The fingerprint was run through LAPD's updated automated fingerprint system and returned with a hit.

Investigators found that the fingerprint belonged to Francis J. Fico, also known as Rodney H. Wallace. Fico had a multistate criminal history dating back to 1958, including two bank robberies, one in New York in 1969 and the other in Los Angeles in 1973. The West Coast robbery occurred just 2 months after Akopian's murder. Fico had spent most of his adult life in and out of prison.

Closure has been bittersweet, because Fico died in 1995 from injuries he sustained in a traffic accident in Spokane, Washington, where he was living.

Detective Jackson conceded that "There is pleasure in closing a case, but the true satisfaction comes from providing justice to the families of victims." In spite of the disappointment of not having the opportunity to hold the suspect accountable for this crime, detectives expressed satisfaction in knowing that they were successful in solving an age-old crime.

The preceding case information comes from http://lapdblog.typepad.com/lapd_blog/2007/02/thirtyyearold_c.html

BIOMETRICS: APPLYING FINGERPRINT TECHNOLOGY

In 1901, the first official use of fingerprints for systematic personal identification in the U.S. was adopted by the New York City Civil Service Commission to certify all civil service applications. The use of **biometrics** has grown considerably in the more than a century since then. Biometrics are measurements of physical characteristics of an individual that can be used to verify his or her identity when checked against a known exemplar in a database. Fingerprints are probably the best known biometric, but others include palm prints, facial recognition, and iris scans. Most of the advances have taken place in the last 10 years, driven by enhanced technology and efforts to control terrorism. For example, many countries have adopted machine-readable passports with biometrics to help ensure better border security.

In the Enhanced Border Security and Visa Entry Reform Act of 2002, the U.S. Congress mandated the use of biometrics for travelers who want U.S. visas. Digital photos and electronic fingerprint scans were chosen as the standard biometric. Both index fingers of a visa applicant are electronically scanned during the required interview with a consular officer at a U.S. embassy. The process is quick, painless, and inkless. The fingerprint scans are stored in a database and made available at U.S. ports of entry to Department of Homeland Security (DHS) immigration inspectors.

Scanned fingerprints are sent electronically with a photo and biographic data to the Consular Consolidated Database (CCD) in Washington, DC. The CCD relays the information to the Department of Homeland Security's IDENT system over a reliable, direct transmission line, which sends the results back to the CCD for relay back to the post. Until a good report from IDENT is received, the visa system is locked with regards to that visa application. For the remaining posts, the IDENT checks are being reviewed in the department and posts are notified of any hits.

If no hit is returned from the IDENT lookout database, then the applicant's data are stored in the US-VISIT database in IDENT and a fingerprint identification number (FIN) is generated. Once the visa has been issued, the nonimmigrant visa system sends to the DHS Interagency Border Inspection System (IBIS) the applicant's photo and the fingerprint identification number. When the visa applicant arrives at a port of entry, the US-VISIT system will use the fingerprint identification number to match the visa with the file in IDENT and will compare the visa holder's fingerprints with those on file. This comparison ensures that the person presenting the visa at the port of entry is the same person to whom the visa was issued.

SUMMARY

Fingerprints are the impression of friction skin ridges of the fingers and thumbs. Visible prints and plastic prints, those left as an actual impression in soft material, both can be seen with the unaided eye. Latent prints, those that cannot be immediately seen, must be developed chemically or dusted with a contact powder to be detected. Once visualized, the print must be photographed and either preserved in place or lifted. Techniques are employed from the least destructive to the most destructive.

Francis Galton outlined three basic principles of fingerprints that provide the basis for their use in law enforcement: Fingerprints are unique to the individual, remain unchanged during an individual's lifetime, and have sufficient detail in their ridge patterns to permit them to be systematically classified.

Fingerprint patterns can be divided into three basic types that occur in different frequency: loops (60–65%), whorls (30–35%), and arches (5%).

Verification that a fingerprint belongs to a certain individual is determined by a point-by-point comparison. Today there are databases such as AFIS and IDENT, which store images of fingerprints and analyses of their ridge details, but a trained expert still must make the determination of identity.

75

PROBLEMS

1. Give the word or phrase for the following definitions:
   a. a reproduction or impression of the friction skin ridges of the fingers
   b. a fingerprint pattern containing one delta and a defined core
   c. a fingerprint pattern with no delta, core, or type line
   d. a fingerprint that can be seen with the unaided eye
   e. a fingerprint not readily seen with the unaided eye
   f. a circular fingerprint pattern that tilts toward the little finger
   g. the simultaneous printing of all the fingers of each hand
   h. a fingerprint pattern composed of an arch and a loop
2. List the three principles of fingerprints.
3. List the three general patterns of fingerprints in order of decreasing frequency of occurrence.

4. Look at the fingerprint at the bottom center of the introductory illustration to the chapter and identify
   a. a bifurcation point
   b. an island
   c. a ridge ending
5. Look at the photograph and identify the
   a. whorl, arch, or loop if present
   b. delta if present
   c. any other feature that could be used to classify the print
6. Print your right index finger and make a list of as many features as you can find.
7. Describe the appropriate use of the following developing agents:
   a. iodine fixed with starch
   b. ninhydrin
   c. cyanoacrylate fumes
   d. physical developer
   e. high-contrast dusting powder
8. What is the best order to deploy visualization techniques to preserve evidence for additional testing?
9. What techniques can be used to preserve fingerprint information once a latent print has been visualized?
10. Describe the process for determining the primary classification in the Henry system. How are the categories determined? Which is the most populated category?
11. Describe the use of alternative light sources in discovering latent prints.
12. Define fluorescence, phosphorescence, and incandescence.

GLOSSARY

Accidental a pattern of ridge details that does not fit into one of the regular categories.

ACE-V the standard procedure used in the U.S. for fingerprint comparison.

Bifurcation the division of one ridge into two.

Biometrics the use of physical characteristics to establish the identity of someone.

Central pocket loop whorls a pattern with two deltas and at least one recurring ridge that makes a round shape. If the two deltas were connected by an imaginary line, this line would not touch or cut any recurving ridge within the pattern.

Core the center of a loop pattern.

Cyanoacrylate using cyanoacrylate (Superglue) vapor as a method to visualize latent fingerprints.

Dactyloscopy a system of identification developed by Sir Edward R. Henry from work done by Sir Francis Galton.

Delta a triangular formation made by interacting ridge lines.

Dermal papillae the region between the dermis and epidermis responsible for the ridge patterns on the surface of skin.

Double loop two separate loops, each with a distinct core in the same fingerprint.

FBI classification the FBI use eight different types of patterns: radial loop, ulnar loop, double loop, central pocket loop whorls, plain arch, tented arch, plain whorl, and accidental.

Iodine developer the use of sublimating iodine to visualize latent fingerprints. Because iodine turns from a solid to a gas under ordinary conditions, the developed fingerprints are often fixed with a starch solution.

Island a very short ridge giving the appearance of a dot in a fingerprint.

Latent fingerprint a fingerprint for which the detail cannot be seen with the unaided eye. There are a variety of techniques for visualizing latent fingerprints.

Loop fingerprints with concentric hairpin ridges that enter and exit from the same side of the pattern. This pattern containing one delta is found in about 65% of fingerprints.

Minutiae the fine details of a fingerprint such as bifurcations and ridge endings that allow for comparison of samples.

Ninhydrin developer the use of this chemical is to react with amino acids and visualize latent fingerprints.

Physical developer a reagent containing silver ions that is used to locate latent prints on paper or wood.

Plain arch a delta-less pattern that rises in the middle but does not form a loop.

Plain impression/flat impression the simultaneous printing of all the fingers of each hand and then the thumbs without rolling used to verify the sequence and accuracy of rolled impressions.

Plastic print the impression of a fingerprint left in soft or malleable material.

Radial loop a loop that tilts toward the radius bone or index finger and is most often found there.

Ridge ending the terminal point of a ridge.

Rolled impression the individual printing of the thumb, index, middle, ring, and little fingers of each hand done by rolling the finger from one edge of the fingernail to the other.

Silver developer the use of silver salts, which oxidize to silver oxide when exposed to air or other chemicals, as a method to visualize latent fingerprints.

Tented arch a delta-less pattern that rises sharply in the middle but does not form a loop.

Ulnar loop a loop that tilts toward the ulna bone, or little finger, the most typical loop of all.

Visible print a fingerprint that can be detected with the naked eye.

Whorl a circularly shaped pattern containing at least two deltas and occurring in about 30% of fingerprints.

Some examples of document examination. Clockwise from top:
- Use of infrared luminescence to reveal obliterated writing.
- Examination of currency.
- Authentication of signatures.
- Use of Electrostatic Detection Apparatus (ESDA) to reveal indented writings.

Obliterated writing and ESDA courtesy of Foster and Freeman; currency from http://www.moneyfactory.gov/section.cfm/4; signature from Stockxpert.

CHAPTER 5

Documents

Case Study

The Hitler Diaries

There was a buzz in the air in the offices of *Stern*, the German newsmagazine: The cover story for its April 1983 edition was the publication of the hitherto unknown diaries of Adolph Hitler. The publishers had purchased the material 2 years earlier for the sum of $2.3 million, without conducting any validation of origin. However, after acquisition but before publication, they had the documents compared to a sample of Hitler's handwriting and received the report that they wanted: The handwriting specimens were the same.

Unfortunately for *Stern*, although they were the same, they were not from the hand of Adolph Hitler. Both experts consulted by the publisher had relied on comparisons of the materials provided by *Stern* — alleged authentic writing as well as the diaries — and, in the absence of any of the usual signs of handwriting forgery, had declared the work to be that of Hitler. Not everyone was convinced that Hitler had kept a diary, and the documents were subjected to other investigations. For example, testing carried out by Dr. Louis Werner of the German police focused on the paper the diaries were written on and not the handwriting. Werner showed that the paper contained a whitening agent not used until after 1954 and that the ink was less than 12 months old. The diaries were a fraud.

The subsequent criminal investigation focused on Gerd Heidemann, the *Stern* journalist who had broken the story and banked most of the payment for the material. He eventually confessed that the work—the diaries and the exemplar writings—was a fabrication and had been written for him by a petty criminal, Konrad Kujau.

The case is an excellent illustration of some of the principles of questioned document analysis. Firstly, the fundamental question is the authenticity of the document. There are many elements to resolving that issue, not just handwriting comparison. Secondly, many of the signs of forged writing arise from the attempts to simulate the authentic writing—Kujau did not do that; he simply wrote in what he imagined to be the style of German handwriting of the 1930s and 40s. Finally, the validity of conclusions in document examination is always governed by the quality of the test and exemplar materials presented—in this case the exemplar writing was taken on trust as being from Hitler.

INTRODUCTION

A *questioned document* is one where the source or authenticity of the material is disputed. From checks and lottery tickets to wills and ransom notes, documents feature in a variety of crimes, including forgery, counterfeiting, fraud, theft, and homicide. Many fraudulent documents are intended to pass for printed material such as currency or identity papers and do not contain handwriting. Hence, a questioned document examiner does much more than compare handwriting and signatures. Paper, ink, and the machine that produced the document itself may be examined. Using special techniques, a criminalist may be able to determine if a document has been altered by obliteration or erasure and even recover some of the original information.

CENTRAL QUESTIONS

- Is the document authentic?
- Was anything added to or removed from the document?
- Does the handwriting belong to the individual or the typescript to a particular machine?
- What is the age of the document?
- If the document has been altered, can we recover any of the original?

DOCUMENTS

As with fingerprints, techniques must be applied from the least to most destructive.

Today "documents" can include electronic files, but we shall restrict this chapter to physical documents, primarily those in paper form. With that qualification, it is convenient to classify documents into handwritten or machine produced. Examinations usually involve comparing the questioned document to a known or an exemplar. Machine-produced text can be compared for typeface and other characteristics imparted by the machine, including incorporation of security features, and for the make and model of the instrument used to produce it. Analyzing handwriting is slightly more complex. The shapes of letters are just a place to start. However the document is produced, both the paper and ink also must be examined. Paper can be compared macroscopically for finish and watermarks. Microscopically, its fiber content may be analyzed. The paper also may be subjected to dating procedures. Similarly, inks may be examined for optical properties and using chemical techniques. In this chapter, we will investigate these topics in more detail.

Document examiners deal with the authenticity of documents. Graphologists claim to be able to draw conclusions about character from the examination of the writing of an individual. This is a highly controversial area and not considered by questioned document examiners to have a scientific basis.

Handwritten Documents

Most of the work presented to document examiners consists of signatures and other handwritten material. Children are taught to print in kindergarten with cursive introduced in second or third grade. Printing is taught first because it is thought that children more easily identify with the style of letters they find in books and the newspaper. Students "learn" by copying standard practice letters. At this stage, they are making a conscious effort to conform their writing to the standard letters, and their copies may look very similar. With practice, whether in cursive or print, writing eventually becomes a subconscious effort and takes on individual characteristics. Physical, physiologic, and psychologic factors such as muscle coordination, motor skills, and innate attention to detail impart a uniqueness to each individual's handwriting. By adulthood, most people have a distinctive style that will vary very slowly over time. For example, the letter *E*, when written in block capital style, has a limited number of ways in which it can be constructed; most adult writers adopt one of them as a matter of convenience. For example, right-handed people construct the loop of the letter *O* in a counterclockwise direction, but hand anatomy means that left-handed people will form the loop in a clockwise direction. However, some left-handed children copy the style of their right-handed teacher and make counterclockwise loops. (See Figure 5.1.)

Cursive was considered faster and less fatiguing than printing because the pen leaves the paper less often. However, many adults print more quickly and legibly than they write "longhand." With the advent of computers, some people are turning away from cursive altogether.

Handwriting can be analyzed for variations of letter size, shape, slant, and spacing. **Ligature**, pen movement, pressure, and pen lifts also play parts in the determination. Even the page itself, taken as a whole, may provide clues. While changing writing styles may be easy for a few words, it is difficult to sustain the effort because natural habits of the writer will try to assert themselves. An examiner must consider the layout of a document for consistency in spacing, line use, and margins.

81

Block capital *E* showing the three most common forms of construction. These are, left to right, the letter *L* with a central and upper cross stroke; a Greek sigma-like form made by adding the central cross stroke to a *C* form; and a four-stroke form with a vertical dash to which are added the top, central, and bottom cross strokes.	Two forms of the letter *O*. The character on the left was written as normal by a right-handed person and shows the counterclockwise formation of the loop. The character on the right was written by a right-handed person but using his left hand. The loop shows a clockwise formation and a point of hesitancy where the writer paused.

FIGURE 5.1
Some basic handwriting features. Original work of author.

The basic underlying principle is that under normal circumstances, and considering a sufficient amount of writing, two different skilled writers are unlikely to produce handwriting that is identical in terms of the combination of construction, line quality, formation variation, and text formatting. As individuals, we are able to recognize our own writings and those of family, friends, and colleagues because we store a pictorial memory of the material. The memory increases in reliability with exposure to the writing. The document examiner does not have that advantage and is essentially comparing two sets of unknown writings. Each set contains the features that the brain subconsciously considered when creating the pictorial memory, but the examiner has to identify them individually.

It is interesting to watch experienced and skilled document examiners at work. At some point they essentially try to recreate that pictorial memory by concentrating on the overall appearance of the writings, rather than the detail contained in them.

The features that make up the rational evaluation of the writing fall into four general types: style, execution, variation, and horizontal dimensions.

- *Elements of style:* These include placement of text, formatting, connections between characters and words, feature proportions, size, slant, and spacing.
- *Elements of execution:* These include the use of abbreviations; alignment with real or imaginary baseline, length, direction, path, and taper of the line trace; punctuation and embellishments; legibility; pen stops; and pen lifts.
- *Consistency of natural variation:* There is always within-writer variation in writings. The extent of this is a feature in its own right.
- *Lateral expansion and word proportion:* The horizontal spread of words and characters and the size and spacing of writing components contribute to the pictorial character of the writing.

The examiner records specific characteristics of the features, typically the stroke order and line directions of character construction. Pen direction is determined by observation, usually under low-power magnification, of stroke connections and striation marks in the lines. Embellishments present are described and added to the record. The features may be presented as charts, where similar allographs are grouped and described. (An **allograph** is a letter of an alphabet in a particular shape, for example, *a* and *A*, or a letter or combination of letters that is a way of representing a phoneme, for example, *pp* representing the phoneme *p* in the word *hopping*.) The examiner now has to determine what constitutes a similarity or dissimilarity in the writings, beginning by discarding dissimilarities such as vertical pen movement that are the result of differences in the speed of writing. (See Figure 5.2.)

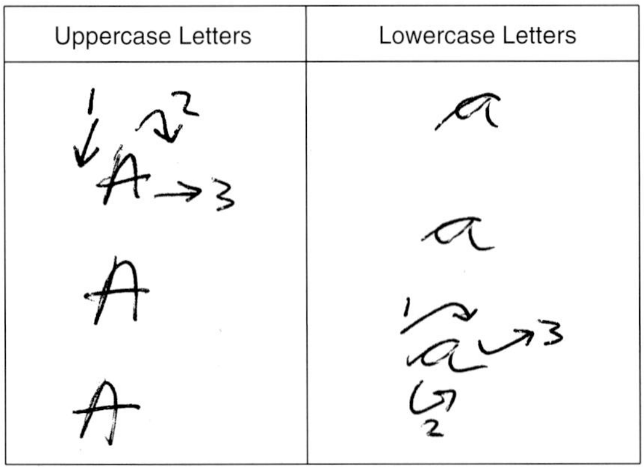

Figure 5.3 shows the allograph combination *OK* as written by two different people. Although this is a very simple example of writing, the differences in character formation and in construction of the combination are clear.

FIGURE 5.2
Chart showing analysis of the construction of three examples of the allograph *A* and the allograph *a*. All were written by the same person. The arrows and numbers indicate the sequence of strokes in formation of the allograph. Original work of author.

Uppercase Letters	Lowercase Letters

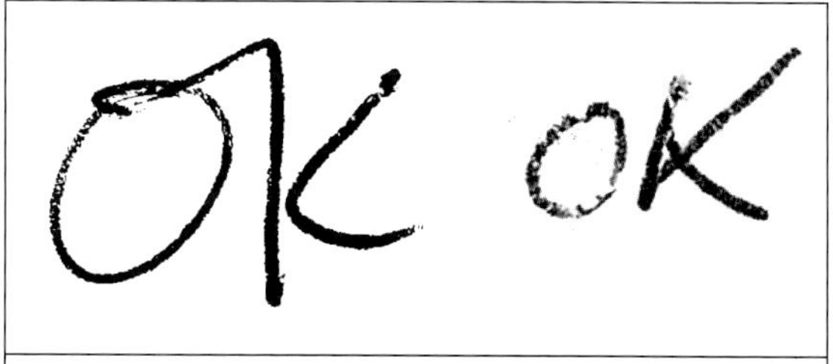

The images shown in Figure 5.3 are deceptive. The writings were made by two different people with no attempt at copying. Although there are only two allographs, they contain enough features to support the obvious conclusion that most people would draw on first seeing the writing, namely, they are not the same. However, things are different when attempts are made to forge writing. Depending on the skill of the forger and the complexity of the writing, it may not be at all easy to discern the fraudulent writing. Figure 5.4 shows two passages; the one marked "Questioned" was written as an attempt to copy the writing of the exemplar. Superficially, the writings are similar but different enough to question the authorship of the "Questioned."

The allograph combination *OK* written by two different people. Note the obvious differences in construction of the *O* and *K* and the linkage of the two allographs in the left image but not in the right.

FIGURE 5.3
Differences in letter constructions. Original work of author.

The forged writing is close to the original in elements of style, except that the "forger" did not realize that the writer of the original had missed the *L* in the word *COMPLEX* and inserted it afterward. The forger copied this as *COMREY* (even although there is no such word). The writings are also similar in the element of proportion, but that could reflect the constraints imposed by asking

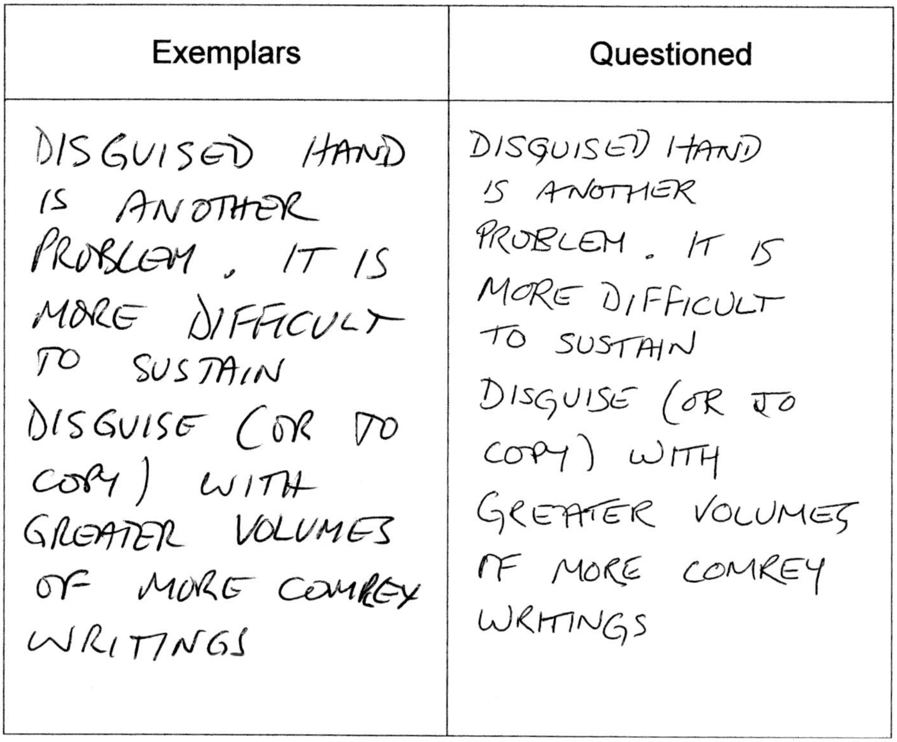

Exemplars	Questioned
DISGUISED HAND IS ANOTHER PROBLEM , IT IS MORE DIFFICULT TO SUSTAIN DISGUISE (OR TO COPY) WITH GREATER VOLUMES OF MORE COMPLEX WRITINGS	DISGUISED HAND IS ANOTHER PROBLEM . IT IS MORE DIFFICULT TO SUSTAIN DISGUISE (OR TO COPY) WITH GREATER VOLUMES OF MORE COMREY WRITINGS

FIGURE 5.4
A worksheet showing examples of writing made to copy an original. Original work of author.

the "forger" to copy the original into a defined space. Most of the clues are to be found in the elements of construction, such as the letters *R, H, G,* and *P.* These writings are presented to illustrate the general points. In a real case, more extensive samples of the writing of both authors would provide a better database on which to draw a conclusion. Figure 5.2 shows the consistency in formation of "a" and "A" when writing is by the same person.

Other problems encountered by the document examiner dealing with handwriting include the nature of the case. The situation described in the content of the writing in Figure 5.4 is one such problem. In contrast, sometimes a writer will try to disguise his or her handwriting—ransom notes or holdup demands, for example. Because of their nature, the amount of questioned writing can be insufficient for a confident conclusion to be drawn. Changes in writing with age or illness underscore the importance of obtaining exemplars that are authentic not only in the sense of being written by the author of the valid document but that also are contemporaneous.

Case Study

The Howard Hughes Mormon Will

The billionaire recluse Howard Hughes died in 1976, leaving no apparent will. There were rumors that he had left a holographic will, that is, one written entirely in his own hand. Shortly after this possibility was made public, an alleged holographic will was found in the building of the Church of Jesus Christ of Latter Day Saints. The will, which became known as the "Mormon will," left a large sum of money to a man, Melvin Dummar, with no known significant connection to Howard Hughes.

The authenticity of the will was contested. The court held that the will was a forgery and that Howard Hughes had died intestate. The conclusion of the several document examiners who worked on the case was clear. The Mormon will was three pages long, and there was a large body of contemporaneous exemplar writings. Added to the quantitative data was the significant qualitative feature that Mr. Hughes had undergone an obvious change in some of his handwriting habits during a 2-year period just before the alleged will was written.

EXEMPLARS AND CONCLUSIONS IN EXAMINATION OF HANDWRITING

The previously described Hitler diaries and Howard Hughes will cases show how important it is to obtain appropriate references samples, or **exemplars**. The reference exemplars can be existing, known writings of the authentic writer and the suspected forger or can be created to look as much like the questioned document as possible. The writer might be asked to write out a sample of text using the same type of pen on the same kind of paper. A good exemplar will contain the same combinations of letters and words used in the suspect material, written several times. The repetition of the sample text will reveal **natural variation**, subtle differences between the same letters in the writing. It may also help reveal conscious attempts to alter a writing style.

To avoid bias, the writer is given dictation or a selection of text to write rather than be shown the questioned document itself.

Unlike more invasive sampling such as a blood swatch, handwriting samples may be ordered by the court. The Supreme Court has decided that handwriting samples do not constitute an unreasonable search and seizure under the Fourth

Amendment and are not protected as identifying physical characteristics under the Fifth Amendment.

In the end, an examiner may not be able to make a determination if a particular questioned sample is only a few words in length. In those cases, and in situations where the writing style of the exemplar may have been made to look like (or unlike) a suspect item, the examiner may be able to give only a qualified opinion.

Machine-Produced Scripts

TYPEFACE

A typeface is a set of characters designed to share a particular look. The set usually contains alphabet letters and numerals and may be extended to include punctuation, **diacritic marks**, and decorative characters. To investigate differences in machine-produced lettering, it helps to know a little about typeface and how it originated. (See Figure 5.5.)

Characters are textual units. The letter *a* can be thought of as the first character in the word *apple.* In typography, the graphical units are **glyphs**. Because they are graphical representations, glyphs may be part of a character, a single character, or several characters combined into a ligature (for example, *st, nd,* or *th*). When type was cast, the printing surface—the "face"—was a glyph mounted on a block of metal called the *body.*

The Geography of a Typeface

Most characters are designed to sit on a *baseline,* an imaginary "ground" used for alignment and measurement of glyphs. The most important measurement is the *x-height,* or the distance from the baseline to the top of a lowercase glyph. A solid stroke of this height is a called a *stem.* For letters like *h* that rise above the x-height, the stem is topped with an ascender. For letters like *y* that extend below

Perhaps the most widely used font in international signage today is Helvetica, a sans serif font remarkable for its clarity. Originally designed and drawn by Linotype™ artist Max Miedinger in 1957, the font premiered under the name Neue Haas Grotesk, which was changed to Helvetica (from the Latin word meaning Swiss) in 1960.

85

FIGURE 5.5
Machine-produced scripts. Left to right: Combination printer–copier–fax; printer type; typewriter. From Stockxpert.

A similar but less well known feature to look for is the ear, which can sometimes be found on a lowercase *g*.

86

Long passages also highlight issues of proportionality and spacing. Condensed and extended type, because of their spacing, can lower readability.

Pitch and point are two different kinds of size. A pica is actually ⅙ of an inch (an older unit of measure for document layout) but also refers to a size of type with 10 characters to the linear inch, or 10 pitch. A **point** is the standard unit for measuring font size in height and corresponds to ¹⁄₁₂ of a pica, or ¹⁄₇₂ of an inch.

the baseline, a descender is added to the stem. The glyph may be modified further with a diacritic mark. (See Figure 5.6.)

The presence or absence of **serifs** is another important characteristic of a glyph. Serifs are the short, perpendicular lines added to the ends of strokes on traditional typefaces such as the New Times Roman used here. The more modern sans serif fonts, also called *grotesques,* do not bear these marks. Most newspapers are published in serifed type because it is thought that these typefaces increase readability over long passages. However, sans serif fonts are favored for signage due to their clarity. To show all the elements and give a sense of the impact of a particular **font**, characters are often displayed in *pangrams,* a text using every letter of the alphabet. (See Figure 5.7.)

Font weight is another consideration. A font is actually a specific size and style (like bold or italic) of type. An individual font weight is a set of characters of the same design and line thickness. Taken together, all the font weights for a particular type form a font family. (See Figure 5.8.)

Proportionality

The spacing of font characters is called *proportionality.* In nonproportional, or fixed, fonts, the width of each character—whether *i* or *w*—is identical. Fixed fonts can be measured in **pitch**, the number of characters per linear distance. Lines of text with the same number of characters will always be the same width. When typewriters dominated machine text production, the two most popular sizes of text were **pica** (10 characters to the inch, also called *10 pitch*) and **elite** (12 characters to the inch, also called *12 pitch*).

Proportional fonts have characters of varying width. While not good for producing columns, proportional fonts make for excellent newsprint. To make the text even more readable, the font can be *kerned.* **Kerning** is a process of adjusting the white space (or side bearings) on each side of a glyph to produce a better eye-spacing.

TYPEWRITERS

Although almost entirely replaced by computers in the more industrialized countries, typewriters are still a major historical source of machine-produced text and of text from developing nations. By comparing the typeface of a document (or its digitized image) to a database of manufacturers' offerings, it is possible to determine the make and model of the typewriter that may have produced the text. This might also be done through photographic enlargement and comparison. Usually, however, this is not enough to satisfy an investigator who would be happier with attribution by being able to say a document came from a specific typewriter.

If the typewriter alleged to have produced the document is available, exemplars—known samples—can be collected for comparison. This might involve an attempt to duplicate the text of the questioned document. If the machine is damaged, destroyed, or missing, the examiner must secure exemplars known to have been produced on the machine in question and which contain similar words and phrases to the questioned document. Ideally, these exemplars would be produced on similar paper and at about the same time as the questioned document. This is essentially a tool mark comparison.

AaBbCc	AaBbCc	The Quick Brown Fox Jumps Over The Lazy Dog. g
Serif typeface (Serif in red)	Sans serif typeface	Slab serif typeface

FIGURE 5.7
Examples of serif and sans serif typefaces. Note that the slab serif typeface incorporates the simplicity of the sans serif style into a serif format. Serif type from en.wikipedia.org/wiki/Image: Serif_and_sans-serif_03.svg; sans serif from en.wikipedia.org/wiki/Image:serif_and_sans_serif_01.svg; slab serif type from upload.wikipedia.org/wikipedia/commons/9/90/Rockwell_sample.svg

Time frame is important. The moving parts of typewriters suffer from mechanical wear with use. Such wear may develop into attributable traits but also may change over time. Examples of this would include type where the characters have become displaced (vertically) or misaligned (horizontally) along the baseline. Again, photographic enlargement or digital mapping can play an important role in identifying details too fine for the unaided eye.

Helvetica 10 pt.	The quick brown fox jumps over a lazy dog.
Times New Roman 10 pt.	The quick brown fox jumps over a lazy dog.
Georgia 10 pt.	The quick brown fox jumps over a lazy dog.

FIGURE 5.8
The "quick brown fox" pangram in three 10-point fonts. Note the difference in line weight and in the serif on the descenders in the two serif typefaces.

The typewriter's ribbon may also afford clues. For "self-correcting" ribbon typewriters, the examiner may discover whole sections of the questioned text or critical changes to it "on tape." For older, woven, inked ribbons, it might be possible to look at keystroke impressions on the ribbon itself.

Case Study

Bobby Franks

Bobby Franks was kidnapped and murdered on his way home from high school in 1924. That evening his parents received a phone call saying he had been kidnapped, followed the next morning by delivery of a typewritten ransom demand. Before the parents could respond to the demand, the body of Bobby was discovered. The police investigation centered on Richard Loeb and Nathan Leopold. Both were well educated and from well-off families, and neither had an obvious motive. Leopold owned a typewriter, but it was excluded as the source of the ransom note. By chance, police found that he also had a portable machine that he used to type notes from a study group. Comparison of pages of notes with the ransom demand showed them to be identical. Leopold and Loeb were tried and convicted. The Bobby Franks case is significant to forensic science, as it established the acceptability of typewriter examination as evidence.

87

OTHER BUSINESS MACHINES

With the explosion of home printing technology comes an explosion of techniques an examiner may be asked to identify. Toners, inks, and papers may give away a printing method or even identify the make and model of machine used. This is especially telling with toner in noting the appearance and chemical components of the pigment.

When creating an exemplar to attempt to identify printing technology, criminalists must minimize the differences from the questioned document—especially with respect to paper and toner—as much as possible. The best comparisons use the same type of machine, paper, and pigment. A sample of 10–15 pages, labeled to preserve the order in which they were produced, is usually large enough.

No matter how the document was printed, an individual machine may leave behind distinguishing clues to help identify it. Some moving parts that shepherd paper through machines leave tool marks. These marks—dents, creases, or small tears—can occur anywhere on the page but are often found on an edge. Defects or damage to the drum or platen will be reproduced as marks on every copy. Machines may also make reproducible stray marks or overpigmented or underpigmented patches that can be used as points of individuation. (See Figure 5.9.)

PRINTERS

Numerous types of computer printers are in use today. Most printers fall into two broad categories based on how the machine creates an image. Impact printers are usually older machines with mechanical parts, not unlike typewriters, that "strike" the image onto paper. Examples include thermal, daisy wheel, and dot matrix printers. Some of these still use ribbon cartridges! These printers suffer the same aging effects as typewriters and—in certain cases—sometimes create unique tool marks as artifacts of their mechanisms.

Ink-jet and laser printers are examples of nonimpact processes. The appearance of toner and how it is adhered to the document may assist the examiner in individuation. For example, toner that is improperly fused may indicate problems in a laser printer.

The combination of computerized font libraries with the reliability of laser and ink-jet printing offers the forger a way to create seemingly authentic documents that are either in the style of an original or intended to be copies of an original. However, the forger may not identify the correct typeface—many look very similar, and kerning or other computer printer idiosyncrasies may result in a printed document that is not in fact identical to the authentic one. The technique of superimposition, using equipment such as the Foster and Freeman VSC 6000, can identify these close calls by showing the minute physical displacements when the questioned document is superimposed on the authentic one. This is illustrated in Figure 5.10.

FIGURE 5.9
Blank page from photocopier showing marks produced by the paper transport mechanism. These are tool marks and can display class characteristics typical of the make and model because of the manufacture of its transport mechanism, and individual characteristics arising from wear and damage. From Stockxpert.

FAX MACHINES

Fax machines and "all-in-one" machines employ technology similar to that found in printers. However, fax machines usually stamp documents with a code called the *transmitting terminal identifier*. This label is often found at the top or bottom of a fax printout. Analyzing the typestyle of the TTI can help examiners identify the correct machine.

PHOTOCOPIERS

A printer may be shipped to the laboratory for analysis, but, due to size and weight, a photocopier is usually sampled in place. Because it may take several copies for the drum to make a complete revolution, noting the order in which the sheets of an exemplar were produced is desirable.

Inside the copier, a camera captures the image of the document that is transferred to a cylindrical drum. The drum has a static-charged, light-sensitive surface. When exposed to light from the image of the document, areas of more or less static electric charge (which will correspond to light and dark areas on the copy) are created. The drum is then exposed to a toner that will adhere to the surface of the drum in proportion with the amount of static electric charge. Then the toner is transferred to a piece of paper and fused in place by a heating element. (See Figure 5.11.)

Elements of Documents

PAPER

The paper of a document itself provides an important comparison. Examiners must consider both physical and chemical characteristics. Papers may be distinguished by the presence of watermarks, fiber content, security threads and inclusions, reflectivity, interaction with inks, and chemical sensitivity.

Physical Measurements

In the United States, the standard sizes for paper are "letter" ($8\frac{1}{2}" \times 11"$) and "legal" ($8\frac{1}{2}" \times 14"$). Europe uses a size between these based on a system of sizes produced by folding a sheet in half. The normal letter size is A4, which is $8.26" \times 11.69"$, or 21×30 cm. Thus, A5 is 10.5×15 cm. Differences in lengths and widths often can be determined by observation. For thickness, however, most examiners rely on a paper micrometer, which can detect differences in thousandths of an inch.

Fibers

Though usually made from wood or cotton, paper may incorporate a variety of fibers. The fiber content of a paper can affect the way that paper absorbs ink or reacts to chemicals. Tests can identify and quantify fiber content (down to the type of wood) of a paper sample, but these chemical methods destroy the sample.

FIGURE 5.10
Screen shot from Foster and Freeman VSC 6000 showing superimposed authentic and forged printing. The documents are aligned with the word *Trustee* in the center. Although it looks identical in both, as the text gets displaced from the centered word, the misalignments become clear. Courtesy of Foster and Freeman.

89

Old copiers were called *photostatic copiers*, and the copies were called *photostats*.

Because image quality degenerates over successive copies, it is important to compare copies of the same generation.

FIGURE 5.11

How a photocopier works. 1: Charging: the surface of a cylindrical drum is electrostatically charged by either a high voltage wire called a corona wire or a charge roller. The drum has a coating of a photoconductive material. A photoconductor is a semiconductor that becomes conductive when exposed to light; 2: Exposure: a bright lamp illuminates the original document, and the white areas of the original document reflect the light onto the surface of the photoconductive drum. The areas of the drum that are exposed to light (those areas that correspond to white areas of the original document) become conductive and therefore discharge to ground. The area of the drum not exposed to light (those areas that correspond to black portions of the original document) remain negatively charged. The result is a latent electrical image on the surface of the drum. (In digital machines, the original document is scanned and digitized and a laser is employed to discharge the drum in a similar fashion.); 3: Developing: the toner is positively charged. When it is applied to the drum to develop the image, it is attracted and sticks to the areas that are negatively charged (black areas), just as paper sticks to a toy balloon with a static charge; 4: Transfer: the resulting toner image on the surface of the drum is transferred from the drum onto a piece of paper with a higher negative charge than the drum. The toner is melted and bonded to the paper by heat and pressure rollers. The drum is wiped clean with a rubber blade and completely discharged by light. From http://en.wikipedia.org/wiki/Image:Xerographic_photocopy_process_en.svg and http://en.wikipedia.org/wiki/Photocopier

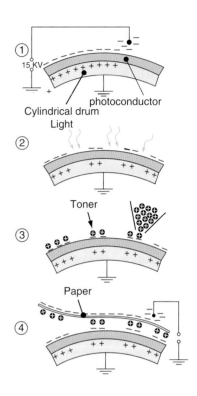

Inclusions and Other Security Marks

The U.S. Treasury incorporates red and blue security fibers in the paper on which its currency is printed. Surface fibers can be seen, but these small colored fibers are distributed throughout the paper. Secure labels and badges can be made incorporating visible or ultraviolet fluorescent fibers. These fibers may appear invisible until viewed under an appropriate light source. They also may appear to change color when illuminated.

Many currencies employ a security thread or other larger inclusion. Though large enough to be seen with the unaided eye, these elements cannot be photocopied. Further, they cannot be removed from the document without destroying the thread or the paper. These threads can contain machine-readable information, microprinted text, or other information.

Identity papers and modern travel documents also incorporate similar features as security measures. Some examples are shown in Figure 5.12.

Watermarks

True watermarks are incorporated into the fiber of a sheet of paper during its manufacture. When held up to a light source, a true watermark appears as a translucent area of the document that can be seen from either side. True watermarks deter alteration since they cannot be erased, photocopied, or faked. Better still, a true watermark identifies the manufacturer and may aid in dating the paper. (See Figure 5.13.)

91

Dutch passport showing the security images visible only when the page is illuminated with coaxial light. These images are invisible in normal light.	Fluorescent security image in Portuguese visa, rendered visible under long wavelength UV light.	Window showing personal information embedded in the machine-readable zone of a passport.	Demonstration screen of how personal information can be embedded in the image in an identity card or passport.

FIGURE 5.12

Examples of security features that can be incorporated into travel and identity documents to prevent forgery or misuse. Images are from the Foster and Freeman VSC 5000 or VSC 6000. Courtesy of Foster and Freeman.

Some documents have printed watermarks. Though these are also created during the manufacturing process, they sit on the surface of a page the way any decorative element does. Printed watermarks may use inks that must be viewed at an angle or under an alternative light source. They may also be created with very fine lines that appear altered or missing when photocopied.

Chemicals Can Affect the Characteristics of Paper

Chemicals such as fillers, sizings, and coatings introduced during paper formulation affect the opacity, color, and brightness of finished products. Characterizing a sample by its chemical properties can aid in identifying a manufacturer or production year. Fillers—such as titanium dioxide—improve the opacity and whiteness of paper. Differences in opacity too slight for the unaided eye are measured with a light meter. Color differences, "optical whiteness," are best compared under short- and long-wave ultraviolet light. Sizings (including rosin) and coatings (including waxes) change the surface properties of paper in smoothness, color, and ability to hold inks and toners. For example, papers with highly adherent surfaces resist lifting or scraping the toner off the document.

Starch is a sizing used when ironing. Consider the finish of a shirt subject to the heat and chemical process of ironing compared to one just taken out of the dryer or allowed to air-dry.

Papers may also be formulated with additives that make them more reactive. Such chemically sensitized papers deter attempts to alter documents with acids, bases, and solvents. Very secure papers may thwart alteration under a variety of chemical conditions.

INKS

Inks are made by incorporating pigments or dyes into a carrier vehicle. The carrier contains many other components, added to control properties such as thickness, drying, adhesion to paper, and flow from the ink reservoir, as well as the appearance of the dried ink. Different ink manufacturers use different ink compositions, but the colored components of ink contain only a few basic

FIGURE 5.13

Watermark in paper used in Australian travel document. Courtesy Foster and Freeman.

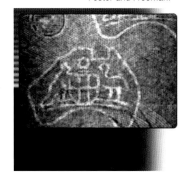

substances. The oldest form of ink is that made by suspending carbon black in a binder solution. The product, India ink, is the most permanent of all inks.

Iron gallotannate ink, composed of tannic acid, gallic acid, ferrous sulfate, and an aniline-based dye, is the basis for many commercial writing inks. The aniline dye produces the immediate pigment, but the other components react together with time to produce the permanent dye.

Most of today's inks are composed of a basic acidic or neutral organic dye, derived mainly from coal tar or petroleum. Inks that have the same dried color to the naked eye can have quite different chemical compositions. The components of different dye inks vary sufficiently to allow comparison and determination of whether known or questioned writings were prepared with the same type of ink.

Nondestructive Methods for Ink Comparisons

Did your badge turn you in? Day passes can be printed with inks formulated to be light, oxygen, or heat sensitive. After a certain period of time or amount of exposure, the badge will undergo an irreversible color change or even turn black.

There are several instrumental processes available for examining inks in written documents, ranging from the simple alternate light source to complex multifunction devices such as the Foster and Freeman VSC 6000. The basic principles are the same in most cases. Some dyes will absorb UV light and emit fluorescent light in the visible region of the spectrum. Tuning the wavelength of the excitation source and capturing the emitted light at various wavelengths increase the value of the technique. The related technique of **infrared luminescence** uses longer wavelengths (visible region) for excitation, which pushes the emitted light wavelengths into the infrared (IR) ranges. UV fluorescence and IR luminescence both depend on the electrons being raised to a higher energy orbital by the irradiated light and then emitting light of a longer wavelength when they decay to their ground state.

Fluorescence and luminescence are valuable tools in identifying altered writings where documents have been changed using an ink of the same visible appearance but different composition to add text. (See Figure 5.14.)

Amount written in check, photographed with visible light.	Screen capture of same writing but with UV incident light and detecting fluorescence activity in the ink used to add a zero to the writing.	The same writing but capturing the reflected infrared light. The lower intensity of the added character is because of absorption of the incident light.

FIGURE 5.14
Use of UV and IR light to detect alterations made by adding writing. Images are from the Foster and Freeman VSC 6000. Courtesy of Foster and Freeman.

Some dyes exhibit a form of Raman scattering, called an *anti-Stokes effect*, in which photons in the irradiating beam striking an atom or molecules are scattered but the scattered photons have a higher energy level than that of the incident photons. This means that dyes invisible to the naked eye can be rendered visible by visible-length light emitted on irradiating with infrared light. These anti-Stokes inks are used as a security feature. Figure 5.15 illustrates this for a Chinese banknote.

Destructive Methods for Ink Comparisons

Thin-layer chromatography (TLC) and high-performance liquid chromatography (HPLC) are well-established separation science techniques that can be used to exploit the molecular differences of ink components. Though destructive to the sample, they can help a criminalist determine which dyes, pigments, or other chemicals are present in an ink sample. Microdots of ink can be punched out of a writing sample using a hollow needle. Alternatively, if small amounts of fiber containing the ink can be teased from the surface, these can be mounted on the plate as a sample.

HPLC is the more powerful tool in regards to its capability to separate dye components, but TLC is simpler and gives a good visual representation. Once developed, the TLC plate is examined under visible and ultraviolet light. Figure 5.16 shows the component dyes in a black ink sample, separated by TLC.

OBLITERATIONS AND ERASURES

Obliteration is the process of writing over text with the intention of hiding or destroying the original information. Whether at the time the document was created or at a later date, obliteration made with the same ink used in the original is virtually impossible to recover. If a different ink was used to obliterate the text, illumination with alternative light sources may show differences in reflection or infrared luminescence, which can be photographed. Similar techniques, combined with handwriting analysis, are applied to detect additive alterations. (See Figure 5.17.)

Erasure, removing information from the original document, can be accomplished by abrasive or chemical means. Abrasive erasure, the kind one normally does with a pencil eraser, disturbs the finish of the paper surface. Depending on the degree of damage, the evidence of erasure can be seen with the unaided eye or a microscope. Some samples require *side lighting*, placing a light source at an angle to the surface of the paper, to detect an erasure.

FIGURE 5.15
Security printing in banknote. The number 100 is printed just above the visible denomination of 100, but using an anti-Stokes ink. The security print is invisible in normal light but can be seen when the note is viewed in IR light. Courtesy of Foster and Freeman.

FIGURE 5.16
Colored-dye components of black ink separated by TLC. From en.wikipedia.org/wiki/Image:TLC_black_ink.jpg

93

Information from charred documents can sometimes be recovered by employing side lighting with alternate light sources. The digitized images recorded from the document are then subjected to software filters that may enhance the contrast enough to recoup the information.

FIGURE 5.17
The writing concealed by the obliteration in the top frame becomes visible by detection of the IR luminescence of the ink in the concealed writing. Courtesy of Foster and Freeman.

INDENTED WRITINGS

Indented writings are valuable as evidence. Rather than an alteration, indented writings are impressions of the original made in a soft surface such as the next sheet of paper in a pad. The indentations, which may be visible to the unaided eye, are often enhanced by side lighting and photographed. However, by far the best technique is that of electrostatic document analysis (ESDA). ESDA works by creating an invisible electrostatic image of indented writing, which is then visualized by the application of charge-sensitive toners. The sensitive imaging process reacts to sites of microscopic damage to fibers at the surface of a document, which have been created by abrasive interaction with overlying surfaces during the act of handwriting. (See Figure 5.18.)

DATING

Many indicators can be used to date a document. For paper, the date of a document may be established by its fiber content or fiber inclusions. Physically, paper may also bear a true watermark—a manufacturer's seal—that changes from year to year. Chemically, finishing and brightening agents used in paper formulation as well as the ink used in a printed watermark may furnish clues to its date.

For inks, dating may depend on a variety of chemicals. **Taggants**, dyes, pigments, solvent mediums, and shellacs all contribute to ink composition. A particular ink may be traced through a constellation of components that identify the formula.

FIGURE 5.18
The barely discernible indented writing in the top image is made clearly readable after processing in the ESDA apparatus. Courtesy of Foster and Freeman.

SUMMARY

A questioned document is any handwriting or machine-produced writing where the source or authenticity of the material is disputed.

Characters are textual units. In typography, the graphical units are called *glyphs*. They compose a typeface, characters designed to share a particular look. The most important measurement is the x-height, the distance from the baseline to the top of a lowercase glyph, which forms the stem. The presence or absence of serifs is also an important characteristic.

The spacing of font characters is called *proportionality*. Pitch measures horizontal spacing, while point measures height.

When an exemplar is produced is important. In machine-produced writing, moving parts suffer from mechanical wear with use. Similarly, though it becomes more stable during adulthood, handwriting changes slowly with time.

Uniqueness of handwriting can provide clues to the identity of the individual who produced it; however, many factors, including the writer's state of mind, influence penmanship. While changing writing styles may be easy for a few words, it is difficult to sustain the effort because natural habits of the writer will try to assert themselves.

Like typescript, handwriting can be analyzed for variations of letter size, shape, slant, and spacing. Ligature, pen movement, pressure, and pen lifts also play parts in the determination. Even the page itself, taken as a whole, may provide clues. An examiner must consider the layout of a document for consistency in spacing, line use, and margins.

Exemplars are often created to look as much like the questioned document as possible. The writer might be asked to write out a sample of text using the same type of pen on the same kind of paper. A good exemplar will contain the same combinations of letters and words used in the suspect material, written several times.

Papers may be distinguished by the presence of watermarks, fiber content, security threads and inclusions, reflectivity, interaction with inks, and chemical sensitivity.

Inks are dyes or pigments suspended in a carrier medium. A single ink may contain more than one color or medium component. Inks may be compared by infrared luminescence (a nondestructive method), thin-layer chromatography (TLC, destructive to the sample), and other methods.

Questioned documents may show obliteration, erasure, indented writing marks, or alterations. Obliteration is the process of writing over text with the intention of hiding or destroying the original information. Erasure, removing information from the original document, can be accomplished by abrasive or chemical means. Indented writing marks can be made clearer by using obligue lighting or ESDA.

PROBLEMS

1. Give the word or phrase for the following definitions:
    a. a known specimen or sample used for comparison
    b. the emission of infrared light from a sample when stimulated with another light source
    c. the adjustment of spacing between characters
    d. the printing or writing of two or more letterforms as a unit, such as *th*
    e. normally occurring differences between repeated characters in the writing of an individual
    f. short horizontal lines added to the tops and bottoms of traditional typefaces
    g. the height of the body of a character without ascenders or descenders
    h. molecules used as internal markers for an ink
2. Describe the difference between the following terms:
    a. ascender and descender
    b. erasure and obliteration

c. elite and pica

d. kerning and pitch

e. individual and class characteristics

3. Give several examples of questioned documents.

4. Analyze the typeface of this book. What features do you see?

5. Write out the old typing practice sentence "The quick brown fox jumped over the lazy dog" three times each in pen and pencil. Note the natural variations in your handwriting.

6. Describe the effects of wear on mechanically produced handwriting such as that done by typewriters or mechanical printers.

7. Describe how alternate light sources can be used to

a. discover if an alteration has been made

b. recover writing from indentations

c. discover which writing was done first

8. Describe how thin-layer chromatography may be used to identify inks.

9. Describe some methods to compare paper samples.

10. Obtain a one-page writing sample from a friend and attempt to copy it. What was successful? Did the copy look more like your natural writing at the end?

11. Cut a section of paper towel (about $1'' \times 6''$). Mark the paper with ink about $1''$ from one end. Place the sample, marked end down, into a glass with $1/4''$ of water and allow the liquid to wick upward. (Be sure not to let the paper towel "stick" to the side of the glass with water. You may want to suspend your paper towel from a straw. What happens?)

12. Take a piece of paper towel and mark it with ink. You might also want to make samples of colored markers or fruit juices. Let the samples dry well. Wearing appropriate protection, mix 1 tablespoon of dishwashing detergent into a large glass of water. Take a small amount of this solution and mix it with an equal portion of hydrogen peroxide (often found in the first aid aisle of the drugstore). Dab your samples with the mixture. What happens?

GLOSSARY

Allograph a letter of the alphabet in a particular shape, or a coordination of letters.

Diacritic marks character modifiers used for pronunciation guidance, such as accents or umlauts, positioned above or below a character.

Elite a size of type with 12 characters to the inch; also called *12 pitch*.

Erasure removal of a written or printed element from a document by abrasion or chemical methods.

Exemplar a known specimen or sample used for comparison.

Font a specific size and style of type within a type family.

Font weight a set of characters of identical stroke thickness, width, or design characteristics.

Glyph graphical representation of a character or ligature.

Infrared luminescence the emission of infrared light from a sample when stimulated with another light source.

Kerning the adjustment of spacing between characters.

Ligature the printing or writing of two or more letterforms as a unit.

Natural variation the normal differences between repeated characters within a sample.

Obliteration often overwriting, but generally any attempt to render an original unreadable by adding to the document.

Pica one-sixth of an inch, a unit of measure for document layout; a size of type with 10 characters to the inch, also called *10 pitch.*

Pitch the number of characters per inch.

Point the standard unit for measuring font size, $1/12$ of a pica or $1/72$ of an inch.

Proportional font a font where the characters vary in width.

Serif short horizontal lines added to the tops and bottoms of traditional typefaces such as Times New Roman.

Taggants small molecules incorporated into the formula of an ink that are used as markers to identify it.

Clockwise from top left:
- Colored bottles—color is a feature that can assist in identifying the source of broken glass, and bottles are sometimes used as weapons.
- Michigan soil strata—soil composition varies by geographical location and by depth below the surface.
- The distorted filament from a light bulb that was broken while the lamp was on and therefore the filament hot.
- A paint fragment removed from a prybar—the color and chemical composition of paint fragments recovered from crime scenes or tools can be compared to that of possible sources.

Bottles: From Stockxpert; Soil: From http://soils.usda.gov/education/resources/k_12/lessons/color/mi.html;
Paint: Courtesy Faye Springer Filament: original image made by author.

CHAPTER 6
Physical Evidence

The Two Pias

Late one Friday evening, 17-year-old Pia K. borrowed a clean white shirt from her sister and a clean blue denim jacket from a friend and set out for a night on the town. The next day, at around 7:00 AM, her body was found by a fisherman in shallow water near the shore. She was wearing the shirt, jacket, and jeans from the night before but her pantyhose, panties, and shoes were missing. The body and clothing were meticulously examined to recover any trace evidence that might have been transferred from the locus of the murderer. Police investigations identified several suspects, but no evidence was found to link them to the crime.

The case looked as if it was going to remain unsolved, but almost exactly 3 years later, 20-year-old Pia T. disappeared in the same part of Finland as had Pia K. It was presumed that she too had been raped and murdered. In the 3 years between the disappearance of the two young women, police collated information on several rapes in the region where the girls lived, and eventually a suspect was developed and taken into custody. His apartment and car, which he had owned since before the disappearance of Pia K., were thoroughly searched and reference and evidence samples collected. However, he was released due to insufficient evidence.

Six months after her disappearance, the body of Pia T. was found in a lake. The tailor-made red coat, the artificial leather waistcoat, and the watch that she wore the night she was last seen alive were missing, as was her purse. Her outer clothing (jeans and tee shirt) was in poor condition, but her underclothing (bra, panties, and pantyhose) was practically undamaged though extensively soiled with silt from the lake. The case received considerable media coverage, as a result of which her purse was handed in to police. It had been found on the riverbank a few miles from the home of the suspect just one day after her disappearance.

Extensive laboratory examinations on trace material recovered from the body and clothing of both victims, and the car and residence of the suspect, produced several independent examples of association. These included

- **Pia K.:** Fibers from tapings from Pia's clothing were similar to those from the blanket covering the seat of the suspect's car; numerous welding-fume particles were found on her clothing; and a navy blue paint chip found on her jeans was similar in color and chemical composition to paint on a jack found in the trunk of the suspect's car.

- **Pia T.:** The tailor-made red coat was never found, but red wool fibers found on tapings from her panties, pantyhose, clothing, and furniture from her apartment, as well as cloth samples provided by the tailor, were selected as target reference fibers. Forty similar red wool fibers were found in the suspect's car. Numerous welding-fume particles similar to those found on Pia K.'s clothing were recovered from Pia T.'s clothing. A pile of ashes found in the backyard of the suspect's apartment yielded four partially burned brass buttons and an intact steel buckle that were similar to those seen in photographs showing Pia T.'s waistcoat.

- **Pia K. and Pia T.:** The suspect was involved in welding, and numerous welding-fume particles were recovered from the clothing of both young women. Neither had any work or environmental exposure to welding operations.

The trace evidence and associations derived from it are shown in Figures 6.1 and 6.2. The colored arrows indicate the different type of evidence and show the direction of transfer (from source to recipient).

The identification and bringing to justice of the perpetrator in the preceding case depended almost entirely on the scientific evidence uncovered in the laboratory from examination of materials from the deceased, the crime scenes, and the home of the suspect. The physical material ranged from the microscopic — for example, the welding-fume particles—to those visible to the naked eye—for example, buttons and buckle from Pia T.'s waistcoat.

This brings us to the question, what is physical evidence? Some people say physical evidence is an object that "speaks for itself," meaning a real object that does not require an inference to be made. The term *silent witness* also often is used. Of

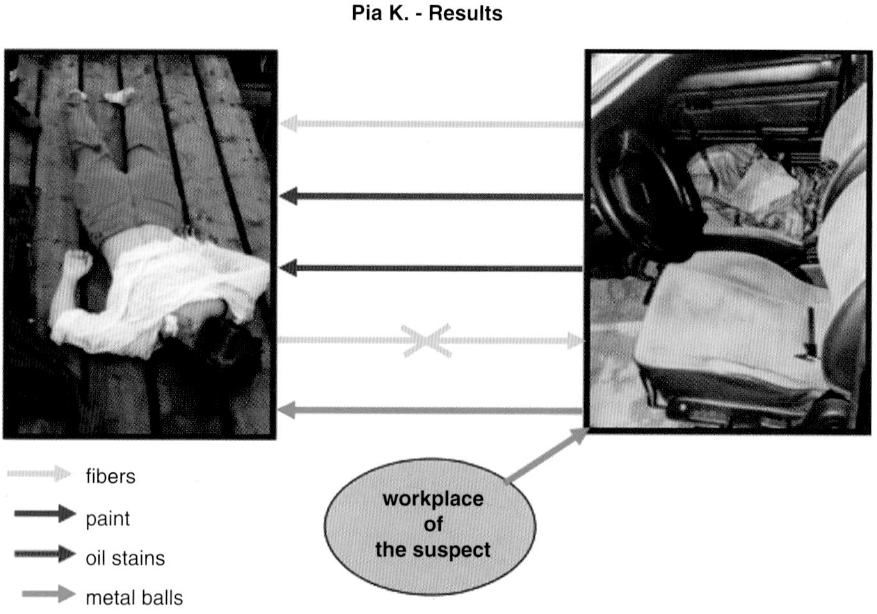

Pia K. - Results

FIGURE 6.1
Illustration of the multiple transfer of trace evidence in the case of Pia K. Fibers, paint, oil stains, and metal particles from the car of the accused were found on Pia's clothing. The metal particles originated at the workplace of the accused. Courtesy Dr. Sulkava.

fibers
paint
oil stains
metal balls

workplace of the suspect

Pia T.-Results

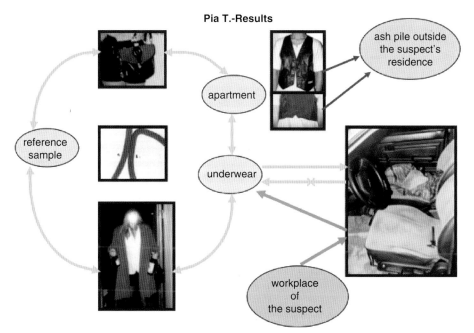

FIGURE 6.2
Physical evidence — Pia T. The associative evidence in this case was strengthened by the finding of materials that could have originated with Pia in the environment of the accused. For example, red clothing fibers in his car and residues in the burned debris at his house. Courtesy Dr. Sulkava.

course, it is the forensic examiner who ultimately must explain an object's meaning in court. As we just saw, physical evidence may include microscopic materials such as hairs, fibers, soil, glass, metal, paint, and other objects. This has led to the term *trace evidence* often being used synonymously with physical evidence, but it is probably more appropriate to use the less restrictive term *physical evidence,* since macroscopic evidence also can be used to infer or establish associations between persons and places. (See Figure 6.3.)

CENTRAL QUESTIONS

What can be answered:

- Could the physical materials recovered from objects associated with the crime, including clothing and vehicles, have a common origin with reference samples?

What we cannot answer:

- When were the materials deposited?

What we may be able to answer:

- What weight can be attached to the association; for example, are there databases of the frequency of occurrence of the materials in the environment?

What we are learning or researching:

- Can we test the materials to the point at which we have an identity?

101

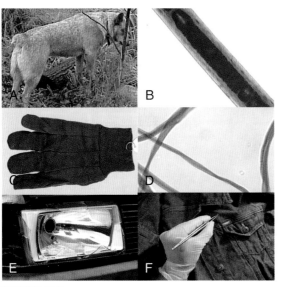

PHYSICAL MATERIALS

We will now consider the nature and properties of some of the physical materials that are encountered in physical evidence examination in the forensic science laboratory.

Properties of Materials

Scientists use chemical and physical properties to describe materials including physical evidence. **Chemical properties** describe what happened to a substance during a chemical reaction. These properties depend on the nature and amount of material present. When gasoline burns in the presence of oxygen, it creates carbon dioxide and water. The amount of oxygen needed depends on the amount of gasoline available to burn. (See Figure 6.4.)

Physical properties depend only on the nature of the substance measured. These properties are completely independent of that amount of material present. Physical properties include **nonderivable** properties such as freezing, melting, or boiling point and **derivable properties** such as density.

FIGURE 6.3
Macro and trace evidence. Microscopic trace evidence usually originates from a much larger source. Sometimes the nature of the source is such that it too can provide useful evidence. The figure illustrates this: A is a dog identified as being part of a scene and B is a recovered hair that provided evidence of a possible link between the dog and victim; C is a woolen glove from the DC sniper case and D shows recovered trace evidence fibers that linked two of the shooting scenes to the glove. E is a broken headlamp on a car involved in a hit-run, the break in itself providing relevant information, and F shows a forensic scientist removing a glass fragment from the jacket of the victim. A and B courtesy Faye Springer. C and D courtesy Foster and Freeman. E and F, U.S. government (ATF).

System International

International professional organizations such as the International Union of Pure and Applied Chemistry (IUPAC), the International Union of Pure and Applied Physics (IUPAP), and the International Organization for Standardization (ISO) make nomenclature suggestions that must be agreed upon internationally. The definition of standard physical properties is determined by international consensus. Each country has a national metrology institute (NMI). The NMI in the United States is the National Institute of Standards and Technology (NIST).

FIGURE 6.4
Properties of materials. A burning candle illustrates chemical and physical properties of materials. The original candle is an inert solid made of wax. When the wick is lit, chemical combustion takes place producing light and heat, and changing the solid candle wax to liquid. From Stockxpert.

The **System International (SI)** was established in 1960 by the General Conference on Weights and Measures (CGPM, *Conférence Générale des Poids et Mesures*). This intergovernmental treaty organization dates back to the Meter Convention of 1875, one of the first agreements for international standardization of measures. Signatory countries, those having ratified and adopted the treaty, agree to use the SI and meet to modify it as science and technology change.

SI BASE UNITS

The SI defines seven nonderivable physical properties, or base units. They have absolute definitions and must be measured directly. Most were originally defined by reference to physical artifacts; for example the meter was the distance between marks on a platinum-iridium alloy bar calculated to be equal to 10^{-7} of the meridian through Paris from the North Pole to the equator. The definitions have been refined to be absolute and not dependent on a reference artifact, the kilogram being the only exception. (See Table 6.1.)

While we commonly use the terms **mass** and **weight** to mean the same thing, weight (w) is actually mass (m) multiplied by the acceleration due to gravity (g). Mass is the quantity of matter in an object that can be acted on by gravity. Weight

Two of the units are named after famous physicists. The kelvin recognizes the nineteenth-century Scottish physicist William Thomson (Lord Kelvin), and the ampere recognizes the eighteenth-century French physicist Andre-Marie Ampere.

Table 6.1	SI base units	
Base Unit	**Name**	**Definition**
Length	**Meter (m)**	The distance light travels in a vacuum in 1/299792458*th* of a second.
Mass	**Kilogram (kg)**	The mass of the international prototype, a platinum-iridium cylinder housed under special conditions in Sevres, France.
Time	**Second (s)**	The duration of 9192631770 periods of the radiation corresponding to the transition between the two hyperfine levels of the ground state of the cesium 133 atom.
Electric current	**Ampere (amp)**	The ampere is that constant current which, if maintained in two straight parallel conductors of infinite length of negligible circular cross section and placed 1 meter apart in vacuum, would produce between these conductors a force equal to 2×10^{-7} newton per meter of length.
Thermodynamic temperature	Kelvin (K)	The kelvin is 1/273.16*th* of the thermodynamic temperature of the triple point of water.
Amount of substance	**Mole (mol)**	The amount of substance of a system that contains as many elementary entities as there are atoms in 0.012 kilogram of carbon 12.
Luminous intensity	**Candela (cd)**	The candela is the luminous intensity in a given direction of a source that emits monochromatic radiation of frequency 540×10^{12} hertz, and that has a radiant intensity in that direction of 1/683 watt per steradian.

103

is relative to the force of gravity acting on the mass. Astronauts who travel to the moon can bounce on its surface or appear weightless in space because the g-force acting on them is small. The astronauts themselves, however, have not been reduced in size. Hence, it is the mass of a substance or piece of evidence that is recorded, though we say it was "weighed." Figure 6.5 shows some reference artifacts used in the SI system.

Some things to remember when using SI units:

- When the mole is used, the elementary entities must be specified and may be atoms, molecules, ions, electrons, other particles, or specified groups of such particles.
- Kelvin is not expressed in degrees, but conventional temperature measurement is made in degrees **Celsius** (°C). One Celsius degree is equal in magnitude to one kelvin, allowing a temperature difference to be expressed in either unit. Therefore, the value of a Celsius temperature t expressed in degrees Celsius is given by t (°C) = T(K) – 273.15. Centigrade and degrees centigrade were replaced by Celsius as part of an international naming convention. The thermometer is what the name implies: a tiny meter for measuring temperature change. If we have a Celsius thermometer, we can calculate the temperature in degrees Fahrenheit (°F) by using the conversion formula °F = (9/5) °C + 32.

Derivable Properties

Many properties of matter can be derived from the standard set of units. Some relationships are very helpful to the forensic examiner. Simple derived units include area (length × width), volume (length × width × height), speed (distance per unit time), density, and concentration.

DENSITY

Density is the mass per unit volume of a substance:

$$D = m/v$$

In SI units, it is expressed in kilograms per cubic meter (kg/m³); however, in the laboratory, it often is more useful to use g/cm³. Cubic centimeters (cc) are the same as milliliters (mL) under a specific definition.

FIGURE 6.5
SI unit reference artifacts. Left to right: U.S. national reference kilogram; NIST cesium clock; platinum-iridium meter reference bar. Kilogram: http://www. mel.nist.gov/galleryph/ calres/pages/049a.htm. Cesium clock: Public domain U.S. government (http://tf.nist.gov/ timefreq/cesium/ fountain.htm). Meter: http://www.mel.nist.gov/ div821/museum/length. htm.

One way to determine density is to use water displacement. After a material is weighed, it is immersed in water. The volume of the object is equal to the volume of water it displaces. Other methods must be used for liquids and gases because they have variable volumes under different conditions.

Bubble tea is an excellent example of a solid (tapioca) and liquid (tea) having equal densities. The tapioca remains suspended throughout the liquid.

CONCENTRATION

Related to density, concentration is the amount of substance per unit volume, moles per cubic meter (mol/m^3). In the laboratory, mmol/mL is a more commonly used unit. Concentration and density are linked by the molar mass of a substance.

 **Case Study**   **The Williams Brothers**

In the early hours of June 18, 1999, law enforcement and emergency services personnel were notified of three fires at synagogues in the Sacramento area. It was clear from examination of the scene that these were related, hate-crime motivated arson attacks. Crime scene and laboratory examination of the sites recovered several items of potential evidential value, including oil jugs that had been used as containers for the accelerant.

On July 1, police were called to a house in a rural area near Redding, California. The occupants, two gay male partners, had been murdered and their car and other personal effects stolen.

The next day saw an arson attack on a Sacramento abortion clinic. Access had been gained by breaking the reinforced glass windows on the clinic doors. The stolen vehicle from the Redding double homicide was recovered nearby,

and several days later police responded to a reported attempt to use the credit cards stolen from the homicide scene. This led to the arrest of Matthew and Tyler Williams on suspicion of the synagogue arsons, the Redding homicides, and the abortion clinic attack.

Searches of the vehicle and the Williams brothers' home yielded considerable physical evidence, including a black pry bar and black wrecking bar found in the vehicle trunk. Glass fragments recovered from the bars, the car, and coveralls found at the Williams' home matched that on the broken window of the clinic.

The case had many unpleasant features, but ultimately it appeared likely that the accused had links with white supremacy groups. They pled guilty to the arsons, but Matthew committed suicide before the homicide trial. Tyler pled guilty and is serving a life imprisonment sentence.

105

Glass

Glass is an isotropic amorphous vitreous substance (meaning that it has the same **refractive index** regardless of the direction of vibration of light passing through it and that it does not have a regular crystal structure). A forensic examiner may encounter glass in several different situations; for example, headlight and windshield glass in automobile hit-run investigations, container glass in bar fights, and window glass in break-and-enter cases.

TYPES OF GLASS

Glass is made of silicon oxides found in sand, which can be formulated with different metal oxides to give color, strength, and other properties. (See Figure 6.6.)

FIGURE 6.6
Some types of glass. Glass has many uses and products are manufactured in many forms. Left to right: colored glass bottles; reinforced glass window showing the damage from an impact; stained glass window. From Stockxpert.

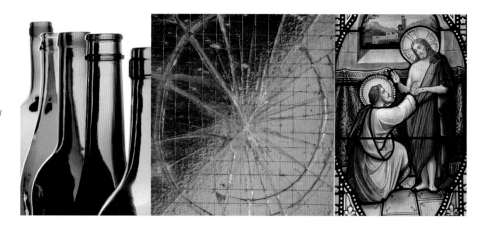

Soda–Lime Glass

The most typical glass for windows and regular uses, soda–lime glass is made by adding sodium carbonate (Na_2CO_3, the soda) and calcium oxide (CaO, the lime). Because of its low melting point and low viscosity, it sometimes is referred to as "soft glass."

Pyrex–Borosilicate Glass

This type of glass is formulated with boron oxide to impart heat resistance.

Tempered Glass

Like a sword, **tempered glass** is made by rapidly heating and cooling the material's surface. This thermal cycling, called *annealing*, during production stresses the glass material such that it forms "cubes" rather than shards on breaking. Annealing also changes the refractive index of the material.

Laminated Glass

This is actually two layers of glass with plastic between them. If the glass is broken, the plastic can keep all the fragments in place.

Stained Glass

The brilliant colors of stained glass are due to the incorporation of metal salts and the process by which the glass is manufactured.

GLASS MANUFACTURE

Flat window glass was first made around 1 AD. Early manufacturing processes, such as drawing the molten glass through a block, resulted in imperfections in the sheets. Today window glass is made by floating the molten mix on a bath of molten tin, producing a product of very uniform thickness. The surface of the glass retains traces of the tin from the flotation.

Container glass is made by automated processes that use a combination of pressing and blowing to produce the hollow body and open end of the container.

COLLECTING AND PRESERVING GLASS

After photographing the evidence, every effort must be made to collect as much of any glass evidence as possible. Having as many fragments as possible may help to show how the object was broken or may show missing pieces that could have been transferred during the commission of a crime. Glass collected at the crime scene should be kept separate from that collected on or near a suspect at another location. To avoid damage to the fragments, glass evidence should be packed to prevent breakage.

Tiny particles can be collected by tape lifts, shaking over collecting paper, or any of the other procedures commonly used to collect trace evidence. Large pieces can be picked up and packaged in rigid containers in order to prevent further breakage and protect handlers against cuts. Small pieces visible to the naked eye can be removed with forceps (see Figure 6.3).

EXAMINING GLASS

The examination of glass in the laboratory is conducted to show whether evidence fragments, for example, recovered from the clothing or footwear of a suspect, could have come from the scene, for example, the broken window at the entry point of a house break-in. Glass also can be examined to provide information about the events at the scene, for example, whether a window was broken from the inside or outside.

The first step should always be careful visual examination, for example, to see if larger evidence fragments can make a physical fit to scene fragments. When dealing with small particles, the material may first be tested to show that it is glass. A few simple tests can be applied to eliminate particles that might be confused with glass: Plastics can be eliminated by testing for indentation with a needle; cubic crystals such as salt can be identified by shape, fracture, and water solubility; and mineral grains can be identified using polarized light. Under the polarized light microscope, glass isotropic particles remain dark, whereas anisotropic or birefringent particles show up colored or bright.

Laboratory testing is based on the physical and chemical properties of glass. The physical properties most commonly used in the forensic science laboratory are **refractive index (RI)** and density. Because glass formulation changes little from manufacturer to manufacturer, and even less so between batches produced by the same manufacturer, it is difficult to describe beyond class characteristics unless the glass is tested for trace elemental composition. Though density and refractive index cannot provide individualization, these physical properties are used to describe glass particles and narrow down the possibilities. RI in particular can provide a high degree of discrimination between fragments from different sources.

The bulk materials, such as sand, soda, and lime, used to manufacture glass all contain low to trace quantities of other metals. Analysis of these can produce profiles that are specific enough to be considered as individualizing. However, because glass is an amorphous solid, the chemical composition, density, and refractive index of a sheet of glass will exhibit small variances that depend on the area tested. The forensic examiner must explain that these natural variances are very small by comparison to test data. The differences also limit the potential of chemical and physical methods to individualize glass fragments.

For example, an international collaborative study of 61 float glasses of global origin found that 90% of them could be differentiated using RI, and all could be differentiated using inductively coupled plasma-mass spectrometry (ICP-MS) to measure the relative concentrations of 30 trace elements in the glasses.

PHYSICAL PROPERTIES OF GLASS

Refractive Index (RI)

Light has both wave- and particle-like properties. Both forms of light interact with matter in unique ways. *Refraction* is the bending of light that takes place when it interacts with a material. It accounts for the look of a "break" in a straw inserted in a glass of water. (See Figure 6.7.)

The refractive index of a material is the factor by which light slows down when it travels inside that material relative to its speed in a vacuum. The expression is

$$n = c/v; \quad c = \text{speed of light} \quad v = \text{velocity of light in material}$$

This physical property can be used as a class characteristic to define a material; however, the refractive index of a material changes with both temperature and the frequency wavelength of light shining. To make a standard for comparison, the reference wavelength used is usually the bright school bus yellow color emitted at 589.3 nanometers by excited sodium atoms, often called the *sodium D-line*.

FIGURE 6.7
Refraction. "Bending" of straw in a glass of water as a result of refraction. From Stockxpert.

A prism disperses "white" light into its component colors because the glass has a different index of refraction for each "color" (frequency) of light passing through it.

108

FIGURE 6.8
Birefringence. Birefringence illustrated by double image of letters when read through transparent calcite crystal. From http://en.wikipedia.org/wiki/Image:Calcite.jpg

---

BOX 6.1 CRYSTALS

As you may have learned in general chemistry, **crystalline** solids have regular geometric structures. The smallest representation of that structure is called the *unit cell*. Cubic crystals, by nature of the definition of a cubic cell, have only one refractive index. However, most crystals are not cubic. Noncubic crystals exhibit double refraction: They bend incident light into two rays to give two different refractive indices. The difference between the two indices is called **birefringence,** an important characteristic to describe a crystal. For example, the indices of refraction for calcite are 1.486 and 1.658. The difference between these values is 0.172, calcite's birefringence. (See Figure 6.8.)

Refractive Index Measurement and Becke Lines. The Becke line is a bright outline of light that plays around a glass chip immersed in a liquid with a different refractive index than the glass. This "halo" moves toward the higher refractive index medium when the distance is increased from the point of critical focus under a plane-polarized microscope. (See Figure 6.9.)

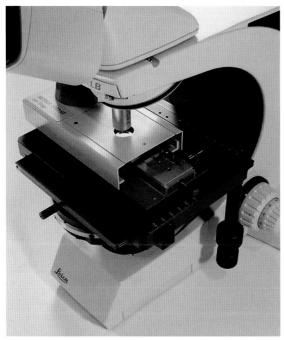

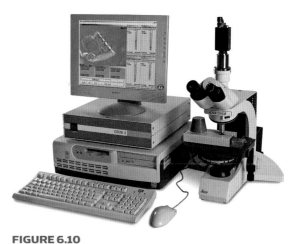

FIGURE 6.10
The GRIM 3. The glass-refractive index measurement apparatus captures images of the edge of a glass fragment suspended in oil. The "edge" is only visible as a Becke line and will disappear when the refractive index of the oil is the same as that of the glass. The sampling points can be seen on the screen image. Courtesy Foster and Freeman.

FIGURE 6.9
Refractive index. The heated microscope stage of the GRIM 3. The glass fragment is suspended in oil, the refractive index of which changes with temperature (see Figure 6.10). Courtesy Foster and Freeman.

To test for refractive index in this manner, glass chips are immersed in a silicone oil whose refractive index is slowly varied by heating until it matches that of the glass. If the liquid has a similar refractive index to the glass, the Becke line disappears and the glass seems to "dissolve" in the liquid. This is called the *match point*. The test is performed on a microscope fitted with a hot stage that can heat elements while they are viewed.

The process of measuring the RI of glass fragments is now highly automated and reliable, using the GRIM 3 apparatus designed and manufactured by Foster and Freeman (see Figure 6.10). The acronym GRIM stands for *glass-refractive index measurement*. The instrument locates and scans the interface between the fragment and the oil in which it is suspended. Measurements are taken at four sites and the average oil temperature when the Becke line disappears measured.

The Becke line is named for Friedrich Johann Karl Becke, an Austrian geologist who developed a method using microscopy to determine the relationship between light refraction and refractive index changes.

DENSITY TESTING

Using the flotation method, standard glass particles are immersed in a liquid matrix such as bromoform and bromobenzene. Glass chips will sink if their density is greater than the matrix, and they will float if their density is less. The matrix is adjusted by adding one component or the other until the glass chips

Bromoform (CHBr₃) is a small molecule with a density of 2.894 g/mL and a refractive index of 1.596. Bromobenzene, a moderately carcinogenic component of "new car smell," is a ring-shaped, planar molecule with a density of 1.495 g/mL and a refractive index of 1.5597. Remember that density is a ratio of mass to volume, so big pieces and small pieces of the same density behave the same way.

are suspended. When suspension occurs, the glass and liquid have equal density. Evidence is then compared by adding it to the matrix and observing its behavior. If the shards of evidence are suspended, their densities are equal to the reference. If not, the matrix can be adjusted until the particles are suspended. The liquid then can be measured for density using a densitometer. Density measurement is a simple but not very discriminating test.

CHEMICAL EXAMINATION OF GLASS FRAGMENTS

The chemical composition of glass fragments can be measured in several ways: scanning electron microscopy–energy dispersive X-ray spectrometry (SEM-EDX); X-ray fluorescence spectrometry (XRF); inductively coupled plasma–optical emission spectrophotometry (ICP-OES); and inductively coupled plasma-mass spectrometry (ICP-MS), including laser-ablation sampling (LA-ICP-MS).

Scanning Electron Microscopy

In scanning electron microscopy, a focused electron beam is scanned over the surface of a sample, causing, among other things, the emission of X-rays. The wavelengths or energies of the detected X-rays are used to identify the elements, and the intensities of the X-ray peaks in the measured spectrum correlate with the quantities of each element present in the sample area exposed to the electron beam.

X-Ray Fluorescence Spectrometry

X-ray fluorescence spectrometry is an elemental analysis technique based upon the measurement of characteristic X-rays emitted from a sample following excitation by an X-ray source. The energies or wavelengths of the detected X-rays are used to identify the elements, and the intensities of the X-ray peaks in the measured spectrum correlate with the quantities of each element present in the sample area exposed to the X-ray beam.

Inductively Coupled Spectrophotometry

In most inductively coupled plasmas, an electrical discharge is initiated in a flowing stream of inert gas, usually argon, and then sustained by a surrounding radio frequency field. The resulting stable discharge, or plasma, has the appearance of a small, continuously glowing flame, with temperatures in the range of 7000–10,000 K. When a sample is introduced into the plasma, extensive atomization, ionization, and excitation of the sample atoms occur. As the ions and atoms present in the sample enter cooler portions of the plasma and drop to lower excited states, they emit light at characteristic wavelengths. In an inductively coupled plasma-optical emission spectrophotometer, this emission is dispersed with a spectrophotometer and its intensity is measured.

ICP Mass Spectrometry

The inductively coupled plasma torch is an excellent ionization device. Instruments made by coupling inductively coupled plasma with mass spectrometry as an ion isolator and detector have shown improved analytical capabilities suitable for glass fragment analysis. Mass spectrometry instruments may be of quadrupole, time-of-flight, or magnetic-sector design with single or multiple electron multiplier detectors.

Laser Ablation ICP-MS

The relatively new technique of laser ablation–inductively coupled plasma-mass spectrometry (LA-ICP-MS) offers considerable advantages over all earlier methods. It can measure the elemental composition in a fragment as small as 0.5 mm. The technique uses a laser beam to vaporize a tiny spot on the sample; the vapor is carried to an ICP furnace by a stream of inert gas, and the elements in the plasma sample are identified by MS. (See Figure 6.11.)

The dimension of the crater created in the LA step is of the order of 75 μm, or less than the width of a human hair. The technique preserves the bulk of the sample, can process very small fragments, is highly effective in discriminating between samples of the same type of glass, and can differentiate between different types of glass. However, at this time the cost of the equipment and the relatively small number of cases in which it can be used do not justify its widespread implementation.

FIGURE 6.11
ICP-MS. A Varian ICP-MS instrument. Laser ablation instruments use a laser to vaporize the sample for introduction to the ICP-MS. From http://en.wikipedia.org/wiki/Image:ICP-MS.jpg

GLASS FRACTURES

Glass is brittle and breaks without much elongation or stretching. Individualizing fragments to a source occurs only if the evidence recovered is fitted together to reconstruct the object. Still, breakage patterns in glass may give information about the force and direction of impact.

111

Reconstruction

Pieces of glass that align but were obtained from different locations are valuable for evidence. Examiners can look at the broken edges under a microscope to reveal corresponding features such as Wallner lines, hackle marks, and ream lines. *Wallner lines* are rib-shaped marks with a wavelike pattern and are almost always concave in the direction from which the crack was propagating. A *hackle mark* is a line on the crack surface running parallel to the local direction of crack spreading, and *ream lines* are imperfections in the glass that may match across a fracture line.

FIGURE 6.12
The Four R rule. Photograph of fragment of broken glass illustrating the Four R rule. The Wallner lines are at right angles to the top edge in the illustration; the glass was broken by impact from the bottom side. Original photograph by author.

Direction

The direction of breaking force can be determined by observing Wallner lines on the radial cracks nearest the point of impact. In untempered glass, the Wallner lines on radial cracks nearest the point of impact follow a rule of thumb called the *four R rule*: *r*idges on *r*adial cracks appear at a *r*ight angle to the *r*ear (see Figure 6.12). However this "rule" does not apply in all situations; for example,

it is unreliable for tempered and laminated glasses. If the impact site has been destroyed because the object shattered, the glass must be reconstructed and its original orientation determined before direction of impact can be assigned.

Sequence

The sequence of impact from multiple projectiles, such as bullets, can be determined because cracks caused by the later impacts will stop at cracks made from the previously fired shot.

Low-Velocity Impact

Low-velocity projectiles produce cracks that radiate outward from the point of impact (radial cracks). If a pane is firmly held on all sides, concentric cracks can form around the point of impact, as is seen in Figure 6.6.

High-Velocity Impact

A high-speed projectile striking a piece of glass will produce a cone or crater with its tip on the entry side and its base at the exit. If the impact site is shattered, the object must be reconstructed to observe any coning effects. This may prove difficult due to the very small size of the shards near the impact site. Like with fabric, if the projectile was a bullet, the diameter of the hole and the crater cannot be used to determine its caliber. (See Figure 6.13.)

112

FIGURE 6.13
Bullet hole (high velocity impact) in glass window. Note cratering effect from front to rear. From Stockxpert.

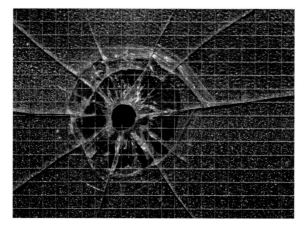

Case Study

Paint Evidence in the Williams Brothers' Case

The identification of Mathew and Tyler Williams as suspects in the hate crimes that took place in the Sacramento area in the summer of 1999 depended on many factors, as did the evidence that led to their subsequent arrest and conviction.

The role of glass examination was described previously, but paint evidence was also important.

The sequence of crimes was first the arson of three synagogues, then the double homicide of Gary Matson and Winfield Mowder, and finally the arson attack on an abortion clinic. The Williams's made several errors in regard to the homicide, principally the theft of the Toyota car and the theft and attempted use of credit cards owned by the deceased. The power of physical evidence is often related to the extent that it links people and objects in circumstances where there are no grounds—other than the commission of the crime being investigated—to believe they have ever been in contact with each other.

The brothers abandoned the Toyota near the clinic. A search of the vehicle yielded a pry bar and a wrecking bar in the trunk. Examination of the bars revealed paint evidence as follows:

Black paint found on the window at the point of entry to the B'Nai Israel could have come from the black wrecking bar.

Black paint on the broken glass on the point of entry to the abortion clinic could have come from the black pry bar.

Green paint on the pry bar could have come from the clinic door (see Figure 6.14).

FIGURE 6.14
Paint associative evidence. The image on the left is a close-up photograph of the tip of the pry bar showing a paint fragment (arrowed) adhering to it. The image on the right is the recovered paint fragment. The evidence linked the Williams brothers to the abortion clinic arson attack in the Sacramento area in 1999. Analysis showed that the green paint flake recovered from the pry bar could have come from the clinic door that was forced open to gain entry to the premises. Courtesy Faye Springer.

113

Paint

Paints, lacquers, and coatings can be found on almost any surface. Transfer of paint evidence is readily understood by the misfortune of a car accident. Paint from one vehicle is deposited on the other and vice versa. Using minute amounts of paint, forensic examiners can often identify the make, model, and color of a vehicle even if it has left the scene. Paint evidence often has a layered structure that is key to individualization of a sample.

WHAT IS PAINT?

Whether intended for automotive or architectural use, paint consists of pigments and additives suspended in a binder whose consistency is adjusted by a solvent. The color of a paint is determined by organic or inorganic chemicals called **pigments**. The most manufactured pigment for architectural paint is titanium dioxide (TiO_2), which by itself provides a bright white color and lends opacity to other colors. In automotive paints, additives give shine and opalescence. Paint binders are often polymers that hold together the ingredients in a paint formulation. Binders help paint dry into a smooth layer as the solvent, sometimes called *float media,* evaporates. The length of drying time may vary with the type of solvent used; however, whether water based or oil based, there is no use watching and waiting.

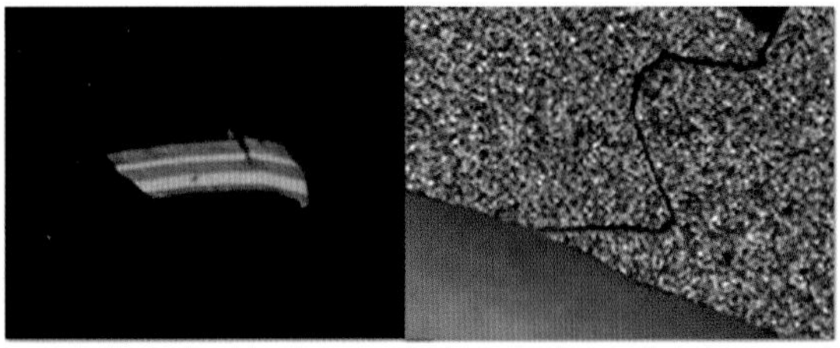

PAINT LAYERING

Rarely does an object have just one coat of paint. Whether from the design of a car finish to redecorating a living room, paint is often found with a layered structure. The sequence, thickness, and chemical compositions of the layering are useful in helping individualize a sample. The same principles regarding the study of layering apply to both automotive and architectural paint; however, automotive paint is slightly more defined. Basic automotive paint usually has several layers. (See Figure 6.15.)

FIGURE 6.15
Automobile paint evidence. Paint flakes or chips created in vehicular incidents such as hit-runs can provide good evidence. In some cases, the layer structure of the paint, created by the successive application of coats, will be distinct (left). In others, flakes may be large enough to permit physical fit of material recovered from the scene with that on the source vehicle (right). From http://www.state.nj.us/njsp/aivorg/invest/criminalistics.html

Electrocoat Primer

Applied to the bare metal of a car body, electrocoat primer is a mixture of epoxy-based resins that provide rust proofing. To ensure thorough coating, the frame is usually dipped into a tank of primer.

Primer Surfacer

In "primerless" paint, the electrocoat and primer surfacer are combined into a dip that provides the base for the color coat.

Applied over the electrocoat, primer surfacers are epoxy-modified polyesters or urethanes that dry to a very smooth finish, preparing the body of the car for the color coat. Unlike the "Bondo gray" of regular primer, automobile primer surfacers come in a variety of colors suited to what the color coat may be.

Color Coat (Base Coat)

Color coat provides the color of the finished car with fade-resistant organic or inorganic pigments bound in an acrylic-based polymer. Additives, such as microparticles of aluminum, which give a metallic finish, can alter the final look of the coating.

Because of the cumulative toxicity of heavy metals, lead- and chrome-based pigments are being replaced by more environmentally friendly organic pigments.

Clear Coat (Topcoat)

To give a glassy surface to the vehicle, a colorless clear coat of acrylic or polyurethane material is applied last. This coating is also applied as a detailing to older cars to renew their finish.

COLLECTING AND PRESERVING PAINT EVIDENCE

Paints and coatings can be collected from a variety of surfaces after they are documented in place. Loose paint flakes can be fragile, so they must be collected carefully to avoid fragmentation. The chips can be collected with tweezers, a scalpel, or a tape lift. They may be stored in any properly labeled container that will minimize damage due to breakage. Embedded paint transfer in clothing, fabric, or on a hard surface should be taken to the laboratory as is. If this is not possible, as in a car accident, a sample of transferred paint should be taken to the base of the surface containing the paint evidence. If both of the surfaces involved in a transfer are available, both should be sampled.

Particularly in car accidents, exemplars of the paint of each vehicle should be collected from an undamaged area near their impact site. The exemplars must be cut all the way to the base metal, documented for location, and properly labeled. Consideration should be given as to whether the damaged area or the one from which the exemplar is taken has been repainted.

To better observe paint layering, it is advisable to cut paint exemplars at an angle using a thin blade. Sometimes, such angular cuts facilitate peeling the layers from one another. To study the strata of paint, thin sections may be cut. If the sample is brittle or small, an embedded preparation may be made by coating the paint chip with a stabilizing material before sectioning it.

Paint evidence may also be a component of a tool mark, whether on the surface of the tool or by providing a soft surface that bears an impression. Rather than lift paint off a tool at the scene, the examiner is wise to take the tool itself to the laboratory for further examination. Similarly, the examiner should never attempt to recover a paint sample from an impression mark. Instead, the entire impression should be collected, if possible, and an exemplar taken from the surrounding area (see Figures 6.14 and 6.16).

Although the tape lift is an excellent procedure for recovery of trace physical evidence such as hairs, fibers, and glass, it can be a forensic examiner's "last resort" for recovery of paint fragments because adhesives and chemical components in the tape may make certain tests more difficult.

115

EXAMINING PAINT EVIDENCE

Paint can be analyzed by a variety of microscopy, chemical, and instrumental methods to provide class characteristics or component identification. The sample size often dictates the selection and sequence of techniques used. Because paint is often found in layers, microscopy is a good place to start the examination of paint evidence. Afterward, paint may be examined for its optical and chemical properties.

Microscopy

Though the layering of a paint sample is not enough to individuate it, such strata can provide an excellent descriptive correlation when matched by sequence, color, and further chemical testing. Exemplars and evidence are viewed side by side under a comparison microscope or stereomicroscope. The samples should be described in terms of condition, size, shape, color, wear, and identifiable layers as well as documented with photography. Paint chips with a large surface area may bear witness to the surface over which they were coated. Impressions and striations in the paint fragment's details by microscopy can prove very useful.

While color is the most obvious distinguishing characteristic, the overall texture of the paint is also important. Even when a color is identified, it may not identify the make, model, and year of manufacture of an automobile since popular paint formulations might be used by one manufacturer in more than one product line over more than 1 year. Hence, the composition of underlying layers becomes important.

Solubility and Microchemical Tests

Solubility and microchemical tests are destructive techniques and not especially powerful at distinguishing between different paints. They may be applied to single layers of paint components or to the entire sample. Often the exemplar is tested first to see how it responds to the conditions. On a single layer of paint, microsolvent extraction can be used to prepare samples for further experiments such as IR, GC (gas chromatography), and GC-MS. It can also be used to separate pigments from binders, making the analysis of either component less complicated.

When a whole sample of automotive paint is tested, the layers may react differently. Changes in the appearance of the layer, such as change of color, swelling, distortion (curling, wrinkling, or puckering), and dissolution, must be carefully described.

Why test the exemplar first? Most likely there is a lot more of it, so the best method for analyzing the evidence can be worked out without destroying the evidence.

Infrared (IR) Spectroscopy

Both transmittance and reflectance infrared (IR) spectroscopy are used to discover more information about the chemical composition of the paint layers; however, transmittance spectra are more prevalent in reference collections. Functional groups within chemicals absorb infrared radiation at different frequencies, yielding a spectrum indicative of the chemicals present (see Figure 6.16). The technique is most useful for organic materials. Inorganic pigments have lower frequency absorptions in an area of the spectrum called the *fingerprint region*, below 700 cm^{-1}. While specially equipped spectrometers can collect data to the far end of the infrared (220 cm^{-1}), the process is less sensitive and hence requires longer analysis times. When possible, the layers should be tested separately. However, because the chemical composition of an adjacent layer may affect the spectrum of one tested, IR spectroscopy can help provide data on the order of the layers.

Pyrolysis Gas Chromatography (PGC)

Pyrolysis gas chromatography (PGC) is a destructive technique in which small samples of paint chips (a few micrograms) are heated until they break down. The volatilized gases and decomposition products are injected into a gas chromatograph that separates the constituents by properties such as polarity. The pattern of elution of pyrolytic components is called a *pyrogram*. The pattern of peaks in the pyrogram may be used for comparison. PGC is best employed on individual layers of paint where the sample runs are separated by **blanks**.

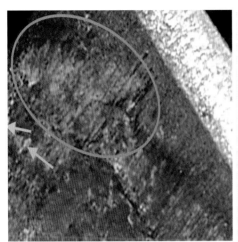

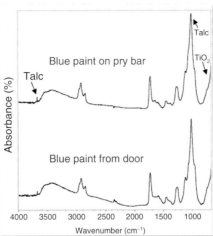

FIGURE 6.16
FT-IR spectroscopy of paint. Left: A multi-colored paint chip recovered from a pry bar suspected of being used in a burglary. Right: FTIR spectra of the evidence paint chip and the paint source/ IR spectrum reproduced courtesy of Dr. Patrick Buzzini; paint chip image from Buzzini, P., Massonnet, G., and Monard Sermier, F. 2006. The micro Raman analysis of paint evidence in criminalistics: case studies. *J. Raman Spectrosc.* **37**, 922–931, Wiley-Blackwell.

Fragments may be identified more closely by coupling the PGC procedure with mass spectrometry (PGC-MS). Data from the reconstructed total ion chromatogram, a list of the pyrolysis fragments by weight and prevalence, can sometimes be used to piece together information about chemicals present in the sample.

Scanning Electron Microscopy

Scanning electron microscopy–energy dispersive X-ray analysis (SEM-EDX) can be used to characterize the morphology and elemental composition of paint samples. The SEM rasters an electron beam over a selected area of a sample, producing emission of signals including X-rays, backscattered electrons, and secondary electrons. Emitted X-rays produce information regarding the presence of specific elements, and the electron signals produce compositional and topographical visualization of a sample (see Figure 3.23.)

The X-rays are produced as a result of high-energy electrons creating inner-shell ionizations in sample atoms, with subsequent emission of X-rays unique to those atoms. The minimum detection limit under many conditions is 0.1%. The technique does not work well with elements with atomic numbers less than 11.

X-Ray Fluorescence and X-Ray Diffraction (XRF and XRD)

Excitation of a sample by an X-ray source results in the emission of longer wavelength X-rays, or X-ray fluorescence, characteristic of the element excited. The limits of detection for most elements are generally better than for SEM-EDX, and the higher energy X-ray lines produced by higher energy excitation typical of XRF can be useful during qualitative analysis. Because of the significant penetration depth of the primary X-rays, XRF analysis will generally yield elemental data from several, if not all, layers of a typical multilayer paint fragment simultaneously. Because variations in layer thickness may cause variations in the X-ray ratios of elements present, this technique can be used only comparatively or qualitatively.

XRD is a nondestructive technique for the identification of the crystal form of pigments and extenders or fillers. This method is usually not suitable for the identification of organic pigments. XRD instruments usually employ a copper target X-ray tube to generate the X-ray beam and a diffractometer to measure both the diffraction angles and peak intensities characteristic of the crystal structure. The diffraction patterns are characteristic of the crystalline material irradiated.

PAINT DATA QUERY (PDQ)

Started by the Royal Canadian Mounted Police (RCMP) in 1975, the Paint Data Query (PDQ) is a worldwide database of automotive finishes from electroprimer to topcoat. The RCMP opened the database to the European Union and Japan in exchange for data in 1998. Similarly, the FBI acquired the use of the database in 2000 in exchange for data on North American car manufacturers. The database allows forensic scientists access to more than 50,000 automotive paint components based on their layering sequence, color, optical properties, and chemistry with the hope of providing information as to the year, make, and model of a vehicle used during a crime.

Case Study

The Green River Homicides

In July 1982, the bodies of four women were recovered from the Green River, near Seattle, Washington. It soon became apparent that they were the victims of a serial killer whose prey was young prostitutes. Over the next 10 years the number of victims rose to over 60, and a special team, the Green River task force, was established to lead the investigation.

No successful leads were developed until 2001, when DNA analysis linked four of the deaths to Gary Ridgway, a painter at the Kenworth truck factory. Ridgway conceded that he had been a customer of the four women but that he was innocent of their murder. However, having been given an opening that identified a suspect, the task force contacted Skip Palenik and his colleagues to conduct microscopic trace evidence analysis, focused on the possibility of transfer of physical evidence originating in Ridgway's occupation as a painter.

The scientists found minute particles of Imron paint on the clothing of Ridgway and in debris removed from clothing of six of the victims, two of whom also had yielded positive DNA associative evidence (see Figure 6.17). Imron paint is a

FIGURE 6.17
Imron paint. Bicycle frames painted with DuPont's Imron polyurethane paint, incorporating reflective metallic flake particles. From http://www.flickr.com/photos/27209537@N00/2481077317/

specialty product not available to the general public but used by Ridgway in his work. The spheres were identified specifically as coming from Imron paint produced pre-1984.

Ridgway pled to the murder of 48 of the women in return for avoiding the death penalty.

Metals

As we have seen, the metal content of materials such as glass and paint can be used to characterize them. However, metal objects themselves are seldom encountered in the forensic science laboratory. For example, the examination of metal components in investigation of accidents can yield very strong evidence but is usually conducted by a specialist metallurgist as part of an accident investigation team.

Two examples of metal objects that are tested in the physical evidence section of a forensic science laboratory are metal filaments in vehicle lights, and weld particles.

FILAMENTS

Filament tests are a good example of physical evidence. A conventional incandescent lightbulb consists of a resistance wire mounted in either a low-pressure inert gas atmosphere or a vacuum contained within the glass envelope of the bulb. When the light is switched on, current flows through the resistance, resulting in the emission of light and heat. (See Figure 6.18.)

The question is often raised in vehicle accidents that occur at night, was the light on or off at the time of the impact? Because the filament is heated, the force produced by the sudden deceleration of the impact will make it stretch if the light was on at the time. In contrast, a cold filament either will be unaffected or may even break. It is important to be aware that the distinction is a general one and that it is not inevitable that there will be observable stretching of an "on" filament or cold breaking of one that was off. (See Figure 6.19.)

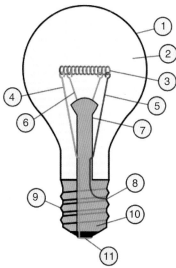

FIGURE 6.18
Incandescent lightbulb. 1. Glass bulb 2. Low-pressure inert gas 3. Tungsten filament 4. Contact wire (goes out of stem) 5. Contact wire (goes into stem) 6. Support wires 7. Stem (glass mount) 8. Contact wire (goes out of stem) 9. Cap (sleeve) 10. Insulation (vitrite) 11. Electrical contact. From http://en.wikipedia.org/wiki/Image:Incandescent_light_bulb.svg

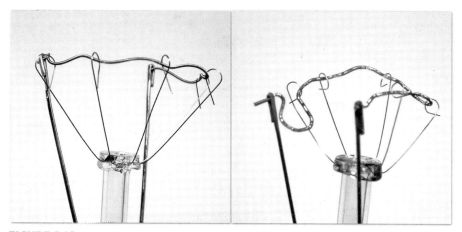

FIGURE 6.19
Filaments. Left to right: Filaments from incandescent bulbs that were broken while off (filament cold) or on (filament hot). Note the deformation of the hot filament. Original photograph by author.

Traditional incandescent bulbs are inefficient, with less than 5% of the energy being emitted as light. Halogen bulbs protect the filament by fusing it in quartz and encase it in high-pressure halogen gas. They operate at a much higher temperature than incandescent bulbs. When a bulb that is "on" is broken, the fine dust of glass from the outer envelope often will fuse on the hot filament, giving another indicator as to illumination status.

WELD PARTICLES

Welding produces microscopic particles similar to those encountered in spray painting. Weld particles were mentioned in the opening case of this chapter, as they were part of the extensive physical evidence recovered in the investigations of the murders of Pia T. and Pia K. The particles had considerable evidential value because the normal environment of the two young women was not one in which they would have encountered welding. The same applies to the spray paint particles in the Green River homicides. However, this is not always so, as the case study below illustrates.

Case Study
The Conviction and Exoneration of Edward Splatt

Rosa Simper was a widow who lived alone in a suburb of the South Australian capital of Adelaide. On December 3, 1977, an intruder broke into her house by forcing open a window. He raped and killed her. Police inquiries identified Charles Edward Splatt as a suspect. Examination of his clothing revealed the presence of weld and spray paint particles that were similar to those on the outside sill of the window used to gain entry to Mrs. Simper's home.

The house was located adjacent to a factory that conducted welding and painting, and the debris easily would have been transferred to the window in the air.

There were other items of physical evidence that could have resulted from Mr. Splatt being in the house, but the particles from the window were considered by the prosecution to be highly significant. Mr. Splatt was tried and convicted. However, a very strong campaign in the local press resulted in a review of the case, and the conviction was overturned on the basis that the associations inferred from the physical evidence were unsound.

Many aspects of the forensic evidence were explored at the review, but the principal objection was that Mr. Splatt worked as a welder in the factory. It therefore would be impossible to determine whether or not the particles recovered from his clothing were deposited during the course of his work or during entry through the window.

Soil

Forensic soil examiners look at far more than dirt. For their purposes, soil can be thought of more like a laundry stain. Soil is dirt and anything in it that will mark it as belonging uniquely to a particular location: dust, chemicals, building materials, glass fragments, organic matter, micro-organisms, and a wide range of minerals. Soil is ubiquitous and, as anyone who has ever walked mud into the house knows, easily transferred from the crime scene to other locations—clothes, cars, houses—by the criminal. If the soil can be matched to a crime scene, it may put the criminal there as well. (See Figure 6.20.)

TYPES OF SOIL

Soil generally is made up of minerals, organic material, air, and water. It is defined by texture, really the size of the mineral or rock fragments within the soil, into three main categories: sand, silt, and clay. The U.S. Department of Agriculture further defines soils into eight categories according to particle size (see Table 6.2).

Soil type is determined by sorting a soil sample with a series of sieves. Most soils are a mixture of types. A set of sieves, for example, 2 > 1 > 0.5 > 0.25 > 0.125 > 0.05 mm can be used not only to give a gross categorization of a sample but also to produce a characteristic particle size distribution within it.

COLLECTING AND PRESERVING SOIL EVIDENCE

Exemplars of soil should be sampled at the suspected crime scene, at regular intervals radiating away from it (to an appropriate perimeter distance), and from any alibi location. Unless the earth was disturbed at depth—to dig a grave, for example—a sample of the surface soil is sufficient. The locations should be photographed and the samples stored in properly labeled glass or plastic vials. Though samples may be collected wet or dry, samples suspected of containing chemicals can be packaged into vials fitted with septa to allow sampling of the headspace.

Recovery of soil samples from automobiles should be performed in this sequence: exterior of front fender and grill; interior of front fender; wheel wells and tires;

There's nothing pedestrian about it: A forensic soil scientist, or pedologist, with field expertise in the botany or geology of a particular area may be able to help pinpoint a crime scene from soil data.

121

Table 6.2	Types of Soil
Particle Size	**Name**
1.0–2.0 mm	Very coarse sand
0.5–1.0 mm	Coarse sand
0.25–0.5 mm	Medium sand
0.125–0.25 mm	Fine sand
0.05–0.125 mm	Very fine sand
0.02–0.05 mm	Coarse silt
0.002–0.02 mm	Medium and fine silt
0.002 mm	Clay

Digging deeper does not always help the investigator. Material unearthed by digging may dilute the information provided by the surface soil.

engine compartment; suspension components; muffler components; interior, including trunk; inner and outer surfaces of rear fender; rain gutters and exterior trim; and finally swabs from body panels.

Soil evidence found away from the crime scene should be sampled in place at the lab. Soil embedded in clothing or footwear should not be removed but rather the entire garment or shoe sent to the laboratory. Similar care should be taken with soils embedded in tires or collected on vehicles.

EXAMINING SOILS

Sieving

How close can you get? While variations in soil do exist, the only way to pinpoint a location is to have a unique soil component.

Soil is often described by a series of physical tests. There is no definitive protocol for handling soils. Hence, examiners have to give the best description possible using agreed-upon standards. Sieving to give a particle size distribution, as described previously, is a good place to begin. More detailed discrimination can be added from other tests.

Microscopy

After determining the type of soil by sieving, soil samples can be compared with one another under the microscope. Low-power microscopy will reveal traces of minerals as well as many types of debris. Any unique findings—building dust, glass fragments, minerals, or plants—may help differentiate the soil, individuate it to a crime scene, or link the suspect or victim to a location.

Munsell's Test: The Color of Dirt

Developed by Alfred Henry Munsell and the U.S. Department of Agriculture's Soil Conservation Service, the **Munsell system** is a notation that soil scientists can use to compare soils from anywhere in the world. The system has three descriptors: hue (color), value (brightness), and chroma (color intensity). Soil samples are compared to a book of color chips—quite like a paint index—and assigned the Munsell notation of closest match. Because wet soil appears darker than dry soil, samples to be compared are often dried or conditioned (brought to a specific temperature and humidity) together. See Box 6.2.

DENSITY

The ratios of sand, silt, and clay determine the amount and size of pore spaces (air pockets) and, hence, the density of a soil sample. Because it is difficult to judge this volume with the eye, soil is submitted to density testing not unlike

BOX 6.2   GROUND-IN DIRT

Pedologists use a soil classification system (soil taxonomy) to describe soil horizons (layers) in a profile. From the black beaches of Hawaii to the red desert in California to White Sands in New Mexico, the color of soil can become a defining feature of an area. What gives soil its color?

As rocks and minerals containing iron or manganese weather, the elements oxidize. Small crystals of compounds containing iron range from yellow ($FeOOH$, goethite) to red (Fe_2O_3, hematite) to black (FeS_2, iron sulfide), depending on their size and chemical composition. Manganese can form black crystals on oxidation to MnO_4.

Mineral	Formula	Size	Munsell Color	
Goethite	$FeO(OH)$	(1–2 mm)	10YR 8/6	Yellow
Hematite	Fe_2O_3	(~0.4 mm)	5R 3/6	Red
Lepidocrocite	$FeO(OH)$	(~0.5 mm)	5YR 6/8	Reddish yellow
Ferrihydrite	$Fe(OH)_3$		2.5YR 3/6	Dark red
Iron sulfide	FeS		10YR 2/1	Black
Pyrite	FeS_2		10YR 2/1	Black (metallic)
Todorokite	MnO_4		10YR 2/1	Black
Humus			10YR 2/1	Black
Calcite	$CaCO_3$		10YR 8/2	White
Dolomite	$CaMg(CO_3)_2$		10YR 8/2	White
Gypsum	$CaSO_4 Å \sim 2H_2O$		10YR 8/3	Very pale brown
Quartz	SiO_2		10YR 6/1	Light gray

Color can also yield clues to the environment of a soil sample. Yellowy goethite soils occur more often in temperate climates, while blood-red hematite soils appear in hot deserts and tropical climates. When standing water covers soil, the aerobic bacteria making humus becomes dormant. Anaerobic bacteria reduces ferric iron (Fe^{3+}) in minerals to water-soluble ferrous iron (Fe^{2+}). This bacterial leaching turns the surface of the red soil gray. The same gray color can be seen when anaerobic bacteria attack humus. Drying and reoxidation of the irons salts in the soil renew its red color.

Adapted from Lynn, W. C., and Pearson, M. J., "The Color of Soil," *The Science Teacher,* May 2000.

that of glass. Samples of the soil are added to density-gradient tubes stacked with bands of differing-density liquids (the heaviest at the bottom). The soil particles become suspended in the band that matches their own density. While not a definitive test, density analysis is an excellent way to describe varying soil samples by comparison.

ORGANICS

Identifying specific organic compounds in soils is a way to differentiate soils that are otherwise similar. Organics in soils can be measured in a variety of ways. Headspace over soil wet with chemicals can be sampled by gas chromatography (GC) or a combination of gas chromatography followed by mass spectroscopy (GC-MS). Alternatively, an aliquot of soil may be washed or extracted and the resulting solution tested. In a relatively new technique, the IR spectrum of a soil sample that was oxidatively pyrolyzed (a process that destroys organic materials) is subtracted from the spectrum of the same sample prior to pyrolysis. The difference between the IR spectra represents the organics lost in the oxidation. (See Box 6.3.) Sources of biologic materials include pollens.

BOX 6.3   PALYNOLOGY

Palynology is the study of pollens, the male gametes of flowering plants, and spores, asexual reproductive bodies from other plants. In a broader context, forensic use of palynology may include the study of diatoms, dinoflagellates, and other microscopic organisms. Forensic palynology in combination with soil testing has proved a useful tool in identifying crime scenes.

Researchers used pollen analysis to help in the prosecution of war crimes in Bosnia. To prevent being tried for acts against humanity, Bosnian war criminals exhumed mass graves and reburied bodies in smaller graves. They claimed that, rather than a mass execution, the dead were the result of minor clashes. Researchers analyzed soil samples from skeletal cavities in bodies from "secondary" burial sites to prove that a mass grave had initially existed. In one case, the bodies from a secondary burial site were linked to the site of the execution by the presence of distinctive wheat pollen. The finding was confirmed by ballistics analysis.

SUMMARY

Physical evidence does not require an inference to be made. Physical evidence may include microscopic and macroscopic amounts of hairs, fibers, soil, glass, metal, paint, and other objects.

Scientists use chemical and physical properties to describe materials including physical evidence. Chemical properties describe what happened to a substance during a chemical reaction. These properties depend on the amount of material present. Physical properties depend only on the substance measured.

These properties are completely independent of that amount of material present. Physical properties include nonderivable properties such as freezing, melting, or boiling point and derivable properties such as density. Scientists use the System International (SI), a standard set of units used worldwide to communicate. There are seven nonderivable properties that must be measured: length, mass, amount of substance (moles), time, temperature, luminosity, and electric current. Other properties such as density or concentration can be derived from these base units.

Glass is an amorphous solid made of silicon oxides that may appear in several forms. Glass is studied in terms of its density and refractive index. Refraction is the bending of light that takes place when it interacts with a material. The refractive index (RI) of a material is the factor by which light slows down when it travels inside that material relative to its speed in a vacuum. Noncubic crystals exhibit double refraction. The difference between the two indices is called *birefringence.* The examiner may also look at glass for the Becke line to help determine RI.

Glass is brittle and breaks without much elongation or stretching. While some objects allow reconstruction, breakage patterns in glass can give information about the force and direction of impact. In untempered glass, the Wallner lines on radial cracks nearest the point of impact follow a rule of thumb called the *four R rule*: Ridges on radial cracks appear at a right angle to the rear.

Paint consists of colored pigments and additives suspended in a binder whose consistency is adjusted by a solvent. The sequence, thickness, and chemical compositions of the layering are useful in helping individualize a sample. Paint can be analyzed by a variety of microscopy, chemical, and instrumental methods to provide class characteristics or component identification.

125

Plants are also subject to DNA testing.

Soil is dirt and anything in it that will mark it as belonging uniquely to a particular location: dust, chemicals, building materials, glass fragments, or plant particles. Soil is categorized as sand, silt, and clay by particle size. After determining the type of soil by sieving, soil samples can be compared with one another under the microscope for unique mineral fragments and debris. Samples are also described by the Munsell system for hue (color), value (brightness), and chroma (color intensity). In some cases, soils will be tested for density and organic material content.

PROBLEMS

1. Give the word or phrase for the following definitions:
   a. amount of substance present
   b. amount of substance per unit volume
   c. number of moles per unit volume
   d. solids with random orientation of atoms, ions, or molecules
   e. difference between two indices of refraction
   f. fracture lines radiating outward from a crack in glass
   g. test to determine hue, brightness, and intensity of soil color
   h. mixtures of metals
   i. coloring in paint

2. List three physical properties for water.
3. List three chemical properties of water.
4. Explain the importance of the System International units and list the non-derivable properties.
5. Which of the following is larger?
    a. meter or yard
    b. liter or quart
    c. kilogram or pound
    d. kilometer or mile
    e. degree Celsius or degree Fahrenheit
6. Convert the following:
    a. 1.45 m to feet
    b. 0.3 L to cups
    c. 0.5 kg to pounds
    d. 100 km to miles
    e. 37 °Celsius to Fahrenheit
7. Describe a method to compare glass fragments by relative density.
8. Describe the importance of the Becke line and how to test for it.
9. Describe the types and meanings of fragmentation patterns in glass.
10. Describe a protocol for the analysis of a paint chip.
11. Describe a protocol for the analysis of a metal fragment.
12. Describe a protocol for the analysis of a soil sample.

GLOSSARY

Amorphous a material in which the constituent atoms, molecules, or ions are arranged randomly.

Ampere (A) the SI unit of current that produces 2×10^{-7} newton/meter between two parallel wires of infinite length and negligible cross section placed 1 meter apart in a vacuum.

Becke line a line of light observed near the edge of a transparent material immersed in a liquid with a different refractive index.

Blank a sample without any analyte used to test instrumentation.

Birefringence the property of a crystal that causes double refraction; the difference between the two indices of refraction.

Candela (cd) the basic unit for luminous intensity. It is the monochromatic radiation of frequency 540×10^{12} hertz with an intensity in a given direction of $1/683$ watt per steradian.

Celsius a unit of temperature abbreviated as C, also known as centigrade. Zero degrees Celsius is equal to 273 Kelvin. Fahrenheit = degrees Celsius × ($9/5$) + 32.

Celsius scale a temperature scale defined by 0°C at the ice point and 100 °C at the boiling point of water at sea level.

Chemical property a property that becomes apparent during a chemical reaction; a property observed when a substance undergoes a transformation into one or more new substances.

Crystalline (crystal) a material in which the constituent atoms, molecules, or ions are packed in a regularly ordered, repeating pattern extending in all three spatial dimensions.

Density a measure of mass per unit of volume.

Derivable property a physical property that can be calculated based on the relationship of nonderivable properties.

Fahrenheit scale a temperature scale defined by 32° at the ice point and 212° at the boiling point of water at sea level.

Kilogram (kg) the SI unit of mass, the only basic unit still defined in terms of an artifact.

Kelvin 1/273.16th of the thermodynamic temperature of the triple point of water.

Mass the quantity of matter in a body that causes it to have weight in a gravitational field.

Meter (m) the SI unit for length defined as the distance light travels, in a vacuum, in 1/299792458th of a second.

Mole (mol) the SI basic unit of substance, it is the same number of electrons, particles, atoms, ions, or molecules as there are atoms in 0.012 kg of carbon-12.

Munsell system a set of soil descriptors rating soil by hue (color), value (brightness), and chroma (color intensity).

Nonderivable properties physical properties such as length, which must be measured.

Physical property a property that is not dependent on the amount of material present; a property that can be measured without changing the chemical composition of a substance.

Pigment the colored portion of a paint or dye.

Refractive index (RI) the ratio of the speed of light in a vacuum to the speed of light in a material.

Second (s) the basic unit of time defined as the time increment for 9192631770 vibrations of a cesium 133 atom to occur.

Steradian (sr) the SI unit of solid angular measure. A sphere measures 4 pi (about 12.5664) steradians.

System International (SI) a standard set of units that scientists use to communicate data.

Tempered glass glass that has been thermal-cycled during manufacture to give greater strength; it breaks into "cubic" shapes rather than shards.

Weight the force exerted by a mass as a result of gravity.

Clockwise from top left:
- Human pub hair root.
- Human head hairs.
- Polyester fiber.
- Wool fibers.

Human hair: From http://www.fbi.gov/hq/fsc/backissu/jan2004/research/2004_01_research01b; polyester fiber: original work of author; wool fibers from http://commons.wikimedia.org/wiki/Image:Lana_ scaglie3.jpg; pubic hair: original photograph by author.

CHAPTER 7
Hair and Fiber

Case Study

Bevan von Einem

It was the evening of June 15, 1983. Fifteen-year-old Richard Kelvin was returning to his home in the up-market suburb of North Adelaide after visiting a friend. Richard was never seen alive again. His body was found in the countryside outside the city of Adelaide by a hill walker on July 24. Postmortem tests revealed that death had been caused by massive bleeding from an anal injury and that he had been administered sedatives, including methaqualone, which was available legitimately only as the prescription drug Mandrax. Investigators reviewed pharmacy records for Mandrax prescriptions. One name jumped out at them: Bevan von Einem.

The city of Adelaide, capital of the state of South Australia, is known as the "city of churches," but in the late 1970s and early 1980s it was well known for a darker reason. It was a center of homosexual-related crime. Von Einem was already known to police as a possible member of a group of homosexual predators, and the police questioned him about Richard's death. At first von Einem denied any contact between them. However, hair and fiber evidence at the preliminary hearing provided sufficient evidence of association between Kelvin and von Einem's home and von Einem himself for the case to proceed to trial. It also led von Einem to change his story to one in which Richard had indeed

been with him on the night of his disappearance but that nothing untoward had occurred, and he had taken Richard back to the city 2 hours after they met.

The trial had several important elements. Pathology and entomology evidence indicated that Kelvin had been killed and his body dumped around July 11. Recovery of trace materials from his clothing produced 925 fibers, 250 of which could have come from von Einem's home environment and only 7 that could have come from Richard's. Sources of the fibers included the carpet and bedding from the home and a cardigan owned by von Einem. Hairs that could have come from von Einem were found on Richard, including some inside his underclothing. The hair comparison included matching of dye on the recovered and exemplar hairs.

The defense argued that the associative evidence did not disprove von Einem's version of events; namely, that Richard had been in von Einem's house briefly on the night of Richard's disappearance. However, the very large number of foreign fibers on his clothing, the persistence of hairs, and the long time interval between the date of his disappearance on the one hand, and the likely date of death and disposal of the body and its subsequent discovery on the other, argued very powerfully against that explanation. Von Einem was found guilty and is serving a life sentence.

CENTRAL QUESTIONS

What can be answered:

- Where could hairs or fibers found at a crime scene have come from?

What we cannot answer:

- Are the hairs from a particular individual, or the fibers from a particular garment?

What we are learning or researching:

- The dynamics of the transfer and retention of hairs and fibers, and the building of fiber databases.
- To what extent can hair be used as a body tissue representative of the donor in regard to genetic and acquired attributes?

HAIR

As anyone who has ever come in contact with a pet knows, hair is easily transferred during a physical encounter! Hair is useful to the forensic scientist because it is more stable than most other tissues and because it contains a record of the person's environment and habits over time. However, the characteristics of hairs collected from the same individual can vary widely. While hair has no chemical or physical properties that can permit individuation, some information can be gained by studying its morphology (shape) and characteristics. Hair samples may also yield **nuclear** or **mitochondrial DNA** for analysis.

What Is Hair?

Hair is an outgrowth of the skin of most mammals. Each hair has a follicle, buried deeply in the skin, and a shaft, the visible external growth. While it may look healthy, hair is actually dead. Hairs have no blood vessels or nerves. The main chemical component of hair is **keratin**, a protein found in claws, hoofs, and fingernails too. Hair also contains water, fats, **melanin** (hair's pigment), and traces of zinc and other metals. The water content of hair, usually 10 to 13% of its weight, gives rise to many of its physical and chemical properties. As it grows, hair may incorporate a variety of other chemicals in small amounts. (See Figure 7.1.)

Human Hair

Like most mammals, humans produce hair over most of their body. However, some of the hairs

Hair samples from 1000-year-old Andean mummies have been analyzed for alcohol, cocaine, and nicotine use.

130

FIGURE 7.1
Drawing showing hair growing from the follicle in the skin. From http://en.wikipedia.org/wiki/Image:HairFollicle.png

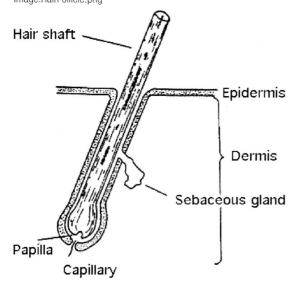

Hair shaft

Epidermis

Dermis

Sebaceous gland

Papilla

Capillary

are so tiny, they are difficult to see. In fact, human beings produce three types of hairs:

- *Lanugo hairs*: **Lanugo hairs** grow on unborn babies as soon as 3 months after conception and are shed about 4 weeks before birth. Some premature babies are born with them, but they soon fall out.
- *Vellus hairs*: Grown from follicles that do not have sebaceous glands (oil glands), **vellus hairs** are short hairs with little to no pigment.
- *Terminal hairs*: Most of the hairs on the body are **terminal hairs**. Produced by follicles with sebaceous glands, they are larger in diameter and more robust than vellus hairs.

Without DNA, the sex of a donor is also difficult to determine. However, sex determination can be made by staining and observing the sex chromatin in the cells of a **follicular tag**.

Hair has two important parts: the follicle, which is deeply buried in the skin, and the shaft, the visible external growth. The **follicle**, the part of the skin that grows hair, is a tiny cup-shaped organ. While the shaft has no blood supply, the follicle is supported by blood vessels. This contact with the blood allows hair to grow a record of the person's environment and habits. Inside the follicle, the bulb produces cells that will become hairs. Cells are formed at the bottom and pushed upward until they are arranged in a series of layers at the top of the bulb. The outer layers form the lining of the hair follicle, while the inner layers become the hair itself. The color of a hair is produced by cells called *melanocytes* that put melanin into the cortex of the hair.

The hair shaft is composed of three layers: the cuticle, cortex, and medulla:

- *Cuticle*: The **cuticle**, the outside covering of hair, is marked by overlapping scales that point away from the root in the direction of hair growth. The scales are made of dead cells that have been hardened with keratin protein. Unfortunately, the scale pattern is random. While it cannot be used to individualize hairs, the scale pattern can be used to identify the animal that grew the hair.
- *Cortex*: Contained within the protective layer of the cuticle, the **cortex** gives hair its strength, elasticity, and curl. The cortex is filled with a matrix of low-sulfur keratin fibers that run along the length of the hair bound together with high-sulfur keratins. The result is an internal structure like that of a high-tension cable. The cortex also contains melanin-containing pigment granules. Microscopic examination shows two other structures in the cortex, called *ovoid bodies* and *cortical fusi*, which are used by some microscopists in characterizing hairs. (See Figure 7.2.)
- *Medulla*: The **medulla**, a group of nonpigmented cells or an air-filled channel in the center of a hair, is not found in all hairs. When present, medullae are classified as continuous, interrupted, or discontinuous, or as fragmented or trace. In humans, medullae measure less than one-third of the diameter of the hair and are fragmented (randomly placed, small groups) or absent entirely in head hairs.

It is difficult to tell much about the age of a hair's donor with the exception of infants and the elderly. Both baby hair and an older person's hairs are finer than that of a middle-aged person. Older people also exhibit graying, a loss or sputtering of pigment in their hair. However, some people go gray at a very early age, so this is hardly a definitive descriptor.

The strength of hair is related to its sulfur content and based on the amino acid cysteine. Keratins in the matrix of a hair can form bonds between different strands when the sulfur atoms of two cysteines link to create a disulfide bridge (sometimes called a cysteine–cysteine cross-link). This oxidation product is called cystine.

131

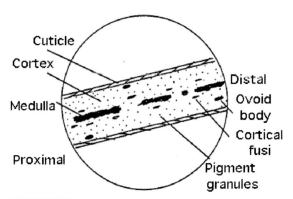

FIGURE 7.2
Drawing showing the internal anatomy of a hair. From http://www.fbi.gov/hq/lab/fsc/backissu/jan2004/research/2004_01_research01b.htm

The ultimate length of a hair is a matter of cell programming. For example, follicles that make arm or eyebrow hairs are coded with a short growth cycle. After a few months, the hair stops growing and is shed, but on the head, follicles are programmed to grow hair for several years. This is why body hairs do not grow long, unlike those on the head. Animals like horses that shed seasonally have hair follicles with short growth periods and synchronized rest phases. In the spring, their winter coat falls out.

HAIR GROWTH CYCLE

There are three stages to the growth cycle of human head hair. Each stage produces a change in the hair root where growth takes place.

- *Anagen*: The **anagen phase** is the time during which the root is growing hair continuously and has a duration that depends on the anatomical site. The root is bound to the follicle, giving the structure a tear or flame shape. If pulled out from the root, the hair may retain a DNA-rich follicular tag. (See Figure 7.3.)
- *Catagen*: While it does not become catatonic, in this **catagen phase**, the root rests and hair grows more slowly until it stops. During this 2- to 3-week period, no pigment is pumped into the hair. The phase is marked by an elongation of the root structure.
- *Telogen*: After hair stops growing, the root begins to look like a match head or a club. Over the next few months, the hair will be shed. About 10% of follicles are in the **telogen phase** at any time.

FUR

To make a distinction, animal hair is usually called *fur*. While fur has largely the same keratin makeup as human hair, the organization and productivity of follicles vary widely from species to species. Animals may produce more than one type of hair from the same follicle at the same time. In dogs, for example, a follicle may produce 1 primary hair and up to 15 secondary hairs.

FIGURE 7.3
Anagen, catagen and telogen hairs. From left to right: Roots of hairs in the anagen (A), catagen (C) and telogen (T) growth phase. The tissue tag is typical of anagen hairs. From http://www.fbi.gov/hq/lab/fsc/backissu/jan2004/research/2004_01_research01b.htm

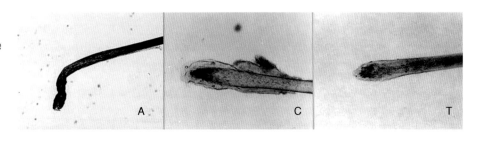

GUARD HAIR

These long, pigmented hairs give the animal's coat its color and appearance. The primary function of the **guard hair** is to protect the underlying skin and channel away rain or snow.

UNDERCOAT (GROUND HAIR)

The **undercoat (ground hairs)** is shorter than a guard hair and may not contain the same pigment. This hair provides temperature regulation for the animal. The wool of sheep and some types of rabbits is mostly undercoat.

TACTILE HAIRS (VIBRISSAE)

More commonly called *whiskers* or *feelers,* **tactile hairs (vibrissae)** are thick hairs found on the face. Like other hairs, they have no nerves in them; rather, they are surrounded by a larger number of nerve endings in the skin making them more sensitive to touch.

The structure of animal hair varies widely with species. While most animals, including humans, have cylindrical medullae, the shape of the medulla may give information about the species generating the hair. In animals, the medullae often measure more than half the diameter of the hair and appear continuous (running the length of the hair) or interrupted (in several large pieces). Some animals have medullae that are hollow bubbles of air. (See Figure 7.4.)

Hair Evidence

COLLECTION AND PRESERVATION

Hair can be stored in appropriately labeled plastic or paper envelopes. While vials also work well, hair can slide out of paper folds. Evidentiary hair can be collected with the fingers, forceps, taping, or a comb. Hairs removed by tape lift can be stored by sticking the tape onto a glass slide or small sheet of plastic film.

Because of the variability of hair, a suitable number of full-length exemplar hairs should be taken from the same area of the body as the evidentiary hair.

Mercury poisoning is less common than it used to be. During the days of the stylish blacktop hat, tanners and hatters would shear fur down to pelt and soak it in a mixture of chemicals that contained mercury salts. This gave the pelt weight and made it easier to form. Hatters absorbed mercury through the skin and by inhalation. The toxic metal accumulated in the brain, giving rise to damage mislabeled as insanity. Hence, the saying "mad as a hatter."

133

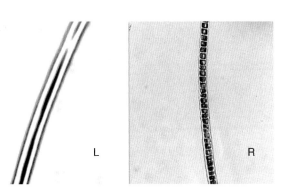

L R C

FIGURE 7.4
Animal hair medullae. Left to right: Photomicrographs of llama (L), rabbit (R), and cat (C) hair showing the variety in medulla morphology. Llama original photograph by author. Other images from http://www.fbi.gov/hq/lab/fsc/backissu/july2004/research/2004_03_research02.htm

Exemplar hairs may be shaved off or pulled out. In rape cases, the pubic area is combed for loose hairs and the comb itself may be retained as evidence. After all loose hairs, which could include hairs transferred from the assailant, have been removed, samples can be collected from the victim. Hair is highly durable, and it is often sampled and saved at autopsy.

EXAMINING HAIR EVIDENCE

Morphology is the study of form and structure. Hair can be examined by microscopy to study its morphology for speciation and — in some cases—points of comparison toward individuation. It is generally recognized today that morphologic features are best used for screening for body site of origin, race, and elimination of source, and that reliable individuation is best conducted through DNA testing.

Additionally, hair may be subjected to chemical testing for heavy metals and drugs, as well as for cosmetic treatments such as dyeing.

Measurement and Comparison Microscopy

A forensic hair examiner may begin by simply measuring the length and diameter of a hair and observing its color. Using a comparison microscope, hairs are viewed side by side. With the help of appropriate exemplars, variations and point of comparison may be discovered and recorded. (See Figure 7.5.)

Examination of the root can help tell whether the hair was shed or pulled out of the skin. Hair that is pulled out—especially when pulled rapidly—often comes with a **follicular tag** (sheath cells). Shed hairs have a club-shaped root without sheath cells. However, the presence or absence of the sheath cell is not a reliable indicator of whether or not the hair was pulled out or shed naturally.

Looking at the shape of the hair can tell the examiner from what part of the body it was removed. Head hairs exhibit nearly uniform diameter and distribution of pigment over their length. Beard hairs have a triangular cross section and are thicker than head hairs. Pubic hairs are often wiry with tapered ends (unless they have been cut or shaved). Whether straight or curly, these hairs exhibit buckling, tight bends, and wide variations in shaft diameter giving a ribbon-like appearance. Limb hairs are short and slightly curved in shape. While they are not as useful for comparison, their presence may help investigators place a person at a crime scene, especially if they retain a follicular tag. (See Figure 7.6.)

Dry-Mount Light Microscopy

Using low-power light microscopy, a hair examiner can detail many of the surface features of a hair. Intact cuticle cells are smooth, glossy, and

134

FIGURE 7.5
Human head hairs. Photomicrograph of human head hairs showing range of color and medullary morphology. From http://www.fbi.gov/hq/lab/fsc/backissu/jan2004/research/2004_01_research01b.htm

FIGURE 7.6
Human body hairs. Left to right: Tip of head hair (H) showing sharp edge from recent haircut; tip of limb hair (L) showing slightly narrower size and rounded tip; section of pubic hair (P) showing buckling site — pubic hairs are generally coarser than those from the head or limbs and twisted or buckled. All images from http://www.fbi.gov/hq/lab/fsc/backissu/jan2004/research/2004_01_research01b.htm

reflect light well. They may be observed directly or by making a casting of the scale pattern in a gel or clear nail polish. Scale patterns can distinguish human hair from the hair of animals. With expertise, the examiner may be able to identify the species or even the breed of animal from which the hair came.

Examination of the cuticle will reveal three basic scale types: coronal (which look like a stack of crowns or paper cups), spinous (appearing like flower petals), and imbricate (flattened). Of course, natural variation and rough combinations of scale types are possible. Coronal scales are a distinguishing feature of rodent and bat hairs; they are rarely seen in human hairs. Protruding from the hair shaft like flower petals, spinous scales are found in cats but never seen in humans. People have hair covered mainly with flat-shaped imbricate scales. At the ends of long hair, the stripping away of the surface scales leads to split ends and breakage. (See Figure 7.8.)

Damage to or color in the cuticle can provide evidence of cosmetic treatment. Yellowish hairs that have been depigmented are likely to have been bleached. Such hairs often have damaged cuticles. Similarly, dye present in the cuticle (and throughout the cortex) is evidence that hair has been colored. Dyes can be extracted and analyzed chemically. Further, because hair grows at the rate

The shape of a hair's cross section can give information about the donor's race. Hair from Caucasians is round- to oval-shaped, while Negroid hair is oval to almost flat or ribbon-like. Because many people are of mixed racial origin, cross-sectional shape can vary widely. (See Figure 7.7.)

135

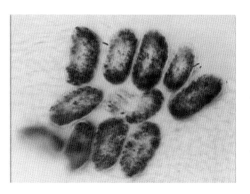

FIGURE 7.7
Racial characteristics. Photomicrographs of negroid hair length (left) and cross sections (right) showing heavy pigmentation and ovoid, flattened shape. Left image original by author; right image from http://www.fbi.gov/hq/lab/fsc/backissu/jan2004/research/2004_01_research01b.htm

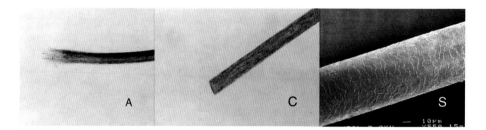

FIGURE 7.8
Hair features. From left to right: Tip of human head hair showing abraded end arising from wear (A); tip of human head hear showing clean edge from recent cutting (C); SEM of human head hair surface showing scale pattern (S). From http://www.fbi.gov/hq/lab/fsc/backissu/jan2004/research/2004_01_research01b.htm

of about one-half inch (one centimeter) each month, it is possible to estimate when it was treated. (See Figure 7.9.)

When collected from a decomposing body, hairs may exhibit a postmortem root band. This is a short, dark mark near the root of the hair. (See Figure 7.10.)

The presence or absence of a medulla, the medullary index (ratio of the medulla width to the diameter of the hair), and the shape of the medulla can also be studied under transmitted light. While the medullae of humans are somewhat amorphous, some animals exhibit more characteristic shapes and patterns. In rabbit hair, ladder and multiserial (more than one concurrent) ladders can be found (see Figure 7.4). Deer hairs bear a latticework pattern. Hairs are vacuolated and can look like a series of spheres.

Wet-Mount Light Microscopy

Because light normally reflects off the glossy surface of the cuticle, hair can be mounted with a resin (or other material with a similar refractive index) to allow more light to enter the hair and illuminate the details of the cortex. The distribution, shape, and color intensity of the pigment granules

FIGURE 7.9
Dyed hair. Dyeing of hair can leave a characteristic color and the chemical dyestuff can sometimes be extracted and analyzed to give further identification. http://www.fbi.gov/hq/lab/fsc/backissu/jan2004/research/2004_01_research01b.htm

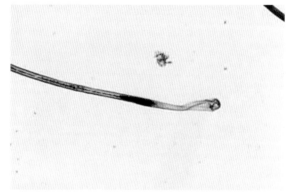

FIGURE 7.10
Postmortem banding. Human hair showing the dark banding artifact sometimes found in hairs collected from the deceased. From http://www.fbi.gov/hq/lab/fsc/backissu/jan2004/research/2004_01_research01b.htm

within the cortex can provide information about the donor's race. Hair from Caucasians has evenly distributed, regularly shaped pigment granules that can be very fine to coarse in size. Negroid hairs have uneven distribution of pigment granules.

BOX 7.1 IS METAL THE CULPRIT?

The body does not metabolize or excrete most metals easily. Some—like mercury, lead, and arsenic—accumulate in the body to toxic result. Metals have been implicated in brain damage, attention-deficit/hyperactivity disorder, autism, Alzheimer's disease, and kidney disease. Because hair follicles are fed by tiny blood vessels, minute amounts of metals present in the blood can be incorporated into the hair as it grows. Elemental analysis of hair can reveal exposure to many toxic elements, including the following:

- Aluminum
- Arsenic
- Cadmium
- Copper
- Lead
- Mercury
- Nickel

DNA from Hair

Despite claims to the contrary some years ago, it is accepted that microscopic analysis of hair can compare only class characteristics. DNA analysis must be done for individuation to be determined. Of course, DNA analysis also provides the sex of the hair donor. Because DNA analysis is destructive, it must be performed after other examinations. See Chapter 12 for information on DNA in hair.

FIBERS

Fibers come from a wide variety of plant, animal, and chemical sources. Like hairs, fibers can be easily transferred on contact between people and people or people and objects. Fibers may be recovered from tools, clothing, fingernails, shoes, and vehicles. The identification of a fiber is based mainly on microscopic examination of morphological characteristics, followed by chemical and instrumental analysis. The chemical analysis may be of the fiber itself or of dyes used to color it. Though it is rare that fibers can provide individuation to an article of clothing or an object such as the carpet in the trunk of a car, they are useful as evidentiary links between people and from people to a crime scene.

Hair today gone tomorrow? Hairs may be easily transferred but also are easily lost. Generally speaking, they will fall off recipient surfaces in a matter of hours. The duration will depend on the surface—obviously they are retained longer on an immobile flat surface such as a chair than on a shirt worn by someone moving around.

The Atlanta Child Murders

Edward Smith, a 14-year-old African American, disappeared from his home in Atlanta, Georgia, on July 21, 1979. Alfred Evans, a 13-year-old African American, disappeared the next day. Between then and 1981, Atlanta police found themselves faced with up to 30 possibly linked homicides of black males, mostly young men or children. By that time, there was considerable evidence linking the deaths: Most of the victims had been bludgeoned and asphyxiated. Many of the bodies had been dumped in the Chattahoochee River. Examination of the clothing of many yielded very characteristic fibers, with two main kinds. One was a violet-colored acetate fiber; the other was a trilobed yellow-green nylon fiber of the type used in carpet manufacture. Efforts to locate the manufacturer of the carpet were unsuccessful.

By May 1981, the police decided to focus on the only lead they had: the Chattahoochee River. The strategy paid off on May 22 when the stakeout patrol investigated a splash and identified a vehicle driving away from the location as belonging to Wayne Williams. A search of Williams's home revealed a floor covering of yellow-green carpeting. Fibers from the carpet could have been the source of the fibers recovered from the victims.

The investigation did not stop there but went on to explore how common the carpet was so that some idea of the weight of the evidence could be adduced. The fibers were traced to a specific manufacturer who sold the material to several carpet makers. However, each then colored the fibers with their own dye, and the Williams carpet was sourced to a Georgia company. The particular carpet had had a limited run, and it was estimated that it would have been in fewer than 100 homes in the Atlanta region.

Williams was tried for two of the murders and found guilty. The case was built mainly on the association with Williams's home shown by the carpet fibers, but other supporting fiber evidence and data from other cases also was introduced in evidence. Evidence included hairs found on the bodies that could have come from Williams's dog. This was recently the subject of a challenge, but DNA testing failed to exclude the dog as the source.

The exact number of deaths attributable to Williams is uncertain, and he well may not have been responsible for them all. (See Figure 7.11.)

138

Types of Fibers

There are two broad classes of fibers: natural and man made. The delineation is clear for **natural fibers**, those derived from animal or plant sources, but is slightly more complicated in **man-made fibers** that can be regenerated from cellulose supplied by plants or created entirely from chemicals. The main distinguishing feature is how the final material is formed: Natural fibers are exactly what the name says: The fiber is a natural component that is converted to a material for use in fabrics. In man-made fibers, the final fiber is made by a process known as *extrusion*. (See Figure 7.12.)

Spinning is an ancient process for making wool from the fleece of a sheep. It essentially consists of twisting the animal hairs in the fleece together to form a continuous yarn. Spinning in the manufacture of man-made fibers is entirely different; it derives its name from the extrusion of the fiber filament through nozzles in a device called a *spinneret.*

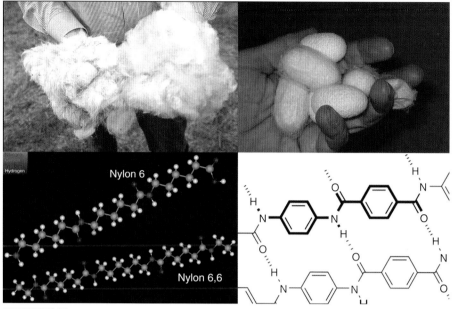

FIGURE 7.11

Natural and synthetic fibers. Origins of natural and synthetic fibers. Top row, left to right: woolen fleece; silk worm cocoons. Bottom row, left to right: the chemical structure of nylon; the base monomer of the Kevlar molecule. Wool: http://en.wikipedia.org/wiki/Image:Wool. www.usda.gov.jpg; silk worm cocoons: From http://commons.wikimedia.org/wiki/Image:Tkalnia.jedwabiu.Shuzhou-kokony.JPG; nylon molecule: From http://en.wikipedia.org/wiki/Image:Nylon6_and_Nylon_66.png; kevlar: From http://en.wikipedia.org/wiki/Image:kevlar_chemical_structure_H-bonds.png

NATURAL FIBERS

Wool

Wool is the most common natural fiber sourced from an animal. It is derived mainly from the fleece or coat of sheep and similar animals, including goats and llamas. The main characteristic that distinguishes wool from other animal coats is the high degree of crimping in the hair. A high-quality wool such as that from a merino sheep can have as many as 100 bends or crimps per inch. Wool is a good insulator and relatively flame retardant. (See Figure 7.13.)

Despite the antiquity and value of wool as a textile fiber, most natural fibers are made from plants.

Cotton

Cotton fabric is produced from a unicellular filament that grows in the seed pod (boll) of

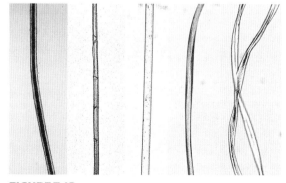

FIGURE 7.12

Fibers. Left to right: wool (this is a coarse wool fiber from a Scottish Blackface breed, note heavily pigmented cortex and compare with the finer fiber examples in Figure 7.13); linen (note bamboo-like structure); nylon (featureless, regular-shape fiber); polyester (this example is dyed light brown and is triangular in cross section); cotton (note characteristic twisting of the fibers). Images courtesy Dr. N. Watson and Dr. K. Savage, Strathclyde University Forensic Science Centre.

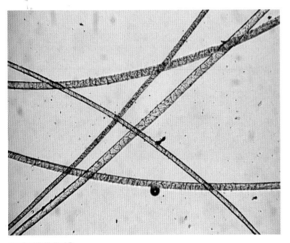

FIGURE 7.13
Some fine woolen fibers. Note the scale patterns and also that these finer fibers do not have the heavy cortex seen in the wool in Figure 7.12. From http://commons.wikimedia.org/wiki/Image:Lana_scaglie3.jpg

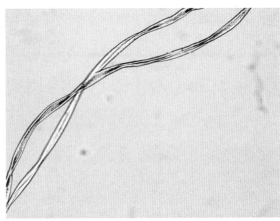

FIGURE 7.14
Cotton fibers. Image courtesy of Dr. N. Watson and Dr. K. Savage, Strathclyde University Forensic Science Centre.

the cotton plant. These filaments, called *staple fibers*, range from about 1–5 cm in length. Pima and Egyptian varieties produce the longest fibers. Longer fibers mean fewer ends to fray in yarns and, hence, the highest quality cotton fabrics. Cotton fibers are ribbon shaped with irregularly spaced twists. (See Figure 7.14.)

Flax

Cultivated for thousands of years, common flax, also called *linseed,* is a blue flowering plant that produces the bast fiber used to make linen. It contains a natural clockwise S twist. *Bast* refers to the strong woody fibers obtained from the phloem of plants.

Hemp

Hemp is the older name for abaca (also called Manila hemp because it originated in the Philippines), the leaf fiber of which is used to make paper and rope. This tough bast fiber is highly water resistant. Today many people associate the word *hemp* with nondrug-related use for the bast fiber of *Cannabis sativa*. (See Figure 7.15.)

Jute

Made from plants in the linden tree family, jute is a weak fiber with low cellulose content used to make twine, burlap, and carpet backing. Raw jute is yellow to brown in color and may appear slightly lustrous. It consists of bundles of fiber held together by gummy substances that make the fiber difficult to bleach. The fiber does, however, spin well.

Mercerization is treatment for cotton yarn or fabric that increases its shine, luster, strength, and ability to absorb dyes. Named after the Scottish textile finisher, John Mercer, the process involves soaking the material in alkali solution (caustic soda) under tension, followed by neutralization in acid. The treatment causes permanent swelling of the fiber and, hence, increases the luster.

FIGURE 7.15
A bundle of hemp fibers. From http://commons.wikimedia.org/wiki/
Image:Hennepvezel_Cannabis_sativa_fibre.jpg

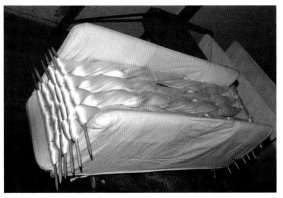

FIGURE 7.16
Raw silk. From http://commons.wikimedia.org/wiki/Image:Silk_
raw_01.jpg

Ramie

This lustrous fiber comes from a nettle plant related to flax. In fabric, its strong, staple fibers can be mistaken for linen or cotton, but—in many areas of the world—it often is less expensive. Ramie is used in clothing and papermaking. It resists mildew and rotting.

Cultivated Silk

Silk fiber is produced by a variety of insects that build cocoons. It is not a hair but a long, strong protein filament composed mainly of the amino acids alanine and glycine.

Wild Silk

Also called *Tussah silk,* wild silk is a beige-colored filament of two protein fibers stuck together with a gum produced by the silkworm in the construction of its cocoon. Wild silk is often a thicker and shorter fiber than that of cultivated silk, giving its fabrics a slightly rough feel. (See Figure 7.16.)

Papyrus

Used in papermaking in ancient times, the pith of papyrus stalks was cut into strips that were flattened, layered at right angles, and pounded to produce a smooth surface. The mechanical agitation of the pounding released starches from the plant material, causing the fibers to adhere to each other and dry into a sheet.

MANUFACTURE OF MAN-MADE FIBERS

Man-made fibers are made by the extrusion of a thick solution of polymer through the tiny holes in a *spinneret,* a device almost like a bathroom showerhead.

Silk is the warmest fiber by weight. Its fibers are nearly five times stronger than steel and twice as strong as Kevlar of the same weight. It has amazing elasticity and can stretch up to 30% without breaking. Silk produces a soft fabric with excellent drape, shine, and dyeability.

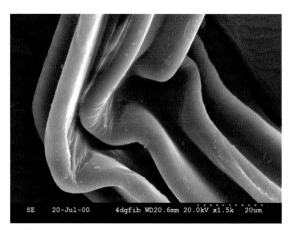

FIGURE 7.17
SEM image of a 7-lobed polyester fiber. Polyester fibers are made by extruding molten polymer through nozzles and manufacturers use different nozzle shapes to make fibers that have different characteristics. Public domain image from http://commons.wikimedia.org/wiki/Image:SEMexample.jpg

The extruded material solidifies into the fiber strands, or filaments. The process of extrusion and solidification is what is termed *spinning.* Filaments can be made by wet, dry, melt, or gel spinning.

In wet spinning, the spinnerets are submerged in a bath, and the polymer is fed into the spinneret as a solution from which it precipitates as it is extruded into the bath. This is the oldest form of manufacture, and acrylic, modacrylic, rayon, aramid, and spandex are made this way. In dry spinning, the filament is formed by the solvent being evaporated by a steam of inert gas as the polymer solution is extruded. Acetate, triacetate, acrylic, modacrylic, and spandex are made by dry spinning.

In melt spinning, the polymer is liquified by melting, and the filament forms as the polymer cools on extrusion. Nylon, olefin, polyester, and saran are made this way. One of the features of extrusion is that the spinneret nozzles can be shaped and form filaments of different cross-sectional profiles, such as oval, trilobal, pentagonal, octagonal, or even hollow. Trilobal fibers reflect more light and give a sparkle to the finished textile product. Pentagonal and hollow fibers are used in carpets, as they tend to show less dirt. Octagonal fibers produce glitter-free materials. (See Figure 7.17.)

Gel spinning is a special process used to make high-strength filament. The polymer is processed in a liquid crystal state that results in interchain attraction of polymer molecules. High-tensile-strength polyethylene and aramid fibers, such as Kevlar, are made this way.

Regenerated Man-Made Fibers

FIGURE 7.18:
Close up of fabric made from rayon thread. From http://en.wikipedia.org/wiki/Image:Rayon_closeup_1.jpg

Regenerated fibers are made from cellulose extracted from cotton, wood, and other sources. The polymer that is extruded is a solution of cellulose.

Rayon

Created from a solution of cellulose as an artificial silk by French chemist Hilaire de Chardonnet, this fiber is soft, strong, absorbent, and dyeable. It shrinks but does not melt in high temperatures. Rayon is also resistant to moths. (See Figure 7.18.)

Acetate

Acetate is produced from cellulose dissolved in acetic acid. It is a moderately absorbent, fast-drying fiber that resists stretching. Unfortunately, it does not withstand heat well.

Triacetate

Triacetate is made by modifying cellulose with acetic acid until more than 90% of the hydroxyl groups are acetylated. Fabric produced from the fiber is wrinkle resistant, less absorbent, and less heat-sensitive than acetate.

SYNTHETIC MAN-MADE FIBERS

Synthetic man-made fibers are the products of chemistry. Many are **polymers**, which are very large molecules formed when many (*poly*) small molecules or parts (*mers*) react together to form a chain. A polymer may be made from many repeats of a single **monomer** (a homopolymer) or from repeats of two or more different repeating monomers (copolymer). Most synthetic fibers are polyamides or polyesters. (See Figure 7.19.)

Nylon

Invented by DuPont scientists in 1938 as the world's first synthetic fiber, nylon is a *polyamide*, a polymer of repeating bonds between a carboxylic acid and an amine (amide units). Nylon 6,6 (nylon 66) denotes that both hexamethylene diamine and adipic acid have six carbons. Because the diacid and diamine monomers alternate, unlike proteins, the direction of the amide bond reverses at carbonyl. Though dyeable, nylon is strong and resistant to water, insects, and many chemicals. Intended as an artificial silk, uses range from women's hose to carpets to gear wheels in machinery.

The DuPont patent was for nylon 6,6; other polyamides with similar properties have been marketed, including nylon-6. (See Figure 7.20.)

Polyester

Polyester is a category of condensation polymers containing ester functional groups in their chain. These synthetic plastics include polycarbonate and polyethylene terephthalate. In fabric, polyester becomes a soft, slightly shiny material that dyes well. Examples of polyesters include terylene, Mylar, arnite, and Dacron. Many modern textiles incorporate polyester with natural fibers to give

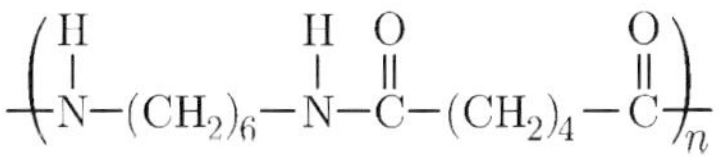

FIGURE 7.19
Synthetic fiber cross section. Synthetic fibers are manufactured in a variety of colors and cross-section shapes. This figure shows some nylon fibers. From http://www.state.nj.us/njsp/divorg/invest/criminalistics.html

Unlike its flammable cousin nitrocellulose, cellulose acetate is fairly slow to burn, making it safe for motion picture film.

Ballistic nylon was developed by DuPont for the U.S. Department of Defense for use in flak jackets. Eventually, it was replaced by Kevlar.

143

Denier is a weight-per-unit-length measure for filaments and nonspun yarns. It is the weight in grams of 9000 meters of the fiber. A low denier number means a fine, thin fiber. Ultra-sheer pantyhose are 7–10 denier, nearly the limit of too thin.

$$\left(\!\!\begin{array}{c}\overset{H}{\underset{|}{N}}-(CH_2)_6-\overset{H}{\underset{|}{N}}-\overset{O}{\overset{\|}{C}}-(CH_2)_4-\overset{O}{\overset{\|}{C}}\end{array}\!\!\right)_{\!n}$$
Nylon 66

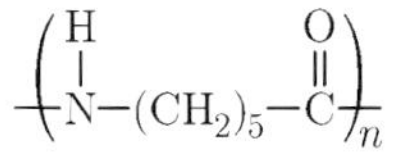

$$\left(\!\!\begin{array}{c}\overset{H}{\underset{|}{N}}-(CH_2)_5-\overset{O}{\overset{\|}{C}}\end{array}\!\!\right)_{\!n}$$
Nylon-6

FIGURE 7.20
Nylon polymer. The figure shows the chemical structure of the monomer units that are polymerized in the manufacture of nylon. Note that nylon 6,6 is a copolymer of the amide formed from hexamethylene diamine and adipic acid, each of which has 6 carbon atoms, hence the "66" notation. From http://commons.wikimedia.org/wiki/Image:PA6-PA66.png

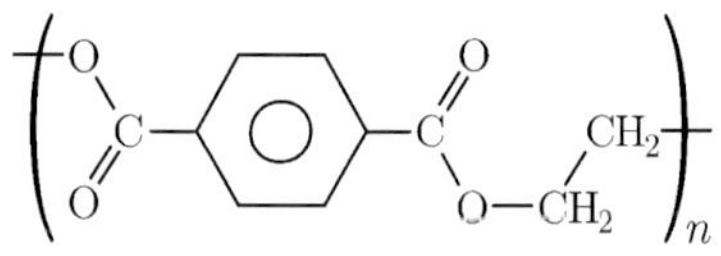

FIGURE 7.21
PET monomer.
Polyethylene terephthalate (PET) is a polymer of ethylene terephthalate, and is widely used in the manufacture of fibers and food and beverage containers. From http://en.wikipedia.org/wiki/Image:PET.png

One common polyester is polyethylene terephthalate (PET), the polymer used in soda bottles. PET is made from ethylene glycol and either terephthalic acid or its methyl ester. To recycle PET, the bottles are melted, chemically cleaned, and re-extruded.

Face too shiny? Apply powder. Titanium dioxide, the chemical that gives opacity to house paint, is a stable, white salt used to dull the shine of some fibers.

the benefits of the feel of the natural fiber and the crease resistance of polyester (see Figure 7.21). It is the most common artificial textile fiber in the U.S.

Acrylic

Acrylic fibers are produced from acrylonitrile, a petrochemical, and other chemicals to improve dyeability. Acrylic fibers are unique among synthetic fibers because their surface is not smooth. Hence, these fibers are often blended into fabric with animal hair, like angoras. It also resists degradation from sunlight. Acrylic textiles are lightweight, soft, and warm and are used to produce low-cost fabrics that mimic cashmere. Acrilan and Orlon are trade names for acrylics once made in the U.S., but production is now centered in the Far East.

Spandex

Manufactured as a replacement for rubber, the polyurethane chain of spandex can repeatedly stretch to 500% of its length and recover its original shape. It resists degradation from detergents and body soil. Lycra is the most common brand name for textiles made using spandex. The fiber is a clever mix of soft, rubbery, and rigid elements that give the stretchability without deformation to textiles made from spandex. (See Figure 7.21.)

Aramid

Another long-chain synthetic polyamide, aramid contains linked aromatic rings. It is produced as a multifilament by DuPont and valued for its high heat resistance as an alternative to asbestos. Kevlar, used in lightweight body armor, is a para-aramid. (See Figure 7.22.)

Collecting and Preserving Fiber Evidence

Large loose fibers can be collected with forceps or gloved hands. Similarly, large single fibers may be tape-lifted or collected into folded paper or into a vial. Because transferred fibers may be very small, clothing from the victim and suspect should be packaged for examination at the laboratory. To avoid cross-contamination, each article of clothing should be placed in its own paper bag and properly labeled with information detailing who was wearing the item and where it was found. Bodies may also be a source for fiber evidence. If fibers are seen under the victim's fingernails, these should be collected or the hands placed in plastic bags so that collection can take place at autopsy. (See Figure 7.23.)

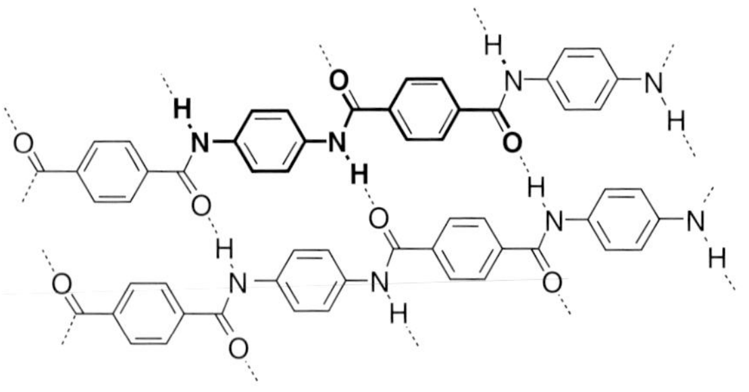

FIGURE 7.22
Kevlar. The figure shows the monomeric units in Kevlar and the hydrogen bonding between them. From http://en.wikipedia.org/wiki/Image:Kevlar_chemical_structure_H-bonds.png

Large items such as bedding or carpeting should be folded to protect the fiber-bearing area while transporting them. If moving the item is not possible, it can be sampled with a lift tape kit or a small vacuum cleaner (the entire vacuum trap is then taken in for analysis). Whenever possible, exemplar fibers should be collected for comparison.

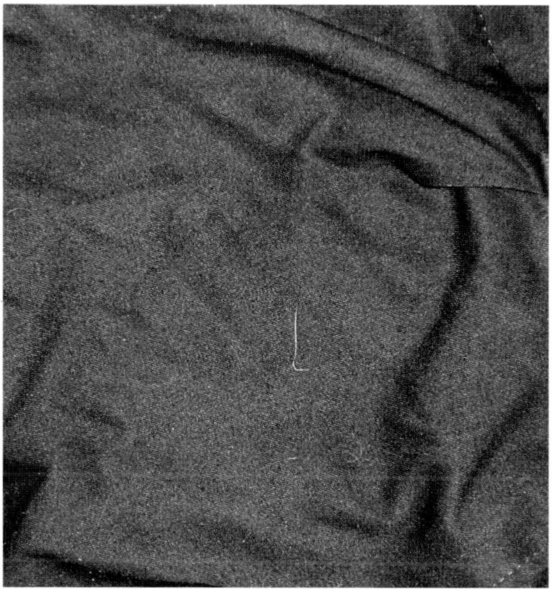

Examination of Fiber Evidence

TESTING FIBERS

Fiber examiners use microscopy, instrumental, and chemical techniques to identify fibers. Often, because there is so much more of the exemplar fiber than the evidentiary fiber, a test procedure will be run on the known first.

Fitting

If a large piece of a fabric is torn or cut away and the piece is recovered, the examiner may be able to match the piece to its parent. This may require folding the garment or fabric into an unusual form. This is especially true of stabbing cases where a cut may pass through several layers of the fabric.

Light and Comparison Microscopy

If an exemplar is available, the features of the exemplar and evidentiary fiber can be analyzed using comparison microscopy. If not, the evidentiary fiber should be examined for morphological features under a light microscope. All fibers should be examined for color, length, and diameter–cross section. The examiner will also note the presence of delustering agents such as titanium dioxide. Scale patterns indicate animal hair. They should be cast or recorded for species

FIGURE 7.23
Hair evidence. Photograph of an animal hair on a pair of trousers. The hair should be removed by tape lifting or with forceps for microscopy. Original work of author.

Never test a possible stab cut by inserting the suspected knife through it. This will contaminate the knife, possibly alter the physical characteristics of the cut, and compromise the integrity of the evidence.

Optical brighteners are best detected under a UV light.

145

BOX 7.2   A TIMELINE OF SYNTHETIC FIBERS

In the late 1910s, DuPont was a chemical company working on cellulose-based explosives. Having the equipment and expertise to work on cellulose technology and seeking to diversify out of munitions, DuPont moved into fiber manufacturing. By early 1920, the company was the American licensee for Chardonnet's artificial silk patents. In 1921, the company changed its name to The DuPont Fibersilk Company. Its first rayon yarns were produced in 1922. It renamed its fiber subsidiary again in 1924 to become The DuPont Rayon Company, the predecessor of DuPont's Textile Fibers Department. The 1930s was a boom time for chemical materials development. This decade saw the creation of artificial rubber (DuPont), fiberglass (Owens and Corning), Plexiglas™ (Rohm and Haas), and Teflon (DuPont).

- 1880s: French chemist Hilaire de Chardonnet creates artificial silk from a solution of cellulose.

(continued)

(continued)
- 1924: The textile industry names the artificial silk "rayon."
- 1930: Building on German innovation, Wallace Carothers and a team at DuPont create artificial rubber.
- 1935: Carothers and team create nylon.
- 1936: Polymethyl acrylate, the forematerial of plexiglass, is developed by Rohm and Haas.
- 1938: Nylon, the first fiber created from chemicals, is introduced.
- 1938: DuPont chemist Roy Plunkett discovers that a tank of tetrafluoroethylene gas has polymerized on its walls and creates Teflon.
- 1941: British chemists create polyethylene terephthalate, a high-melting fiber produced under the name Dacron by DuPont in 1953.
- 1953: Chemist Karl Zeigler develops a method for creating a high-density polyethylene (PET) found in soda bottles.
- 1964: British engineer Leslie Phillips develops carbon fibers by stretching and heating synthetic fibers.
- 1965: At DuPont, Stephanie Kwolek and Herbert Blades create poly-paraphenylene terephthalamide (Twaron) sold as Kevlar, the heat- and impact-resistant material of bulletproof vests.

FIGURE 7.24
Polarized light microscopy is a valuable tool in the examination of trace evidence. The figure shows flax (or linen) fibers — compare to the image in Figure 7.12. From http://www.fbi.gov/hq/lab/fsc/backissu/july2000/deedric3.htm

BOX 7.3   WHAT IS A POLYMER?

A polymer is a large molecule composed of many small molecules—called **monomers** or *feedstock*—joined together in a regular, repeating structure. Natural polymers include the long glucose chains that make up cellulose. Others polymers are created synthetically. Polymers often have characteristics vastly different from their constituent monomers.

identification. Striations and twists, indicating a natural fiber, should be noted. Similarly, the cross section of a man-made fiber may offer information as to its origin. Fiber features should be documented with photography.

Refractive Index and Birefringence

The refractive index of a fiber can be determined in the same way it is for glass.

Some fibers show birefringence (a value based on the difference between two different indices of refraction). Melt-spun polymers cool with their molecules aligned along the length of the filament. This arrangement lends a crystallinity to the fiber. This crystallinity, in turn, gives rise to double refraction and, hence, birefringence. Using a polarizing microscope, by immersing the fiber in a fluid with a matching refractive index, the examiner will observe the disappearance of the Becke line as with glass. Because determining the refractive index or birefringence is nondestructive, it can be performed on an evidentiary fiber. (See Figure 7.24.)

Visible Light Spectrophotometry

Visible region spectrophotometry (the region of 400–700 nm) is useful for *colorimetry*, measuring color. Hence, spectral analysis makes a good tool with which to compare dyes. By sampling at intervals (perhaps 10 nm) across the visible region, the spectrophotometer can build a spectral reflectance curve indicative of the color of the material. To measure fluorescence in dyes, a bispectral fluorescent spectrophotometer can be used.

Infrared Spectrophotometry

Organic compounds absorb infrared light according to functional groups present. As a consequence, infrared spectrophotometry allows the forensic examiner to identify functional groups in a fiber such as amide or ester bonds. While it is difficult to interpret the complexity of a spectrograph to an individual fiber, the functional groups present often tell to what family a fiber belongs. Additionally, dyes extracted from the fiber may be tested by infrared analysis.

Thin-Layer Chromatography (TLC)

Though a destructive technique, thin-layer chromatography may offer information about a dye formulation by separating its components. Dye is extracted from fiber samples using an appropriate solvent and spotted onto a TLC plate. A spot of dye from an exemplar and a commixed spot are run in separate channels on the same plate to allow direct comparison. After development, the plate will show any components in common. In some cases, bands may be scraped from the TLC plate, extracted into a suitable solvent, and submitted for GC or GC-MS analysis.

Solubility

The chemical structure of a fiber determines its properties. Diagnostic solubility tests are more often used by textile analysts—where a large sample of material is available—than by forensic fiber examiners. However, differential solubility can help differentiate members of the same class of fibers. For example, acetate dissolves in acetone while triacetate does not. Solubility tests are done in a specific order to permit a presumptive test for fiber categories.

SUMMARY

Hair is useful to the forensic scientist because it is more stable than most other tissues. While hair has no chemical or physical properties that can permit individuation, some information can be gained by studying its morphology (shape) and characteristics. Hair samples may also yield DNA for analysis.

Hair is an outgrowth of the skin of most mammals. Hair is made of keratin, a protein found in claws, hoofs, and fingernails. As it grows, hair may incorporate a variety of other chemicals in small amounts. Because the growth

Some microscopes are fitted with light sources and detectors that enable them to be used as spectrophotometers.

147

rate is known, exposure time frames to environmental occurrences may be calculated.

Human beings produce three types of hairs: lanugo, vellus, and terminal hairs. Each hair has two important parts: the follicle, which is deeply buried in the skin, and the shaft, the visible external growth.

The hair shaft is composed of three layers: the cuticle, cortex, and medulla. In humans, medullae measure less than one-third of the diameter of the hair and are fragmented (randomly placed, small groups) or absent entirely in head hairs.

There are three stages to the growth cycle of hair: anagen phase (growth phase), catagen phase (rest phase), and telogen phase (shed phase). Each stage produces a change in the hair root where growth takes place.

To make a distinction, animal hair is usually called *fur*. While fur has largely the same keratin makeup as human hair, the organization and productivity of follicles vary widely from species to species. Animals may produce more than one type of hair from the same follicle at the same time. The hairs found in animals include guard hairs, undercoat (ground hair), and tactile hairs. In animals, the medullae often measure more than half the diameter of the hair and appear continuous (running the length of the hair) or interrupted (in several large pieces).

Scale patterns can distinguish human hair from the hair of animals. With expertise, the examiner may be able to identify the species or even the breed of animal from which the hair came. There are three basic scale types: coronal, spinous, and imbricate (flattened).

Morphology is the study of form and structure. Hair can be examined by microscopy to study its morphology for speciation and—in some cases—points of comparison toward individuation. The information gathered in the physical examination of hair may be confirmed with DNA testing. Additionally, hair may be subjected to chemical testing for heavy metals and drugs.

Examination of the root can help tell whether the hair was shed or pulled out of the skin. Looking at the shape of the hair may tell the examiner from what part of the body it was removed. The shape of a hair's cross section can give information about the donor's race.

Fibers come from a wide variety of plant, animal, and chemical sources. The identification of a fiber is based on microscopic examination of morphological characteristics as well as chemical and instrumental analysis. There are two broad classes of fibers: natural and man made. The delineation is clear for natural fibers, those derived from animal or plant sources, but is slightly more complicated in man-made fibers that can be regenerated from cellulose supplied by plants or created entirely from chemicals.

Regenerated fibers are made from cellulose extracted from cotton, wood, and other sources. A solution of cellulose is extruded through the nozzle of a spinneret at a steady rate. As the solvent evaporates, the fiber is "regenerated."

Synthetic man-made fibers are the products of chemistry. Many are polymers, long chains of feedstock called *monomers.*

Fibers should be examined for morphological features under a light microscope for color, length, and diameter–cross section.

Some crystalline polymers exhibit birefringence.

Because organic compounds absorb infrared light according to functional groups present, infrared spectrophotometry allows the forensic examiner to identify functional groups in a fiber such as amide or ester bonds.

PROBLEMS

1. Give the word or phrase for the following definitions:
   a. exterior layer of hair
   b. the part of hair containing pigment granules
   c. the central empty space found in some hairs
   d. the diameter of the medulla relative to the diameter of the hair shaft
   e. a weight-to-length ratio for filaments and nonspun yarns
   f. fibers derived from plant or animal sources that have not been chemically altered
   g. a naturally occurring polymer of glucose molecules found in plants
   h. the protein found in hair
   i. a fiber made solely from chemicals
   j. a large molecule made of repeating subunits
2. Name and define the three types of hairs found on the human body.
3. Name and describe the three phases of the hair growth cycle.
4. Name and describe the three layers of a hair.
5. Describe the appearance of head, beard, and pubic hairs.
6. Describe the medulla pattern in people and animals.
7. Can the examiner tell
   a. when a hair was shed?
   b. when a hair was dyed?
   c. if a hair was pulled?
   d. the age of a hair donor?
   e. the race of a hair donor?
   f. the sex of a hair donor?
8. How does DNA technology complement hair analysis?
9. Describe the process for creating a regenerated fiber.
10. Describe a natural and a synthetic polymer.
11. Describe microscopy procedures for examining hair.
12. Describe microscopy procedures for examining fiber.

149

GLOSSARY

Anagen phase the growth phase during which a hair follicle is producing hair.

Catagen phase a slowing of hair production marked by elongation of the hair root; the transition between hair growth and shedding.

Cortex the main portion of the shaft of a hair; cortex cells contain the hair's pigment granules.

Cuticle the tough, scalelike protective covering on the outside of a hair.

Denier a weight-per-unit-length measure for filaments and nonspun yarns; a number equal to the weight in grams of 9000 meters of the fiber.

Follicular tag a small, light-colored piece of tissue that coats the hair shaft near the root; it can be used in DNA testing.

Follicle the part of the skin that grows hair.

Guard hair in animals, long hairs that extend above the undercoat.

Keratin the protein that makes up hair.

Lanugo hair the hairs found on unborn babies.

Man-made fibers fibers created by a chemical or mechanical process.

Medulla a central canal-like structure running through the center of a hair; generally, one-third the width of the hair in humans.

Melanin the pigment in hair.

Mitochondrial DNA matrilineal DNA found in the mitochondria, an organelle responsible for supplying energy to the cell.

Monomer the repeating unit of a polymer.

Morphology the study of the shape of objects and their parts.

Natural fibers fibers from arachnid, animal, or plant sources.

Nuclear DNA genetic material representing both parents, found in the nucleus of all cells.

Polymer a large molecule made up of repeating units of smaller molecules joined in a regular order.

Regenerated fiber cellulose that is chemically converted to a soluble compound and then converted back to a filament of fiber.

Synthetic fiber a man-made fiber, often chemically manufactured.

Tactile hairs (vibrissae) in animals, thick hairs on the face whose roots are surrounded by extra nerve endings.

Telogen phase the terminal phase of hair growth marked by a club-shaped appearance of the root; the phase during which hair is shed naturally.

Terminal hairs regular, pigmented hairs.

Undercoat (ground hairs) in animals, short hairs that help regulate body temperature.

Vellus hairs thin, colorless hairs produced from follicles that do not contain oil glands.

SECTION III
Chemical Evidence

Clockwise from top left: Cannabis plant, cocaine molecule, poppy capsule, alcohol. Cocaine from http://en.wikipedia.org/wiki/Image:Cocaine-from-xtal-3D-balls.png; poppy from Stockxpert; wine from http://en.wikipedia.org/wiki/Image:Tempranillowine.jpg; cannibis from http://commons.wikimedia.org/wiki/Image:Marijuanasmall.jpg

CHAPTER 8

Drugs and Pharmaceuticals

Case Study

Californian Cannabis Cultivation

Clandestine indoor grow operations are becoming a significant contributor to the illicit production of marijuana and derivatives. In July 2008, the DEA and local law enforcement officers raided five homes in the Riverside County area of southern California. Each house had been converted to a covert grow facility, with artificial sunlight and irrigation lines. Electricity meters had been bypassed to conceal the power used. Holes had been cut through floors, ceilings, walls, and doors to accommodate electrical wires, water lines, and ventilation duct work; every room contained either growing marijuana plants or, in the case of closets and bathrooms, light ballasts, extra chemical supplies, and fertilizer; windows had drywall covering them on the inside, as did any sliding glass doors.

Agents seized 5600 plants and estimated that each house had the potential to raise approximately $3 million a year.

Identification of the grow sites depended on good intelligence information, but the analysis of the scene depended on forensic experts with knowledge and expertise in identification of cannabis, awareness of indoor cultivation techniques, and the know-how to convert the physical findings of plants into an estimated street value of the production.

153

INTRODUCTION

Drugs are chemicals with pharmacological activity related to their structures. They may be derived from natural sources (plants or fungi) or synthesized from chemicals. Forensic drug analysts must be able to identify a drug, whether created by a pharmaceutical laboratory or made in a clandestine facility.

CENTRAL QUESTIONS

What can be answered:

- What type of drug is it?
- How much is present?

What we are learning or researching:

- Where did the drug come from?

DRUGS AND THE LAW

Today's drug regulations were built up from a series of laws that control the legal and illicit formulation, distribution, and sale of drugs. Drugs are often classified by weighing efficacy and use against the potential for harm and abuse. Hence, pharmaceutical descriptions of drugs have little to do with how they are ultimately classified.

The United States Pure Food and Drug Act of 1906

Passed by Congress, the Pure Food and Drug Act (PFDA) banned the manufacture, sale, or transport of fraudulent medicines and adulterated food products. It also contained provisions for meat inspection. A major provision of the PFDA was proper labeling of foods, drugs, and related products. The PFDA also created the Food, Drug, and Insecticide Administration under the Department of Agriculture, the precursor to today's FDA.

The Food, Drug, and Cosmetic Law of 1938

Properly labeling treatments that contained harmful substances proved to be a terrible plan. Elixirs containing radium and a chemical similar to antifreeze killed their users. The 1938 law gave the FDA jurisdiction over cosmetics and medical devices. Beyond labeling, it required that manufacturers give directions for using products. The law also provided that manufacturers show drugs were safe before they were put on the market, defined standards, set parameters for foreign material in products, and created a system for inspecting plants and manufacturing facilities.

The Comprehensive Drug Abuse Prevention and Control Act of 1970

Title II of this large document is the Controlled Substances Act (CSA), a law that acts as a summary of many amendments to the 1938 act and other laws regarding the manufacture, distribution, and sale of drugs, controlled substances, and the chemicals used to produce them. The CSA places regulated chemicals into five categories, called *schedules*, based on the material's pharmaceutical use, potential harmfulness, and how likely it is to cause dependency. So that the law will be more organic, the CSA provides a means by which substances can be added to the schedules, reclassified among them, or removed from them by the U.S. attorney general. The CSA also specifies penalties for certain criminal offenses.

Here is a summary of the schedules:

- Schedule I: Highly addictive substances with little or no medical use. The U.S. attorney general sets manufacturing caps on materials classified under Schedule I. Schedule I drugs include marijuana, heroin, 3,4-methylenedioxymethamphetamine (Ecstasy), and LSD.

154

Products containing cocaine and other chemicals were not illegal under the act if the materials were properly labeled. A supporter of the law, Coca-Cola advertised its product as "Guaranteed under the Pure Food and Drug Act." In 1909, a few years after Coca-Cola removed cocaine from its products, scientist Harvey W. Wiley sued to stop Coca-Cola from manufacturing the "pause that refreshes" on the basis of its high caffeine content. The judge found in favor of Coca-Cola's right to use caffeine in its products, though the soft drink manufacturer reduced the amount in its formulations.

BOX 8.1   DESIGNER DRUGS

To get around the Controlled Substances Act, creative chemists changed molecules very slightly such that their names were not actually listed in the schedules. These new chemicals were called *designer drugs*. However, changing a molecule even slightly can produce dangerous unknown effects in the body. These drugs are made without any medical testing to ensure their efficacy and safety. A bad batch of Ecstasy, made in a clandestine laboratory, caused many of the users to develop a Parkinson's-like syndrome. Some so-called designer drugs are now treated as if they were part of Schedule I.

- Schedule II: Highly addictive substances with a severely restricted medical use. The prescription distribution of these drugs is monitored by the DEA. The U.S. attorney general also sets manufacturing caps on materials classified under the Schedule. Schedule II drugs include cocaine, phencyclidine (PCP), oxycodone, methylphenidate (Ritalin), and many amphetamine and barbiturate formulations.
- Schedule III: Substances with less potential for abuse than Schedule I and II drugs and that have a recognized medical use. These are also prescription drugs. Schedule III drugs include codeine, some LSD precursors, ketamine, and many anabolic steroids.
- Schedule IV: Substances with lower potential for abuse than Schedule III drugs and that possess a medical use. They are also prescription drugs and treated similarly to Schedule III substances. Schedule IV drugs include chlordiazepoxide (Librium), dexfenfluramine (Redux), ethchlorvynol (Placidyl), zolpidem (Ambien), and many tranquilizers and weight control agents.
- Schedule V: Substances with less abuse potential than Schedule IV drugs and that have medical use. Many of these preparations are available without a prescription. Schedule V drugs include codeine and opiate preparations used in cough syrups.

Controlled drugs or *controlled substances* are expressions sometimes used for scheduled drugs because of the additional controls placed on them (beyond the need for a prescription).

BOX 8.2   MEDICAL USE OF MARIJUANA

The medical use of marijuana was ruled outside of the CSA in 2003 by the United States Court of Appeals for the Ninth Circuit (*Raich v. Ashcroft*, 352 F.3d 1222, 9th Cir. 2003). In 2005, the Supreme Court ruled in favor of the federal government in that the CSA did apply, making so-called "Schedule VI" use illegal. Dronabinol, the synthetic version of THC, remains in Schedule II because of its therapeutic use in reducing intraocular pressure in glaucoma sufferers as well as its ability to increase the appetite in AIDS and chemotherapy patients.

The central nervous system is the brain and the spinal cord. Together with the peripheral nervous system, it controls vertebrates' movements. The central nervous system is protected from the blood vessels that feed it by a physical barrier. This blood–brain barrier prevents many chemicals from passing from the blood to the brain.

NARCOTICS

Narcotic drugs are classified as **analgesics** (pain relievers) and soporifics (sleep aids). They work by depressing the action of the central nervous system. Narcotics are often prescribed for short periods of time to reduce the risk of developing **physical dependence**. Depressant drugs include ethanol.

Opium

The parent narcotic is often considered to be opium, a mixture of chemical compounds including morphine produced by lightly scoring the unripened seedpod of an opium poppy (*Papaver somniferum* or *paeoniflorum*). These superficial cuts "bleed" a milky white juice. When the juice has dried to a gummy consistency, it is collected from the seedpod. Combined scrapings from several flowers are pressed into cakes that darken from grayish to tan or brown as they dry. Drugs derived from opium are called *opiates* or *opioids*. Afghanistan, Pakistan, and Laos provide much of the world's opium cache. (See Figures 8.1 and 8.2.)

FIGURE 8.1
Opium poppies. Field of opium poppies growing in Burma. From DEA.

FIGURE 8.2
Heroin harvest. Exudate weeping from scores in the unripened seedpod of *Papaver somniferum*. From DEA.

Morphine

morphine

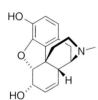

Raw opium may contain as much as 25% morphine, which can be extracted and purified. Morphine is a painkiller that causes central nervous system excitation followed by depression. Its prolonged use or abuse leads to physical addiction. Morphine is administered by mouth, subcutaneously, or intravenously (single injection or continuous pump). Longer-lasting MS-Contin pills last up to 12 hours.

Heroin (3,6-diacetylmorphine)

heroin

Heroin can appear in forms from a dull white powder (usually a salt of heroin) to a dirty black tar (usually the freebase of heroin). Heroin is made by acetylating morphine to its 3,6-diacetyl derivative with acetyl chloride, an ester of acetic acid, or acetic anhydride. Formulated as a painkiller and cough suppressant in Europe, the U.S. medical community withdrew heroin from the commercial markets in the 1920s citing its addictive properties. (See Figures 8.3 and 8.4.)

FIGURE 8.3
Heroin powder. Off-white colored powder that results from
treatment of the raw opium. From DEA.

FIGURE 8.4
Black tar heroin. "Black tar" is a variety of heroin produced in
Mexico and typically found in the western United States. From DEA.

Codeine

Codeine is another component of opium (usually less than
1%), but it can also be made from morphine. Used as a
painkiller, sedative, and cough suppressant, codeine—with
roughly one-sixth the analgesic strength of morphine—can
be mixed with acetaminophen. Its weaker high makes it less
likely to be abused.

Oxycodone (14-hydroxydihydrocodeinone)

Oxycodone is similar in chemical structure to morphine and
heroin and has similar effects. The *one* in the name refers to
the ketone functional group. OxyContin, the time-release
formulation of this powerful analgesic, is very attractive to
addicts for its sustained, heroin-like high. Pills and prescriptions for these pills are often stolen or diverted for purposes
other than those originally intended. (See Figure 8.5.)

Methadone (6-(N,N-dimethylamino)-4,4-diphenyl-3-heptanone)

Though it does not contain the heroin core structure, the synthetic
opiate methadone has many of heroin's parts and similar pharmacology. In heroin addicts, methadone is used to suppress heroin's
highs and alleviate **withdrawal sickness**. Because of its lower potential for abuse, methadone is also used as a prescription analgesic.

Many street drugs are called *narcotics*. In the laboratory, the section that handles drugs is often called the *narcotics unit*. However,

codeine

oxycodone

methadone

157

European poppies and
ornamental "California"
poppies produce little-
to-no opium.

Contins are continuous
(sustained) release
drugs. Because most
opiates wear off in 3–4
hours, contins were
formulated to keep a
slow, steady stream of
drug in the bloodstream.

Alkaloids are
nitrogen-containing
chemicals that have
pharmacological effects
on people or animals.
They come from a
variety of sources, but
many are extracted
from plants. The name
comes from an Arabic
word describing their
characteristic bitter
taste, often descriptive
of basic compounds.

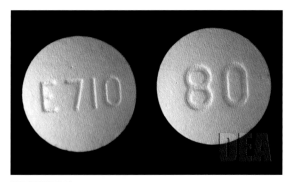

FIGURE 8.5
OxyContin tablets. Different strength OxyContin tablets are manufactured with a different color to the final product. These pale green tablets are 80 mg strength. From DEA.

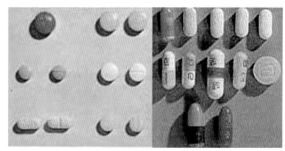

FIGURE 8.6
Assortment of barbiturate tablets and capsules. Image from CA state stopdrugs.org; see http://www.stopdrugs.org/idpills_1. html. Reproduced with permission of the California Department of Justice.

the term *narcotics* is properly applied to drugs that depress the central nervous system, causing sleep and relieving pain. Cocaine, a powerful stimulant, is the very opposite of a narcotic yet is classified as such under federal law.

BARBITURATES, DEPRESSANTS, AND TRANQUILIZERS

Barbiturates

Exotic-sounding *acetic acid* is the same chemical as vinegar used in salad dressing.

158

A metabolite of heroin, 6-monoacetylmorphine can be detected in hair and in urine. The concentration of this metabolite prevents those who enjoy poppy seed bagels from being mistaken for heroin users in drug tests.

Like narcotics and alcohol, barbiturates produce a feeling of well-being and induce sleep by suppressing the action of the central nervous system. Once prescribed as sleep aids, they are not prescribed for insomnia today due to their overall safety risks. People who did not sleep after taking the drug experienced effects similar to those of alcohol intoxication: euphoria, confusion, and impaired judgment. However, low doses are still used to suppress seizures, as sedatives, and anxiolytics (to reduce anxiety). These latter effects have earned them the collective name "downers."

Chemically, barbiturates are derivatives of barbituric acid. Though more than 20 barbituric acid derivatives and formulations are sold, the most often prescribed are amobarbital, pentobarbital, phenobarbital, and secobarbital, which come in tablet form. In hospitals, ultra-fast-acting barbiturates (effective in under a minute) are administered by injection. (See Figure 8.6.)

AMOBARBITAL

Intermediate-acting amobarbital is used as a sedative and to control convulsions and seizures. It is fast acting and long acting enough to have some potential for abuse.

amobarbital   pentobarbital

PENTOBARBITAL

While also used as a hypnotic, pentobarbital can be prescribed as an antispasmodic for muscle tremors. Like amobarbital, it has some potential for abuse.

Homebake Heroin

It was 2 AM on a cold and wet winter night. The telephone of the duty on-call forensic scientist rang, with someone requesting assistance at a suspected drug scene located in a remote farm cottage. Two hours later, the weather still dark and very wet, the scientist arrived to find two frightened suspects, four drug squad officers, and a request to "tell me what those bags out there are."

The bags in question consisted of approximately 20 5-gallon garbage sacks, all filled with residues of tablets that were disintegrating further in the rain. The couple had been making "homebake," a particularly ineffective way

of synthesizing narcotics and one that has been largely restricted to Australia and New Zealand. The process begins with codeine tablets — usually stolen from a pharmacy, but in this case purchased over several months. The codeine is demethylated with pyridine hydrochloride to give morphine, which is then acetylated with acetic anhydride to give a mixture of heroin and 3- and 6-monoacetyl morphine.

It probably would have been more cost effective for the couple to have saved their money and found a dealer!

PHENOBARBITAL

Peak plasma concentrations of phenobarbital are not attained until 8 to 12 hours after an oral dose, and, with a half-life of 2 to 7 days, it is classified as a long-acting barbiturate. Phenobarbital is still one of the most effective anticonvulsant drugs available. It has a low potential for abuse.

phenobarbital

159

SECOBARBITAL

Secobarbital has no anxiolytic properties but is prescribed as a sedative and anticonvulsant.

Barbituric acid was first synthesized by German dye chemist Adolf Von Baeyer on St. Barbara's Day. Baeyer went on to found the chemical company where Felix Hoffman would produce aspirin bearing the Bayer imprint.

Depressants

METHAQUALONE (QUAALUDE, SOPOR)

Introduced in 1965 as a "safer" alternative to barbiturates, the powerful sedative and muscle relaxant was pulled from the market in 1984 because of its very high potential for abuse.

ALCOHOL (ETHANOL)

Found in beer, wine, and liquor, alcohol is a very common (and legal) central nervous system depressant. Alcohol is a by-product of fermentation when sugars from grains or fruits are processed by yeast. Alcoholic drinks have varying strengths measured in percent alcohol by volume (the higher the percent, the stronger the drink). Most wines range from 10 to 14% alcohol by volume. Beer has about half that. (See Figure 8.7.)

secobarbital   methaqualone

FIGURE 8.7
Alcohol. Illustrations of a range of alcoholic beverages. Although legal and widely accepted socially, alcohol is a drug with potential for addiction and harm to health. From Stockxpert.

In the body, alcohol passes the blood–brain barrier and suppresses cognitive processes and muscle coordination. As the amount of alcohol ingested becomes greater, the ability to think and perform simple tasks degrades. If enough alcohol is consumed, a person may pass out. In some cases, enough alcohol may be consumed to cause a person to stop breathing or induce cardiac arrest. Alcohol is discussed in more detail in Chapter 10.

Tranquilizers

Tranquilizers differ from barbiturates in that they do not affect the central nervous system as strongly. They are divided into major and minor categories. Major tranquilizers, also called *neuroleptics,* include indoles, thioxanthenes, butyrophenones, phenothiazines, piperazine derivatives, and piperidine compounds. These drugs are prescribed as antipsychotics and in the treatment of dementia and Alzheimer's disease. They have a low potential for abuse. Minor tranquilizers are more prevalent and prescribed as anxiolytics, sedatives, and hypnotics. These include the benzodiazepines and meprobamate. While they can produce relaxation and reduce anxieties without inducing sleep, minor tranquilizers are more likely to be abused.

chlorpromazine

CHLORPROMAZINE (THORAZINE)

Chlorpromazine is used as an antipsychotic. It also has sedative, hypotensive, and antiemetic properties. Chlorpromazine's mode of action is as an anticholinergic and antidopaminergic.

meprobamate

MEPROBAMATE (MILTOWN)

Meprobamate is an older insomnia treatment largely replaced by benzodiazepines. It has some muscle relaxing capabilities but not enough to be used as an antiseizure medication.

CHLORDIAZEPOXIDE (LIBRIUM)

The first commercially available benzodiazepine, chlordiazepoxide is an anxiolytic with a long half-life, used as adjuvant therapy in the treatment of alcoholism.

DIAZEPAM (VALIUM)

A benzodiazepine sedative used as an antiepileptic and antiseizure medication, it is not recommended for long-term management of epilepsy due to its sedative effects and because patients develop **tolerance**. Diazepam enhances the inhibitory actions of the neurotransmitter GABA. It is more commonly used as an anxiolytic.

TRIAZOLAM (HALCION)

A benzodiazepine sedative and hypnotic prescribed for insomnia, this drug has a short half-life, helping patients avoid lingering effects in the morning.

BUSPIRONE (BUSPAR)

One of the newer drugs, like many before it, buspirone is being touted as a safe, nonaddictive, and nonsedative treatment for anxieties.

chlordiazepoxide

diazepam

triazolam

buspirone

Stimulants

Stimulants increase the activity of the central nervous system, earning them the name "uppers." Medicinally, they are used to suppress appetite and fatigue, though they may be abused for the same reasons. These drugs may also create a feeling of euphoria, hyperactivity, delusions, and hallucinations. As the drug wears off, depression and fatigue return. The main illicit stimulant drugs are amphetamines and cocaine. Amphetamines belong to a class of drugs called *phenethylamines*. They have medicinal value for weight control as anorectics (appetite suppressants). Legal stimulants include caffeine and nicotine.

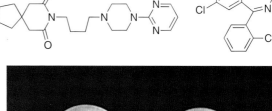

FIGURE 8.8
Methamphetamine. Desoxyn gradumet 15 mg tablets. These are a sustained-release formulation of methamphetamine that has been used to treat attention-deficit/hyperactivity disorder. Note that although medicinal tablet presentations can seem very similar, there are usually unique coloring, size, or marking characteristics that permit identification of the solid dosage forms. From DEA.

METHAMPHETAMINE

Methamphetamine can be injected or inhaled. On injection, the drug produces an intense "rush" and a deep sensation of well-being. (See Figure 8.8.) When a solution of methamphetamine is slowly evaporated from solvent, much the way rock candy is produced, it forms large, colorless crystals. "Ice" is a smokable form of methamphetamine, the effects of which are similar to those of crack cocaine. (See Figure 8.9.)

methamphetamine

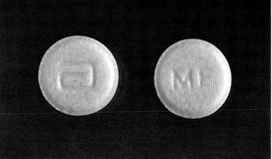

FIGURE 8.9
Methamphetamine "ice." Methamphetamine ice crystals. From DEA.

PHENMETRAZINE (PRELUDIN)

A sympathomimetic amine used in the treatment of obesity, phendimetrazine is an anorectic that stimulates the central nervous system. This drug produces many of the same actions as methamphetamine but is less potent.

PHENDIMETRAZINE (STATOBEX, TANOREX)

Similar in effect to phenmetrazine, this drug is less likely to be abused.

Use of methamphetamine and other similar drugs can result in **psychological dependency**. Long-term abuse may result in symptoms similar to those of schizophrenia.

Anesthetics

COCAINE

Cocaine is part of the family of drugs that are used as anesthetics. At one time, cocaine was found in Coca-Cola and used as an anesthetic for its vascular constricting effects. It may be injected or snorted. In the nose, it is absorbed through the mucous membranes. (See Figure 8.10.)

In the Andes, farmers chew coca leaves (*Erythroxylon coca*; see Figure 8.11) the way we would drink coffee. Extracted and concentrated, cocaine is a powerful central nervous system stimulant suppressing hunger and fatigue. It is usually supplied as a hydrochloride salt, a white to off-white powder, which may be injected or snorted.

Crack

Crack is cocaine *freebase*, a smokable form of cocaine. Inhalation causes the drug to be absorbed more rapidly, producing an intense high that has been described as a feeling of superpower, a feeling of euphoria combined with ability, that makes it very addictive. The high is short lived, making addicts "bump" or "chase" the good feeling. Crack, sometimes called "rock" cocaine, may come in small cubes or even be pressed into the shape of sugar cookies (see Figure 8.12).

Cocaine may be adulterated with a number of cutting agents. These include lidocaine, procaine, vitamins, and other materials.

Procaine

Sold under the name Novocain, procaine is a common dental anesthetic. It may be administered topically or by injection.

phenmetrazine

cocaine

procaine

162

FIGURE 8.10

Cocaine. Cocaine is traded, used, and taken in many different forms. Clockwise from top left: Cocaine bricks—a common form for trading large quantities (DEA); crack pipe—smoking crack cocaine gives a rapid, intense- and short-lived high (from Stockxpert); crack—named after the noise made when the rocklike preparation is heated. Crack is a potent form of freebase cocaine that is particularly addictive because of the intense high that it produces (DEA); lines —the stereotype action of a cocaine addict is snorting lines of the drug (from Stockxpert).

FIGURE 8.11

Coca plant. Foliage of the coca plant *Erythroxylon coca.* From http://commons.wikimedia.org/wiki/Image:Colcoca03.jpg

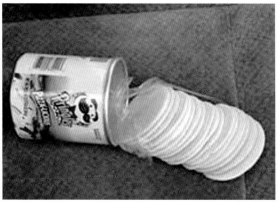

FIGURE 8.12

Crack cookies. Crack cookies found in Pringles can. From http://www.boingboing.net/2006/07/13/crack-cookies-hidden.html

lidocaine

Lidocaine

Marketed under the name Xylocaine, lidocaine is a local anesthetic and antiar-rhythmic. This drug may also be administered topically or by injection.

Hallucinogens

Whether derived from plants or made in a lab, **hallucinogens** are chemical sub-stances that distort perception and induce delusions. Hallucinogens cause a wide variety of experiences ranging from altered perception (streaming lights or colors from objects) to the perception of sensations (auditory, visual, tactile, and gusta-tory) not present. These drugs do not have a common chemical structure. They are grouped in this category because of their mode of action. (See Figure 8.13.)

lysergic acid diethylamide

LYSERGIC ACID DIETHYLAMIDE (LSD)

First synthesized in 1943 by Swiss chemist Albert Hoffman, LSD is an extremely potent hallucinogen taking effect at doses of a few micrograms. LSD is derived from lysergic acid, the chemical produced by ergot fungus. While LSD does not cause physical dependence, heavy users (or even an individual who took one large dose) may experience psychotic episodes after taking the drug. A momen-tary return to the intoxicated state or "flashback" may also occur.

"Rocking up" cocaine into crack often involves the use of baking soda. The resulting material may be waxy or brittle. Sometimes bubbles formed from carbon dioxide liberated in making the freebase give it the look of crumble candy.

Sigmund Freud, the father of modern psychoanalysis, was very interested in cocaine. In a letter to Martha Bernays (1884), Freud wrote, "Woe to you, my princess, when I come. I will kiss you quite red and feed you till you are plump. And if you are forward you shall see who is the stronger, a gentle little girl who doesn't eat enough or a big wild man who has cocaine in his body."

164

FIGURE 8.13

Hallucinogens. From top left, clockwise: magic mushrooms (*Psilocybe zapotecorum*) (from http://en.wikipedia.org/wiki/Image:Psilocybe.zapotecorum.1.jpg); phencyclidine (PCP) crystals, powder, and aqueous solution (DEA); cannabis plant (*Cannabis sativa*) (from http://commons.wikimedia.org/wiki/Image:Marijuanasmall.jpg); lysergic acid diethylamide (LSD) powder and capsules (DEA).

LSD is available in many dosage forms. One of the most popular is produced by placing drops on squares of blotting paper marked out with cartoon-style illustrations. (See Figure 8.14.)

PHENCYCLIDINE (PCP)

Originally developed as an anesthetic, patients treated with phencyclidine experienced a number of side effects while recovering from it. PCP may appear as liquid or powder. It can be smoked, ingested, or snorted. Regular cigarettes and marijuana cigarettes are often sold after being dipped into a solution of PCP. A few milligrams of the drug are all it takes to create visual hallucinations, paranoia, and a sense of invulnerability.

MAGIC MUSHROOMS

Psilocybin (4-phosphoryloxy-N,N-dimethyltryptamine) and related, naturally occurring hallucinogens are found in many species of mushrooms. Psilocybin is converted by the body to psilocin (about 1.5 times as potent as its precursor). The effects are similar to those of LSD but shorter in duration. While the dosage may run in the milligram range, users often take an unknown amount of the drug. This is because the users may ingest the mushrooms or make tea from them.

PEYOTE/MESCAL (MESCALINE)

Used by the indigenous people of Mexico in religious ceremonies, peyote are the buttons found on several types of cactus that grow in the area (see Figure 8.15). Peyote may contain a number of phenethylamine alkaloids, but its primary psychoactive ingredient is mescaline. The drug may also be produced synthetically.

PCP users may feel hot and take off their clothing. Some users feel strong and invincible to the point where they will try to break handcuffs, sometimes injuring their wrists and arms.

phencyclidine

FIGURE 8.14
LSD blotter. LSD "Dancing Condom" blotter. LSD is available in many dosage forms. One of the most popular is produced by placing drops on squares of blotting paper marked out with cartoon-style illustrations. From DEA.

FIGURE 8.15
Peyote cactus. Peyote cactus is the source of the hallucinogen mescaline Public domain image (U.S. government, Fish and Wildlife).

MDMA (ECSTASY, 3,4-METHYLENEDIOXYMETHAMPHETAMINE)

MDMA is an interesting drug with a variety of hallucinogenic and stimulant properties. It is related chemically to mescaline and amphetamine. Developed as an adjuvant therapy for psychotherapy, its primary effect is to stimulate the brain to secrete serotonin and dopamine, giving the user a sense of well-being, empathy, and openness. It is a favorite of club goers for its ability to increase tactile sensations. Clinically, it may used to treat post-traumatic stress disorder and extreme phobias. (See Figure 8.16.)

3,4-methylenedioxymethamphetamine (Ecstasy)

Club Drugs

Like hallucinogens, club drugs are not chemically related. In fact, they may even have different modes of action. What makes them a class is their use at dance clubs, nightclubs, and bars to keep people going and "enhance" their club-going experience. We already discussed MDMA (Ecstasy), methamphetamine, and cocaine. Now let us look at some other popular drugs. Many of these are connected to date rape and other criminal activity.

gamma-hydroxybutyric acid

GHB (GAMMA HYDROXYBUTYRATE, LIQUID X, GAMMA-OH)

GHB is a colorless, odorless central nervous system depressant with a slightly salty taste. It is a naturally occurring compound that may function

What ever happened to the Mickey Finn? Chloral hydrate was a popular sedative and hypnotic. Clinically used as an anesthetic, an anxiolytic, and to treat porphyria patients, chloral hydrate retains some use as an animal tranquilizer. The term *Mickey Finn* originally applied to a solution of chloral hydrate in alcohol. Later, it became the term for any drink tainted with the drug intended to knock a person out.

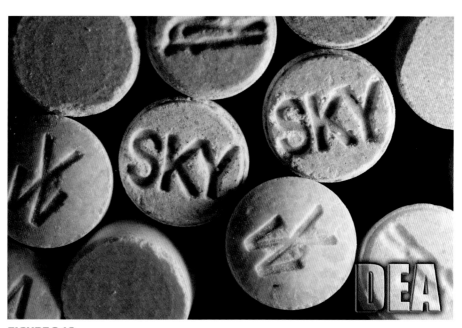

FIGURE 8.16
Ecstasy tablets. These are made by illicit producers in a wide range of shapes, colors, and markings (DEA).

as a neurotransmitter in the brain where it inhibits the release of dopamine. When mixed with alcohol, it can cause a person to black out. A date rape drug, it induces amnesia and is removed from the bloodstream very rapidly, which makes it difficult to prove administration.

ROHYPNOL (FLUNITRAZEPAM, ROCHE, "ROOFIES")

Another colorless, odorless central nervous system depressant, Rohypnol has earned the name "the date rape drug." The drug has sedative and muscle relaxant effects that are amplified when mixed with alcohol. (See Figure 8.17.)

flunitrazepam

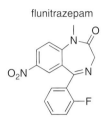

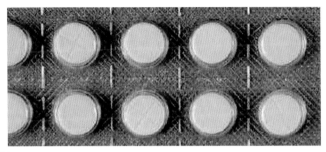

FIGURE 8.17
Foil pack of Rohypnol tablets. These contain the benzodiazepine flunitrazepam, and although produced as a legitimate medicine, the product has obtained a reputation as "roofies" used illicitly especially in the context of date rape (DEA).

KETAMINE (SPECIAL K, VITAMIN K)

Ketamine is a short-acting, dissociative anesthetic produced as an injectable liquid for use by veterinarians. Ketamine may appear as a powder or tablet in a club. In humans, it has hypnotic, analgesic, euphoric, and amnesic (causing short-term memory loss) properties. In some, it is a mild hallucinogen.

ketamine

Study Drugs

Study drugs are amphetamines or amphetamine derivatives that have been diverted from their original purpose. These drugs are often prescribed for attention-deficit/hyperactivity disorder (ADHD) or attention deficit disorder (ADD). The mechanism by which they work is unclear. Rather than demonstrating a stimulating effect, these drugs exhibit paradoxic reactions. That is, they have a sedative effect on hyperactive people.

RITALIN (METHYLPHENIDATE HYDROCHLORIDE)

methylphenidate (Ritalin)

Ritalin is a central nervous system stimulant similar to amphetamines. It is used to treat ADHD in children and adults. It is also used to treat narcolepsy in adults. (See Figure 8.18.)

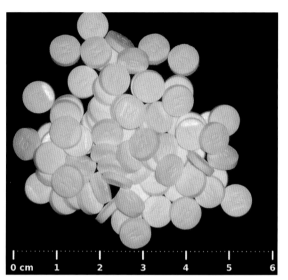

FIGURE 8.18
Ritalin tablets. Ritalin (methylphenidate) is a potentially addictive drug that is sometimes abused as a "study drug." From http://en.wikipedia.org/wiki/Image:Methylin2.jpg.

DEXEDRINE

Originally a prescription diet aid, this drug is also prescribed for narcolepsy and ADHD. The drug has a high abuse potential, and users may become physically addicted.

ADDERALL

Also developed as an anorectic, Adderall serves as a treatment for narcolepsy and ADHD. It may also cause physical and psychological dependence. In the brain, Adderall increases the levels of dopamine. It is often diverted to a study drug.

Steroids

The preceding information from a DEA press release shows that steroid abuse is a major criminal activity with health consequences as serious as those from other illicit drugs. Steroids are hormones, part of the endocrine system that tells the body to take specific actions. The adrenal glands, gonads, and other glands produce many types of steroids chemically related by a common skeleton. However, most drug cases involve anabolic and androgenic steroids,

168

Operation Raw Deal

In September 2007 the DEA successfully concluded Operation Raw Deal, an international case targeting the global underground trade of anabolic steroids. The investigation was the largest steroid enforcement action in U.S. history and took place in conjunction with enforcement operations in nine countries worldwide (Figure 8.19).

Federal search warrants totaling 143 were executed, resulting in 124 arrests and the seizure of 56 steroid labs across the United States. In total, 11.4 million steroid dosage units were seized, as well as 242 kilograms of raw steroid powder of Chinese origin.

Operation Raw Deal was a four-prong strategy focusing on raw material manufacturers/suppliers in China and other countries; underground anabolic laboratories in the United

States, Canada, and Mexico; numerous U.S.-based websites distributing materials, or conversion kits, necessary to convert raw steroid powders into finished product; and Internet bodybuilding discussion boards that were the catalysts for individuals to learn how to illicitly use, locate, and discretely purchase performance-enhancing drugs, including anabolic steroids. Many of the underground steroid labs targeted in this case advertised and were endorsed on these message boards. A concerning aspect of the bust was the unclean and unsafe environment at many of the manufacturing sites.

Besides steroids, many websites targeted also offered other dangerous drugs and chemicals such as ketamine, fentanyl, ephedrine, pseudoephedrine, and GHB.

a group of naturally occurring and synthetic compounds that closely resemble the male sex hormone testosterone. Most professional sports and the International Olympic Commission prohibit the use of anabolic steroids, yet abuse of these drugs continues because of the belief that they enhance performance.

In the body, testosterone has both androgenic, regulating the development of male secondary sex characteristics, and anabolic, regulating tissue, muscle and bone development, effects. Synthetic efforts have been made to maximize the anabolic effect of these drugs while minimizing the androgenic side effects.

Medically, anabolic steroids are available with a prescription to treat anemia and muscle atrophy. They are delivered by injection or as tablets. When taken for non-medical reasons, anabolic steroids exhibit a wide range of side effects. They can stunt bone growth and height development in teens. Women taking anabolic steroids may disrupt their menstrual cycle and cause the development of male secondary sex characteristics: body hair, deepening of the voice, and increased sexual desire. Conversely, men taking these drugs see atrophy of the genitals and gynecomastia (the growth of breasts), diminished sex drive, and infertility (decreased sperm production). Continued use has also been linked to cancer (brain and liver), liver disease, and depression. The jury is still out on the controversial idea of *road rage*—bouts of explosive temper and violent personality shifts attributed to the drugs.

While little peer-reviewed research exists to support the claim that anabolic steroids enhance physical performance, athletes caught using these drugs at the top of their game do nothing to dispel the myth. Anabolic steroids were added to the list of controlled substances in 1991.

On Valentine's Day 2005, former baseball player Jose Canseco released his book, *Juiced: Wild Times, Rampant 'Roids, Smash Hits & How Baseball Got Big* (Morrow, NY, 2005) which alleged that many of the stars of major league baseball were, in fact, steroid users. Mark McGwire was found with androstenedione in his locker and eventually admitted to its use.

169

FIGURE 8.19
Illicit steroid manufacture uncovered during the DEA Operation Raw Deal in 2007 (DEA).

androstenedione

oxandrolone

nandrolone

methandrostenolone

testosterone

Users may inject drugs or "stack" them by injecting and taking tablets and mixing the steroids. Some of the more popular anabolic steroids include the following.

ANDROSTENEDIONE

Secreted by the testicles, ovaries, and adrenal cortex, this steroid has weaker potency than testosterone. It exists in three isomeric forms that are converted to testosterone in the body. It has both anabolic and androgenic properties. Users call the drug "Andro."

OXANDROLONE (ANAVAR)

Available in tablets, this drug has been used clinically to promote growth in boys with delayed adolescence and to treat obesity. It has few androgenic side effects and is often stacked with other drugs.

NANDROLONE (DECA-DURABOLIN)

The body does not convert nandrolone to testosterone. The injectable drug has fewer androgenic side effects than many of its counterparts.

METHANDROSTENOLONE (DIANABOL)

Originally used to treat dwarfism and assist burn victims in recovery, methandrostenolone is available as creams or tablets. The drug converts to estradiol in the body, a process users seek to avoid by stacking with other drugs.

TESTOSTERONE CYPIONATE

Testosterone is the naturally occurring male sex hormone. The body converts testosterone both to estrogen and to dihydrotestosterone (DHT). This second conversion is highly desirable, as dihydrotestosterone produces stronger effects in the body. (See Figure 8.20.)

SUSTANON 250

This drug is actually a premixed injectable cocktail of testosterone propionate (30 mg), testosterone phenylpropionate (60 mg), testosterone isocaproate (60 mg), and testosterone decanoate (100 mg). It comes in a one-shot ampule and is used for about 10 days at a time. It is also known as Sostenon.

Drugs that produce feminizing effects are called aromatizing.

Marijuana

Marijuana, a drug prepared from the plant *Cannabis sativa,* is perhaps the most commonly used recreational drug worldwide. A hardy weed that grows to a height of 15 feet, marijuana came to the United States from Mexico and quickly became popular (see Figure 8.21).

In 1964, scientists isolated tetrahydrocannabinol (delta-9-tetrahydrocannabinol, THC). Among the 400-some chemicals present in marijuana, THC is the chemical most responsible for its hallucinogenic properties. The potency and dosage of marijuana may be compared by using the amount of THC by weight in a sample. Marijuana may also contain other cannabinoids such as cannabinol (CBN) and cannabidiol (CBD).

While many botanists believe that *Cannabis sativa* is the only species of marijuana, other plant specialists and many users believe that two others exist: *Cannabis indica* and *Cannabis ruderalis.* The marijuana leaf is palmately compound, with each leaf composed of 5–9 serrated leaflets. The leaves of *sativa* plants are long and thin, while *indica* leaves are wider and shorter. Users believe the difference is that *Cannabis sativa* produces more cognitive and perceptual effects, while *Cannabis indica* generates more physical effects. All plants exhibit three types of hairs:

- Glandular trichomes: Hairs that the produce THC-rich resin. These are often seen as having a little ball of red or colorless resin at the top (see Figure 8.22).
- Nonglandular trichomes: Similar in appearance to glandular trichomes, these hairs do not produce resin or appear to have a ball at their tips.
- Cystolithic hairs: Broad, often colorless hairs resembling claws.

Marijuana comes in a variety of preparations.

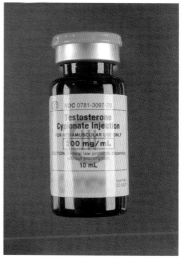

FIGURE 8.20
Vial of injectable testosterone cypionate. Steroid abuse includes illegal sale and distribution of legitimate preparations as well as illicit manufacture. From DEA.

171

FIGURE 8.21
Cannabis plants being cultivated indoors. Note this is from the scene described in the introductory case. From DEA.

FIGURE 8.22
Cannabis glandular trichomes. Characteristic glandular trichomes on *Cannabis* leaf. Courtesy of Eirik at Overgrow.com/norcan.org

In metabolism, *anabolism* is the process during which smaller molecules are used to create more complex materials. For example, a tree could make cellulose out of smaller sugars during anabolic metabolism. When applied to steroids, the term is used to describe drugs that promote a gain in muscle mass. The opposite process, *catabolism*, is the consumption of tissues—muscle and fat—to provide heat and do work.

LEAF (SHAKE)

Leaf or "shake" is a collection of dried leaves, stems, and seeds that is considered a poor-quality mixture by users because of the low (about 3%) THC content of material.

FIGURE 8.23
Cannabis bud. From
http://en.wikipedia.
org/wiki/Image:Macro_
cannabis_bud.jpg

BUD

The flowering tops of the marijuana plant are called *buds* (see Figure 8.23). This part of the plant is richer in THC, especially the females. Depending on the variety of material, THC content may range up to 8%.

SINSEMILLA

Sinsemilla refers to marijuana composed of the unfertilized flowering tops of female plants (see Figure 8.24). The name means "without seeds." To achieve sinsemilla, male plants are killed as soon as they are identified, to produce an environment free of pollen. The flowering tops of these unfertilized female plants contain up to 10% THC.

HASHISH (HASH)

Stronger than shake, hashish is formed by rubbing or shaking the glandular trichomes from the flowering tops. The resin and bits of plant material are then pressed together in a cake or bar and dried, creating a drug with 10 to 12% THC. (See Figure 8.25.)

KIEF (KIF)

Sometimes also called *crystals* or *red shake*, kief is a powder composed mainly of dried resin hairs and very small leaf particles produced by shaking dried marijuana in a sieve.

FIGURE 8.24
Sinsemilla. Sinsemilla
(Spanish for "without
seeds") is obtained from
plants that have been
grown in an environment
with no male plants
present. The females
then produce more
calyces to increase the
chance of pollination,
and the more calyces
on the plant, the more
THC in the harvest. From
http://en.wikipedia.org/
wiki/Image:Comparison_
between_bud_and_
cigar_pack.jpg

FIGURE 8.25
Hash block. A hash block, made by
harvesting and compressing the trichomes
from cannabis plants. From http://
en.wikipedia.org/wiki/Image:Hashish-2.jpg

HASH OIL (HASHISH OIL)

Hash oil, a dark liquid containing the extract of THC from plant materials, is created by soaking flowering tops in a solvent and then concentrating the extract. While most hash oil contains up to 20% THC, some may contain as much as 70% THC once concentrated. A drop of hash oil is often placed on a regular cigarette before smoking. It is an especially popular practice with menthol cigarettes. A lighter-colored variant called *golden* or *honey oil* is sometimes used. (See Figure 8.26.)

FIGURE 8.26
Golden oil. Hash oil is a potent preparation with high levels of THC. Its color has led to the names "golden oil" and "honey oil." From http://en.wikipedia.org/wiki/Image:Golden_Cannabis_Oil.jpg

Marijuana may be prepared for use in a variety of ways. It may be smoked as a cigarette (joint) or in a water pipe (bong). Industrious users may remove the tobacco from a regular cigarette or cigar and replace it with marijuana, forming a "blunt." Hash users may mix the drug with tobacco or use it alone either as a cigarette or in a pipe. Users may drink marijuana tea or marijuana "steamers," a preparation of marijuana in hot milk. Still other users may bake marijuana into brownies (see Figure 8.27) or prepare it in other foods.

Marijuana is a hallucinogen that does not produce marked behavioral changes in the user at low doses. The person may experience a sense of well-being, relaxation, and increased sensitivity of the senses. Undesirable effects include dry mouth, red eyes, impaired judgment, and impaired coordination. Use of the drug is often followed by increased hunger. Higher dosages may lead to delusions and hallucinations. Marijuana does not seem to cause physical dependency, but prolonged heavy use may result in psychological dependence.

BOX 8.4 MARIJUANA AND THE LAW

Marijuana has been used in societies since prehistory, but in modern times in the U.S. it grew markedly in popularity and in regulation from the 1920s. Though almost every state and the federal government regulated its use, often classifying it as a dangerous narcotic, it was not until the Marijuana Tax Act of 1937 that the law carried enough weight to be obeyed. A campaign to stop marijuana use ensued. Posters from the U.S. Federal Bureau of Narcotics said marijuana caused "murder, insanity, and death."

In 1969, the 1937 act was struck down by the Supreme Court in a case brought by counter-culture guru Timothy Leary. The Court noted that the act's provision that marijuana users register with the IRS—essentially providing a database of scofflaws to law enforcement officials—violated Fifth Amendment rights regarding self-incrimination. However, the next year, the Controlled Substances Act scheduled marijuana, making it federally illegal.

Possible medical uses of marijuana include relief of pain, increase of appetite, reduction of nausea, dilation of blood vessels, and lowering of intraocular pressure. Because marijuana contains more than 400 chemicals, many of which are harmful chemicals common to tobacco smoke, smoking marijuana is not the best delivery option. Marijuana cigarettes contain as much as four times the tar of regular tobacco cigarettes. However, the benefits of THC are available by prescription in the form of a pill called Marinol. In the future, researchers hope to be able to deliver THC by inhaler or patch.

DRUG ANALYSIS

Collecting and Preserving Drug Evidence

Drugs may be packaged in a variety of forms, including pills, plant material, cigarettes, stamped papers, jars of liquid, and powders in a variety of colors. The evidence may be wrapped in a piece of magazine, a plastic bag, fiberglass, plastic wrap, or a balloon. First, drug evidence should be photographed in place with a scale. Then it should be documented, properly labeled, and packaged to ensure no contamination between samples occurs. Many jurisdictions provide specialized envelopes for drug cases on which an investigator may write the results of screening tests to identify a drug family. At the laboratory, chemical analysts will examine the evidence further.

FIGURE 8.27
Cannabis brownies. Cannabis can be consumed in the form of baked products such as brownies. From en.wikipedia.org/wiki/Image:Three_space_brownies.jpg

How to tell the boys from the girls? Before flowering, female plants will develop small hairs at every bract, which is the start of bud production. If these hairs are pollinated they will develop into seeds.

Drug Analysis

Because drugs come in so many different forms, forensic drug examiners use an arsenal of color tests, crystal tests, microscopy, chromatography, and instrumental methods to identify and quantify them. The protocols involved in drug identification include screening tests and identification or **confirmatory** tests. **Screening tests**, such as color tests, can identify a drug family but not a specific drug. Identification tests, such as infrared spectroscopy, confirm the presence of the specific drug and may even individuate the sample. Some drugs must be identified by a series of presumptive (nonspecific) tests, which, taken together, prove a drug is present.

The forensic drug examiner must be able to identify not only the drug but also any binder, excipient, or other component present.

COLOR TESTS

Color tests are wet chemical processes used to screen unknown materials for the presence of drug families. Officers in the field may use these presumptive tests to help sort the type of case coming into the lab. However, the forensic drug examiner will perform the test again as part of his or her analysis. Though there are many color tests, the most commonly used are described in Table 8.1.

MICROSCOPY: MICROCRYSTALLINE TESTS

The **microcrystalline test** is a nearly instantaneous process whereby a specific drug and reagent react to form crystals of characteristic morphology. A solution

Table 8.1 Some Common Color Tests Used in Screening for Drugs

Test	Result
Dillie–Koppanyi Sample is treated with a drop of 1% cobalt acetate in methanol, followed by 5% isopropylamine in methanol.	A violet-blue solution indicates barbiturates.
Duquenois–Levine (Solution A: 2% vanillin and 1% acetaldehyde in ethanol; Solution B: concentrated aqueous hydrochloric acid followed by dilution chloroform)	Transfer of purple color into the chloroform layer indicates marijuana.
Marquis (2% formaldehyde in sulfuric acid)	A purple color indicates opiates, including heroin and morphine. An orange-brown color indicates amphetamines or methamphetamines.
Scott (Solution A: 2% cobalt thiocyanate in water/glycerine (1:1); Solution B: concentrated aqueous hydrochloric acid; followed by chloroform)	On application, Solution A will turn blue in the presence of cocaine. When Solution B is added, the mixture will turn pink. Addition of chloroform will extract a blue color, indicating cocaine.
Van Urk (1% p-dimethylaminobenzaldehyde in 10% concentrated hydrochloric acid/ethanol)	A blue-violet color indicates LSD.

of unknown drug in an appropriate solvent or a small sample of powder is placed on the microscope slide and mixed with the reagent. Any precipitate formed will be tiny crystals. For example, cocaine reacts with gold chloride to form cross-shaped crystals with chevrons that look like frost. When treated with a solution of lead iodide, cocaine in potassium acetate forms spiked balls. Some crystals show up, and are best described by, the changes they undergo in polarized microscopy.

LOW-POWER MICROSCOPY: MARIJUANA MORPHOLOGY

The Duquenois color test is not sufficient to identify marijuana, even with the Levine modification in which the color is extracted into the chloroform layer. The forensic examiner must also use microscopy. Under a low-power microscope, the hairs of marijuana may be clearly seen. On the upper side of the leaf, cystolithic hairs with a characteristic "bear claw" shape will be present. Glandular hairs with red or colorless resin tips should also be seen. On the underside of the leaf, there will be nonglandular hairs.

Forensic drug examiners must be able to account for all drug material in their possession and explain every chemical test protocol along with its results in court. They must also be able to explain the use of instrumentation.

Using the unaided eye, forensic examiners may determine if the plant is male or female. If female, development in the bracts will determine if the plant is fertilized or unfertilized.

CHROMATOGRAPHY

Depending on the size of the sample, thin-layer chromatography (TLC), high-performance liquid chromatography (HPLC), gas chromatography (GC), and gas chromatography–mass spectroscopy (GC-MS) may be used to identify both the drug and any excipients.

Thin-Layer and Liquid Chromatography

Thin-layer chromatography is employed when the sample is small. Compounds are compared by reference to the solvent front. High-performance liquid chromatography is an excellent technique to separate a drug from mixtures of similar compounds and from a binder in solid samples. In any type of liquid chromatography, materials are compared by retention time. It is important to note that retention time must be compared to a reference standard. Also, while retention time is related to structure, it is not to be used alone for identity. Chemicals may be ill-resolved and have overlapping or near-overlapping retention times. HPLC has the advantage that the sample is not destroyed in the analysis. Recent advances in instrumentation have meant the HPLC combined with MS is feasible in a routine laboratory. HPLC-MS offers all the advantages of HPLC and MS in one instrument and, especially with tandem MS, greatly simplifies preanalysis sample preparation. (See Figure 8.28.)

Gas Chromatography and Gas Chromatography–Mass Spectroscopy

Comparison of retention time is also used as a parameter for identification of compounds by gas chromatography. However, GC provides much greater separation power than TLC, so samples with some cutting agents or other contaminants can be separated and identified. With gas chromatography followed by mass spectroscopy, the fragmentation pattern is indicative of the structure of the molecule. With high-resolution mass spectroscopy or elemental analysis, GC-MS is accepted as providing molecular confirmation of a structure. The major disadvantages of GC-based methods are that the compound must be sufficiently volatile to be transported through the instrument in the gaseous phase, and that it is not suitable for thermolabile compounds.

INFRARED SPECTROSCOPY

Infrared spectroscopy tests for the functional groups present in a molecule. Because each bond of the molecule absorbs light and releases light at a different frequency, the infrared spectrum for each chemical compound is unique. This also means that the chemical must be fairly pure to be submitted for infrared spectroscopy. The recorded chart of an infrared spectrum can be divided into a functional group region and a "fingerprint" region. A trained chemist can interpret infrared spectra and determine the identity of a molecule.

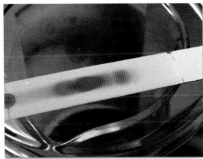

FIGURE 8.28
Chromatographic procedures used in the analysis of drugs. Clockwise from top left: A typical chromatogram from a gas chromatograph (GC) showing the elution of two components of a mixture (see http://commons.wikimedia.org/wiki/Image:Rt_5_9.png); a Liquid Chromatograph–Mass Spectrometer (LC-MS) (see http://commons.wikimedia.org/wiki/Image:LC_and_LTQ.jpg); and separation of dyes by thin-layer chromatography (TLC) (see http://commons.wikimedia.org/wiki/Image:TLC_black_ink.jpg).

SUMMARY

Pharmaceutical descriptions of drug have little to do with their classification. The Comprehensive Drug Abuse Prevention and Control Act of 1970 includes the Controlled Substances Act (CSA) which governs the manufacture, distribution, and sale of drugs and controlled substances and the chemicals used to produce them. The CSA places regulated chemicals into five categories, called *schedules,* based on the material's pharmaceutical use, potential harmfulness, and how likely it is to cause dependency.

Narcotic drugs are classified as analgesics (pain relievers) and soporifics (sleep aids). They work by depressing the action of the central nervous system. Narcotics are often prescribed for short periods of time to reduce the risk of developing physical dependence. Opiates are part of the narcotic family.

Like narcotics and alcohol, barbiturates produce a feeling of well-being and induce sleep by suppressing the action of the central nervous system. These drugs have earned the nickname "downers." Tranquilizers differ from barbiturates in that they do not affect the central nervous system as strongly. They are divided into major and minor categories.

Stimulants increase the activity of the central nervous system, earning them the name "uppers." Medicinally, they are used to suppress appetite and fatigue, though they may be abused for the same reasons. This category includes amphetamines and cocaine.

Whether derived from plants or made in a lab, hallucinogens are chemical substances that distort perception and induce delusions. These drugs do not have a common chemical structure. They are grouped in this category because of their pharmacologic action.

Like hallucinogens, club drugs are not chemically related. In fact, they may even have different modes of action. What makes them a class is their use at dance clubs, nightclubs, and bars to keep people going and to "enhance" their club-going experience. Stimulants such as MDMA (Ecstasy), methamphetamine, and cocaine belong in this category. Other drugs include GHB, Rohypnol, and ketamine.

Some amphetamines prescribed for attention-deficit/hyperactivity disorder (ADHD) such as Ritalin and Adderall are recently increasingly diverted to "study drugs."

Steroids are hormones, part of the endocrine system that tells the body to take specific actions. Most steroid drug cases involve anabolic and androgenic steroids, a group of naturally occurring and synthetic compounds that closely resemble the male sex hormone testosterone. In the body, testosterone has both androgenic, regulating the development of male secondary sex characteristics, and anabolic, regulating tissue development, effects. Synthetic efforts have been made to maximize the anabolic effect of these drugs while minimizing the androgenic side effects.

Marijuana, a drug prepared from the plant cannabis, is perhaps the most commonly used drug. Tetrahydrocannabinol (delta-9-tetrahydrocannabinol, THC) is the most important of 400-some chemicals present in marijuana and the one that is the most responsible for hallucinogenic properties. The potency and dosage of marijuana may be compared by using the amount of THC by weight in a sample. Marijuana may also contain other cannabinoids such as cannabinol (CBN) and cannabidiol (CBD).

Drugs may be packaged in a variety of forms, including tablets, plant material, cigarettes, stamped papers, jars of liquid, and powders in a variety of colors. The evidence may be wrapped in a piece of magazine, a plastic bag, fiberglass, plastic wrap, or a balloon. First, drug evidence should be photographed in place with a scale. Then it should be documented, properly labeled, and packaged to ensure no contamination between samples occurs.

Because drugs come in so many different forms, forensic drug examiners use an arsenal of color tests, crystal tests, microscopy, chromatography, and instrumental methods to identify and quantify them. The protocols involved in drug identification include screening tests and identification tests. Screening tests, such as color tests, can identify a drug family but not a specific drug. Identification tests, such as infrared spectroscopy, confirm the presence of the specific drug and may even individuate the sample. Some drugs must be identified by a series of presumptive (nonspecific) tests, which, taken together, prove a drug is present.

Color tests are wet chemical processes that are used to screen unknown materials for the presence of drug families. The most commonly used include Dillie–Koppanyi for barbiturates, Duquenois–Levine for marijuana, Marquis for opiates and amphetamines, Scott for cocaine, and Van Urk for LSD.

The microcrystalline test is a nearly instantaneous process whereby a specific drug and reagent react to form crystals of characteristic morphology. Some crystals show up and are best described by the changes they undergo in polarized light microscopy.

The Duquenois color test is not sufficient to identify marijuana, even with the Levine modification. The forensic examiner must also use microscopy to note the presence of cystolithic, glandular, and nonglandular hairs. Using the unaided eye, forensic examiners may also determine if the plant is male or female. If female, development in the bracts will determine if the plant is fertilized or unfertilized.

PROBLEMS

1. Give the word or phrase for the following definitions:
   a. the perceived need for a drug
   b. a physiological need for a drug, developed with continued use
   c. the need for an ever-increasing amount of drug to achieve the same effect
   d. drugs given to reduce pain
   e. drugs that facilitate tissue growth
   f. drugs that alter perception
   g. tests that may rule out a class of drugs
   h. a test that identifies a specific drug
   i. drugs chemically altered to skirt inclusion on a schedule
   j. the process of separating a drug from other material (e.g., excipient)
2. List three narcotics.
3. List three stimulants.
4. List any drugs that cause physical dependency.
5. List any drugs that cause psychological dependency.
6. Describe the system by which controlled substances are classified.
7. Describe the relationship between opium and heroin.
8. List several drugs derived from plant sources, their active ingredient, and how they are used.
9. Describe the features of marijuana plant material.

10. Classify each of the following drugs:
    a. LSD
    b. heroin
    c. methamphetamine
    d. androstenedione
    e. alcohol
    f. Rohypnol
11. Give a definition for the following medicinal terms:
    a. anxiolytic
    b. anorectic
    c. soporific
    d. anesthetic
    e. analgesic
    f. amnesic
12. Give the possible drug based on the result of the color test:
    a. Marquis test: purple
    b. Marquis test: orange
    c. Duquenois–Levine test: purple color in the chloroform layer
    d. Van Urk test: blue-violet color appears on paper
    e. Dillie–Koppanyi test: violet-blue solution
    f. Scott test: blue present in the chloroform layer
13. Describe some of the ways in which drugs are packaged.
14. Describe the difference between presumptive and confirmatory tests.
15. Explain the use of color and crystal tests.
16. Describe a protocol for analyzing an unknown white powder.

GLOSSARY

Analgesic a drug used to treat pain.

Confirmatory test (confirmation test) a test that identifies a substance.

Depressant a drug that decreases the functions of the central nervous system, increasing relaxation or inducing sleep; depressants may include barbiturates and alcohol; downers.

Hallucinogen a naturally occurring or synthetic chemical that alters cognition and perception.

Microcrystalline test a reagent that, when mixed with an unknown, can help to identify the substance by the color and shape of the crystals formed.

Narcotic drugs drugs classified as analgesics (pain relievers) and soporifics (sleep aids), which work by depressing the action of the central nervous system; continued use of these drugs can produce physical dependence.

Physical dependence a physiological need for a drug developed as a result of regular use.

Psychological dependence a perceived need for a drug.

Screening test a preliminary test that, when applied to an unknown, may rule out several class possibilities.

Stimulant a drug that increases the functions of the central nervous system, increasing wakefulness and decreasing appetite; stimulants include amphetamines, cocaine, and caffeine; uppers.

Tolerance the need for ever-increasing doses of a drug to have the same level of effect; tolerance can become physical dependence.

Withdrawal (withdrawal sickness) symptoms that develop when a drug to which a patient has a physiological dependence is removed.

Photo By Bureau of ATF 1993 Explosives Incident Report

Clockwise from top left: house on fire (from Stockxpert); charred remains after fire extinguished (note "crocodiling" burn patterns) (from Stockxpert); World Trade Center bomb site (ATF); illustration of dynamite and a timer-detonator (from Stockxpert).

CHAPTER 9

Arson and Explosives

Case Study

Ash Wednesday

Ash Wednesday 1983 fell in the middle of a long, extremely hot dry spell in the Australian summer that year. At first it looked like just another dreadful, searingly hot day, with temperatures around 110 °F in the southern states of Victoria and South Australia. But this Ash Wednesday was to live up to its name. The tinder-dry bushland was pitted with spot fires that spread relentlessly. The first major fire near an urban area was reported in the country town of Clare in South Australia just after 1 PM. By late afternoon the major city of Melbourne in Victoria was surrounded by fires. The indigenous eucalyptus trees and introduced pines are a rich source of volatile oils that acted as their own accelerants to further propagate the fires.

Worse was on the way. A weather front driven by winds of between 40 and 70 mph and relative humidity of less than 6% were rushing in from the desert north. Inevitably, the winds encountered the hundreds of fires in the country areas and fanned them to massive conflagrations with fronts many miles wide. Over 1 million acres of land were burned and more than 2500 homes destroyed. Seventy-five people, including 17 firefighters, lost their lives.

Although a natural disaster, the fires were the cause of major forensic investigations. Some sites became potential crime scenes as experts investigated reports of deliberate lighting. In this case, however, no instances of arson were proven. The cause of many of the first out-breaks of fire was found to be sparks from power lines: They sagged in the intense heat, and the winds drove them together, with the resulting short circuits producing hot sparks that ignited fires in trees and uncut dry grass alongside and beneath the lines. As a result, many of the lines were replaced by insulated cables and the land alongside subjected to active clearance and maintenance. Home design (low-profile roofs and eaves sealed against wind-blown embers) and safety advice ("Don't seek refuge in your swimming pool" — some people literally were boiled alive) were improved.

Investigation of the dead produced many sad tales. In South Australia, the capital city of Adelaide lies between the Southern Ocean and the Adelaide Hills, a picturesque area favored by many as a cooler place to live than the hot plains. As the main fire fronts neared the residential towns in the Adelaide Hills, the police closed the freeway to and from the city. Nine people lost their lives trying to get home to protect their families and property by taking a detour along a secondary road. They got caught in a fire front that was so hot and rapid that they were flash-incinerated in their cars.

INTRODUCTION

Arson, **explosions**, and terrorism can be planned in advance to allow the criminal time to escape and cover his or her tracks. While evidence from such crimes may be difficult to gather because much of it is burned, destroyed, removed by firefighters extinguishing the blaze, or blown up at the crime scene, the trained examiner may be able to identify **accelerants**, ignition sources, or detonation devices as well as determine whether or not the situation was accidental.

BOX 9.1 PROVING ARSON

There is no "test" for arson. While an arsonist often leaves clues such as accelerant traces, it may be impossible for even an experienced forensic fire investigator to determine that a fire has been set deliberately or tell exactly how it was started. Some arsonists, like those who set fire to churches, may be profiled and eventually caught by their patterned behavior or **modus operandi**. In other cases, such as the bombing of the World Trade Center or Murrow building, the perpetrator must be caught by extensive detective work.

Energy may be defined in many units. While scientists measure energy in kilojoules or kilocalories, others still use older units, such as the British thermal unit (Btu, the amount of heat required to raise 1 pound of water 1°).

ENERGY

Energy is the capacity of a system to do work. It is manifest in many forms, including heat, light, and sound, and may be described in terms of potential, kinetic, or chemical nature. Like matter, energy may be converted from one form to another but cannot be created or destroyed. This conversion is often accomplished by breaking and making chemical bonds. Burning wood (chemical energy) creates heat (thermal energy). The process also creates light and sound, as in the case of a wildfire. (See Figure 9.1.)

FIGURE 9.1
Trees burning in wildfire. From Stockxpert.

Many homes are heated with natural gas, a combination of methane and other light **hydrocarbons**. The combustion of methane is a form of **oxidation**. When methane burns in the presence of oxygen from the air, it forms carbon dioxide and water and liberates heat and light. Reactions that give off energy are called **exothermic** or *exergonic*. The amount of energy released as heat is the difference in energy between the bonds of methane and the bonds of the products, carbon dioxide and water. This quantity is called the **heat of combustion** (see Figure 9.2 and Table 9.1). All the events considered in this chapter are examples of exothermic reactions.

FIRES

Introduction

Fires are important to life. We use them to cook food and keep us warm in winter. The efficiency of the fuel as an energy source can be expressed as its heat of combustion (see Table 9.1).

Unfortunately, fires are important to the forensic scientist too, in the form of arson, or deliberately lit fires. Arson may be simple property crime with a building burned down to allow the arsonist to claim the insurance. It may be a hate crime (see Chapter 6, the Williams brothers) or to kill or to conceal a death. Forest fires are some of the most terrifying natural disasters, but unfortunately some are deliberately lit, sometimes by people who just want to see the effect.

Some fires may start due to **spontaneous combustion**, but most require an ignition source, a fuel, and oxygen.

Ignition Source

Every reaction requires a certain amount of energy to proceed. This "impulse" is called the *activation energy.* It is that energy required to get over a barrier of reactivity. The energy applied may come in the form of mechanical agitation, electrical stimulation, or heat. Whether it is intentionally applied or accidental, the forensic fire examiner must try to determine what ignition source might have been applied to provide the energy needed to start the reaction. Once started, the reaction is self-sustaining. Combustion proceeds until the oxygen or fuel is consumed.

There are more ways to start a fire than simply striking a match. Fires may be started by a variety of ignition sources. Deliberately set fires may be started with a match or sparker, as if lighting a fireplace. Alternatively, the arsonist may use a delay device such as a cigarette, candle, or more complicated timing mechanism designed to apply heat to the fuel source. However, accidental sources of ignition must not be overlooked. These may include lightning strike, electrical failure, or even nothing at all, in the case of spontaneous combustion where the local environmental temperature exceeds the ignition temperature of the fuel (see Table 9.2). The success of the fire depends on other factors too, such as the rate of reaction.

Rate of Reaction

Not all reactions proceed at the same rate. While every oxidation liberates energy, not all oxidations produce flames or proceed rapidly. The process by which patina develops on bronze is very slow compared to the burning of wood. The chemical reaction rate is dependent on several factors, including pressure, volume, temperature, and the amount of fuel present.

Some reactions absorb energy from the surroundings as they proceed. These "uphill battles" are called **endothermic** (or *endergonic)* **reactions**. While interesting to chemists, these reactions are not important to forensic fire examiners. Endothermic reactions have positive values for (Δ) H.

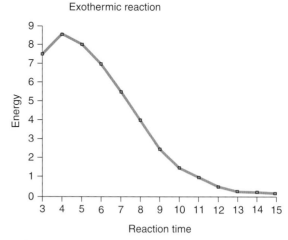

FIGURE 9.2

Energy changes during an exothermic reaction. The y-axis represents the potential energy of the chemical system. The initial rise is due to the energy required to break the chemical bonds; however, once the reaction is under way it releases more energy (in this example, in the form of heat), and the potential energy of the system falls. The net energy change is called the *enthalpy change,* ΔH. Because the system is losing energy, ΔH is always negative for an exothermic reaction. Graphic created by author.

185

Table 9.1	Heat of Combustion of Some Common Fuels		
	Heat of Combustion		
Fuel	**MJ/kg**	**MCal/kg**	**Btu/lb**
Hydrogen	141.9	33.9	61,000
Gasoline	47	11.3	20,400
Diesel	45	10.7	19,300
Ethanol	29.8	7.1	12,800
Propane	49.9	11.9	21,500
Butane	49.2	11.8	21,200
Wood	15	3.6	6,500
Coal	15–27	4.4–7.8	8,000–14,000
Natural Gas	~54	~13	~23,000

Data from http://en.wikipedia.org/wiki/Heat_of_combustion

For a fire to burn, there must be three elements: heat, fuel, and oxygen. **Oxidation**, the chemical reaction by which substances combine with oxygen to form new compounds, is one way to look at combustion reactions. The reaction for the burning of propane, a common fuel for camping and home use, is balanced according to the principles of stoichiometry. Such a reaction produces heat and flame. Other oxidations, such as the formation of patina on a roof or statue, are oxidations that proceed at a slower rate and do not produce a flame.

Table 9.2	Autoignition Temperatures and Flash Points of Some Common Fuels	
Fuel	**Ignition Temperature °C**	**Flash Point °C**
Gasoline	280	<–40
Ethanol	365	13
Natural gas	580	–188
Coal	400	N/A
Kerosene	210	38–72

The autoignition temperature of a substance is the lowest temperature at which it will spontaneously ignite in a normal atmosphere without an external source of ignition. The flash point of a flammable liquid is the lowest temperature at which it can form an ignitable mixture in air.

Range of Combustibility

While fuel, oxygen, and heat are necessary to produce a flame, not all such mixtures burn. The fuel-to-oxygen ratio must fall in a range of combustibility. Mixtures containing too little fuel are called *lean*, while mixtures containing too much fuel are called *rich*. The range of combustibility (**flammable range**) contains the mixtures between lean and rich that will burn. For gasoline, mixtures from 1.3 to 6.0% fuel in air will burn.

Temperature

As the amount of heat increases, the rate at which the reaction proceeds will increase. This helps to explain why fire spreads so quickly. Burning fuel causes the temperature of the surroundings to increase, accelerating the reaction. Additionally, temperature may start a fire. In forest fires, the intense heat of the burning fuel draws air into itself, creating gale-force winds that feed oxygen to the fire.

Flash Point

Only fuel in the gas phase can support flame. The **flash point** is the minimum temperature at which liquid gives off enough vapor to support combustion. At the flash point, the vaporized fuel may be ignited to start a fire. However, the ignition temperature for most fuels is considerably higher than the flash point (see Table 9.2).

For a solid fuel to burn, it must be brought into the gaseous state. Some fuels can be heated enough to vaporize. Other fuels decompose in a process known as **pyrolysis (thermal decomposition)**. When wood burns, heat causes chemicals to be liberated into the vapor phase. These vapors ignite and burn as flame. If there is not enough heat to vaporize flammable materials from the fuel, it will undergo glowing combustion or smoldering.

Is It a Fire?

There are many words to describe oxidative processes, depending on the nature of the ignition, fuel, and oxygen supply.

- *Glowing combustion* or *smoldering* is the process of burning fuel without producing a flame. Cigarettes, charcoal, and embers are examples of smoldering. The process occurs when there is not enough heat to pyrolyze the fuel. (See Figure 9.3.)
- *Combustion* is a chemical reaction between a fuel and oxygen, producing heat and light (often as flame). The process is more often called *burning*. (See Figures 9.1 and 9.2.)
- *Spontaneous combustion* is a rare but real phenomenon caused by an exothermic reaction producing sufficient heat to ignite a fuel. This is often seen with decomposition of compost heaps or the evaporation and oxidation of linseed oil (a highly unsaturated oil) from rags.
- A *subsonic combustion* process is driven by thermoconductivity (burning material ignites adjacent material). The burning rate of **deflagration** is less than 2000 meters per second.
- An extremely rapid, *exothermic combustion* process creates a supersonic shock wave within the burning material. The burning rate of a **detonation** is greater than 2000 meters per second.

Do solids burn? Metals such as sodium, potassium, and magnesium can oxidize very rapidly. In water, sodium and potassium appear to burn. These metals react with water to form hydroxide and hydrogen. The reaction involves so much heat that the metal may melt. The heat also ignites the hydrogen, producing a flame. Such metal fires must be put out with the special category of extinguisher, a D-class or "star" extinguisher.

187

FIGURE 9.3
Smoldering charcoal.
From Stockxpert.

Collecting and Preserving Arson Evidence

In order to preserve evidence, the investigation should begin as soon as the fire is extinguished. A timely investigation also ensures that salvage operations and cleanup procedures will begin as soon as possible.

Unlike other crime scenes, for an arson or explosion crime scene a determination of structural integrity may need to be made before an investigation may begin. Access to the crime scene should be photographed. The first order of business is to find the fire or explosion's origin.

ORIGIN DETERMINATION

It can be difficult to find the origin of a fire. Because fire moves upward, the origin is most often found at a low point marked by very intense burning. It is best to sample a larger area than one might initially think. Drafts, fuel sources, techniques used to extinguish the fire, and other factors may obscure the origin. Once detected, the area around the origin should be photographed and protected from foot traffic until searching for evidence of accelerants, ignition devices, and indications of arson is done. Suspicious circumstances to be mindful of near the origin include a number of small fires in several areas, the use of devices to spread fire ("streamers") such as paper or clothing, and ignition in unusual places. Containers found near the origin, even when empty, should be collected, as should anything that could have been used as a fuse. Signs of accidental ignition should also be noted.

188

BOX 9.2   FURNISHING AND APPLIANCES

When accelerants are used on a floor, nearby furniture may show intense burning on its underside compared to upper surfaces. Electrical appliances such as stoves, dryers, and electronics may be burned in a fire. The first step in answering the question of whether an appliance was burned because it was faulty and caused the fire is to dismantle the object and look inside. If a fault in the appliance caused the fire, there will be signs of burning and sooting inside it. If it was burned as a result of the fire, the sooting will be on the outside.

Dogs are being used in a wide range of law enforcement and public safety situations. The ATF has a canine academy to train dogs to sniff explosive and accelerant traces. The U.S. Transportation Security Administration has more than 400 dogs trained to detect explosives and drugs. (See Figure 9.5.)

VAPOR DETECTION

The same technology used by the gas company to detect leaks is employed by forensic fire investigators, both to detect the origin of a fire and to screen it for traces of flammable substances. A portable vapor detector or "sniffer" provides a rapid screening test for volatile organic compounds at a fire crime scene. Air around the scene is sampled with a handheld device. Inside the device, volatile organics are oxidized, and the heat from this reaction is detected as a positive. Materials in the area that may have absorbed flammable liquids can then be collected. (See Figure 9.4.)

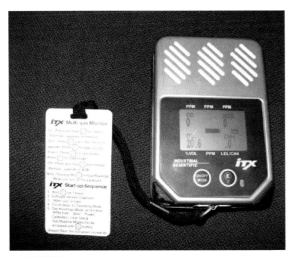

FIGURE 9.4
The Omni GDP portable gas detector. From http://www.
omniinstruments.co.uk

FIGURE 9.5
Detector dog on duty at Dulles International Airport. From http://
commons.wikimedia.org/wiki/Category:Police_dogs

189

ASH AND DEBRIS

Absorbent material such as wood, paper, fabric, and carpeting should be collected from the scene, as these can retain traces of accelerant. Collection containers must be clean and airtight. Clean lined or unlined quart or 1-gallon-size paint cans are often used, as are glass jars with screw-top lids. Paper should never be used, as is the case with nylon bags. Polyethylene or Kapak bags are suitable. Containers should not be more than 3/4 filled. Objects with sharp edges should be collected in cans as they may puncture plastic bags.

Liquid samples, including the contents of cans that may have been used to transport accelerant to the scene, should be sampled into small Teflon-lined glass vials. Care should be taken not to contaminate or destroy potential fingerprint evidence.

UNBURNED MATERIALS

The floor and ground are great places to look for evidence. Items such as floorings, rugs, pillows, cushions, furniture, rubbish, clothing, and rags should also be sampled into properly labeled airtight containers. Very large items may be sampled by cutting pieces small enough to fit into containers. Outdoors, soil, along with any plants, can be collected the same way as flooring.

The ATF Fire Research Laboratory is a new facility established to conduct scientIflc research that validates fire scene indicators and improves fire scene reconstruction and fire evidence analysis; support fire investigations and the resolution of fire-related crimes; and develops improved investigative and prosecution procedures using scientifically validated methods that integrate the assets of ATF and its partners to enhance fire investigation personnel expertise.

It is not permitted to send flammable or combustible liquids through the U.S. mail.

SUBSTRATE CONTROL: AN EXEMPLAR

While collecting evidence, it is important that the forensic fire examiner collect from areas in the room far away from the origin. This process, called *substrate control,* is essential for establishing an exemplar of the normal conditions of a room. If sufficient material is available, a large sample may be taken for pyrolysis experiments. The control should be from an area where it reasonably can be expected that there are no accelerant traces. The main reason for the control is that materials such as synthetic fiber carpets can give false positive results in tests used to identify accelerants.

All debris, ash, clothing, soil, and substrate control samples should be stored in airtight containers a cool place to prevent the loss of lighter, volatile components until ready to process.

IGNITION SOURCES

Delay devices such as candles, cigarettes, and homemade wicks made of clothing or paper may provide vital information if recovered. Mechanical devices such as mercury switches, alarm clocks, mechanical strikers, or sparking devices often survive fire scenes. If possible, they should be packaged in airtight containers the same as regular samples.

Analytical Methods

Gas chromatography (GC) is the universal tool used in identification of accelerant residues in fire debris samples. There are several variants of the technique, and also of the procedures used to treat the samples before analysis.

Most fire accelerants are mixtures of volatile organic compounds such as gasoline, paint thinners, and lighter fluids (see Table 9.3). The heat of the fire will distort the relative concentrations of the mixture components, with the more volatile ones being evaporated preferentially. Standards used in the analysis include ones prepared from the pure accelerant by heating. The concentrated samples are often referred to as *weathered.*

ACCELERANT RECOVERY

The techniques available for accelerant recovery are shown in Table 9.4.

ACCELERANT IDENTIFICATION

Gas chromatography (GC) is the national standard method for identification of accelerant residues in the laboratory. There are some smaller, portable GCs that can be used in the field in addition to electronic detectors and canines. Capillary column GC is favored because of its excellent resolution of volatiles

Table 9.3   **Classification of Arson Accelerants**

Class	Boiling Point °C	Examples
Class 1: Light petroleum distillates (LPD)	<120	Petroleum ethers; lighter fuels; rubber cement solvents; lacquer thinners
Class 2: Gasolines	50–120	All brands and grades of automotive gasolines
Class 3: Medium petroleum	60–200	Charcoal starters; paint thinners; mineral spirits; dry-cleaning solvents
Class 4: Kerosene	90–290	No. 1 fuel oil; jet-A fuel; insect sprays; lighter fuels
Class 5: Heavy petroleum	210–410	No. 2 fuel oil; diesel fuel
Class 0: Unclassified	Variable	Single components: alcohols; acetone; toluene; camping fuels; lamp oils; lacquer thinners

Table 9.4   **Methods for Recovery of Accelerant Traces from Fire Debris Samples**

Technique	Process
Direct headspace	Samples are drawn by syringe from the vapor space in the container above the debris sample, which may be either heated or at room temperature.
Static headspace	A material such as activated charcoal bound to an inert strip is suspended in the headspace of the can or bag containing the debris. The charcoal adsorbs the volatile compounds present.
Dynamic headspace	Similar to static, but the headspace is swept by air and the activated charcoal, which will adsorb the volatile compounds present in the vapor stream.
Solvent extraction	A solvent such as carbon disulfide (CS_2) is added to the container and samples removed for analysis.
Steam distillation	No longer used because it is the least sensitive and most time consuming.

and the consequent ability to give a profile of the components in an accelerant mixture. The GC detector may be a simple flame ionization detector, but a mass spectrometer is the *de facto* standard detector used today.

EXPLOSIVES

World Trade Center Bombing

Just after noon on February 26, 1993, lower Manhattan was rocked by a huge explosion. Almost a decade before 9/11/01, the World Trade Center was the target of a terrorist attack. The bomb had detonated in the underground car park and created a 100-foot crater several stories deep; it killed six people and injured over a thousand. The explosion disrupted all power to the building; the critical investigation to recover evidence had to be made in the poor lighting provided by portable generators and in freezing winter weather. Indeed, the weather was so cold that water from the firemen's hoses froze and made physical access to the site dangerous.

A multiagency task force consisting of the Bureau of Alcohol, Tobacco and Firearms (ATF); the Federal Bureau of Investigation (FBI); and the New York Police Department (NYPD) bomb squad was set up. Despite the hazardous conditions, they set themselves to the immensely difficult task of working through the rubble to identify the source of the bomb. An ATF investigator found a vehicle identification tag on an axle located at the center of the explosion. The number allowed the vehicle to be identified as a Ryder rental truck and led from there to the rental office and name and address of the renter.

The truck had been rented by Mohammad Salameh, a known associate of Abdul Rahman Yazin, a known terrorist bomb maker. From there, several other conspirators were identified and the details of the plot and the bomb pieced together.

The 1300-pound bomb used urea nitrate as its main charge, along with aluminum, magnesium, and ferric oxide. Boosters of bottled hydrogen were incorporated into the device to enhance its incendiary effects. Ignition was by means of 20-foot-long fuses that gave the bombers approximately 12 minutes to flee the scene.

Introduction

Explosives are high-energy materials that participate in rapid exothermic reactions. An **explosion** is characterized by its rapid rate of reaction. In fact, the speed of detonation is so great because these chemicals already have their own oxygen supply or **oxidizing agent** (whether internal or another chemical). These oxidative processes produce light, heat, sound, and large amounts of gas. The damage done by explosions comes from both shrapnel (flying debris) and the pressure wave of the blast itself. Depending on the rate of reaction, materials are classified as either *low explosives* or *high explosives.*

As is clear from the World Trade Center bomb and others, considerable damage can be inflicted with devices that do not contain commercial or military high explosives (see Figure 9.6).

Low Explosives

Most **low explosives** are mixtures of fuel and an oxidizing agent. Low explosives include gunpowder (both black and smokeless powders), methane or ethane gas and air mixtures, and sugar–potassium chlorate mixtures. For low explosives, the rate of reaction is called the *rate* (sometimes *speed*) *of deflagration* or *burning*. **Deflagration** is characterized as a subsonic pressure wave driven by thermoconductivity (burning material ignites adjacent material); the burning rate is usually less than 2000 meters per second. While the slow burn rate indicates that most of the damage will be done by debris, in sufficient quantity or when contained in a device such as a pipe bomb, low explosives still can yield powerful results.

Photo By Bureau of ATF 1993 Explosives Incident Report

FIGURE 9.6
The World Trade Center bomb site (ATF).

The difference between a bomb and an explosive, apart from the purpose to which the material is put, often lies in the physical presentation. The explosive in a bomb is contained, as in the very basic pipe bomb, and there may be other materials present too. One very dangerous type of pipe bomb is the flechette bomb. Packed with screws or nails and rat poison, it is meant to be detonated in a crowd where the shrapnel will cause wounds with the bleeding difficult to control.

Some explosions save lives. Sodium azide is a solid that releases nitrogen gas when detonated by an electrical spark from a sensor detecting a car accident. The reaction is very rapid. Once the sensor is activated, the air bag is triggered within 0.05 s and takes 0.1 s to fully inflate (the burst of gas causes initial inflation at over 1000 pounds of pressure). In another 0.5 s, the air bag deflates through side vents. The "smoke" seen after deployment is talc or cornstarch (used to pack the bag) and sodium hydroxide dust formed as a byproduct during the reaction.

Got oxygen? Most low explosives are mixtures of fuel and an oxidizing agent. For example, in black powder, oxygen is provided by potassium nitrate—a separate chemical from the fuel, carbon. High explosives, such as triacetone triperoxide, incorporate the oxidizing agent in the material itself. Rocketeers, seeking to control the burn to their advantage, exploit knowledge of these mixtures.

The burn rate of gunpowder makes it useful for firing ammunition from a gun without making the barrel or breech explode.

POWDER EXPLOSIVES

Gunpowder

Gunpowders contain nitrate compounds, which are used as a source of oxygen to react with carbon, sulfur, and other chemicals. (See Figure 9.7.)

Black Powder

Black powder is a mixture of potassium nitrate (KNO_3, 75%), charcoal (C, 15%), and sulfur (S, 10%). The smoke in this powder comes from the charcoal component. While it can be found in gun and sporting goods stores, it can also be made at home. Black powder can be used as a "fuse" for other explosives when prepared in special cords or poured in a line.

FIGURE 9.7
Gunpowder. Gunpowder is an explosive that has been known for more than 8 centuries. From http://en.wikipedia.org/wiki/Image:Pyrodex_powder_ffg.jpg

Smokeless Powder

More powerful than black powder, **smokeless powder** comes in a variety of mixtures, grain sizes, and shapes. Single-based gunpowder usually contains nitrocellulose (cellulose hexanitrate). While "smoke free," this powder still leaves residues. Double-based powder is a mixture of nitrocellulose and nitroglycerin (glyceryl trinitrate). Triple-based powders, used by the military but rarely seen among game or target shooters, may contain nitroguanidine in addition to a double-based mixture. (See Figure 9.8.)

FIGURE 9.8
Smokeless powder. From http://en.wikipedia.org/wiki/Image:N110_ruuti.jpg

Other Low Explosives

METHANE, ETHANE, OR PROPANE–AIR MIXTURES

If contained in a small vessel or even a small room, these light hydrocarbons will produce a great explosion if the mixture is within the range of combustibility. Outside this range, the mixture will not ignite. *Lean mixtures,* those at the low end of the scale, will explode but may not burn. *Rich mixtures,* those heavy in fuel, will explode, causing the hot gas to rise. Cooler air is sucked in underneath the hot air, diluting any remaining fuel and allowing for continued combustion. Such a blast fills the room it is in and then may cause fire.

An excellent model for experimenting with lean and rich fuel mixtures is a "woofing" bottle. A small amount of alcohol is placed in a carboy (or water-cooler bottle) and shaken to disperse air into it. The bottle is then lit by bringing a match to its mouth. Air rushing into the bottle creates a jet of flame and a loud rushing noise. The bottle will not explode because it is open. However, it may become very hot.

POTASSIUM CHLORATE–SUGAR

Potassium chlorate, a white powder, is a very strong oxidizing agent used in fireworks and matches. On heating, it decomposes to release molecular oxygen. This process is accelerated by magnesium filings. When mixed with ordinary table sugar and ignited with sulfuric acid or a match, it produces purple smoke, flames, and considerable heat. While often used as a chemistry demonstration, when large amounts of the mixture are placed in a small container, this seemingly innocuous mixture can produce the same explosion as one-half stick of dynamite.

> **BOX 9.4   POWDER EXPLOSIONS**
>
> When dispersed in the air, even very finely divided powders from grain or flour can become an explosive if a spark is applied. Grain elevators and bakeries have met their end in such explosions. Many violent explosions in coal mines resulted from ignition of methane–coal dust mixtures. The bombs that caused the deaths of 52 commuters in London on July 7, 2005, had the power of several pounds of high explosive but were homemade from flour and hydrogen peroxide.

High Explosives

In contrast to low explosives, **high explosives** are often chemicals that incorporate their own oxygen supply. Another contrast is that they must be detonated or initiated by another explosion. High explosives include dynamite, azides, TNT, and so-called "plastic" explosives such as RDX (C-4). For high explosives, the rate of reaction is called the *rate* (or *speed*) *of detonation.* **Detonation** is characterized by a supersonic pressure wave (shock wave or blast) within the burning material; the burning rate is usually greater than 2000 meters per second. High explosives are further classified into primary and secondary explosives.

Certain solvent storage sheds and other small buildings are designed with a blast in mind. The walls will blow out, causing the ceiling to collapse and smother any fire.

methane

ethane

$H_3C–CH_3$

195

propane

potassium chlorate

$KClO_3$

sugar

PRIMARY EXPLOSIVES

Primary explosives have low tolerance for heat (including sparks), shock, or friction. These explosives are sometimes called *primers* because they can be used in blasting caps and other devices to detonate other types of explosives such as RDX (C-4). Blasting caps can be set off with an electrical current or a **safety fuse**. However, the sensitivity of these explosives makes them dangerous when handled alone by amateurs. Some uses of primary explosives are shown in Table 9.5.

Table 9.5	**Some Primary Explosives and Their Uses**
Primary Explosive	**Uses**
Lead azide	Detonator, primer, exploding bullets.
Lead styphnate	Primer and detonator.
DDNP	Used with other materials as a primer–detonator in situations where high sensitivity to flame or heat is required but sensitivity to impact is not important.
Mercury fulminate	Used in percussion caps and blasting caps but generally avoided because of sensitivity to initiators.
Silver fulminate	Extreme sensitivity makes it of little practical use in explosives. Small amounts mixed with potassium chlorate are used in "popper" and "cracker" novelty fireworks.

Lead Azide (Pb(N3)$_2$)

Like many azides, lead azide is an impact-sensitive, white, crystalline powder. It is made by metathesis (an exchange reaction) between sodium azide and lead nitrate. While sodium azide is often used to cut lead azide, the sugar dextrose provides greater use as a stabilizing agent. Lead azide is used in blasting caps as a detonator for secondary explosives. Its rate of detonation is about 5.18 km/s. It resists absorbing water, and moisture does not decrease its sensitivity to impact; however, it metathesizes with copper to form the more explosive, more sensitive copper azide.

Lead Styphnate (lead 2,4,6-trinitroresorcinate, $C_6H_3N_3O_8Pb$)

Lead styphnate is detonated by fire or electrical discharge. It is so sensitive to electrical discharge that it can be set off by touch from a person. The salt appears yellow to brown in color and has two isomorphic crystal shapes for its monohydrate. It is only slightly soluble in water and methanol and does not react with metals.

Diazodinitrophenol (DDNP)

Though slightly less sensitive than its counterparts to friction and shock, this yellowish brown powder is often used in primer devices. It is soluble in most

Exploding bullets: Lead azide was incorporated into the rounds used by John Hinckley Jr. in his attempted assassination of President Ronald Reagan on March 30, 1981. The bullets had lead azide centers intended to explode on impact. Fortunately, none made a direct hit and none exploded.

solvents, including hydrochloric acid, acetic acid, and acetone, but is insoluble in water. It is desensitized to detonation in water.

diazodinitrophenol

Mercury Fulminate (Hg(ONC)$_2$)

Mercury fulminate is detonated by sparks, heat, flame, friction, and shock. The heavy, white-to-gray-colored powder does not absorb water. It is very sensitive to initiators and associated with accidents.

Silver Fulminate (AgONC)

Used in fireworks and noisemakers, silver fulminate is extremely sensitive to impact. The grayish white salt is not soluble in water and is so sensitive that it can be used in underwater blasting.

Shock-sensitive sodium azide is one of the chemicals used in air bags.

SECONDARY EXPLOSIVES

Secondary explosives are more stable to heat, electrical discharge, friction, and shock, making them safer than primary explosives for use. When ignited, these explosives will burn rather than detonate. They are detonated with a blasting cap or safety fuse. For this reason, they are sometimes called *noninitiating explosives.*

Dynamite (Stabilized Nitroglycerin)

nitroglycerin

Invented by the Swedish chemist Alfred Nobel in 1866, dynamite was nitroglycerin-stabilized with clay or diatomaceous earth. Later, pulp was used as a stabilizing agent. Due to the danger of dynamite sweating nitroglycerin, the explosive was gradually reformulated. Today's dynamite uses sodium nitrate and calcium carbonate as oxidizing agent and stabilizing agent, yet it has given way to other explosives.

Cyclotrimethylene Trinitramine (RDX)

Dating from World War II and perhaps the most ubiquitous military explosive, RDX is found in a variety of formulations. When mixed with wax or plasticizers, it becomes pliable and can be shaped forming the base of many "plastic" explosives. The two best-known plastic explosives are C-4 and Semtex. C-4 is made of about 91% RDX, 5% plasticizer (di(2-ethylhexyl) or dioctyl sebacate), 4% binder (2% polyisobutylene), and filler (2% petroleum oil). Semtex is available in two forms: Semtex A is approximately equal quantities of RDX and PETN with di-n-octyl phthalate and tri-n-butyl citrate as plasticizers; Semtex H is 94.3% PETN and 5.7% RDX. A taggant is often then added to the mixture to help identify it.

RDX is stable to being dropped, shot, or burned and must be detonated with a blasting cap or safety fuse. Because it is common and easily used, it is popularly diverted from military use to terrorism. In the form of Semtex, it was the explosive used to bring down PanAm flight 103 in December 1998. Ironically, it was originally developed as a medicine.

Most explosives are toxic. Some contain heavy metals. Others, like TNT, pose health and environmental risks.

Trinitrotoluene (TNT)

Unlike nitroglycerin, TNT is stable to friction and impact. Produced in massive amounts during World Wars I and II, it became the standard against which other explosives were measured. TNT does not react with water or metals but can be converted to unstable compounds by treatment with base.

trinitrotoluene

Pentaerythritol Tetranitrate (PETN, Penthrite)

More sensitive to shock and friction than TNT, PETN it is used in mixtures with TNT as a booster for grenades, shells, and small-caliber ammunition. It is used by the military in land mines and is manufactured in **detonation cord**. Its speed of detonation is approximately 7000 meters per second. Interestingly, it is also given medicinally as a vasodilator.

pentaerythritol tetranitrate

2,4,6-trinitrophenyl-N-methylnitramine (Tetryl, Tetrile, Nitramine)

Used to make detonators, tetryl can be ignited by flame, friction, and shock. In large quantities, it may detonate rather than burn. The off-white to yellow solid is commonly used as a booster explosive because it tolerates compression well.

2,4,6-trinitrophenyl-N-methylnitramine

Triacetone Triperoxide (TATP)

This explosive is relatively easy to make from acetone, hydrogen peroxide, and a small amount of acid such as hydrochloric acid. It is sensitive to friction and impact. Because it is fairly easily made and packs a large punch when enclosed, it is used in pipe bombs and terrorist weapons.

Ammonium Nitrate–Fuel Oil

Another easily homemade explosive is the ammonium nitrate–fuel oil mixture called *ANFO*. It can be made by soaking ammonium nitrate fertilizer in fuel oil. This mixture was used in the 1993 bombing of the World Trade Center and in the destruction of the Murrow federal office building.

triacetone triperoxide

TAGGANTS

Taggants for explosives come in two types: detection taggants, used to detect explosives before detonation, and identification taggants, used to determine the source of a material after detonation. Companies such as Microtrace and others manufacture a variety of taggants. The tracers are often layers of color-coded material that may incorporate magnetic or fluorescent materials to aid in locating them. In simple plastic taggants, the layers of material are coded to tell by whom, where, and when a material was created (see Figure 9.9).

Without detection taggants, plastic explosives are very difficult to find. The Antiterrorism and Effective Death Penalty Act of 1996 required manufacturers to incorporate detection taggants in the formulations of plastic explosives. These taggants do not change the performance of the high-energy materials they mark. They are volatile chemicals that can be detected by sniffer dogs or ion mobility detectors. Examples include 2,3-dimethyl-2,3-dinitrobutane (DMDNB) used universally in the U.S. and ethylene glycol dinitrate (EGDN) used in Europe to mark Semtex.

FIGURE 9.9
Laminated plastic identification microtaggants manufactured by Microtrace. Each particle is around 20 microns in size. Courtesy of Microtrace LLC.

Identification taggants have not received wide support from the explosives industry. The 1996 Antiterrorism Act called for a study of identification taggants in explosives, which was done by the Bureau of Alcohol, Tobacco, Firearms, and Explosives (ATF) and The National Academies of Science (NAS). The resulting 1998 report concluded that it was not yet appropriate to require commercial explosives to contain identification taggants due to "concerns about long-range environmental consequences, effectiveness in law enforcement, safety issues, and costs."

Dupont, Hercules, and Atlas Powder all voluntarily use some taggants in their explosive formulations.

Collecting and Preserving Explosives Evidence

Once the origin is determined, sample collection proceeds much like arson investigation. The area is photographed and documented. Debris from the crater can be packed in airtight containers for analysis. While larger plastic containers may be used provided the evidence is not sharp enough to cut its way out, the investigator must take care because explosives can volatilize and both seep away and contaminate nearby samples.

Surfaces near the origin of detonation must be collected. Porous and impregnable surfaces such as wood or rubber may contain bits of debris coated with undetonated explosive residue. Nonporous or hard surfaces such as laminated glass or metals may be coated with small amounts of explosive residue and can be a good place to look for taggants. Items identified as being near the detonation site before the explosion should also be recovered as they may also provide evidence of explosive residue or taggants.

DETONATION SOURCE

Unlike arson investigation, where the ignition source is localized near the origin, because the detonation source was very close to the blast, it may be fragmented over a larger area. Debris may be sifted through a series of metal sieves to find components of the detonation device.

Analysis of Explosive Debris

LOW-POWER MICROSCOPY

Debris from the blast site and any remainder of the detonating device are searched with low-power microscopy. Grains of black or smokeless powder may be identified by their shape and size. The analyst may also look for taggants.

Once examined by microscopy, debris, surfaces near the blast, and portions of the detonation mechanism may be washed with acetone. The washings are collected and submitted for further testing.

THIN-LAYER CHROMATOGRAPHY

Acetone washings are spotted against known explosive standards and compared for Rf value. A co-spot may be performed or the plate subjected to two-dimensional analysis.

Table 9.6	Some Color Tests Used in Screening Materials for Explosive Residues	
Reagent	**Color**	**Explosive residue**
Griess (sulfanilic acid and N-(1-naphthyl) ethylenediamine in methanol)	Pink–red	Nitrites. Used as a screening test for nitroglycerin.
Diphenylamine (diphenylamine in concentrated sulfuric acid)	Blue	Nitrates. Gives positive with smokeless powder residues.
Alcoholic KOH	Red	TNT.

COLOR TESTS

The color tests for common explosives are very general in their results and must be taken in combination to provide presumptive information. See Table 9.6.

CRYSTAL TESTS

A tiny amount of the acetone washing may be swabbed onto a slide. When the solvent evaporates, a film of explosive crystal is left behind.

GAS CHROMATOGRAPHY–MASS SPECTROSCOPY

If there is sufficient material, the debris washing may be submitted to GC or GC-MS.

INFRARED SPECTROSCOPY

Using IR spectroscopy, the analyst looks for the signature of a particular organic component or components of a material.

ARSON, EXPLOSIONS, AND THE LAW

Because evidence at the scene of an arson fire or an explosion may literally evaporate, the Supreme Court ruled that such an investigation could be started without a warrant to enter and search the premises. Its reasoning in the opinion included the following:

Immediate investigation may also be necessary to preserve evidence from intentional or accidental destruction. And, of course, the sooner the officials complete their duties, the less will be their subsequent interference with the privacy and the recovery efforts of the victims. For these reasons, officials need no warrant to remain in a building for a reasonable time to investigate the cause of a blaze after it has been extinguished. And if the warrantless entry to put out the fire and determine its cause is constitutional, the warrantless seizure of evidence while inspecting the premises for these purposes also is constitutional.

However, the Court did mention that officers should take care to make the investigation efficient so as to interfere as little as possible with privacy and cleanup efforts of affected parties.

Other laws affect who can handle high-energy materials. With the passage of the Homeland Security Act of 2002, the regulatory and revenue-collecting functions for alcohol and tobacco were assigned to the newly created Alcohol and Tobacco Tax and Trade Bureau (Department of the Treasury). Functions regarding enforcement of the federal laws for alcohol, tobacco products, firearms, and explosives remained with the ATF as it became a bureau within the Department of Justice.

The Homeland Security Act also amended Title XI of the Organized Crime Control Act of 1970 (the Safe Explosives Act). The new law requires that people who work with explosive materials obtain a federal permit. The act also provided for the ATF to create an explosives training and research center.

SUMMARY

The forensic arson or bomb investigator may arrive long after the crime has taken place and when much of the evidence is burned, destroyed, or blown up at the crime scene.

Energy is the capacity of a system to do work. It is manifest in many forms, including heat, light, and sound, and may be described in terms of a potential, kinetic, or chemical nature. Energy may be converted from one form to another by breaking and making chemical bonds. Every reaction requires activation energy to proceed. The reaction will go in the direction of the more stable products. The heat of combustion is the amount of energy released or the difference in energy between the bonds broken and those produced. Reactions that give off energy in this fashion are called *exothermic*.

Factors affecting fire include rate of reaction, ignition source, range of combustibility, temperature, and flash point of the available fuel. There are many types of "fires" and explosions. Glowing combustion or smoldering is the process of burning fuel without producing a flame. Regular combustion happening in the presence of a flame and is called *burning*. Higher energy materials can produce deflagration, a subsonic combustion process driven by thermoconductivity, or detonation, an extremely rapid, exothermic combustion process that creates a supersonic shock wave within the burning material. The burning rate of a detonation is greater than 2000 meters per second.

A warrant is not needed to begin an arson investigation. To preserve evidence, the investigation should begin as soon as the fire is extinguished. The origin of the fire or blast should be determined and the area documented before further collection of evidence proceeds.

Suspected arson sites should be searched for small fires in several areas, the use of devices to spread fire ("streamers") such as paper or clothing, and ignition in unusual places.

A portable vapor detector or "sniffer" provides a rapid screening test for volatile organic compounds at a fire crime scene. Evidence should be collected in airtight containers to prevent the loss of volatile organic vapors. Substrate control samples, an exemplar of the normal conditions of a room, must also be collected along with any evidence of an ignition device.

In the laboratory, gas chromatography can be used to separate organic compounds present in a sample. Hydrocarbons from accelerants may be matched by retention time to standards. Gas chromatography can be combined with mass spectrometry to identify even the components of very complex mixtures where the carbon chains differ by only one methylene unit.

Explosives are high-energy materials that participate in rapid exothermic reactions. The speed of detonation is so great because these chemicals already have their own oxygen supply or oxidizing agent (whether internal or another chemical). Depending on the rate of reaction, materials are classified as either low explosives or high explosives.

Most low explosives are mixtures of fuel and an oxidizing agent. Low explosives include gunpowder (both black and smokeless powders), methane or ethane gas and air mixtures, and potassium chlorate–sugar mixtures. For low explosives, the rate of reaction is called the *rate* (sometimes *speed*) *of deflagration* or *burning*. Deflagration is characterized as a subsonic pressure wave driven by thermoconductivity.

High explosives are often chemicals that incorporate their own oxygen supply. They must be detonated or initiated by another explosion. High explosives include dynamite, azides, TNT, and so-called "plastic" explosives such as RDX (C-4). For high explosives, the rate of reaction is called the *rate* (or *speed*) *of detonation*. Detonation is characterized by a supersonic pressure wave (shock wave or blast) within the burning material; the burning rate is usually greater than 2000 meters per second. High explosives are further classified into primary and secondary explosives. Primary explosives have low tolerance for heat (including sparks), shock, or friction. Secondary explosives are more stable to heat, electrical discharge, friction, and shock, making them somewhat unsafe for use. When ignited, these explosives will burn rather than detonate.

Taggants for explosives come in two types: detection taggants, used to detect explosives before detonation, and identification taggants, used to determine the source of a material after detonation. Simple taggants have layers of material that code to tell by whom, where, and when a material was created.

Once the origin of an explosion site is determined, sample collection proceeds much like an arson investigation. The investigator must take care because explosives can volatilize and both seep away and contaminate nearby samples.

Surfaces near the origin of detonation must be collected to look for undetonated explosive residue or taggants. Debris in the crater may be sifted through a series of metal sieves to find components of the detonation device. Samples of the debris may be searched by low-power microscopy and washed with acetone. The washings can be submitted for color, crystal, and other testing.

PROBLEMS

1. Give the word or phrase for the following definitions:
   a. the capacity for doing work
   b. reactions that liberate heat
   c. reactions that absorb heat from the surroundings
   d. minimum temperature at which liquid fuel will produce enough vapor to burn
   e. minimum temperature at which fuel will burn
   f. combustion producing a subsonic wave propagated by thermal conductivity
   g. combustion producing a supersonic wave
   h. the addition of oxygen
   i. mixtures of metals
   j. burning without a flame
2. Explain what happens to a combustible mixture above, within, and below the range of combustibility.
3. List the three elements that must be present for a fire to burn.
4. Describe the difference between high and low explosives and give an example of each.
5. Describe the scene at the origin of
   a. a gasoline fire
   b. a low-explosive detonation
   c. a high-explosive detonation
6. Give the chemicals in
   a. black powder
   b. smokeless powder
   c. ANFO
   d. dynamite
   e. detonation cord

7. Describe a procedure for collecting and storing evidence from a suspected arson investigation.
8. Describe a procedure for analyzing arson evidence consisting of several pieces of porous pottery.
9. Describe the uses of a "sniffer" and a vapor concentrator.
10. Explain why the results of the three crystal tests for explosives have to be taken together.

GLOSSARY

Accelerant a flammable liquid or other substance used to start or speed the spread of a fire.

Arson burning a property with criminal or fraudulent intent.

Black powder an explosive consisting of potassium nitrate (75%), carbon (15%), and sulfur (10%).

Combustion the chemical oxidation of a material producing heat and light energy; burning.

Deflagration a subsonic combustion process driven by thermoconductivity (burning material ignites adjacent material); the burning rate is usually less than 2000 meters per second.

Detonation cord (detonating cord, det-cord, primer cord, primacord) an explosive packed in a flexible casing that can be used as a high-speed fuse to set off multiple charges or as a shape charge.

Detonation an extremely rapid, exothermic combustion process that creates a supersonic shock wave within the burning material; the burning rate is usually greater than 2000 meters per second.

Endothermic reaction a chemical reaction that absorbs heat energy from the surroundings.

Energy the capacity of a system to do work; energy may be kinetic, thermal, chemical, potential, electrical, or even light. Energy units include calories, kilocalories, joules, and ergs.

Explosion a violent chemical reaction accompanied by rapid production and expansion of gases. Explosions are categorized as deflagrations (subsonic) and detonations (supersonic), depending on the speed of pressure wave they create.

Exothermic reaction a chemical reaction that liberates heat energy into the surroundings.

Flammable range the range of fuel concentrations in air that can burn.

Flash point the minimum temperature at which a liquid gives off enough vapor to burn when ignited.

Glowing combustion burning without flaming, such as hot charcoal.

Heat of combustion the amount of heat released per unit mass or unit volume of a material when it is burned completely.

High explosive energetic material with a velocity of detonation greater than 1000 meters per second, such as dynamite.

Hydrocarbon a chemical made from carbon and hydrogen.

Ignition temperature the lowest temperature at which a substance will spontaneously ignite and continue burning.

Low explosive energetic material with a velocity of detonation less than 1000 meters per second, such as gunpowders.

Modus operandi from Latin, meaning "method of operation," the repeated action of criminal behavior that may be used in profiling.

Oxidation a chemical reaction in which an atom loses electrons (inorganic process) or a molecule gains oxygen or loses hydrogen (organic process).

Oxidizing agent a chemical reagent that accepts electrons from an atom (inorganic process) or donates oxygen to a molecule (organic process).

Primary explosive a high-energy material detonated by heat or shock.

Pyrolysis (thermal decomposition) literally, breaking by heat; breakdown of materials caused by heat.

Safety fuse less reactive than a detonation cord, it is a flexible tube containing black powder used to set off other charges.

Secondary explosive an explosive that must be detonated by a primary explosive.

Smokeless powder an explosive made of nitrocellulose (single based) or a mixture of nitrocellulose and nitroglycerin (double-based).

Spontaneous combustion combustion caused by an exothermic reaction producing sufficient heat to ignite.

Clockwise from top center: alcohol (whisky); drugs of abuse (Heroin); poison warning sign; natural poisons (foxglove). All images from Stockxpert.

CHAPTER 10

Forensic Toxicology

Case Study

Marie Besnard

When Léon Besnard died on October 25, 1947, apparently from uremia, he was buried without fuss in Loudon, France, where he had lived for many years with his wife, Marie. The Besnards were wealthy, mainly through the good fortune of several inheritances. However, after Léon's death, suspicions began to grow that the inheritances had come about by poisoning at the hand of Marie and not by good fortune. Shortly before his death, Léon had confided in Louise Pintou, the village postmistress who probably was also Léon's lover, that he believed he was being poisoned and that in the event of his death she should alert the police. This she did, and before long the investigators had compiled a list of 13 suspicious deaths linked to Marie, ranging from Léon's parents to Marie's cousins to the Rivets, a childless couple who had formed an attachment to the Besnards and lived with them until the Rivets's deaths. In every case, Marie was either directly named as heir or had a link to the inheritance through Léon or another family member.

The body of Léon was exhumed on May 11, 1949. Tests showed the presence of arsenic in his remains, with this finding leading to the exhumation of the other bodies. Most were highly decomposed, but arsenic was found in each. Marie's trial began in February 1952. The circumstantial case was overwhelming. Thirteen deaths all ultimately benefited Marie financially, and some with strange circumstances. Thus Marie's 88-year-old cousin, Pauline, died in July 1945; Marie reported that Pauline had mistakenly eaten a bowl of lye instead of her desert. Her sister Virginie apparently made the same terrible mistake just a week later. How anyone would consume a whole bowl of corrosive lye, how such a substance would be left around a kitchen in a bowl, and how Virginie would make the same mistake as her sister all added up to a pretty remarkable set of circumstances.

All that was needed was that at the trial believable evidence should be presented of the presence of lethal quantities of arsenic in the bodies. That did not happen.

Four toxicologists had tested remains from the exhumations, and all had identified the presence of arsenic. The first tests, on the body of Léon, were conducted by Dr. Georges Béroud. He had used the Marsh test to recover and identify arsenic in the samples. The end point of the Marsh test is a mirror-like deposit of arsenic that condenses on a cool glass surface. It is known that antimony can produce a similar deposit, but Béroud had not conducted a test that would have confirmed the substance was arsenic and not antimony. Worse, under cross-examination he asserted that he could identify arsenic mirrors by their appearance.

The defense then produced a set of glass tubes and asked him to identify which ones had arsenic mirrors. He studied the set, removed some tubes, and responded that the remaining ones were arsenic. The defense then produced an affidavit from the professor of chemistry in Paris who had prepared the sample and that showed that none contained arsenic. The trial was suspended and a new panel of experts appointed to repeat the tests.

The second trial began 2 years later. This time the testing had been conducted with considerably greater rigor, and five of the cases were dropped. The testing may have been more reliable, but the defense attorneys were able to show that the authenticity of the samples was highly questionable. Once more the trial was abandoned, new experts engaged, and a new trial set.

The third and last trial was held in 1961. The prosecution was confident that it had closed all the loopholes revealed in the earlier trials. For example, it was able to have samples tested by neutron activation analysis, a new but very specific test.

But the defense was not done yet: This time the attorneys were able to show that there were high levels of arsenic in the groundwater at the cemetery and that it was highly likely that the remains — especially those in an advanced state of decomposition—had been contaminated. Public opinion was also changing from perceiving Marie Besnard as a cold-blooded poisoner—"the Black Widow of Loudon"—to the victim of an incompetent and overly drawn-out prosecution. She was acquitted by the jury after a relatively short deliberation.

Too little can be as bad as too much, but sometimes any is more than enough: An epileptic may have contributed to a traffic accident because not taking the right dose of the prescribed medicine at the right time meant that blood levels of the drug were below that required to control seizures. In other cases any amount is too much and the drug is banned: Many sports prohibit performance-enhancing drugs, and several jurisdictions have a zero blood alcohol limit for young drivers.

INTRODUCTION

Toxicology is the science of poisons and their effect on living organisms. In forensic toxicology the poisons are mainly drugs, and the organism is usually a human. A drug becomes a poison when the amount of it in the body is high enough that its chemical action impairs, injures, or kills. All the drugs described in Chapter 8, "Drugs and Pharmaceuticals," can be poisons, as can medicinal drugs and organic and inorganic substances deliberately selected because of their toxicity.

Forensic toxicology is often divided into two areas: **postmortem toxicology**, where the human is dead and the toxicologist is seeking to identify one or more poisons in the body in quantities that could be the cause of death; and **antemortem toxicology**, where the human is alive and the purpose of the investigation is to determine whether or not the drug has resulted in impairment that either contravenes a law or regulation, or could be a contributory factor in a crime (see Table 10.1).

Now more than half a century old, the case of Marie Besnard illustrates many of the challenges facing the forensic toxicologist. The amounts of substance in blood are low, and the accuracy of tests may be compromised by the presence of similar materials in the sample. In the Besnard case, there was the similar response of antimony in the mirror test; in more modern and more typical cases, there is the presence of **metabolites** of organic drugs. The authenticity of samples is vital in all forensic science investigations, in terms of an unchallenged chain of custody from collection to testing, as is protection against contamination.

Table 10.1	Some Examples of Investigations and Drugs Encountered in Toxicology	
Postmortem Toxicology	**Investigation**	**Examples**
	Homicide	Arsenic, insulin, ricin
	Suicide	Hypnotics, tranquilizers, morphine
	Accidental	Herbicides, carbon monoxide
Antemortem Toxicology	**Investigation**	**Examples**
	Vehicle accidents	Alcohol, recreational drugs
	Sexual assault	GHB, Rohypnol, alcohol
	Performance altering	Steroids and HGH, furosemide and anti-inflammatories (horse racing), β-blockers (shooting)

There is considerable overlap; for example, carbon monoxide is encountered in suicide, and the circumstances of the death or alleged offense are important.

The Besnard investigation fell down on both counts. The case also showed that advances in analytical chemistry will not always rescue a fundamentally flawed case; for example, a case with arsenic in samples of dubious origin and possibly present because of contamination remains of no probative value whether the results were obtained from the dated Marsh mirror or a modern neutron activation analysis procedure.

Poisoning homicides are relatively rare, and most of the work of the forensic toxicologist in death investigation is concerned with identification of medicinal or recreational drugs. Antemortem toxicology is concerned with essentially the same substances, and the focus of most of this chapter is therefore on drugs (including alcohol). In the United States, postmortem toxicology is usually conducted in specialized laboratories associated with a medical examiner or coroner facility. The bulk of the toxicology carried out in crime laboratories is related to blood alcohol determination, either direct testing of samples or the calibration and maintenance of breath-testing devices operated by police officers.

Toxicology is one of the least used but most demanding of disciplines in forensic science. It can require a combination of cutting-edge analytical chemistry with a sound knowledge of pharmacology and drug **metabolism**.

Data interpretation in forensic toxicology requires an understanding of the way in which the body is affected by drugs, as well as the way that the drugs themselves are absorbed into the bloodstream, distributed throughout different body tissues, and removed by metabolism—sometimes referred to as **biotransformation**—and **excretion**.

DRUG ABSORPTION

Apart from drugs applied topically to treat lesions on skin, such as steroids or antibiotics used to treat infections or inflammation, drugs must enter the blood to be effective. Intravenous injection administers the drug directly into the blood, but most drugs are administered by mouth and have to pass from the gastrointestinal tract into the blood and then to the rest of the body.

Drug Absorption from the Gastrointestinal Tract

Most drugs are taken orally and **drug absorption** takes place via the gastrointestinal (GI) tract. The amount of intact drug absorbed and the rate at which it reaches the systemic circulation after oral administration is termed the *bioavailability* of the drug. Some drugs are ineffective when given by mouth. This can be because they are destroyed in the gut, as with the peptide hormone insulin, or for other reasons, as with vitamin B12, which requires a cofactor to be absorbed.

BOX 10.1   BIOAVAILABILITY

Factors affecting bioavailability include the following:

- The rate of release of drug from its dosage form: Tablets must dissolve first.
- Solubility in the acid environment of the stomach and alkaline environment of the intestine: Generally, only unionized drugs are absorbed.
- Gastric emptying: Most drugs are mainly absorbed in the small intestine and take about 1 to 2 hours to reach that site; delayed gastric emptying will result in delayed absorption and possibly degradation of alkaline drugs but increased absorption of acidic ones.
- Rate of metabolism in the liver: Blood from the gastrointestinal tract first passes through the liver, and drugs that are extensively metabolized in the liver have a low bioavailability because some drug is metabolized before it can reach the general circulation.

STRUCTURE OF THE GASTROINTESTINAL TRACT

The GI tract has three major regions: stomach, small intestine, and large intestine. As a drug passes through these regions, it encounters changes in pH, enzymes, electrolytes, and surface features, which can influence drug absorption. (See Figure 10.1.)

The digestive secretions of the stomach provide a highly acid environment. Most drugs are weak bases and so do not experience significant **absorption** in the stomach. Acid drugs, such as aspirin, are mainly absorbed here.

The small intestine is the most important GI site for drug absorption. It is a large organ, about 20 feet long, and the digestive secretions of the small intestine provide a mildly alkaline environment. The surface of the intestine is covered with finger-like projections called **villi**, and the surfaces of the villi themselves are covered with *microvilli*. The anatomy and chemistry of the small intestine therefore provide an environment that is ideal for the absorption of most drugs. (See Figure 10.2.)

The large intestine lacks the villi and microvilli of the small intestine but serves as a site for the absorption of a drug that has not been completely absorbed in the small intestine or that has been administered as a rectal suppository.

MECHANISMS OF DRUG TRANSPORT ACROSS THE GASTROINTESTINAL BARRIER

The majority of drugs cross the membrane by passive diffusion. The drug transport rate is determined by its physicochemical properties—only the neutral, unionized drug is absorbed—and its concentration gradient between the solution in the intestinal contents and that in the blood flowing through lining cells.

Drug Absorption at Other Sites

The same principles apply to drugs administered by skin patch as with contraceptive steroids or nicotine replacement, snorted as with cocaine, smoked as with hash joints or in a bong, or given as suppositories as with some anti-inflammatory drugs (see Figure 10.3).

Skin patches are used clinically because diffusion across the skin is not very efficient. The patch therefore provides a way to permit a steady delivery of small amounts to the bloodstream over a relatively long period. In contrast, the nasal cavity has a lining with a rich supply of blood and can deliver snorted drug directly to circulating blood without the delay or loss in the process of absorption and passage through the liver when taken by mouth. Smoking also delivers drug to a blood-rich surface—the lung—and from there to the general circulation. Although drug is obviously lost in the process, smoking produces a rapid and potentially controllable route of administration.

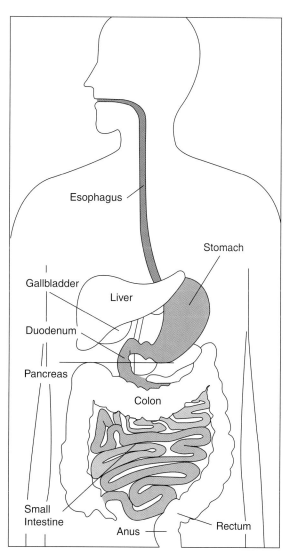

FIGURE 10.1
The digestive system. The organs that are important to drug absorption are the stomach, the duodenum and small intestine, and the liver. From http://digestive.niddk.nih.gov/ddiseases/pubs/uppergi/index.htm

211

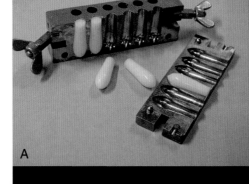

FIGURE 10.2
Intestinal villi. The villi create a very large surface area in the intestine that greatly facilitates absorption of nutrients and of drugs. From Stockxpert.

DRUG DISTRIBUTION

The concentration of drug in the blood varies with time following administration. Figure 10.4 shows the typical pattern that results from oral administration. There is a rise to a peak, usually within 2 hours of administration, followed by a curvilinear fall and finally a linear decline (note that the scale on the concentration axis is logarithmic).

The **absorption curve** reflects the processes of absorption, distribution, and elimination. Absorption and elimination are one-way processes, but distribution is two-way process, with drug leaving the blood into tissues but also being returned, depending on the concentration gradient. Only drug that is in solution in body water is free to distribute between tissues. Substances bound to proteins in blood or tissues or that are preferentially stored in body fat will not participate in the active two-way distribution. See Table 10.2 for examples.

212

FIGURE 10.3
Some routes of drug administration: A, medical suppository mold; B, cocaine lines for snorting; C, bong for smoking hash. These are all used in addition to the normal routes of oral administration and injections. Bong and lines from Stockxpert; suppository, from http://en.wikipedia.org/wiki/Image:Suppository_casting_mould_2.jpg

The early relatively steep fall in concentration is mainly the result of distribution, and indeed this part of the concentration–time curve is called the **distribution phase**. The last part of the curve is called the **elimination phase**; distribution is still taking place but is in equilibrium. The slope of the terminal curve (k), in which the logarithm of the concentration versus time is linear, is used to calculate the half-life ($T_{1/2}$) of the drug in the body thus:

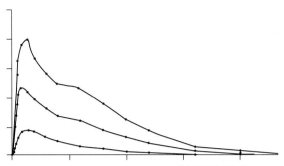

$$\text{Half-life} = 0.693/k$$

The extent of distribution of drug throughout the body will affect its concentration in blood. The more extensive the distribution, the lower the concentration. The concept is usually expressed using the term **volume of distribution (V_d)**, which is the amount of drug in the body divided by its concentration in blood. It is conventional to calculate the V_d from the data in the postdistribution phase of the concentration–time curve. V_d will also depend on the reference body fluid for concentration—whole blood, plasma, or serum. Clinical data mostly are based on serum or plasma, but forensic toxicology data often use whole blood because of the difficulty in obtaining pure serum from postmortem samples.

FIGURE 10.4
Typical concentration–time curve for a drug given by mouth. Each curve represents a doubling of the dose given. Y-axis: Concentration on a logarithmic scale where each mark represents a doubling of concentration. x-axis: Time on a linear scale. Depending on the drug the scale may be anything from minutes to days. Curves generated by the author from typical data.

213

Table 10.2	Some Examples of Toxicity Arising from Distribution of Drug or Poison in the Body	
Substance	**Distribution**	**Effect**
Warfarin	More than 95% bound to plasma protein	Bound warfarin can be displaced by acidic drugs such as aspirin. Reducing the bound fraction to 90% doubles the unbound amount with serious consequences for control of clotting.
Digoxin	Bound to heart tissue	Postmortem biochemical changes result in diffusion of digoxin from the stores back into blood. Tests on postmortem blood may therefore overestimate the predeath levels.
DDT	Sequestered in body fat	Long-term residues in animal tissues with consequences for chronic toxicity and persistence in the food chain.

When is a volume not a volume? When it is the volume of distribution of a drug. With very few exceptions, the V_d of a drug has no real meaning in terms of the volume of a physiological tissue or fluid. It is simply a proportionality constant relating blood concentration to amount of drug in the body.

DRUG METABOLISM
Drug Metabolism in the Liver

The liver is the main site of drug metabolism, primarily through oxidation mediated by the cytochrome P-450 enzyme system. Other metabolic reactions in the liver include dealkylation and conjugation. The common factor is that the drug is converted into a more polar form that can be readily excreted in bile or urine. The main form of conjugation is with glucuronic acid. Some drugs, such as morphine, are extensively conjugated, and their detection in body fluids is made easier by hydrolysis of the glucuronide to increase the amount of drug available for identification and quantitation.

When reviewing concentration–toxicity data for conjugated drugs it is important to know whether or not the assay was performed on samples that have been hydrolyzed, and the process involved. Data can be compared only when the same treatments and assays have been used to generate the sets.

Not all drug metabolic pathways result in the formation of an inactive compound. Many metabolites show similar pharmacologic activity to the parent compound. In some cases the **metabolite** may be more toxic than the parent drug. Thus, a large part of the toxicity of methanol is due to its metabolism to formic acid and formaldehyde. Table 10.3 shows some examples of drugs and their metabolites.

Table 10.3	Examples of Drugs and Their Metabolites	
Drug Class	**Parent Compound**	**Major Metabolites**
Benzodiazepines	Diazepam	Desmethyldiazepam, oxazepam, oxazepam glucuronide
Cannabinoids	Tetrahydrocannabinol (THC)	THC-acid
Cocaine	Cocaine	Benzoylecgonine, ecgonine methyl ester, norcocaine, ecgonine, cocaethylene
Opioids	Codeine	Morphine, norcodeine
	Heroin (diacetylmorphine)	6-Monoacetylmorphine, morphine
	Morphine	Morphine-3- and morphine-6-glucuronide
	Oxycodone	Oxymorphone, noroxycodone
Other	Nicotine	Cotinine, nicotine-1′-N-oxide, hydroxycotinine, norcotinine

The examples include demethylation (desmethyldiazepam, norcodeine), deacetylation (6-monoacetylmorphine and morphine from heroin), and conjugation (morphine glucuronide and ecgonine methyl ester).

Drug Metabolism in Other Tissues

The liver is the primary organ of drug metabolism because of the location of the necessary enzymes for oxidation and conjugation. Other tissues contain enzymes capable of biotransformation. For example, the enzyme pseudocholinesterase found in plasma is responsible for metabolism of the muscle relaxant drugs succinylcholine and mivacurium. Individuals with an inherited deficiency in pseudocholinesterase activity may show toxicity when given these drugs due to impaired clearance from blood.

DRUG EXCRETION

Drugs and their metabolites are removed from the body by excretion. The main pathway is excretion into urine through the kidney, but some conjugated drugs show significant excretion into bile, and volatiles can show slight excretion through the lungs into expired air.

In addition to being a route of elimination, excretion via the kidney is an important process for the toxicologist as urine is often presented as the sample for drug analysis.

BOX 10.2   URINE AND TOXICOLOGY

The advantages of using urine as a substrate in postmortem toxicology are that the amount of drug present can be much higher than that in blood, urine is often available at autopsy, and it is free from contamination due to postmortem redistribution or leakage of gastric contents. In the living, samples are easy to obtain, will contain more of the target drug, and do not require invasive sampling procedures. In both situations, urine has the disadvantage that concentrations of drug in urine cannot be directly compared to those in blood, and the specificity of analyses may be affected by high levels of metabolites in the sample.

Plasma is filtered in the renal corpuscles at the rate of about 125 mL per minute in a healthy adult. The water conservation process is so effective that only about 1 mL of urine is actually excreted each minute. There are specific mechanisms to regulate the reabsorption of electrolytes such as sodium and potassium. Some drugs also undergo active transport in the renal tubules.

The role of the kidney is to eliminate waste products such as urea but conserve essential substances such as water and electrolytes. Figure 10.5 shows the gross anatomy of the kidney. The functional unit of filtration in the renal corpuscle is the glomerulus, a capillary tuft from which arterial pressure filters water together with ions and small neutral molecules dissolved in it through the Bowman's capsule and into the renal tubule. As the filtrate passes through the tubule, water is reabsorbed and the concentration of excreted materials increases by about 100-fold.

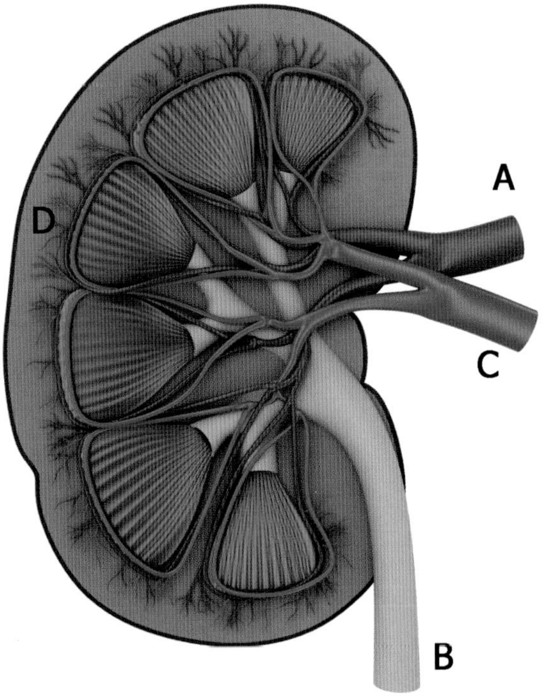

Just as with absorption, the acidity of the drug and the pH of its environment will affect the degree to which it is reabsorbed. Neutral drugs at neutral pH will more or less mimic what happens to water. Their concentration in urine as it is formed will be similar to the concentration in plasma. Basic drugs will be ionized in acidic urine and poorly reabsorbed; it is similar for acidic drugs in alkaline urine.

These basic principles of filtration and reabsorption explain why some drugs are found at high concentration in urine and there is not a one-to-one correspondence in urine and plasma drug levels. Added to this, urine is collected in the bladder until there is sufficient volume stored to promote voiding at a volume of approximately 500 mL. Even if there has been no significant concentration of drug, the volume of urine available for testing means that the amount of drug will be much greater than that which can be obtained from blood.

FIGURE 10.5
The kidney. Drug is delivered to the kidney in arterial blood (A, entering from the right side of the illustration). It is filtered in the renal corpuscles and passed from the kidney dissolved in urine which drains into the bladder through the ureter (cream colored tube B). Some drug will be reabsorbed with water into the blood leaving the kidney (C) and so re-enter the general circulation. The renal corpuscles (D) are located at the outer edge of the kidney; they are not visible in this illustration but the blood supply to (red) and from (blue) the corpuscles can be seen. From StockXpert.

DRUG ANALYSIS IN FORENSIC TOXICOLOGY

Analysis of drugs in toxicology is a much more demanding process than analysis of the same material in bulk samples. The levels of the drug will be many orders of magnitude less, and the presence of metabolites and endogenous materials can complicate the process. Traditionally, toxicology analyses have begun with an extraction to purify and concentrate the drug. The extract is then reconstituted and subjected to qualitative and quantitative analysis. Modern techniques have made the extraction process much more efficient, and some, such as immunoassays (IA) and liquid chromatography–dual mass spectrometry (LC-MS-MS), allow the extraction phase to be bypassed.

Sample Extraction Procedures

LIQUID–LIQUID EXTRACTION

The traditional procedure for **extraction** of drug from body tissues dates back to the late nineteenth century and is often referred to as the Stass–Otto technique of liquid–liquid extraction. The target **analyte** is extracted from an aqueous solution into an organic solvent. How well the analyte extracts into the solvent depends largely on its being in a neutral, unionized form. The degree of drug ionization is dependent on the pH of the environment and the chemical characteristics of the drug. Weak acids (salicylic acid) and bases (cocaine, amphetamine) are incompletely or slightly ionized in solution. **Amphoteric drugs** have both acid and base properties (morphine, BZE).

If an immiscible organic solvent is added to an aqueous solution of a drug, the drug will **partition** between the two phases. The degree to which a drug partitions between an aqueous and an organic medium depends on the relative hydrophilic ("water liking") and lipophilic ("lipid liking") nature of the compound. *Polar drugs,* those with ionized functional groups such as OH⁻ and N⁺, tend to partition into the aqueous phase, whereas nonpolar compounds will partition into the organic solvent. A compound that is ionized has a greater affinity for the aqueous phase than an unionized compound, which will tend to move into the organic phase.

The blood or other tissue is first mixed with an acidic buffer and then shaken with organic solvent. Any acid drugs will be partitioned into the solvent. An alkaline buffer is then added and the extraction repeated to separate the alkaline drugs into the solvent. There are many variants of the technique in regard to the nature of the buffer and solvents employed, but all are based on the preceding principle of partitioning of neutral chemical molecules from an aqueous to an organic phase. If the extraction is being conducted for the analysis of a known target drug, only one extraction is needed; some other variants use finely specified buffers and recover a neutral fraction.

Amphoteric compounds such as morphine exhibit both acid and base properties. While these compounds can be extracted to some extent using acid or base extraction procedures, optimal extraction can be achieved only by carefully adjusting the pH to get the drug into an unionized form. For morphine, this is around pH 8.

217

BOX 10.3   LIQUID AND SOLID PHASE EXTRACTION

Disadvantages of liquid–liquid extraction:

- Emulsions may form, trapping the drug.
- Immiscible solvents are required.
- The process is time consuming.
- Glassware cleanup is required.
- Large volumes of solvents are used, causing health and safety implications.
- The process is operator dependent (some skill is involved).

SPE has these advantages compared to liquid–liquid extractions:

- Selectivity: Extraction processes can be designed to selectively extract an analyte or class of analytes.
- Reproducibility: SPE eliminates emulsion formation, reduces the dependence on operator technique, and improves extraction reproducibility.
- Speed: Vacuum manifolds allow the simultaneous extraction of multiple samples, while low volumes of solvent used reduce the time for evaporation steps. Unlike with liquid extractions, automation is easy.

SOLID-PHASE EXTRACTION

The disadvantages of liquid–liquid extraction led to the development of solid-phase methods.

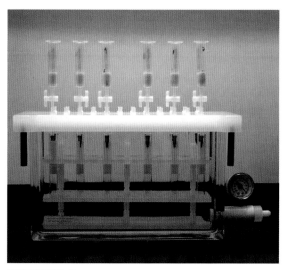

FIGURE 10.6
SPE extraction manifold. The manifold holds six cartridges (top) which elute into sample tubes (bottom) aided by vacuum applied to the manifold at the right side. From http://en.wikipedia.org/wiki/Image:SPE_Manifold.jpg

Solid-phase extraction (SPE) uses inert cartridges filled with a solid stationary phase. There are several stationary phases available, the choice depending on the materials to be separated. Most consist of silica particles with a bonded coating that features a specific functional group: hydrocarbon chains for reverse-phase separation of organics; quaternary ammonium or carboxyl groups for ion exchange.

The exact process used in SPE will depend on the nature of the stationary phase in the cartridge, but generally it consists of preconditioning followed by pH adjustment and then application of the sample and pulling it through the cartridge. The column is then rinsed to remove endogenous substances and analytes in which we have no interest. Finally, the analyte of interest is eluted from the column and collected into a tube using a suitable solvent. (See Figure 10.6.)

The strength of the eluting solvent can be adjusted to optimize the elution of the analyte of interest while at the same time minimizing the amount of endogenous material removed from the column. Solvent strength can be determined by reference to an elutropic series, such as hexane, ethyl ether, chloroform, methylene chloride, acetone, acetonitrile, methanol, and water. In this example, hexane is the least, and water the most, polar solvent. The polarity of aqueous solvents can be increased further by the addition of acids or bases.

Analytical Procedures

IMMUNOASSAYS

Immunoassays work on the principle of competition between a drug (analyte) present in the sample and a labeled drug for binding sites on an antibody specific for the drug of interest. Assays must exhibit *specificity* (the degree to which an assay correctly identifies a compound of interest) and *sensitivity* (the assay's ability to detect an analyte in a sample). The higher the concentration of the drug in the sample, the lower the concentration of labeled drug that will bind to the antibody. The label on the drug can be a radioisotope (radiolabel), an active enzyme, or a fluorescent label (optical label).

The basic technique, known as a **competitive binding assay**, consists of placing a fixed quantity of the antibody in a tube together with a fixed quantity of labeled drug and the drug sample to be assayed. The specific binding sites on the antibody bind both the labeled drug molecules and the unlabeled drug molecules present in the test sample; the proportion of labeled drug molecules bound is inversely proportional to the number of unlabeled drug molecules. A suitable analytical measurement is then made and the results compared against a calibration curve.

For radioimmunoassay, and for optimum sensitivity with optical immunoassays, bound and unbound drug must be separated before analytical measurements are made. Separation steps can be hindered by endogenous components of the body fluid being tested. For example, a separation system that works well with plasma may not work so well with urine.

There are a number of different immunoassay techniques, each a modification of the basic principle explained previously, including the following:

- Radioimmunoassay (RIA)
- Enzyme-linked immunosorbent assay (ELISA)
- Enzyme-multiplied immunoassay technique (EMIT)
- Fluorescent polarization immunoassay (FPIA)
- Cloned enzyme-donor immunoassay (CEDIA)

These systems have their own advantages, disadvantages, and specific applications.

CROSS-REACTIVITY

The specificity of an antibody is determined by comparing the binding of that antibody to the drug against which it is raised with the binding affinity of the same antibody to other related drugs and metabolites. The extent to which other drugs and metabolites interfere is known as **cross-reactivity** and may give false positive assay results (the test indicates the presence of a specific analyte when it's not actually present; instead, it has cross-reacted with a structurally similar molecule). See also in Chapter 11, "Forensic Biology," the section entitled "Immunology and Forensic Biology."

Cross-reactivity means that IA techniques are best reserved for screening. Many are set up with a cut-off level that must be exceeded before a positive result is accepted.

219

Immunoassays have applications in postmortem investigations, workplace drug testing, and human performance investigation. Urine is usually the matrix of choice because it has fewer interfering compounds and decomposition products. Blood assays are more complicated due to interfering compounds. Immunoassays make excellent screening tests and are specified as such in the Substance Abuse and Mental Health Services Administration (SAMHSA) Mandatory Guidelines for Federal Workplace Drug Testing Programs. In addition to being rapid and requiring minimal sample pretreatment, IA techniques can be automated and allow for high-volume throughput.

CHROMATOGRAPHY

Traditional chromatographic methods such as thin-layer chromatography (TLC) and gas chromatography (GC) have been applied to analysis of extracts in forensic toxicology to assist in identifying the presence of drugs and poisons. Some of the techniques, such as GC coupled with mass spectrometry (GC-MS), are sensitive and can provide quantitative information. The various methods and their main advantages and disadvantages are summarized in Table 10.4. Liquid chromatography coupled with dual mass spectrometry (LC-MS-MS) is becoming the method of choice.

Table 10.4	Comparison of Chromatography Systems Used in Toxicology Analyses	
System	**Advantages**	**Disadvantages**
Thin layer (TLC)	Simple to use. When coupled with specific reagent sprays can provide good information as to class of drug present.	Not very good separation of similar substances. Need several different systems for broad screening. Not very sensitive. Not quantitative.
Gas (GC)	Reasonably sensitive. Good separation, especially with capillary columns. Quantitative.	Samples are introduced to the separation column as gases— must be thermostable and capable of vaporization.
GC-MS	Use of mass spectrometer as detector gives high degree of specificity.	Same as GC.
High-performance liquid (HPLC)	Excellent for nonvolatiles and thermolabile drugs. Good separation of similar compounds. Can be very specific, especially when coupled with diode array detector.	Not always very sensitive. Systems can be tricky to maintain.
HPLC-MS	Use of mass spectrometer as detector gives high degree of specificity.	Same as HPLC.

LIQUID CHROMATOGRAPHY–DUAL MASS SPECTROMETRY (LC-MS-MS)

LC-MS and LC-MS-MS combine the wide-ranging separation powers of HPLC (high-performance liquid chromatography) with the specificity of detection that is provided by mass spectrometry. The main hurdle to the introduction of LC-MS was the development of a suitable interface that could take the liquid effluent from the HPLC and introduce it to the MS. The problem was solved by the introduction of electrospray ionization interfaces. Analyte in solvent is pumped at pressure through a capillary from which it exits as a fine aerosol. The neutral solvent is evaporated and the aerosol droplets break up, driven by coulombic forces arising from the presence of like-charged analyte molecules. This results in solvent-free lone ions of analyte being introduced to the analyzer part of the mass spectrometer. Other sample introduction systems used include thermospray, fast atom bombardment, and atmospheric pressure chemical ionization (API (see Figure 10.7)).

In LC-MS-MS, the LC is used mainly as a sample cleanup and introduction system. The mass detector is programmed to select specific ions in the effluent, and they are then fragmented. This process, also known as *tandem mass spectrometry*, is very fast—analyses can be completed in less than a minute—and specific. The technique is extremely sensitive and can detect femtogram quantities of analyte, compared to micrograms with TLC, nanograms with GC and HPLC, and picograms with GC-MS and LC-MS.

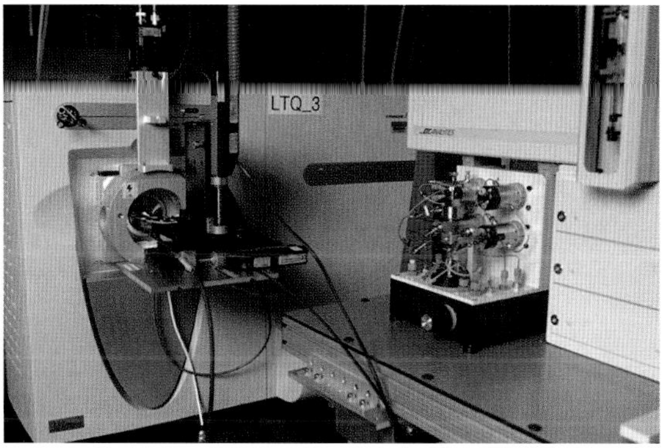

FIGURE 10.7
LC-MS-MS. The instrument shown is the ThermoFinnegan LTQ Liquid Chromatograph–Mass Spectrometer. From http://en.wikipedia.org/wiki/Image:Ltq_lcms.jpg

ALCOHOL

Introduction

Alcohol is ethyl alcohol, or ethanol. It is one of a family of chemicals of the general formula $C_nH_{2n+1}OH$. Ethanol is the second member and has the formula C_2H_5OH. Alcohol has been taken socially for centuries. Alcoholic beverages are appreciated esthetically, and moderate intake of wine has been associated with reduced risk of heart attack. On the other hand, it is an addictive depressant drug, which is poisonous at high concentrations. Chronic abuse can result in liver failure. It is a well-established significant causal factor in road traffic accidents.

Alcohol in alcoholic beverages is produced from fermentation of sugar by yeasts. In beers and wines the concentration of alcohol is about 5% and 13% alcohol by volume, respectively. The final alcohol concentration is determined by the amount of sugar in the starting material and the duration of the fermentation. There is a natural maximum of about 15% as the alcohol kills off the yeast at higher concentration. Stronger alcoholic beverages are produced by distillation of the fermented liquor, or the addition (fortification) of distilled alcohol. Spirits usually have alcohol concentrations around 40%.

Pharmacology

Alcohol is a central nervous system depressant. The observed effects depend on the sequence in which alcohol depresses functions controlled by the brain. The first effect is on the area responsible for inhibitions. The sequence continues through speech (slurring and unmoderated volume) to motor (staggering) to coma (passing out). If enough is taken, death due to depression of the center controlling breathing will result.

Consumption of ethanol can affect a person's judgment, job-performing ability, driving performance, and health. In moderate doses alcohol can induce sociability, reduce inhibitions, and induce relaxation. Increasing doses will lead to negative effects such as inattentiveness, reduced motor reflexes, increased risk taking, confusion, and, at very high doses, dizziness, nausea, loss of coordination and balance, blurred or impaired vision, and possibly respiratory depression.

People vary in their sensitivity to the effects of alcohol intake and the relationship between intake and blood alcohol level. However, the physiological processes are well understood and the variation is a normal biological phenomenon. Blood alcohol concentrations can generally be related to certain behavioral and cognitive skills. In a moderate drinker, alcohol will generally induce unconsciousness at levels of 0.35 g/100 mL and above. Even at this level, death may result from aspirating vomit or respiratory collapse. However, blood levels of 0.5 g/100 mL are quite common, and levels as high as 1.10 g/100 mL have been reported in heavy users who have developed alcohol tolerance.

STAGES OF ACUTE ALCOHOL INTOXICATION

In the U.S., **blood alcohol concentration (BAC)** is usually expressed as grams of ethanol per 100 mL of blood, or simply as percent alcohol. There is a well-established relationship between BAC and effect, and this is summarized in Table 10.5. When reading the table, it is important to bear in mind the preceding and following comments regarding the wide range of individual variation and the effects of tolerance.

TOLERANCE

Many people show marked tolerance to the effects of alcohol. Tolerance results from chronic ethanol or drug use and requires increasingly larger doses of the agent to produce the desired effects. For example, most people will be unconscious at blood alcohol levels of 0.35%, but these sorts of readings are encountered regularly in the laboratory in samples from drunk drivers. There are recorded cases of recovery from alcoholic coma with blood levels greater than 1%.

Absorption, Distribution, and Metabolism of Alcohol

The small intestine is the main site of alcohol absorption. The rate at which the alcohol enters the bloodstream depends on a number of factors.

Alcohol displays two unusual characteristics in regard to the manner in which it is handled by the body. First, it is one of the few drugs where the volume of distribution is indeed a physiological space. After absorption, alcohol is distributed mostly in body water. This means that the same amount of alcohol consumed will result in a blood alcohol level inversely proportional to lean body size. Lean body mass is about 70% of the weight of a man of normal build and about 60% for a woman. The second difference is that the decline in alcohol BAC with time is linear, not log-linear as with other drugs. This makes it relatively easy to relate alcohol consumption, body size, time, and BAC.

Alcohol infusions can be used as energy sources in intravenous nutrition. Some unconscious vehicle accident victims are alcoholics, and the alcohol subdues any **delirium tremens** (the "DTs") as well as provides energy.

222

Table 10.5	Approximate Relation Between BAC and Effects of Alcohol Consumption	
BAC (g/100 mL)	**Stage of Impairment**	**Effects**
Less than 0.02	Basal: There is a low level of endogenous ethanol in the blood, usually less than 0.02%.	None visible.
0.02–0.05	No noticeable effect.	Normal behavior. Specialized sensitive laboratory tests may reveal some impairment.
0.04–0.10	Euphoric.	Behavioral inhibitions are reduced; increased talkativeness and self-confidence. Judgment will begin to be impaired at the lower range, and motor skills and reaction times will begin to be impaired at the higher range.
0.08–0.20	Excitation.	Comprehension, critical judgment, and reaction time are impaired. Emotions are not fully under control; drowsiness.
0.15–0.30	Confusion.	Disorientation, slurred speech, staggering, lethargy.
0.25–0.35	Stupor.	Poor motor control, unable to stand, vomiting, stupor or sleep.
0.30 and higher	Coma.	Unconscious, hypothermia, respiratory depression, respiratory arrest, and death.

Note that the BAC values overlap with those in the category above and below.

The liver metabolizes more than 90% of an ethanol dose, mainly by oxidation by **alcohol dehydrogenase (ADH)**. The average elimination rate is well established as being a reduction in BAC of about 0.015% per hour, with a range of approximately 0.09 to 0.25.

Despite many urban legends and claimed cures, there is nothing effective that can be done to increase the elimination rate of alcohol. Once you have drunk too much you just have to be sure not to drive and be prepared to wait for Mother Nature to run her course.

> ### BOX 10.4 ALCOHOL ABSORPTION
>
> The rate of alcohol absorption is increased by the following:
>
> - Drinking on an empty stomach
> - Drinking when the intestine is irritated and local blood flow is increased
> - Drinking carbonated beverages
> - Drinking beverages with an alcohol concentration of 10 to 30%
>
> The rate of alcohol absorption is reduced by the following:
>
> - Drinking with food
> - Drinking when gastric emptying time is prolonged
>
> Combination effects mean that diluting spirits with carbonated drinks (such as rum and coke, rye and dry, or scotch and soda) will increase the rate of absorption. However, in many cases the diluted drink is consumed more slowly and so the more rapid absorption is offset.

It so happens that the usual volumes of alcoholic beverages and the concentration of alcohol in them are such that there is approximately the same amount of alcohol in a standard drink (shot of liquor, glass of wine, or a glass of beer). It also happens that the amount of alcohol in a standard drink is about the same as is eliminated from the body in an hour. It is emphasized that the normal variation in size, body composition, elimination rates, and absorption rates all come together to result in a very wide range of possible blood alcohol levels per drink and in the time to eliminate the alcohol from the blood. There is thus no "safe" rate of drinking in terms of blood (or breath) alcohol levels.

> ### BOX 10.5 BAC AND DRINKS
>
> The rule of thumb regarding standard drinks and BAC is less valid now than it was 5 or 10 years ago. This is because of a steady rise in the amount of alcohol per drink. Ten years ago the average concentration of alcohol in wine was around 10 to 11%; it is now over 12.5%. Recent times have also seen promotion of "super size" drink offers, with 20-ounce beers being dispensed for only a marginal increase in cost. Overall, the effect is that a "standard" drink is about 20% more than it was a few years ago. (See Figure 10.8.)

Calculating Blood Alcohol Concentration (BAC)

The water weight of the body differs between men (68%) and women (55%). If a man and woman drank the same beverage, the BAC of the woman generally would be higher than that of the man. If two men of different weights drank the same beverage, then the man who weighed more would have the lower BAC. The relationship was first clearly elucidated in Sweden around 1914 by Erik Widmark. He proposed the relationship

$$a = c \times p \times r,$$

where a is the amount of alcohol taken, c is the BAC, and r is a factor (now known as the Widmark factor in his honor) proportional to total body water. The average value of r is around 0.55 for men and 0.68 for women, who have a lesser proportion of their body weight made up of water.

Types of Alcohols

Ethanol is the most commonly encountered toxic substance in forensic toxicology. It is an organic liquid with a low boiling point and is present in beverages, some household cleaning agents, and cosmetics.

Methanol is another type of commonly encountered household alcohol, also known as *wood alcohol*. Methanol is commonly used as a solvent and reagent in the chemical industry and is extremely toxic. In addition to its depressant action on the brain, methanol is metabolized first to formaldehyde and then to formic acid, which can lead to lowered blood pH, causing metabolic acidosis (potentially fatal) and damage to the optic nerve, resulting in blindness.

Isopropyl alcohol, also known as *rubbing alcohol* or *isopropanol*, is a commonly used antiseptic. It isn't as toxic as methanol, but it has more intense CNS depression than alcohol. Isopropanol is metabolized to acetone, requiring analytical methods for suspected intoxication to differentiate and quantify both isopropanol and acetone.

Ethylene glycol is the active component of antifreeze. It is extremely toxic, being metabolized to oxalic acid, which reacts with calcium in the body to form insoluble calcium oxalate. As well as general calcium depletion, calcium oxalate deposits may form in the kidney and brain. Ethylene glycol deaths can usually be determined without analytical testing as the deposits can be seen by polarized light microscopy in tissue sections.

Alcohol and Driving

Consumption of alcoholic beverages is a widely accepted social activity. Unfortunately, there is no doubt that there is a causal relationship between alcohol intake and the likelihood of causing a vehicle accident. Since driving is a major part of everyday life, alcohol cases, specifically drunk driving, probably impact a greater number of citizens than any other aspect of forensic science. There is no doubt that drinking and driving do not mix. There is a well-established relationship between blood alcohol levels and the likelihood of causing an accident.

The benchmark study was performed in the early 1960s in Grand Rapids, Michigan. The blood alcohol levels of drivers who had caused accidents were compared to those in a similar group who had not been involved in an accident. The results showed that the chance of causing an accident increases

FIGURE 10.8
Wine. The normal strength of white and red wines has steadily increased from around 10% to more than 13%. Image created by author.

225

The treatment of methanol poisoning is interesting. Infusions of ethanol are given because it is a preferential substrate for ADH and so inhibits the formation of formaldehyde and formic acid.

FIGURE 10.9

Alcohol and accidents. Relative risk of causing an accident (y-axis) at various BAC levels (x-axis). Redrawn from data from the 1964 Grand Rapids study.

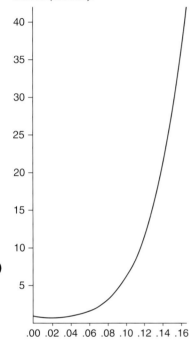

as the blood alcohol level rises above about 0.04%. Someone with a blood alcohol level of 0.1% is five times more likely than normal to cause an accident, and one at 0.15% is 25 times more likely (see Figure 10.9).

Many people claim that their ability to handle the car is not affected at the lower levels. However, the Grand Rapids study showing an increased risk at low levels has been supported in so many other surveys that there is no justification at all for leniency. A British study offered some insight into why accident rates rise at levels where handling skills are probably not affected.

Professional bus drivers were taken to an off-road site. They were divided into groups given no alcohol, one drink, or three drinks. They were then asked to set gates to a gap through which they believed that they could drive their vehicle. They were then allowed to drive through the gates and their performance was measured. Actual performance was as expected. The small amount of alcohol had no effect on the average gap that they could clear (but some individuals did show marked impairment). The larger amount was associated with impairment, the group requiring an increase in the gate width to pass safely through. However, even the low-level group showed clear impairment of judgment in estimating the minimum gap that they would clear with their vehicle.

We thus see that alcohol will impair judgment before motor skills. A low blood alcohol level can indeed leave the drinker able to perform the manipulations required for driving. However, the ability of the driver to respond to a situation requiring judgment will be impaired.

Alcohol Detection in Blood and Breath

Measuring the concentration of alcohol in blood is one of the most straightforward and reliable tests performed in forensic science. The procedure used universally is that of gas chromatography with an internal standard. The alcohol in the sample can be analyzed in either gas or liquid phase. Liquid samples may be introduced by injecting the sample directly or by injecting an extraction or dilution of the sample into the heated GC injection port. To introduce a sample in gaseous phase, the gas may have to be liberated from the test sample using a degassing agent or by heating the closed sample vial until the gas phase has equilibrated with the sample liquid phase. The equilibrium or headspace vapor is then sampled in a gas-tight syringe and injected onto the GC. Liquid and headspace analysis both are used combined with automated injection systems.

The physics of partition between liquid and gas that allow headspace analysis of alcohol in blood samples also permit estimation of blood alcohol by breath testing. Alcohol in the blood is in equilibrium with the concentration of alcohol in the gases in the lungs. The ratio of concentrations is highly in favor of the blood levels, at somewhere between 2100:1 and 2300:1. The measured breath level is converted to a blood equivalent using the blood–air ratio.

There are many devices used in breath testing. The earliest widespread instrument was the Breathalyzer brand. The original Breathalyzer depended on the development of a color due to oxidation of the alcohol in the sample. Modern instruments use a range of detection systems, including infrared spectrometry, electrochemical cells, and miniature gas chromatographs. They have the advantage that they are much more sensitive, specific, and rapid than the Breathalyzer. This means that operators can take more than one sample for greater accuracy, and that potential interferences from natural sources, such as acetone in diabetics, can be allowed for. (See Figure 10.10.)

In Vitro and Postmortem Alcohol Production

Production and decomposition of alcohol have been demonstrated in stored blood samples, but only in samples infected with alcohol producing microorganisms or in postmortem samples where the blood has become contaminated with an opportunistic or gut bacterium prior to collection.

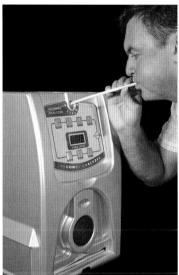

FIGURE 10.10
Breath alcohol testing. A typical breath alcohol instrument. From Stockxpert.

SOME OTHER MATERIALS ENCOUNTERED IN FORENSIC TOXICOLOGY

Carbon Monoxide

Carbon monoxide (CO) is a colorless, odorless gas produced by incomplete combustion. It has a higher affinity for hemoglobin than does carbon dioxide, and its toxic effects are mainly due to lack of available oxygen supply to tissues. CO also binds to cytochrome oxidase in mitochondria, thereby inhibiting cellular respiration. A sign of carbon monoxide poisoning is that someone killed by CO inhalation often takes on a bright cherry pink color caused by the binding of carbon monoxide to the hemoglobin. It is the most common cause of death by poisoning in the U.S.

Carbon monoxide is encountered in accidental deaths associated with poor ventilation and faulty operation of old heaters and stoves. Carbon monoxide also is produced in the exhaust fumes of internal combustion engines, with deaths resulting by accident, suicide, or even homicide.

CARBON MONOXIDE ANALYSIS

Visible absorbance spectrophotometry is the most commonly used technique for determining extent of CO exposure. It works on the principle that reduced hemoglobin, oxyhemoglobin, methemoglobin, and carboxyhemoglobin have different absorbance maxima between 500–600 nm. Results are expressed as percent saturation of hemoglobin by comparing the test sample with blood that has been treated with CO so that all normal oxyhemoglobin has been converted to the carboxy form.

The spectrophotometric assay is simple and reliable for fresh blood samples but may not be suitable for samples from decomposed bodies. In these cases, CO can be assayed by a microdiffusion method based on the reduction of palladium chloride to metallic palladium by carbon monoxide, which is released from specimens by treatment with strong acid. The disappearance of palladium chloride can be measured by monitoring the visible absorbance of the remaining solution at 278 nm. Gas chromatography has also been used.

Cyanide

Cyanide, in the form of the gas hydrogen cyanide and its sodium and potassium salts, is highly toxic. Like CO, it is a potent inhibitor of cytochrome oxidase and therefore disrupts cellular respiration. It has been used as a poison throughout history, including the murder of the Russian "mad monk" Grigori Rasputin, and several notable suicides including Alan Turing, widely regarded as the father of modern computing. Hydrogen cyanide was the agent used in the Nazi gas chambers. Despite its pedigree, cyanide is rarely encountered in forensic toxicology today.

Metals

Readily available as a medicine, rat poison, and a component of wallpaper dyes, it earned the name "inheritance powder."

Certain metal-containing compounds are essential for life, while others are considered to be nonessential or known to have no biological function. Exposure to elevated levels of essential and nonessential metals can result in toxicity and even death. People can be exposed to metals as part of their daily lives through their occupation, living environment, contaminated food and water, or intentional and unintentional poisoning. As with any poisoning, the chemical form of the poison, the age, the physical condition of the person exposed, and the dose play a large role in the resultant toxic response.

Many metals are poisonous, but one—arsenic—has a special place in forensic toxicology. Metallic arsenic is not very poisonous, in contrast to its oxide. Arsenic oxide acts on the gastrointestinal tract, and its symptoms are very similar to those of common pre-twentieth-century diseases, especially cholera.

Botanicals and Fungi

Early poisoners depended on natural sources for their organic poisons. Foxglove, containing digitalis and related compounds, was very effective, as were hemlock, aconite, and opium.

Many potent biological poisons are proteins or polypeptides, including ricin and the toxin in *Cortinarius* mushrooms.

Case Study

Georgi Markov

Ricin featured in the notorious "umbrella murder" that took place in London in 1978. Georgi Markov, a Bulgarian dissident living in London, was murdered by being shot in the leg by a poisoned dart fired from an umbrella. Markov was standing at a bus stop on his way home from work when he felt a sharp jab in his leg. Turning around to look, he saw a man picking up an umbrella. Four days later, Georgi was dead.

A pellet was recovered from his leg and found to contain traces of ricin. Ricin is an extremely potent poison—as little as 50 micrograms can kill a human. It is a protein mainly obtained from castor oil manufacturing waste.

Investigations never were able to prove a link to the Bulgarian or Russian secret police.

Cortinarius is the largest genus of mushrooms in the world. Many of the *Cortinarius* species are potent nephrotoxins, and several fatalities have arisen when mushroom gatherers have picked and eaten *Cortinarius*, thinking it to be another species. The toxin was shown to be a cyclic peptide, which fortunately is found in only three of the many species. (See Figure 10.11.)

FIGURE 10.11
Cortinarius rubellus. C. rubellus is one of the toxic species from the genus *Cortinarius*. Public domain image from http://commons.wikimedia.org/wiki/Image:Cortinarius_rubellus_02.jpg

229

Hormones

Hormones present particular problems to the toxicologist, because they are present naturally in body tissues. Insulin has been encountered in several suspected homicides, especially "angel of death" murders of aged persons in care facilities. Insulin is rapidly eliminated from the blood after administration, and the deceased may have been an insulin-dependent diabetic. Circumstantial evidence, such as discarded vials and syringes, and careful postmortem examination are important. The target for the toxicologist is to work with the pathologist and identify possible injection sites. It has proven possible to identify insulin residues at these sites even when blood insulin levels are normal.

Jessie McTavish, a nurse in charge of a geriatric ward in a Scottish hospital, was convicted of the murder of Elizabeth Lyons, one of her patients, in 1974. The evidence included results indicating the presence of insulin at an injection site (the deceased was not a diabetic). Almost 30 years later, Colin Morris was convicted of the murder of four elderly women in his nursing care, also by insulin injection. Four years later, another British nurse, Benjamin Green, was convicted of the murder of two elderly patients and the assault of 15 others, by injections that included insulin.

SUMMARY

Toxicology is the science of poisons and their effect on living organisms. Toxicologists must understand how a drug is absorbed into the bloodstream, how it is distributed within tissues, its effects, and how it is removed.

Postmortem toxicology seeks to identify poisons that could be the cause of death. In the United States, postmortem toxicology is usually conducted in specialized laboratories associated with a medical examiner or coroner facility.

Antemortem toxicology seeks to determine whether or not the drug has resulted in the impairment of a living person that either contravenes a law or could be a contributory factor in a crime.

Other than topically applied preparations, most drugs must enter the blood to be effective. Drugs administered orally must pass from the gastrointestinal tract into the blood and then to the rest of the body.

Only the neutral, unionized drug is absorbed. The drug transport rate is determined by its physicochemical properties and the concentration gradient between the solution in the intestinal contents and that in the blood flowing through lining cells. The same principles apply to drugs administered by other means.

The absorption curve reflects the concentration of drug in the blood over time following administration; it tracks absorption, distribution, and elimination.

The liver is the main site of drug metabolism. The half-life ($T_{1/2}$) of a drug is the time for its concentrated blood to decline by 50%. Note that not all metabolic pathways result in inactive compounds; some metabolites have activity to their parent compound.

Drugs and their metabolites are removed from the body by excretion—often through the kidney but also into bile and via the lungs.

In the Stass–Otto technique of liquid–liquid extraction, the target analyte is extracted from an aqueous solution into an organic solvent. Solid-phase extraction (SPE) uses inert cartridges filled with a solid stationary phase. The analyte of interest can be eluted and collected.

Amphoteric compounds exhibit both acid and base properties. Optimal extraction is achieved by carefully adjusting the pH to get the drug into an unionized form.

Immunoassays work via competition between a drug (analyte) present in the sample and a labeled drug for binding sites on an antibody specific for the drug of interest.

The specificity of an antibody is determined by comparing the binding of that antibody to the drug against which it is raised with the binding affinity of the same antibody to other related drugs and metabolites. The extent to which other drugs and metabolites interfere is known as cross-reactivity and may give rise to false positive assay results.

Thin-layer chromatography (TLC), gas chromatography (GC), and GC coupled with mass spectrometry (GC-MS) can provide quantitative information about drug samples. However, liquid chromatography coupled with dual mass spectrometry (LC-MS-MS) is becoming the method of choice.

Alcohol is a central nervous system depressant. The linear decline in blood alcohol content with time makes it relatively easy to relate alcohol consumption, body size, time, and BAC. The average elimination rate in the liver is well established as being a reduction in BAC of about 0.015% per hour, with a range of approximately 0.09 to 0.25.

Erik Widmark proposed the relationship $a = c \times p \times r$, where a is the amount of alcohol taken, c is the BAC, and r is a factor (now known as the Widmark factor, in his honor) proportional to total body water. The average value of r is around 0.55 for men and 0.68 for women.

The physics of partition between liquid and gas, which allows headspace analysis of alcohol in blood samples, also permits estimation of blood alcohol by breath testing. Alcohol in the blood is in equilibrium with the concentration of alcohol in the gases in the lungs. The ratio of concentrations is highly in favor of the blood levels, at somewhere between 2100:1 and 2300:1. The measured breath level is converted to a blood equivalent using the blood–air ratio.

Carbon monoxide (CO), a colorless, odorless gas produced by incomplete combustion, can be lethal. Visible absorbance spectrophotometry is the most commonly used technique for determining the extent of CO exposure.

Exposure to elevated levels of metals can result in toxicity and even death. Arsenic oxide earned the name "inheritance powder" for its toxicity.

Many potent biological poisons are proteins or polypeptides, including ricin and the toxin in *Cortinarius* mushrooms.

Hormones present particular problems to the toxicologist because they are present naturally in body tissues. Insulin has been encountered in several suspected homicides.

PROBLEMS

1. Give the word or phrase for the following definitions:
   a. the extent to which a drug can be extracted by aqueous or organic solvents
   b. molecules with both acid and base properties
   c. the extent to which other drugs and metabolites interfere with a test
   d. the change a drug undergoes in the body
   e. the process of making a drug bioavailable
   f. the substance being assayed
   g. the separation of a component from a mixture using differences in solubility properties
   h. a test in which a biologically specific binding agent competes for radioactively labeled or unlabeled compounds

231

2. What is the difference between antemortem and postmortem toxicology?
3. What is a drug absorption curve? What phases does it encompass?
4. Summarize the advantages and disadvantages of the following techniques:
   a. gas chromatography
   b. thin-layer chromatography
   c. high-performance liquid chromatography
   d. mass spectroscopy
5. List several factors that affect bioavailability.
6. How do the kidneys and the liver affect drugs in the body?
7. Describe the differences between liquid–liquid extraction and solid-phase extraction. What are the advantages and disadvantages of each?
8. What is an immunoassay? What principles govern its use? Name several techniques.
9. What is blood alcohol concentration? List several factors that affect blood alcohol concentration.
10. Why is a breath sample a valid way to test for blood alcohol?
11. How is blood alcohol concentration calculated?
12. List several substances other than drugs that may be the subject of forensic toxicology investigations.

GLOSSARY

Absorption the process of making a drug bioavailable.

Absorption curve the change in drug concentration over time after administration, reflecting the processes of absorption, distribution, and elimination.

Alcohol dehydrogenase (ADH) the enzyme responsible for eliminating alcohol from the body; the average elimination rate is 0.015% per hour.

Amphoteric drugs molecules with both acid and base properties, such as morphine.

Analyte the substance being assayed.

Antemortem toxicology the process to determine whether or not the drug has resulted in impairment that either contravenes a law or could be a contributory factor in a crime. The subjects are living persons.

Biotransformation metabolism of a drug; the change a drug undergoes in the body.

Blood alcohol concentration (BAC) the amount of alcohol in the blood, usually expressed as grams of ethanol per 100 mL of blood or as percent alcohol.

Carbon monoxide (CO) a colorless, odorless gas produced by incomplete combustion, which binds to hemoglobin lowering the availability of oxygen supply to tissues.

Competitive binding assay a test in which a biologically specific binding agent competes for radioactively labeled or unlabeled compounds.

Cross-reactivity the extent to which other drugs and metabolites interfere with a test.

Distribution phase the amount of a drug in a certain tissue.

Elimination loss of drug from the body, mainly by metabolism in the liver.

Excretion the elimination of drug in urine.

Extraction separating one component from a mixture, often by utilizing differences in solubility properties.

Immunoassay a technique for identifying a substance using antibodies.

Metabolism the change a drug undergoes in the body. The liver is the main site of drug metabolism, primarily through oxidation mediated by the cytochrome P-450 enzyme system.

Metabolite the result of a change by the body on a drug.

Partition the extent to which a drug can be extracted by aqueous or organic solvents.

Postmortem toxicology the search to identify a toxic compound that could be the cause of death.

Toxicology the science of poisons and their effect on living organisms.

Villi structures in the small intestine that facilitate molecules entering into the bloodstream.

Volume of distribution (V_d) the amount of drug in the body divided by its concentration in blood.

SECTION IV
Biological Evidence

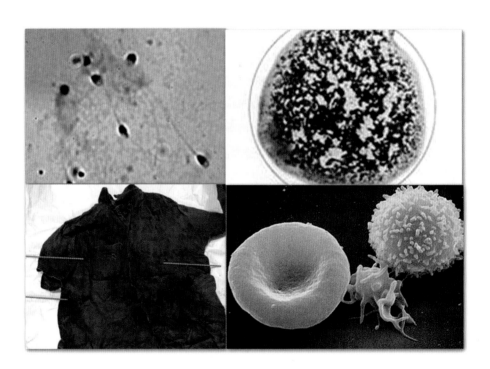

Clockwise from top left: Human sperm; agglutinated blood cells; blood components (left to right: red cell, platelet, white cell) blood-stained shirt from a shooting incident victim (the pink colored lines show the bullet trajectories). Shirt: Courtesy Ronnie Freels; Blood cells: http://commons.wikimedia.org/wiki/Image:Red_White_Blood_cells.jpg; Sperm courtesy of NFSTC; Agglutination from http://en.wikipedia.org/wiki/Image:Bedside_card.jpg

CHAPTER 11

Forensic Biology

Murder in the Mediterranean

Late one summer evening, the police on the small Mediterranean island of Malta were summoned to a shooting scene on a quiet road near the town of Sliema. There they found Angelo Bajada by his car, bleeding from a gunshot wound to his left arm. His wife, Carmen, was inside the car, on the front passenger seat, dead from a shot to the head. A spent cartridge case was found in the folds of her skirt.

The bullet from the gunshot had passed through the fleshy part of Angelo's arm into his chest cavity, where it had nicked a blood vessel. Before being rushed to hospital, he was able to tell police that his and his wife's car was waved down by a man on the roadside. After they stopped to see what the man wanted, he pulled out a gun, threatened them, stole money from Carmen's purse, and shot both of them where they were seated.

The next day, police interviewed Angelo at the hospital and found some discrepancies in his story compared to the account given at the scene and also with some of the evidence in the car. In particular, they were puzzled as to how he had sustained a wound to the upper part of his left arm with a downward trajectory from a gunshot fired from either the passenger or driver side of the vehicle: Cars in Malta have the steering wheel on the right and drive on the left of the road. Angelo explained that

the gunman had made him get out of the driver's seat and sit on the sill of the car by the open passenger door.

Further inquiries revealed information suggesting that Angelo may have been trying to kill his wife. The car was taken for examination. Blood was found inside, but grouping tests revealed only that it was human and group O. However, the investigators at first missed the most important feature of the bloodstains; namely, their physical characteristics. The stains consisted of very fine spots and streaks of blood on the seats, roof, and dash of the car. The simple process of tracing the streaks to their point of origin by aligning fine string with their pattern revealed two points of origin. One was at chest height on the passenger side between the seat and the transmission tunnel and the other about shoulder height on the left side of the driver's seat.

A reconstruction was carried out in which the driver pulled the passenger down and toward himself, simulated firing a handgun to the temple of the passenger, and then sat upright and shot himself in the left arm. The impact points of where the bullet entry holes would have been created matched the two focal points of the reconstructed blood spatter patterns.

Angelo subsequently was convicted of Carmen's homicide.

BODY TISSUES

Biological fluids such as blood and semen may be deposited when a crime is committed, such as blood left at the scene from an injury during forced access to a building or semen deposits from a rape. The presence of the body tissue itself may therefore be of evidential value. The physical distribution of bloodstains at the scene or on clothing may produce additional information; for example, blood spatters indicate the application of force, but smears could be from any direct contact with wet blood.

The detection and identification process begins with a physical examination, followed by a screening test to identify stains that may be body fluids—for example, the identification of possible bloodstains in the car in the Bajada case. The preliminary screen is sometimes referred to as a **presumptive test**, as a positive gives grounds to presume that the material could be the biological fluid of interest. The stains are then processed to provide information about the possible donor, such as species and blood type. Today this last step is performed by identifying markers in the DNA in the sample. DNA testing is covered in Chapter 12; here we deal only with the identification of the biologic material, together with an overview of traditional sample typing.

Most tissues contain biochemicals typical of the source material but not necessarily unique to it. For example, semen has a high concentration of the enzyme acid phosphatase, but the enzyme is found at lower levels in other body fluids, including vaginal secretions. Screening tests target these biochemicals. Confirmatory tests are then used to identify the specific biological material.

The line between screening and identification is not always clear. Experienced forensic biologists know it is highly unlikely that a brown stain found on clothing and that gave a positive presumptive test for blood will be anything other than blood. If the positive screening test is followed by DNA typing and a DNA profile is successfully developed that matches that of the victim, then the material must be body tissue from that source. To prevent any suggestion of providing misleading evidence, the only unqualified conclusion that can be offered is that the stain contains DNA that matches that of the victim. It has not been proven to be blood.

Immunology and Forensic Biology

Many traditional tests used in forensic biology are immunological in nature and depend on antigen–antibody interactions. **Antibodies** are proteins called **immunoglobulins (Ig)**, which are produced by **white blood cells (WBC)** in response to a challenge by foreign materials **(antigens)**. They are found in serum in the gamma globulin fraction. All immunoglobulins have the same basic structure consisting of two pairs of peptide chains linked to form a Y-shaped molecule. The chains in the longer pair are designated as "heavy," or H, chains and those in the shorter pair as "light," or L, chains. The chains within each pair are identical. However, these pairs (H and L) differ from each other. There are five classes of immunoglobulins, each of which can be differentiated by their chemical structure. The specificity of the antibody molecule lies in the chemical structure at the tip of the two arms of the Y. These sites are termed the *Fab regions*, for fragment antigen binding. There is a region of relatively constant composition at the base of the Y, termed the *Fc*, or fragment crystalizable, region. The Fc region plays a role in binding the antibody to receptors during the immune response. (See Figure 11.1 and Table 11.1.)

Antigens are compounds that stimulate production of antibodies in an immune response but are sometimes defined as substances that combine with an antibody. The term **immunogen** is an alternate name for a substance that invokes an immune response, that is, stimulates the production of antibodies. They are usually large molecules, such as proteins. Immunogen challenge results in a wide range of antibodies being produced, each specific to a different structural site on the immunogen, called an *epitope*. The response will include antibodies in all classes, and there will be overlap in the specificity between some of the antibodies.

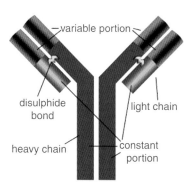

FIGURE 11.1
Antibody. Diagram of immunoglobulin molecule. From http://commons.wikimedia.org/wiki/Image:Antibody_svg.svg

Table 11.1	Immunoglobulin Function and Heavy Chain Structure	
Immunoglobulin	**Function**	**H-Subtype**
IgG	Main Ig that fights infections. Forensic serological interest	gamma (γ)
IgM	Fights infections. Forensic serological interest	mu (μ)
IgA	Fights infection in mucous membranes	alpha (α)
IgD	Function not known	delta (δ)
IgE	Fights parasitic infections, may be associated with allergic reactions	epsilon (ε)

Note: There are two L chain subtypes, namely kappa (κ) and lambda (λ).

The immune response is mediated through a range of white blood cells. The first step is digestion of the immunogenic stimulant by phagocytes. The phagocyte attracts members of a different family of white cells, called *lymphocytes*. Antibodies are produced by a subgroup, the B lymphocytes. Cells in another subgroup, helper T lymphocytes, assist the B lymphocytes to recognize antigens. Each activated B lymphocyte produces one specific antibody, but the activated B lymphocytes undergo repeated cell divisions to produce a clone of antibody-producing cells. The antibody from each clone is identical and termed a **monoclonal antibody**. Many B lymphocytes take part in the immunologic response, and the resultant mixture of antibodies is a **polyclonal mixture**. (See Figure 11.2.)

A chemical complex is formed when an antibody binds to a specific epitope on an antigen. It is possible to have an antibody–antigen reaction where the

FIGURE 11.2
Lymphocyte cloning. Schematic of B lymphocyte cloning in response to antigenic challenge. A stem cell (1) produces families of lymphocytes (2) that learn to ignore the body's own proteins (2) but remember non-self antigens (3). Each non-self is remembered by a different cell line (4). If re-challenged (5) those lymphocytes that recognize the foreign antigen replicate to produce cloned activated B lymphocytes (6) that secrete specific antibodies. From http://commons. wikimedia.org/wiki/ Image:Clonal_selection. svg#file

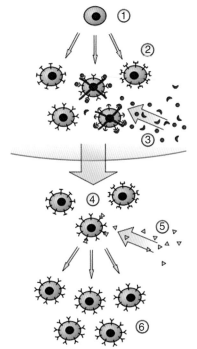

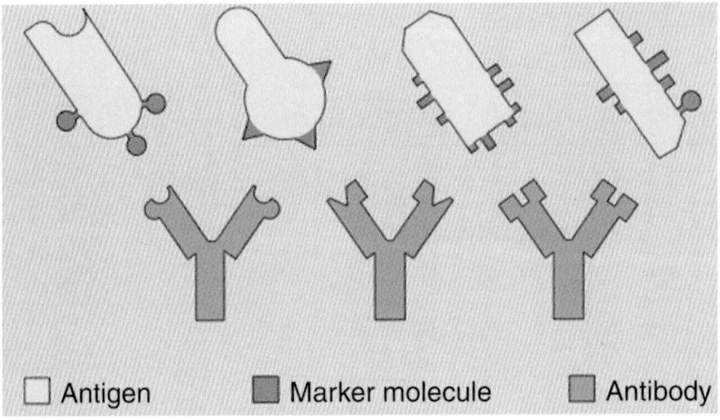

FIGURE 11.3
Lock and key representation of Ag–Ab reaction. Each antibody molecule has specific sites at the antibody binding ends of the "Y," represented here by different shapes. Antigens containing marker molecules that match the sites will bind to them but not to nonmatching sites. Note that the antigen on the right possesses marker molecules that match the binding sites on the left and right of the three diagrammatic antibody molecules and so can bind to both. From NIH Publication No. 03–5423 "Understanding the Immune System."

antigen itself would not produce an immune response, usually because it was too small to be recognized by the B and helper T lymphocytes. However, an antibody can be produced by combining the target antigen with a carrier molecule; such an antigen is termed a **hapten**.

The immune response to an antigen challenge therefore results in the production of antibodies. Commercial laboratory reagents are made by invoking a response in a host animal and harvesting the serum from it. The serum containing antibodies is called **antiserum**. Cell culture techniques can be used to isolate the B cells from blood withdrawn from the host and produce the antiserum *in vitro*. Isolating specific clones of B cells allows the production of monoclonal antibodies. (See Figure 11.3.)

The antibody–antigen reaction is specific. It can be visualized as a lock and key; the binding site on the antibody fits exactly with the epitope region on the antigen. As can be seen in Figure 11.1, each immunoglobulin molecule has two identical receptor sites for each epitope that it recognizes on the antigen. This enables cross-linking to occur, and is the basis of the **precipitin** and agglutination reactions. In the former, divalent IgG molecules cross-link with binding sites on proteins to form a high-molecular weight, insoluble precipitate. In the latter, IgM molecules, which exist as pentamers, can cross-link with binding sites on the surface of cells or other small particles, resulting in clumping, or agglutination. In both cases (precipitin and agglutination), the aggregates can be seen with a low-power microscope or the naked eye. (See Figure 11.4.)

□ Antigen   ■ Marker molecule   ■ Antibody

BLOOD

Blood is a suspension of cells in an isotonic aqueous solution. The main components of blood and their role (if any) in forensic biology are shown in Table 11.2. Figure 11.5 shows blood cells as they appear under the microscope.

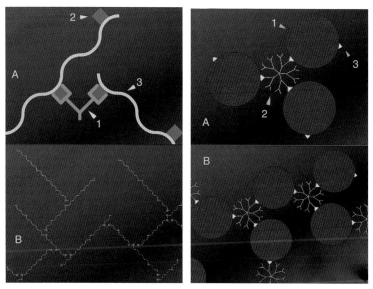

FIGURE 11.4
Precipitin and agglutination reactions. The left panel illustrates the mechanism of precipitin reactions. The top panel (A) shows an IgG antibody molecule (1) combining with a specific antigen site (2) on each of two protein molecules (3). Because each protein has more than one site, the protein molecules are cross-linked to create a lattice as shown in the lower panel (B) that can be large enough to precipitate out of solution—hence the name "precipitin." The right panel illustrates the mechanism of agglutination reactions. In the upper panel, red cells (1) are shown linked together by IgM molecules (2) binding to surface antigens (3). The large pentamer IgM molecules permit extensive linkage of cells in this way to create a visible clumping, or agglutination. Courtesy NFSTC.

Table 11.2	Composition of Blood and Its Forensic Functions	
Cell	**Function**	**Forensic Interest**
Red cell (Erythrocyte)	Transport of oxygen to tissues and removal of carbon dioxide	• Contains many of the typing markers used before DNA • Basis of screening tests for blood • Detection of fetal blood
White cell (Leukocyte)	Fights infections	• Source of DNA in blood stains
Platelets (Thrombocytes)	Essential component of the blood clotting system	• None • Note that serum is the liquid from blood that has clotted and does not contain platelets; plasma is the liquid from unclotted blood and does contain platelets

(Continued)

Table 11.2	Composition of Blood and Its Forensic Functions—cont'd	
Plasma or Serum Component	**Function**	**Forensic Interest**
Proteins	Individual proteins have a range of biologic functions including regulation of blood volume, antibodies, and sequestering of hemoglobin and lipids	• Some proteins such as haptoglobin and transferrin were the basis of some pre-DNA typing methods
Salts	Mainly sodium, potassium, and chloride. Important for maintaining an isotonic medium for survival of cells. Some ions, such as potassium and calcium, have important roles in cellular function	• None
Other organics	Includes hormones and vitamins	• None

FIGURE 11.5
Blood cells as seen under the scanning electron microscope. The large smooth surfaced bi-concave discs are red cell. The rough surfaced cells are lymphocytes and the smaller discs are platelets. From National Cancer Institute, courtesy of Bruce Wetzel (photographer) and Harry Schaefer (photographer).

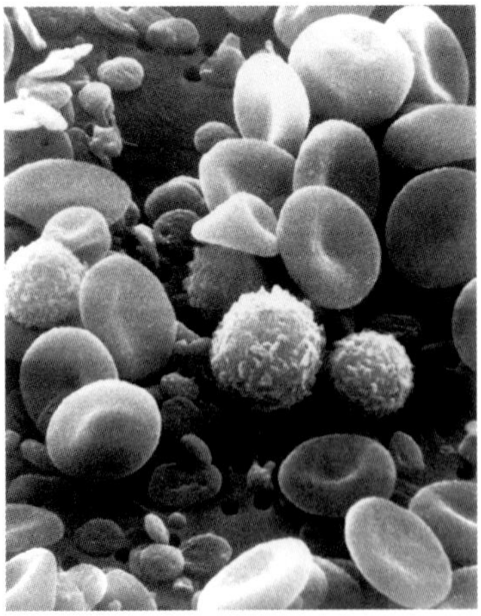

The cellular component of blood is mainly composed of **red blood cells**, which account for about 45% of the total volume. RBCs are unique because the mature circulating cells do not contain a nucleus and so do not contain DNA. Their function is to transport oxygen to tissues as a hemoglobin complex and to remove carbon dioxide.

White blood cells, which possess a nucleus (and therefore DNA) are involved in the body's responses to infection. They are responsible for antibody production. The fluid portion of unclotted blood is called **plasma**. Blood clots through the conversion of a dissolved protein, fibrinogen, to a precipitated polymer, fibrin. Fibrin traps platelets to form the clot. The liquid fraction obtained from clotted blood is called **serum**. Serum can be further separated into fractions by **electrophoresis**. The simple and not very discriminating forms of electrophoresis that were first used, such as those employing cellulose acetate membranes, typically produced only four fractions. These are, in order of electrophoretic mobility, albumin, followed by three globulin fractions designated as alpha, beta, and gamma. These designations have become accepted terms used to describe serum protein fractions.

About half the total amount of serum protein consists of albumin, which is one of the factors that preserves blood volume by regulating osmotic pressure. In contrast, each globulin fraction consists of many different proteins. This is particularly true of the gamma globulin fraction, which contains antibodies.

Screening Tests

Most screening tests for blood depend on the peroxidase activity of hemoglobin. The most common ones depend on the oxidation of colorless reduced indicators, many of which are conjugated systems and known or suspected carcinogens. Table 11.3 lists the most common tests and gives an indication of their sensitivity and safety. The process used is the same for each test other than Luminol. A filter paper is rubbed over the suspect area and a drop of reagent added and allowed to soak in for about 10 seconds. A false positive may develop in this period; if not, the application of the reagent is followed by a drop of hydrogen peroxide. A rapid development of color—in less than 20 seconds—is a positive result. The process is illustrated in Figure 11.6. Luminol is usually sprayed over the area to be screened (note the potential hazard of this process due to the carcinogenic nature of Luminol) and the area illuminated with UV light.

BOX 11.1   BLOOD TEST KITS

The product Hemastix, manufactured by Bayer and widely used in clinical screening tests for detection of blood in urine, provides a safe and simple alternative to the preceding reagents. It contains o-tolidine immobilized behind a membrane. The membrane acts as a barrier to contact by the user but permits aqueous extracts to pass and react with the reagent. Modern tests such as the ABA card HemaTrace also use reagents bound to a test strip and are safe and specific.

Table 11.3   Common Screening Tests for Blood

Test	Indicator	Sensitivity*	Comment
Benzidine	Blue color	++++	Carcinogen
Tetra methyl benzidine	Blue color	+++	Probable carcinogen
o-Tolidine	Dark green	+++	Probable carcinogen
Phenolphthalein or Kastle-Meyer test	Pink color	++	Relatively safe
Leucomalachite green	Green color	++	Relatively safe
Luminol (5-amino-2, 3-dihydro-1,4 phthalazinedione)	Fluorescence	+++++	Probable carcinogen

*+ = least sensitive; +++++ = most sensitive.

FIGURE 11.6
Presumptive blood test. Image A on the left shows the brownish-colored material transferred to filter paper by rubbing a suspected blood stain. Image B on the right is the same stain after treating with Kastle-Meyer reagent and hydrogen peroxide with a bright pink color developed within 20 seconds indicating a positive presumptive test for blood. Courtesy NFSTC.

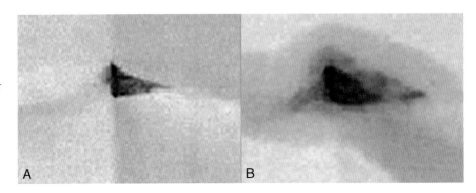

These tests are not specific for blood. Other biological materials, such as fruits, possess peroxidase activity, and other chemicals that are oxidizing agents may be present on surfaces. Some laboratories have used two or more of the tests listed in Table 11.3 and reported the second as confirming the first. However, since they are all presumptive tests that depend on the peroxidase activity of hemoglobin, carrying out two or more tests does not substitute for or constitute a confirmatory test.

Case Study

244

The Disappearance of Azaria Chamberlain

The notorious "Dingo Baby" case provides an example where the lack of specificity of screening tests turned out to be vital. Ayers Rock, now known as Uluru, is an impressive red monolith in the center of the country and regarded as a sacred site by the indigenous population. Michael Chamberlain, his wife, Lindy, their two sons, Aiden and Reagan, and their 10-week-old daughter, Azaria, were on vacation at a campsite near Uluru in August 1980. During the night, Lindy ran from the tent crying out that a dingo (a wild Australian dog) had taken her baby. Subsequent investigations eventually resulted in Lindy's being charged with homicide and Michael charged as an accomplice. A guilty verdict was returned, but there was a strong and continuing movement to establish the innocence of the parents. Eventually, the Australian government ordered an exhaustive inquiry into the circumstances of the conviction.

An important part of the prosecution case was that Lindy Chamberlain, the mother of Azaria, had cut her throat and removed the child's body from the campsite in the family car. The original crime scene examination found what was described as a spray pattern of blood in the car, based on physical appearance and a positive screening test. Subsequent tests showed that the spray pattern was from painting during manufacture of the car, and the positive test was most likely from the copper found in soil in the Australian outback.

Confirmatory tests

CRYSTAL TESTS

Many different tests have been used to confirm that a stain contains blood. The oldest date back to the early twentieth century and depend on chemical confirmation of the presence of hemoglobin or its derivatives by the formation of specific crystals; for example, the **Takayama, or hemochromogen, test,** in which ferrous iron from hemoglobin reacts with pyridine to produce red feathery crystals of pyridine ferroprotoporphyrin. Another confirmatory test uses the **Teichmann** reagent, consisting of a solution of potassium bromide, potassium chloride, and potassium iodide in glacial acetic acid, which is heated to react with hemoglobin. The reaction first converts the hemoglobin to hemin, and then the halides react with the hemin to form characteristic brownish-yellow rhomboid crystals.

PRECIPITIN TESTS

Blood can be identified as being of human origin by mixing it with antisera specific for components of human blood, which then forms an antigen–antibody complex that precipitates from the solution (the precipitin reaction). Traditionally, the antisera contained an antihuman serum serum, that is, an antiserum to human serum. Strictly speaking, this was therefore a test for human origin and not for human blood, as serum constituents such as albumin and some globulins are found in the extravascular space. Modern tests use antihuman hemoglobin and so are specific for human blood.

The original precipitin reaction was carried out by layering a solution of antibody on top of a solution of stain extract in a tube and then leaving for a period of time to allow the development of a precipitin band at the interface (see Figure 11.7). This is referred to as the *tube method*, and, although outdated, it is still used in a few laboratories today.

The tube test for species identification was replaced by the more robust and informative radial diffusion of antigen and antibody through agar gel. This is the Ouchterlony test (see Figure 11.7). A variant of the Ouchterlony test, called **crossover electrophoresis**, uses an electric field rather than diffusion to move the extract and antibody through the gel. Ouchterlony plates can be purchased or made in the laboratory.

245

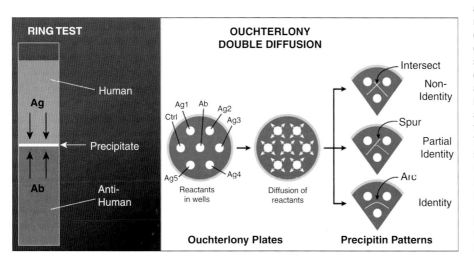

FIGURE 11.7
Identification of human blood. The left hand panel of the figure illustrates the ring test, a traditional precipitin reaction for identification of human blood. An extract of the blood stain is carefully layered on top of antihuman antiserum. If the blood is human an antigen–antibody precipitate is formed at the interface. The right hand panel shows the principles that underpin the Ouchterlony immuno-diffusion procedure as applied to identification of human blood. Compare with Figure 11.4A. Courtesy NFSTC.

Extracts are made from stained areas of interest as well as from nearby unstained areas (substrate controls). Note that the use of unstained controls is a fundamental principle in forensic immunologic testing.

Stains and control samples are loaded in the outer wells, and a drop of anti-human antiserum is loaded into the center well. The process is repeated for antisera to other species, such as dog, cat, and cow; this may include the species from which the antiserum was obtained (e.g., rabbit).

The plates are left to incubate for a suitable period (which can range from a few hours to overnight), and the serum proteins and antibody molecules diffuse outward from the wells. A precipitin band is formed when the diffusing stain contains proteins that are recognized by IgG molecules in the diffusing antiserum. The precipitin band is sometimes clearly visible to the naked eye, but it is normal to stain the plates with amido black or other general protein stain to enhance sensitivity and clarity.

Crossover electrophoresis for species identification is conducted using agar at a pH of 8.6. Stain extracts are loaded into wells arranged in a line at the cathode end of the plate, and the antiserum is loaded into wells at the anode end. During electrophoresis, the electric field drives the serum proteins toward the anode, but the IgG molecules, which are essentially neutral at this pH, are driven to the cathode by the process of electroendosmosis. The antigen–antibody precipitation occurs at the interface between the two rows of wells. Electroendosmosis occurs because the supporting medium acquires a net negative charge. If free, the negatively charged molecules would migrate to the anode, but this is not possible because the agar is immobilized on the plate. Instead, the effect is countered by positively charged water molecules migrating to the cathode. The migrating water molecules carry any dissolved neutral molecules (such as IgG) with them.

Dipstick pregnancy tests are an everyday example of the basic principles that underpin the ABAcard® and similar tests for human blood and semen.

246

IMMUNOLOGIC TEST STRIPS

The method of choice today is the use of test strips that incorporate monoclonal and **polyclonal antibodies** in a series of reactions as stain extract migrates up the strip. The first successful implementation was the ABAcard® HemaTrace test strips manufactured by Abacus Diagnostics, Inc. Stain extract is applied to the bottom of the test strip, where any human hemoglobin present in the extract will combine with a monoclonal antihuman hemoglobin antibody. The antibody is labeled with a pink dye. Any antibody–antigen formed then migrates through an absorbent membrane to the test area of the strip. The test area has an immobilized polyclonal antihuman hemoglobin that will capture the Ag–Ab complex to form an Ab–Ag–Ab sandwich. The pink dye becomes visible as a band in the test region at concentrations of human hemoglobin above about 0.05 µg/mL. An internal control consisting of human hemoglobin antibody–dye conjugate cannot bind to the antibody in the test area but is captured by an antibody in the control area. A correctly functioning positive test will therefore show two pink bands, one in the test area and one in the control area. A correctly functioning negative test will show

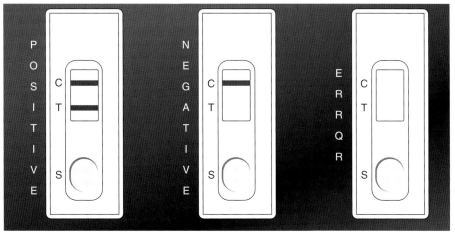

FIGURE 11.8
The ABAcard HemaTrace test for identification of human blood. Stain extract is applied to the sample area (S) which contains monoclonal antihuman hemoglobin tagged with a dye. If the extract is from human blood, the hemoglobin antibody–dye complex migrates in solution to the test area (T) which contains immobilized polyclonal antihuman and captures the complex to form a visible line. As an internal control, any dye-tagged antibody not bound to human hemoglobin continues to migrate to the control area (C) where it is precipitated by an immobilized antibody to the antihuman hemoglobin antibody. A positive test will show two colored lines as the reagents are set up with an excess of the dye-tagged antibody. A negative will only show a line in the C region. A failed test will show no lines in either the T or C regions. "ABAcard" and "HemaTrace" are registered marks of Abacus Diagnostics Inc. Courtesy NFSTC.

only one pink band, in the control area. If there is any problem with the test, there will be no visible bands. The process is illustrated in Figure 11.8.

The ABAcard® test has been extensively validated and shown to be sensitive, specific, and rapid.

BLOOD GROUPING

Once a stain has been identified as blood, the next step is to conduct tests that can provide information as to the possible donor of the material. Today the sensitivity and power of DNA testing means that most of the time tests will provide what in effect is an identification of the origin of the material.

Selection of a Blood Grouping System

Before the advent of DNA testing in the late 1980s, blood grouping depended on the detection of a range of genetically determined characters in the sample. The features of a good typing system are that it does the following:

- Shows variability from person to person but is constant within one individual
- Is stable in shed form
- Can be detected reliably at the concentrations found in forensic samples
- Has a known and stable frequency of occurrence within the population

> **BOX 11.2   POPULATION FREQUENCY AND BLOOD TYPING**
>
> The last point in the preceding list of features of a good typing system—population frequency—is the key to interpretation of results. A marker that meets the other requirements but is present in most of the population will not be very useful in assigning origin to a sample. Some simple statistics illustrate the point. Take a fictitious blood group system, AZ, in which 90% of the population are type A and 10% are type Z. What is the probability that two people at random will have the same AZ blood type? The probability of two type A is 0.9^2, or 0.81; the probability of two type Z is 0.1^2, or 0.01; and the probability of two type AZ is $(0.9 \times 0.1)^2$, or 0.0081. The probability of both being the same is therefore $0.81 + 0.01 + 0.0081$, or 0.828. The probability that two samples taken at random will be different is therefore $1 - 0.828$, or approximately 17%. This statistic is sometimes called the *discriminating power* of the typing system.

In practice, all the typing systems that were used in traditional forensic serology were genetically determined polymorphisms. Provided that the systems are also genetically independent, the population frequency data for each system can be multiplied. This is the product rule and will be addressed in the next chapter, "DNA." However, even with multiple systems, it was unusual to obtain population frequency data much rarer than about 1% for a typical blood or body fluid stain sample.

The only absolute comment that could be made was that when the groups of an evidence stain did not match those of the proposed source, the stain must have come from someone else. When the results gave no exclusion, interpretation of mixtures and of stains with combined population frequencies more common than a few percent was sometimes difficult. The biologic results may have been corroborative of other evidence, such as eyewitness testimony, but the weight that could properly be attached was often overestimated.

ABO Grouping

Hundreds of blood groups characterized on the basis of red cell antigens have been documented. They include clinically important groups such as Rhesus, a range of variants of A and B, and a whole suite of groups, such as Kell, Kidd, and Duffy, which were used in tissue typing before DNA became the method of choice. **Blood grouping** conventionally means assignment of an ABO blood type, and this is the only one that proved to be of value for forensic applications.

The discovery of ABO blood groups was made by Landsteiner in 1901. While investigating the properties of blood, he showed that serum separated from the blood of some individuals would cause clumping, or agglutination, of the red cells isolated from those of some other individuals, but not from those from themselves. Not all serum and not all red cell combinations would react.

Landsteiner identified the response as being due to interaction of antibody in serum with antigens on red cell surfaces, and he was able to describe four blood types and measure their frequency of occurrence in the population (see Table 11.4).

Table 11.4	Blood Types		
Type	**Cells**	**Serum**	**Population Frequency***
A	A antigen	anti-B	42.3%
B	B antigen	anti-A	9.4%
AB	A and B antigen	no antibody	3.5%
O	no antigen	anti-A and anti-B	44.8%

*These are approximate figures for Caucasians in the U.S. There are differences depending on race and geographical location. For example, group B blood is more common in persons of negroid race (around 20%).

It took about 60 years for Landsteiner's work to be developed into a usable test for classifying blood type in stains. The first partially successful attempt was introduced by Lattes in 1915. The basic problem is that the RBCs are destroyed when a stain is formed, and so there is nothing to subject to an agglutination reaction. Lattes realized that antibodies were less susceptible to degradation in stains and might be detectable. He developed a method for extraction of antibody and identification with indicator A and B cells. However, two problems remained. The first was that the low levels of antibody extractable from stains made the test somewhat unreliable. The second was that identification of AB blood depended on making a call from a negative observation (no agglutination with A and no agglutination with B indicator cells), which was not a scientifically acceptable thing to do.

Various attempts to type stains by identifying the antigen were tried for the next 45 years, and a sufficiently reliable method, **absorption–elution**, was eventually introduced in the early 1960s by Kind and by Outterridge.

Absorption–elution depends on detecting antibody that has been bound by A or B antigen on immobilized fragments of the lysed cell surface. The antibody is then eluted and detected with A or B indicator cells. Since group O blood has no antigen, there will be no bound antibody to elute and detect. That means that almost half the samples tested will produce no detectable result. However, group O cells do in fact possess antigen on their surface. It is a precursor of the A and B antigens and designated as *H substance*. Certain botanical extracts called *lectins* can act like antibodies, and the extract from *Ulex europaeus* reacts with H substance to agglutinate group O cells. The extract is called *H-lectin*. The chemistry of A, B, and H is dealt with in the later section, "Semen."

The procedure works because the IgM antibody molecules have an optimum reaction temperature of around 4 °C. The first step, specific binding, is conducted at 4 °C and then the temperature raised to 56 °C, which disrupts the noncovalent Ag–Ab interactions and elutes antibody from its bound state. H-lectin behaves sufficiently

FIGURE 11.9
ABO typing of blood stains. Schematic of the absorption–elution typing of blood stains. Figure A shows a blood-stained fiber (1) that has been attached to an inert base (2). The triangles on the fiber represent group A antigen. Figure B shows anti-A antibody added to the fiber. The antibody (3) is an IgM molecule and is a pentamer. Anti-A binds to the A antigen but other antibodies do not and are removed in the washing step. The absorption phase is conducted at 4 °C, the optimum for the antigen–antibody reaction. Figure C shows the anti-A antibodies being eluted from the bound antigen when the temperature is raised to 56 °C. Figure D shows the eluted antibody combining with added group A indicator cells to produce a visible agglutination reaction. Courtesy NFSTC.

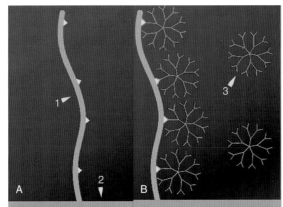
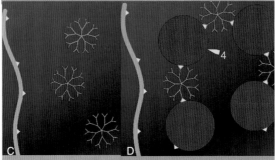

similarly to permit identification of group O stains. Note that since H is a precursor of A and B, and since absorption–elution is very sensitive, A and B stains will usually also display H activity.

Immobilization of stain can be achieved in various ways. The two most widely used are fixing a single thread from the stain (or from a swab of the stain, if it is not on fabric) onto a glass or plastic plate with glue (nail polish) or heat, or making an extract of the stain in 5% ammonia and heat-fixing it to the plate. (See Figure 11.9.)

Characterizing body fluid stains by absorption–elution typing for ABO group was one of the most significant advances in forensic biology. However, the technique has its problems. The major difficulty is that stains can sometimes produce false positive results, especially for group B, due to contamination. Running appropriate negative controls is a vital step, and results from any sample that shows a false positive must be discarded. The sources of contamination include sweat on clothing, as well as cross-reacting materials in substrates such as denim fabric and soiled shoes.

The end point—agglutination of test cells by eluted antibody—is subject to some variability also. Different observers may read weak results differently, and many samples will come up positive if left long enough. Confirmation of test readings by a qualified second reader in a period of time less than 20 minutes from the addition of indicator cells is a key quality control measure. (See Figure 11.10.)

Enzyme Groups

Because of these limitations in ABO grouping and the absence of alternative red cell antigen systems that met the requirements of an effective grouping system, forensic serologists had to look to different kinds of inherited **biochemical markers** to extend the discrimi-

FIGURE 11.10
Agglutination. The agglutination reaction depicted in Figure 11.9B results in red cells clumping together into granular lumps. Agglutination is usually graded between 4+ (all cells in the microscope field are agglutinated) to 0 (no cells in the microscope field are agglutinated). This photograph is typical of a 4+ agglutination. From http://en.wikipedia.org/wiki/Image:Bedside_card.jpg

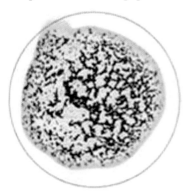

nating power of typing. Attention turned to enzymes found on the red cell membrane, with phosphoglucomutase (PGM) being one of the earliest and most successful examples. PGM catalyzes the reversible conversion of glucose-1-phosphate and glucose-6-phosphate, with glucose-1,6-diphosphate as a cofactor. PGM is an important metabolic enzyme and is found throughout the body. It is expressed at many loci, and the form found in red cells is designated as the PGM 1 locus, usually written as PGM_1. The PGM 1 locus is also expressed in semen, which increased its value in forensic serology. There are two alleles, designated "1" and "2," giving the phenotypes PGM_1 1, PGM_1 2, and PGM_1 2-1. Note that the locus is often assumed and the subscripted identifier omitted. The population frequencies for the three phenotypes are approximately 59%, 36%, and 5%, respectively. The actual frequencies vary by race and ethnicity. Rare variants of the 1 and 2 alleles have been found.

Other red cell enzymes used in forensic biology include the following:

- Erythrocyte acid phosphatase (EAP)
- Esterase D (EsD)
- Edenylate kinase (AK)
- Adenosine deaminase (ADA). (See Figure 11.11.)
- Glyoxalase (GLO)

The enzymes vary in their stability in stains, the reliability of typing, and the sensitivity of tests, as well as in their discriminating power. Although discriminating power can be increased by testing for more than one enzyme, each individual test consumes sample, typically about six 1-centimeter threads from a stain on cotton cloth. One partial solution is to run more than one system at a time, and Multi Enzyme Systems (or MES) became popular for a while. Typical combinations included PGM, EsD and GLO, and PGM, ADA, and AK.

Identification of the polymorphisms in all the preceding systems depends on the same basic principles:

- The changes in structure affect the net charge of the isoenzymes.
- The isoenzymes can be separated by simple electrophoresis.
- The locations of the separated isoenzymes can be visualized by reactions that depend on the specific enzyme activity.

Starch gel was the usual separation medium, but cellulose acetate, polyacrylamide, and agarose were also used. Most of the detection systems used a biochemical chain reaction in which the enzyme of interest reduced nicotinamide adenine dinu-

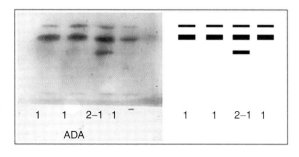

1   1   2–1 1   1   1   2–1 1

ADA

FIGURE 11.11
Red cell enzyme typing. Blood typing using identification of red cell enzyme polymorphism by simple starch gel electrophoresis. The system illustrated is adenosine deaminase (ADA). Left is a photograph of a starch gel electrophoresis plate and right is a diagrammatic representation. Original image by author.

cleotide phosphate (NADP) to NADPH with the concomitant conversion of MTT tetrazolium (3-(4,5-dimethylthiazol-2-yl)-2, 5-diphenyltetrazoliumbromide) to the purple-colored formazan in the presence of phenazine methosulfate (PMS).

Some of the enzymes—EsD and EAP, for example—can hydrolyze esters to produce a fluorescent compound that can be visualized under UV light.

A variant of electrophoresis is isoelectric focusing (IEF), where a pH gradient is formed during the electrophoresis and molecules move until the point in the gel at which they carry no charge. IEF produces much sharper bands than slab gel electrophoresis. Attempts to improve PGM separation by using IEF gave a surprising result; namely, the discovery of a further two alleles, the expression of which was not detected by starch gel separations. Each of the alleles detectable by starch gel electrophoresis had two alternate forms, designated as the "+" and "−" alleles. Thus, the 10 phenotypes were composed of the four homozygous forms PGM 1+, PGM 1−, PGM 2+, PGM 2−, and their heterozygous expressions. (See Figure 11.12.)

Sometimes referred to as *PGM subtyping*, IEF was probably one of the best techniques available before the advent of DNA typing. The technique could type very low concentrations of enzyme, and the enzyme itself was stable in blood and semen stains.

Serum Protein Polymorphisms

Some of the proteins circulating in serum display detectable polymorphisms, with alleles that have sufficient frequency differences to be of value in blood typing. Transferrin (Tf) and group-specific component (Gc) were two that offered considerable promise and were becoming routinely used just before the advent of DNA typing. However, haptoglobin (Hp) was the most widely used of the polymorphic serum proteins in forensic biology.

Haptoglobin is a hemoglobin binding protein found in the α-globulin fraction of serum. There are two alleles, designated Hp 1 and Hp 2, with several rare variants at each allele. The alleles are separated by electrophoresis on a gradient polyacrylamide gel (that is, one in which the concentration of polyacrylamide varies

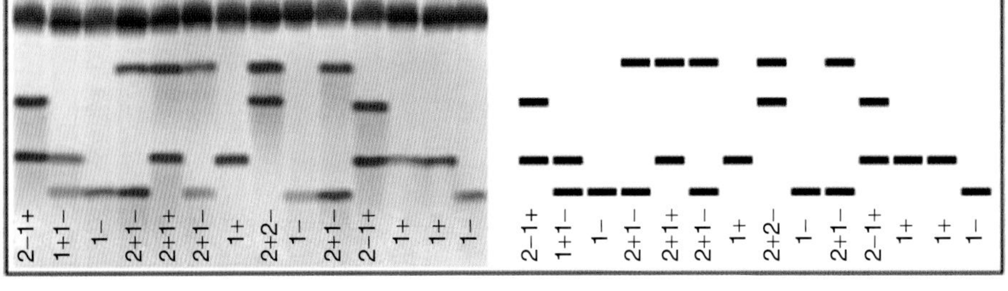

FIGURE 11.12
Isoelectric focusing. Blood typing using identification of red cell enzyme polymorphism by isoelectric focusing of phosphoglucomutase (PGM) in polyacrylamide gels. The left side is the original test result and the right side is a diagrammatic representation. Note that the bands are much sharper than those from starch gel separation as seen in Figure 11.11. Courtesy NFSTC.

from 5% at the top to 30% at the bottom, so giving enhanced separation by molecular sieving).

Haptoglobin 1 is a monomer consisting of two pairs of peptide chains (α and β) joined by disulfide bridges. Electrophoresis of serum from someone who is homozygous for Hp 1

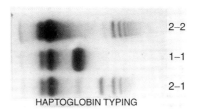

2–2

1–1

2–1

HAPTOGLOBIN TYPING

FIGURE 11.13
Blood typing using identification of serum protein polymorphism by polyacrylamide gradient gel. The system illustrated is haptoglobin (Hp). Original image from author.

shows only one band. In contrast, samples from someone who is homozygous for Hp 2 display multiple bands on electrophoresis. Curiously, electrophoresis of a sample from a heterozygous Hp 2-1 shows a band matching the Hp 1 band along with multiple other bands, but these do not align exactly with those from a haptoglobin 2 homozygous person (see Figure 11.13). The Hp 2 proteins are similar to Hp 1 in that they are composed of α and β peptide chains cross-linked by disulfide bridges. However, the α peptides (α2) are not the same as those in Hp 1. Furthermore, the proteins are found as polymers of the structure $\alpha_{2n}\beta_{n'}$ where n is between 3 and 8. In heterozygotes, some of the polymers incorporate α1 chains as well as α2 ones.

Haptoglobin is a reasonably good system for use in forensic serology. It is stable in stains and the assay is quite sensitive, using one of the hemoglobin screening procedures such as leucomalachite green to visualize the bands by reacting with the bound hemoglobin.

Hemoglobin

Mention has been made of the role of hemoglobin in screening and confirmatory tests for blood. Hemoglobin is yet another protein formed from two pairs of polypeptide chains. There are several variants of hemoglobin. All have the same structure for one of the pairs of polypeptide chains—designated as α. The dominant form found in adult humans is termed *hemoglobin A* (Hb A) and is composed of two α and two β chains. About 2 to 3% of human adult Hb consists of a variant called *HbA2*, in which the β chains are replaced by two δ chains. A more significant variant is HbF, which makes up about 70% of the hemoglobin in fetal blood. HbF has a pair of γ chains instead of β. HbF is rapidly replaced by HbA after birth, and only a trace remains by age 1 year.

Detection of HbF in a bloodstain is an indicator of fetal blood. The usual test is a combination of electrophoresis and the resistance of HbF to alkali denaturation.

SEMEN

Semen is produced by the male sex organs. There is a cellular component, spermatozoa, and a fluid component, seminal plasma. An average ejaculate is 3 to 4 mL, containing 70 to 150 million sperm. Sperm are the male reproductive cells. Each consists of a head, tail, and midpiece. In humans, the head is a tiny disc, about 4.5 μm long and 2.5 μm wide. The tail is about 40 μm long and is rapidly lost in ejaculates. The head is where the DNA is preserved. Ape sperm

FIGURE 11.14
Sperm structure. Diagram of a human sperm showing the three main structural parts. From http://commons. wikimedia.org/wiki/ Image:Simplified_ spermatozoon_diagram. svg

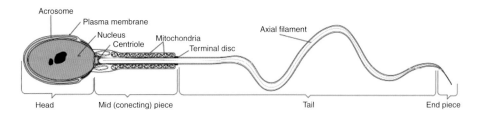

Acrosome
Plasma membrane
Nucleus
Centriole
Mitochondria
Terminal disc
Axial filament

Head   Mid (conecting) piece   Tail   End piece

are similar in size and shape. Dogs have similarly shaped sperm but about one-third the size of human sperm. Other animals have differently shaped sperm. (See Figure 11.14.)

Seminal plasma contains proteins, salts, organics (including flavins, which are the source of its UV fluorescence, and choline, which is the basis of a confirmatory test), and some cellular material. The components originate from several sources, including seminal vesicles and the prostate gland. The prostate is the source of the enzyme **acid phosphatase** and the protein *prostate-specific antigen*, or p30 protein.

Vasectomy severs or ligates the ducts carrying sperm to the penis. Thus, vasectomized men will have no sperm but will have the plasma components present in their ejaculate. These include ABO blood group substances, PGM, and some cellular material, so typing is possible.

After ejaculation during intercourse, semen is lost by drainage and by biochemical change. Microscopical examination of vaginal swab samples shows a sequence of changes with time. Tails are lost first—the damage begins immediately, and about 25% will have no tails by 6 hours. By 12 hours, there will be few sperm with intact tails, and by 24 hours, there will be mainly heads left. These proportions and times are highly variable. Sperm survival in stains outside the body depends on environmental conditions, but a small stain that has dried quickly may have intact sperm preserved for months or even years.

Screening Tests

Human semen contains high concentrations of acid phosphatase, which can therefore be the basis of a screening test. The reaction is based on the hydrolysis of phosphate esters and detection of the liberated organic moiety by production of a color complex; for example, the reaction of acid phosphatase with sodium alphanaphthylphosphate and fast blue B to produce a purple-blue coloration. As with the screening test for blood, a positive result is the rapid formation of the intensely colored product—less than 20 seconds or so, or 30 seconds at most.

Confirmatory Tests

The reliable identification of semen in stains on clothing and in swabs from body orifices is an important piece of evidence that the laboratory can contribute to the investigation of sexual offenses. There are two main approaches: identification of sperm, which is not possible in cases where the man was aspermic or can be extremely difficult in cases where more than a day has passed between the sexual act and the collection of samples; and the identification of components of seminal plasma, which has suffered from lack of specificity in the past.

SPERM MICROSCOPY

The best identification of semen is from its microscopy. The shape and dimensions of the human spermatozoon are unique. Although the morphology of intact sperm is highly characteristic, they can be difficult to locate microscopically, especially in samples that have bacterial or yeast infection and if they have lost their tails. Detection is simplified by histopathological staining. The most usual stain is popularly known as the *Christmas tree stain* because of the bright colors (see Figure 11.15). It utilizes nuclear fast red that differentially stains the DNA-containing head bright crimson, and a counterstain of picric acid–indigo-carmine (PIC) that stains the tails green-blue-gray. The traditional histological staining of hematoxylin and eosin (H&E) is also used, as is Giemsa stain.

IMMUNOLOGIC TEST STRIPS

The currently accepted method of choice for identification of semen in all circumstances is detection of p30 using specific antibody test strips, such as the ABAcard® test strips manufactured by Abacus Diagnostics, Inc. These work in the same way as ABAcards® described earlier for confirmation of blood, except that they use anti-p30 monoclonal and polyclonal antisera, and a pink dye.

OTHER TESTS

Prostate-specific antigen, or p30, has been used in a less specific form than described previously for ABAcards®. Stain extracts can be run against polyclonal anti-p30 using Ouchterlony or crossover electrophoresis. However, these tests are not as reliable as the monoclonal–polyclonal sandwich technique incorporated into the strip methods.

Semen Typing

The ability to draw inferences as to the origin of semen in a sexual assault case is obvious. The power to do this in traditional serology was limited and depended mainly on ABO and PGM typing. The PGM 1 locus is expressed in semen and vaginal secretions, and the methodology and interpretation used in its typing are exactly the same as for blood.

About 80% of the population has very high levels of ABO antigens in body secretions. These persons are described as **secretors**. The remaining 20% of the population are

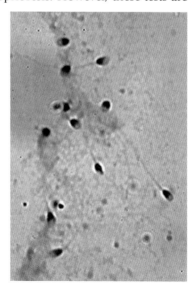

FIGURE 11.15
Human spermatozoa. Extract from semen recovered from vaginal swab and stained with Christmas tree stain. Courtesy NFSTC.

255

John Preece

Early in 1973, the body of Helen Wills was found at the side of a quiet road in the north of England. Police inquiries led to the arrest and trial of John Preece, a truck driver. It was alleged that Helen was a hitchhiker whom he had picked up, and that he had raped and strangled her and dumped her body. At trial, the defense agreed that Mr. Preece had given Ms. Wills a lift in the truck but that she had left at a stop many miles from where the body was found.

The testimony of Dr. Alan Clift, a forensic scientist with the English Home Office, was an important part of the evidence that led to the conviction. Dr. Clift reported that he had found semen of group A on a vaginal swab taken from the body of Ms. Wills, and that since Mr. Preece was a type A secretor, the semen could have been his. Dr. Clift also reported finding many hairs and fibers on the clothing of the deceased that could have originated in the cab of the accused's truck. Although group A semen is quite common, being present in about 32% of men in the United Kingdom, this was taken as corroboration of the sexual element of the allegation, in contrast to the fiber evidence, which would have been present whether or not Ms. Wills had been raped.

The case was appealed in 1981 and the work of Dr. Clift subjected to detailed scrutiny. It so happened that Ms. Wills was also a type A secretor, but this fact and its implications for interpretation of the grouping results had not been disclosed by Dr. Clift in his testimony. Dr. Clift claimed that he had used a variant of the absorption–elution test that was specific for semen components in mixed semen–vaginal secretions.

The court held that Dr. Clift's test had not been demonstrated to be valid, that the onus was on him to reveal any limitations in interpretation of his conclusions, and the fact that Ms. Wills was also a type A secretor made Dr. Clift's results of no probative value. The conviction was overturned.

258

OTHER BODY TISSUES

Saliva

Saliva is the fluid that moistens the mouth. It is secreted from three sets of glands: sublingual, submandibular, and parotid. The saliva from the parotid glands contains **amylases**, which aid in the digestion of carbohydrates. (See Figure 11.16.)

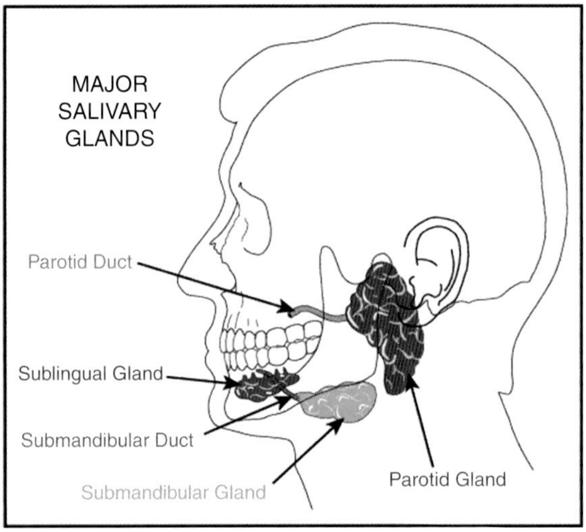

Saliva can be the source of evidence in sexual offenses where oral contact is alleged, where there are bite marks, or on cigarette butts discarded at a scene.

Screening for saliva is based on detection of high levels of amylase in the sample. It is not a confirmatory test, as amylase is found in other body fluids.

FIGURE 11.16
Salivary glands. Diagram of the face showing the location of salivary glands. Courtesy NFSTC.

MAJOR SALIVARY GLANDS

Parotid Duct

Sublingual Gland

Submandibular Duct

Submandibular Gland

Parotid Gland

Vaginal Secretions

Vaginal secretions are a complex mixture of cells and secretions. There is no absolutely reliable test to identify material as being from the vagina. In contrast, vaginal secretions contain acid phosphatase, ABH blood group substances, PGM, and DNA and can contribute to results obtained when vaginal swabs are tested.

Some laboratories attempt to differentiate between vaginal secretions and semen based on the morphology of cellular content. Vaginal epithelial cells are large, and many contain glycogen, which can be demonstrated by staining with iodine in the form of a solution or exposing to iodine vapor. However, the presence of glycogenated cells is variable depending on the stage of the estrous cycle.

Feces

Feces are food residues passed after completion of travel through the digestive system. Feces have a characteristic odor mainly due to skatole. Laboratories may be requested to test stains or other samples for the presence of feces. This occurs in the investigation of anal intercourse or where perpetrators have fouled a crime scene. The screening of samples depends on the detection of **urobilinogen**, a bile pigment excreted in feces, which may be detected using its fluorescent reaction to Edelman's reagent.

Bone

Bone is the tissue that makes up the skeleton. Bone is composed mainly of minerals and collagen, with the minerals (mainly calcium carbonate) making up about 65% of the total mass. The structure makes bones resistant to decay, and skeletal remains may be submitted to the laboratory for identification. Physical attributes such as size and shape, and the presence of injury sites, are probably the most valuable aspects of skeletal remains to examine. However, on occasion serological typing is required. This was not a fruitful area in traditional serology but does yield excellent evidence in DNA typing.

Hair

Hair is an appendage of mammalian skin. It grows outward from its root, which lies below the surface of the skin and is housed within a hair follicle. The root

259

BOX 11.3   HAIR MICROSCOPY

Some authors have suggested that microscopy can be a very discriminating technique for assignment of the source of recovered hairs. However, there is considerable within-person variation in the features used. Samples of at least 20 exemplars are recommended, and even then more modern sources doubt that it is scientifically sound to go beyond exclude or not exclude a nominated source as being the origin of the recovered samples. Where it is not possible to exclude on the basis of microscopy, mitochondrial DNA typing can be conducted.

In contrast to the person who was the source of the hairs, microscopy permits reliable assignment of racial and body region from which the hair came.

FIGURE 11.17
Hair. Roots of hairs in anagen, telogen and catagen phases. Courtesy NFSTC.

Anagen Phase   Catagen Phase   Telogen Phase

is surrounded by an inner root sheath and an outer root sheath. The hair shaft that protrudes above the skin surface is made of a strong structural protein called *keratin*, the same protein that makes up the nails and the outer layer of skin. Microscopy is the main technique used for examination of hair samples.

Hair follicles grow in repeated cycles, termed the *anagen, catagen,* and *telogen* phases. Most hairs are in the anagen or growth phase, during which they have a full-sized and active follicle. (See Figure 11.7.)

At the end of the anagen phase, hairs enter into the transition, or catagen, phase. The hair follicle shrinks, and metabolic activity and hair growth begin to slow down. The hair then enters the resting, or telogen, phase. Metabolism and growth cease. The follicle eventually re-enters the anagen phase, and a new hair grows, pushing out the old dead one.

Although there is some evidence that the hair shaft can contain ABO substances, identification of origin of a hair by the techniques available to traditional serology depends on the shed hair having root material attached. In these cases, ABO and enzyme typing can produce good results.

Today, nuclear and mitochondrial DNA typing allow excellent assignment of origin of hairs even when there is no root material. There is some controversy about nuclear DNA typing of shafts. It may be that results depend on the presence of adsorbed material from sweat or other body fluids, therefore thorough washing is critical. Mitochondrial DNA typing is generally reliable but is, at present, a lengthy and costly procedure. It is best conducted on hairs that have been screened using conventional microscopy and found not to be distinguishable from the target source.

Urine

Urine contains a large amount of **urea**, a chemical by-product of normal metabolic processes in the body. Identification of high levels of urea can therefore serve as a screening test for urine in fluids or stains. The presence of creatinine is also used for screening purposes. Creatinine forms a red compound with picric acid (known as the Jaffe test). Urine also has a characteristic odor, which can help in locating its presence. Gentle heating of urine-stained materials gives rise to a distinctive odor.

Urine from secretors will contain ABH substances. This is a source of contamination in testing underclothing.

SUMMARY

The physical distribution of biological stains—such as blood spatter or smears—at the scene or on clothing may produce additional information about the crime.

A presumptive test for biological materials triggers further testing to identify a possible donor, often done by identifying markers in the DNA in the sample.

Many forensic biology tests depend on antigen–antibody interactions. Antibodies are proteins, called *immunoglobulins* (Ig), produced by white blood cells (WBC) in response to antigens.

Immunogen is an alternate name for a substance that invokes an immune response. Immunogen challenge results in a wide range of antibodies being produced, each specific to a different structural site on the immunogen, called an *epitope*.

Activated B lymphocytes produce one specific antibody, but the activated B lymphocytes undergo repeated cell divisions to produce a clone of antibody-producing cells. The antibody from each clone is identical and termed *monoclonal*. Many B lymphocytes take part in the immunologic response resulting in a polyclonal mixture.

Blood is a suspension of cells in an isotonic aqueous solution. The cellular component of blood is mainly comprised of red blood cells—about 45% of the total volume. These cells do not contain DNA.

White blood cells, which possess a nucleus (and therefore DNA), are involved in the body's responses to infection. They are responsible for antibody production. The fluid portion of unclotted blood is called *plasma*.

Most screening tests for blood depend on the peroxidase activity of hemoglobin. Confirmatory tests include crystallizations and precipitations.

A blood grouping system should show variability from person to person but be constant for one individual, stable in shed form, detected reliably at the concentrations found in forensic samples, and have a known and stable frequency of occurrence within the population.

Landsteiner described the ABO blood groups in 1901. He identified the response as being due to interaction of antibody in serum with antigens on red cell surfaces, and he was able to define four blood types and measure their occurrence in the population.

Characterizing body fluid stains by absorption–elution typing for the ABO group was one of the most significant advances in forensic biology. However, the technique has its problems. The major difficulty is that stains can sometimes produce false positive results, especially for group B, due to contamination.

Enzyme and serum protein polymorphisms can be used to type blood. Identification of the polymorphisms depends on how changes in structure affect the net charge of the isoenzymes, how the isoenzymes can be separated by simple electrophoresis, and how the locations of the separated isoenzymes can be visualized by reactions that depend on the specific enzyme activity.

Some of the enzymes can hydrolyze esters to produce a fluorescent compound that can be visualized under UV light.

Some serum proteins—such as transferrin (Tf), group-specific component (Gc), and haptoglobin (Hp)—display detectable polymorphisms with alleles that have sufficient frequency differences to be of value in blood typing.

Hemoglobin variants all have the same structure for one of the pairs of polypeptide chains—designated as α. In adult humans, hemoglobin A (Hb A) is composed of two α and two β chains. About 2 to 3% of human adult Hb consists of a variant called HbA2 in which the β chains are replaced by two δ chains.

A more significant variant is HbF, which makes up about 70% of the hemoglobin in fetal blood. HbF has a pair of γ chains instead of β. HbF is rapidly replaced by HbA after birth, and only a trace remains by age 1 year.

Semen has a cellular component, spermatozoa, and a fluid component, seminal plasma. Seminal plasma contains flavins, the source of its UV fluorescence; acid phosphatase, identified in screening tests; and choline, the basis of a confirmatory test.

Semen is best identified by microscopy aided by histopathological staining, especially the "Christmas tree stain." Semen degrades rapidly over time. However, a semen stain that has dried quickly may preserve intact sperm for years.

The PGM 1 (PGM_1) locus is expressed in semen and vaginal secretions, and the methodology and interpretation used in its typing are exactly the same as for blood.

The A, B, and H antigens are polysaccharides. They are found on RBC surfaces as lipo-polysaccharides and in secretions as glycoproteins. Secretors—about 80% of the population—have very high levels of these antigens in body secretions.

Screening for saliva is based on detection of high levels of amylase in the sample. It is not a confirmatory test, as amylase is found in other body fluids.

There is no reliable test to identify vaginal materials. While vaginal epithelial cells are large and many contain glycogen, the presence of glycogenated cells varies with the estrous cycle.

Feces screening depends on the detection of urobilinogen, a bile pigment, which may be detected using its fluorescent reaction to Edelman's reagent. Urine contains urea, a metabolic by-product. Identification of high levels of urea can therefore serve as a screening test for urine in fluids or stains.

Nuclear and mitochondrial DNA typing allow excellent assignment of origin of hairs even when there is no root material.

PROBLEMS

1. Give the word or phrase for the following definitions:
   a. a process for separating charged molecules using an electric field
   b. chemicals that can be used to differentiate blood samples
   c. compounds that stimulate production of antibodies in an immune response
   d. a serum containing antibodies
   e. a system of dividing individuals that helps provide information as to the possible donor of the material
   f. a single type of antibody that is directed against a specific epitope
   g. people who express blood type antigens in bodily fluids
   h. a small molecule that can elicit an immune response when attached to a larger carrier such as a protein
2. What are some of the components of blood?
3. What are some of the differences between red and white blood cells?
4. What chemicals can help screen for
   a. semen
   b. urine
   c. feces
   d. saliva
5. What are some of the necessary characteristics of a blood group?
6. Describe the differences between monoclonal and polyclonal antibodies.
7. Describe the use and the positive result for
   a. precipitin test
   b. Takayama or hemochromogen test
   c. Teichmann test
   d. crossover electrophoresis
8. For a semen stain, how do each of the following contribute to analysis?
   a. sperm
   b. flavins
   c. acid phosphatase
   d. choline
9. Why is it difficult to determine if material was a vaginal contribution to a stain?
10. How can rootless hairs be typed?
11. Describe hemoglobin variants and what they may tell an examiner.

263

GLOSSARY

Absorption–elution a technique that detects antibodies that have been bound by A or B antigen on immobilized fragments of the lysed cell surface.

Acid phosphatase a chemical used to screen for semen.

Amylase a chemical used to screen for saliva.

Antibodies proteins, called *immunoglobulins* (Ig), which are produced by white blood cells (WBC) in response to challenge by foreign materials (antigens).

Antigens compounds that stimulate production of antibodies in an immune response but are sometimes defined as substances that combine with an antibody.

Antiserum serum containing antibodies.

Biochemical markers chemicals that can be used to differentiate blood samples.

Blood a suspension of cells in an isotonic aqueous solution.

Blood grouping a system of dividing individuals that helps provide information as to the possible donor of the material. Blood groups include clinically important groups such as Rhesus and the ABO typing system.

Crossover electrophoresis a test to determine blood origin.

Electrophoresis a process for separating charged molecules using an electric field.

Hapten a small molecule that can elicit an immune response when attached to a larger carrier such as a protein.

Immunogen name for a substance that invokes an immune response.

Immunoglobulins (Ig) two pairs of peptide chains linked to form a Y-shaped molecule. The chains in the longer pair are designated as "heavy," or H, and those in the shorter pair as "light," or L, chains. The chains within each pair are identical. There are five classes of immunoglobulins, each of which can be differentiated by their chemical structure.

Monoclonal antibody a single type of antibody that is directed against a specific epitope (antigen, antigenic determinant) and produced by a single clone of cells.

Plasma the unclotted liquid left when cells are removed from a blood sample.

Polyclonal antibody a heterogeneous mix of antibodies from a multiple B cell response to an antigen that will recognize a variety of epitopes on the antigen.

Precipitin test a test for blood origin using antisera.

Presumptive test a screening test used to locate body fluid stains.

Red blood cells these cells contain no DNA. They bring oxygen to tissues as a hemoglobin complex and remove carbon dioxide.

Secretors those who express blood type antigens in bodily fluids.

Semen the secretion produced by male sexual glands.

Serum the liquid left when cells are removed from a clotted blood sample.

Takayama, or hemochromogen, test a confirmatory crystal test for blood in which ferrous iron from hemoglobin reacts with pyridine to produce red feathery crystals of pyridine ferroprotoporphyrin.

Teichmann a confirmatory crystal test for blood where hemoglobin is converted to hemin and then to characteristic brownish-yellow rhomboid crystals.

Urea a chemical used to screen for urine.

Urobilinogen a bile pigment excreted in feces, which may be detected using its fluorescent reaction to Edelman's reagent.

White blood cells (WBC) containing DNA, they are involved in the body's responses to infection.

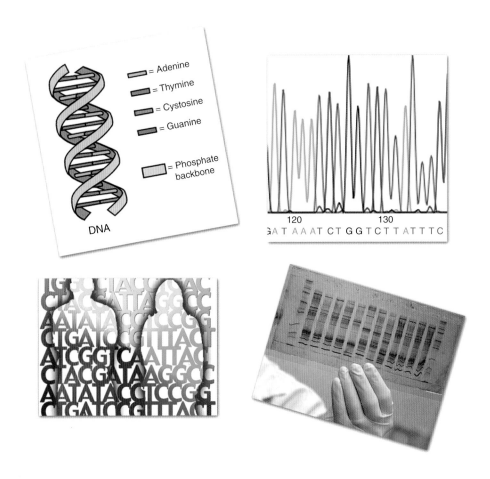

From top left, clockwise: DNA double helix structure; DNA sequencing; Lab scientist viewing RFLP autorad; depiction of human identity and DNA bases. Double helix: http://commons.wikimedia.org/wiki/Image:DNA_simple2.svg; Sequencing: http://commons.wikimedia.org/wiki/Image:DNA_sequence.svg Autorad: http://commons.wikimedia.org/wiki/Image:CBP_chemist_reads_a_DNA_profile.jpg; Identity: http://commons.wikimedia.org/wiki/Image:ATCG.jpg

CHAPTER 12

DNA

Case Study

Colin Pitchfork

The small English country town of Narborough was shocked by the rape and murder of 15-year-old schoolgirl Lynda Mann. A semen sample taken from Lynda's body was found to belong to a person with type A blood and an enzyme profile that matched 10% of the adult male population. At that time, November 1983, this was as far as identification of the semen could go, and the murder hunt was eventually wound down.

But not for long. Three years later the same fate befell 15-year-old Dawn Ashworth. Semen samples recovered from Dawn's body revealed that her attacker had the same blood type as Lynda's murderer. This time the investigation resulted in the development of a suspect, Richard Buckland. Richard was a 17-year-old youth who lived in the area and who revealed knowledge of the circumstances of Dawn's body that had not been made public. He confessed to the murder of Dawn but denied any involvement with the death of Lynda.

Police were convinced that Richard Buckland was responsible for both crimes and contacted Dr. Alec Jeffreys at the University of Leicester for assistance. Dr. Jeffreys had just published a paper on applying DNA profiling to forensic science, together with Dr. Peter Gill and Dr. David Werrett of the English Forensic Science Service (FSS). Significantly, in 1985, they were the first to demonstrate that DNA could be obtained from crime stains, which proved vital in this case. Dr. Jeffreys compared semen samples from both murders against a blood sample from the suspect, which conclusively proved that both girls were killed by the same man, but not Richard Buckland. The police then contacted the FSS, which verified the results.

The police then decided to undertake a comprehensive DNA screen. All adult males in three villages surrounding the location of the murders — a total of 5000 men — were asked to volunteer and provide blood or saliva samples. Blood grouping was performed and DNA profiling carried out by the FSS on the 10% of men who had the same blood type as the killer. None matched the DNA in the semen samples.

Disappointed and baffled, police continued with the investigation, and their patience was rewarded when a local man was overheard in a bar boasting that he had given a sample in the name of a friend, Colin Pitchfork. Pitchfork was located, samples taken and typed and found to match the crime DNA profiles. In 1988 he was sentenced to life imprisonment for the two murders.

INTRODUCTION

The case of Colin Pitchfork is an excellent example of the impact of **DNA profiling** compared to conventional blood typing. Without DNA, Richard Buckland's confession supported by the blood group evidence would almost certainly have resulted in his conviction for the rape and murder of Dawn Ashworth, and possibly Lynda Mann. It also shows the importance of taking a holistic view of crime investigations, as Pitchfork nearly got away with the blood switch.

It was the first criminal case where the perpetrator was identified through DNA profiling. It was the first where there was a mass population screen to narrow the field of possible suspects. It was the first where DNA was used to exonerate an innocent suspect.

The history and role of **deoxyribonucleic acid (DNA)** as the material that carries the genetic blueprint of all biological organisms has been known since Crick and Watson's research that was published in 1953. However, the basis of its use in forensic science is much more recent, beginning just 5 years before the Pitchfork case. Subsequent research showed that genes occupied only a very small part of the total material in a DNA molecule, and in 1980 Dr. Ray White and colleagues at the University of Utah found that some parts of the noncoding DNA were highly variable between individuals. White, a geneticist, suggested that these regions could be used in parentage testing. Dr. Jeffreys went further and showed how the variability could be used to type blood and body fluids in criminal cases.

cytosine

THE BIOCHEMISTRY OF DNA

Structure and Function

guanine

All cells, other than mature red blood cells, contain a nucleus that is where the body's DNA is located. The DNA molecule is a double helix, each strand being composed of four bases, or nucleotides: cytosine, guanine, thymine, and adenine. They are usually referred to by the first letter of their name: C, G, T, and A. The two strands are held together by chemical bonding in which T always pairs with A and G always pairs with C. A gene is a part of the DNA strand in which the order of C, G, T, and A is ultimately responsible for defining which amino acids are assembled in the synthesis of a specific protein. All of the DNA in a cell is known as the *genome*, and there are approximately 3 billion base pairs in the human genome. This description applies only to nuclear DNA. There is an entirely different genome in the mitochondria of cells, and this is described briefly later in the chapter.

thymine

adenine

All cells and therefore all tissues in the body have identical DNA, but every individual (apart from identical twins) has a unique DNA composition. We all have our own unique set of genes, but forensic DNA typing is based on inherited variations in noncoding regions of the DNA molecule. (See Figure 12.1.)

FORENSIC DNA TESTING
Restriction Fragment Length Polymorphisms

The parts of the DNA molecule discovered by White and developed by Jeffreys for typing body fluids and their stains consist of end-to-end repeats of sequences of bases. Hundreds of these sites have been described, with the core unit ranging in size from around 10 bases to more than 30. These systems are sometimes referred to as **variable number tandem repeats (VNTR)**, and the regions in the chromosome where they are located are called *minisatellites*. However, the feature that makes them useful for forensic typing is that the number of end-to-end repeats of the core units varies between individuals. For example, the number of repeats in the VNTR known as D1S80 can vary from 14 to 41. (See Figure 12.2.)

The number of repeats in a VNTR will determine the length of the DNA fragment containing it. The length difference is much too small to be detectable in the whole DNA molecule but is easy to identify if the area containing the VNTR can be isolated. This, the earliest form of DNA typing, therefore depended on incubating the DNA extracted from the body fluid with a restriction enzyme to cut it into hundreds of shorter lengths, separating them by size, and identifying the target sequence by adding a probe. The technique is known as **restriction fragment length polymorphism (RFLP)** analysis. It is no longer used in forensic biology but is described briefly in the following section.

RESTRICTION ENZYMES

Restriction enzymes, or restriction endonucleases, are enzymes that cut double-stranded DNA into smaller fragments. The enzyme targets a small sequence of nucleotides, typically 4 to 12 bases in length, and different endonucleases target different sequences. Because the target sequences are short, there are hundreds randomly distributed along a DNA molecule. Incubating DNA with a restriction enzyme will therefore yield a digest with hundreds of shorter DNA fragments.

The restriction enzyme favored in forensic work is Hae III, named from the bacterium *Haemophilus aegyptius* from which it is extracted. Hae III targets the sequence GGCC. The digest is subjected to electrophoresis through polyacrylamide gel to separate the fragments by size.

MULTILOCUS AND SINGLE-LOCUS PROBES

The final stage in RFLP analysis is to transfer the DNA fragments from the gel onto a stable medium, usually by leaving it in contact with a nylon membrane, and visualize the VNTR region with a probe. Probes

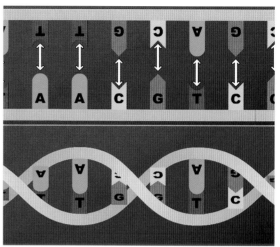

FIGURE 12.1
Base pairing. Each strand of DNA consists of the bases C, T, A, and G. The double helix is formed by chemical bonding between G and C and between A and T so that two complementary strands join up (Top) and then twist into the helix (Bottom). Courtesy NFSTC.

269

FIGURE 12.2
The repeat sequence in the VNTR D1S80. The sequence is repeated between 14 and 41 times. Courtesy NFSTC.

GAAGGAGGACCACCAGGAAGGAGGAC(

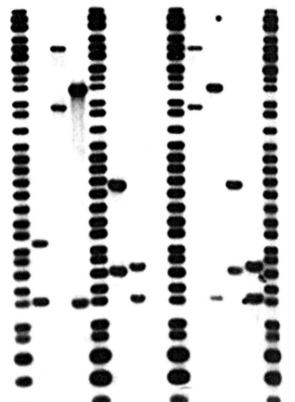

FIGURE 12.3
RFLP Analysis. Auto-radiograph of RFLP analysis of D10S28. From left to right: Lanes 1, 5, 9, and 14 are size markers; lanes 2, 3, 4, 6, 7, 10, 11, 12, and 13 are case samples. Courtesy NFSTC.

are short polymers—oligonucleotides—with nucleotide sequences complementary to the sequences in the target VNTR region. The probes contain a marker such as the radioactive isotope of phosphorus or a chemical tag that can be treated enzymatically to produce fluorescence. The nylon membrane is treated with a solution of probe and washed. Nucleotide sequences on the membrane that are complementary to the probe will hybridize with it; unbound probe is washed off. The radioactive or fluorescent tags can be detected by exposure to sensitive photographic film or electronically.

The original work of Jeffreys used probes that were complementary to several regions in the restriction fragments and resulted in multiple bands being developed on the membrane. These are called *multilocus probes* because of the multiple hybridization locations. However, they were replaced by *single-locus probes* that are much more specific to a defined VNTR. Membranes could be subjected to treatment with several probes, one after the other. (See Figure 12.3.)

The multiple banding results from multilocus probe or repeated single-locus probe development led to the terms *DNA fingerprinting* and *DNA profile* being used to describe the results of DNA identity testing. The term *DNA fingerprinting* is not used now, but the complete set of results from forensic DNA testing is still referred to as the *DNA profile* of the individual.

BOX 12.1   RFLP ANALYSIS

There are five steps in RFLP analysis:

1. Extract DNA.
2. Treat the extract with a restriction enzyme.
3. Separate the restriction fragments based on size using **gel electrophoresis**.
4. Immobilize the fragments by transferring to a nylon membrane (Southern blotting).
5. Locate and identify the fragments by applying a solution containing the probe of interest.

The process can take a long time—as much as 2 weeks—to complete.

Although RFLP analysis revolutionized the typing of forensic samples, it is not without its problems. It is a technically demanding procedure that requires relatively large amounts of sample. The end point of the assay is assignment of a length to the restriction fragments of interest by comparison with markers run on the gel along with the samples, a process that introduces a small but finite variability to the analysis. The length of time to develop profiles on the nylon membrane can be a problem when information is required rapidly for intelligence purposes. The procedure requires good-quality high-molecular-weight DNA and may not work successfully in scene samples that have undergone some degradation. Finally, although the amounts are small, laboratories prefer not to have to deal with the infrastructure and health and safety issues associated with handling radioactive materials.

The Polymerase Chain Reaction

In 1983, 2 years before Jeffreys, Gill, and Werrett used RFLP analysis in the Pitchfork case, Kary Mullis developed the **polymerase chain reaction (PCR)**. PCR mimics the way in which the body makes DNA and allows small target regions of DNA to be copied or replicated up to a million-fold.

The process begins by heating a solution of the DNA to separate it into its single strands. Primers—oligonucleotides synthesized to be complementary with sequences in the DNA that flank the region of interest—are added and the solution cooled to allow the primers to anneal to the binding sites. A reagent mixture containing DNA polymerase and C, G, T, and A is added and the temperature raised. The DNA polymerase adds nucleotides to the primer, pairing them with those on the original strand of DNA. The mixture is cooled to permit annealing. The original region of DNA has now been copied. The cycle is repeated and the two become four, with a doubling each time the cycle is repeated. The product is usually referred to as an **amplicon**.

Because the process depends on heating to temperatures well above those found in the body, a special thermal-resistant DNA polymerase is used. It is extracted from the bacterium *Thermus aquaticus* and is usually referred to as *Taq polymerase.* The process is illustrated in Figure 12.4. The temperatures of each stage are very important, and the apparatus used to rapidly heat and cool the reaction mixture is called a *thermal cycler.* Figure 12.5 shows the exponential growth in the number of amplicons with each cycle.

More from less. The PCR technique is theoretically capable of allowing a DNA profile to be developed from a single cell. However, possible contamination and technical issues limit the practical size of a sample to a tiny pinhead.

271

DQ$_\alpha$ AND POLYMARKER

The PCR process provided the answer to the drawbacks of RFLP analysis, and it was not long before it was applied to typing of body fluids and stains in crime cases. Given that the highly successful RFLP technique depended on identification of noncoding regions, it is ironic that the first successful implementations of the PCR reaction in forensic science were based on identification of genes.

At the time of the discovery of the PCR reaction, the human leukocyte antigen (HLA) had been used in tissue typing for decades. HLA is a large family of related genes, and the antigens are proteins that have been sequenced. Given

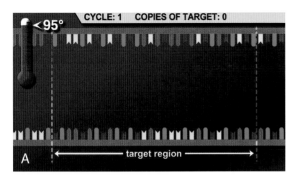

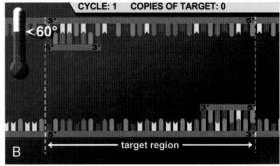

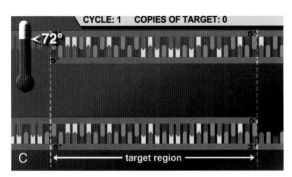

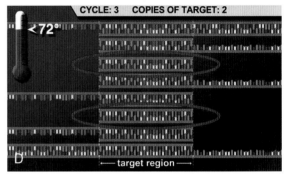

FIGURE 12.4

The PCR process. A: The solution of extracted DNA is heated to 95° and the DNA separates into single strands. B: The reaction is cooled to 60° and added primer anneals to the ends of the target region. C: The reaction temperature is raised to 72° and the DNA polymerase extends the primers to produce double-stranded DNA copies of the target region. D: At the end of the first cycle, although the region has been replicated the extension goes beyond the end of the region of interest and it is not until completion of the third cycle that exact copies are liberated into solution. Courtesy NFSTC.

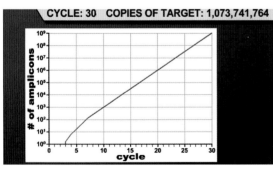

FIGURE 12.5

Cycle number and product. Relationship between number of cycles and number of amplicons produced. Courtesy NFSTC. Created by author from Stills from animation at http://www.nfstc.org/pdi/Subject04/pdi_s04_m01_01.htm

that the protein sequence is known, it is possible to work back and write the DNA code for the gene for any one of the antigens. This was done for the DQ_α (sometimes written as DQA1) system. The system was developed to be as simple as possible and used a technique known as *dot blotting* to produce a series of color reactions on a support membrane. The test membranes have a series of regions in which allele-specific oligonucleotides (ASO) are bound to the membrane matrix. Any matching amplicon will hybridize to the ASO and so itself be immobilized on the membrane. The bound amplicon can then be rendered visible through a colorimetric reaction, which leaves a colored dot or line on the membrane.

The DQ_α system was soon followed by polymarker (PM), which applied the same principles to identification of other genes, including low-density

Case Study

Gary Dotson

On the evening of July 9, 1977, two men forced a young woman into the backseat of a car and raped her. The victim identified Gary Dotson from a police mug book and in a police lineup. The prosecution's evidence at trial included a composite sketch of the assailant that was prepared by the police with the victim's assistance. Further, the state's expert serologist testified that the semen on the victim's undergarment came from a type B secretor and that Dotson was a type B secretor. There was also testimony that pubic hair removed from the victim's underwear was similar to Dotson's and dissimilar to the victim's. In July 1979, Gary Dotson was convicted of aggravated kidnapping and rape. He was sentenced to not less than 25 and not more than 50 years in prison.

In March 1985, the victim recanted her testimony. She said she had fabricated the rape to hide a legitimate sexual encounter with her boyfriend. Dotson contended that the victim's recantation of testimony constituted grounds for a new trial, but this was refused by the trial judge. In 1988, Dotson's attorney was able to have DNA tests conducted that were not available at the time of trial. A sample of semen from the victim's underwear was sent to Dr. Alec Jeffreys in England for RFLP analysis. The sample was badly degraded, however, and results were inconclusive. Samples were then sent to Forensic Science Associates in Richmond, California. DQA1 tests revealed that the spermatozoa on the victim's undergarments could not have come from Dotson but could have come from the victim's boyfriend. Dotson's conviction was overturned on August 14, 1989, after he had served 8 years in prison.

lipoprotein receptor (LDLR), glycophorin A (GYPA), hemoglobin G gamma globulin (HBGG), and group-specific component (Gc). Figure 12.6 shows a developed DQ_{α}–polymarker test strip. As can be seen, although the system has a simple final format, it is not always easy to read.

SHORT TANDEM REPEATS

The most significant advance in DNA typing came from the application of the PCR process to amplify **short tandem repeat (STR) sequences**. STRs are VNTR-like regions in the DNA molecule in which the repeated core unit is 2 to 5 base pair repeats long, sometimes referred to as a *microsatellite* rather than the minisatellite of a VNTR. Most forensic science laboratories now use a battery of between 10 and 20 STRs to characterize biological materials, and all the STRs in common use have core units that are four nucleotides long.

Although each **locus** displays a limited degree to which the core units are repeated, typing samples with the range of STR systems available results in a DNA profile that is essentially unique (other than identical twins). The process is aided by multiplexing in which eight or more loci are amplified at the same time.

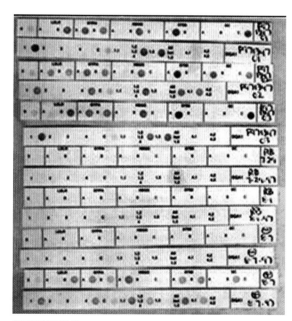

FIGURE 12.6
"Dot blot" techniques. Developed DQ_{α} and PM test strips. Courtesy NFSTC.

> ## BOX 12.2   PCR ANALYSIS
>
> There are four steps in the PCR analysis of STRs in a biological stain. The first is extraction of the DNA. Some substrates require special treatment to remove inhibitors of the PCR reaction. The second step is amplification in the thermal cycler, as illustrated in Figure 12.4; the amplification is usually carried out for 28 to 32 cycles. Next, the amplicons are then separated by capillary electrophoresis and finally, the data processed to identify the components present.

DNA ANALYSIS

Extraction

DNA can be purified and removed from blood or body fluid stains, including vaginal swabs, by organic or inorganic extraction. Organic extraction begins with solubilization of the stain components using a tris–EDTA buffer. The tris renders the cell membranes permeable, and the EDTA stabilizes the DNA by inhibiting nucleases. Cells in the stain are then lysed by the addition of a mixture of proteinase K, detergent (sodium dodecyl sulfate, or SDS), and dithiothreitol. The lysis step is followed by addition of a mixture of phenol, chloroform, and isoamyl alcohol (PCI). Mixing with PCI results in the production of separate organic and aqueous phases. The two-stranded DNA remains in the aqueous phase, and contaminants are removed in the organic phase. The final step is to treat the aqueous extract with ethanol or recover it on a microcentrifugal filter unit with pore sizes small enough to retain the large DNA molecules.

Inorganic extraction uses Chelex 100 ion exchange resin. Samples are boiled in a 5% suspension of Chelex in deionized water. Cell membranes are disrupted, proteins denatured, and the DNA split into its single strands. The suspension is centrifuged, removing the resin and cellular debris and leaving the DNA in aqueous solution.

The steps in the organic extraction, including the final centrifugation, help to remove inhibitors from the sample. Chelex does not achieve this; the boiling at alkaline pH is harsher, and the resin itself is an inhibitor of the PCR reaction. However, Chelex is simpler and less susceptible to introduction of contaminants.

Irrespective of the extraction method used, special techniques have to be used with the mixed male–female material present on vaginal swabs. The samples are subjected to differential extraction to separate the male and female components. Proteinase K is added to lyse epithelial and white blood cells but without affecting spermatozoa. The sample is centrifuged to separate the sperm as a pellet from the soluble lysate. Most laboratories then treat the supernatant with Chelex to extract the DNA from it. The resultant sample contains DNA originating from the female and is referred to as the *F1*, or *female fraction*.

The pellet containing the sperm is subjected to a second incubation with proteinase K and dithiothreitol, to produce the *F2*, or *sperm fraction*.

The concentration of DNA in the F1 and F2 fractions has to be measured so that the optimum amount of DNA can be used in the amplification phase. Typically, around 0.5 ng to 2.0 ng is desired. Several methods have been used, ranging from simple but nonspecific spectrophotometry (Figure 12.7) to modern techniques such as AluQuant or qPCR kits that are sensitive and specific for human DNA.

AluQuant is produced by the Promega Corporation. Alu is a restriction enzyme from *Arthrobacter luteus*, and Alu sequences are sequences of about 300 base pairs found widely throughout the human genome. It is estimated that there are more than 1 million different members of the Alu sequence family, around 7000 of them being unique to humans. The AluQuant reaction starts by enzymically producing deoxynucleoside triphosphate (dNTP) from the Alu sequences. ATP is produced from the dNTP and the amount produced measured enzymically.

Quantitative PCR, or qPCR, is the most accurate, precise, and efficient method currently available to quantify DNA. It is illustrated in Figure 12.8. The initial quantity of DNA in the sample is detected by subjecting it to PCR amplification and monitoring the exponential growth phase of the reaction. The cycle number at which the product exceeds the background "noise" of the process is directly proportional to the quantity of DNA in the reaction.

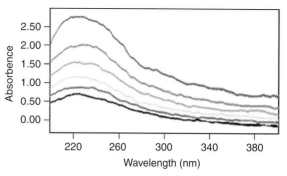

FIGURE 12.7
Quantitation of DNA by spectrophotometry. DNA has a broad absorption maximum around 240 nm and the absorbance increases with the concentration of DNA in the sample. Courtesy NFSTC.

Amplification

The first step in the development of a PCR method is the design of suitable primers. A PCR primer consists of two oligonucleotides of around 18 to 30 bases long that hybridize to complementary strands of the DNA template, and thus identify the region to be copied. A set of primers is used to amplify each DNA target region identified for the reaction. See Figure 12.4 for a diagrammatic representation of the amplification process.

The amplification takes place in small reaction tubes that are placed in a thermal cycler. The main properties of the thermal cycler are that it is capable of rapid heating and cooling to precise temperatures. The main steps requiring temperature control are primer annealing, primer extension, denaturation time and temperature, and cycle number. Figure 12.9 shows a typical thermal cycler. Primer annealing (Figure 12.4B) is generally best conducted in the range of 55 to 72 °C. Stringent annealing temperatures, especially during the first several cycles, will help

275

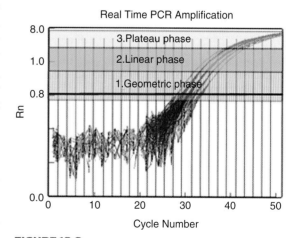

FIGURE 12.8
Quantitative PCR. Diagram of the qPCR reaction as used to identify and quantify human DNA in stain extracts. The family of curves represents different quantities of sample DNA. The curves are well-separated during the geometric phase of the reaction and are computer processed to give the amount of DNA present in the sample. Courtesy NFSTC.

FIGURE 12.9
Thermal cycler. The
Applied Biosystems
9700 thermal cycler,
with its lid open to show
the 96-well reaction
chamber. Courtesy
NFSTC.

FIGURE 12.10
Slab gel electrophoresis
apparatus. From
commons.wikimedia.
org/wiki/Image:
Gel_electrophoresis_
apparatus.jpg

increase specificity. The reaction temperature is briefly cooled to 40 to 60°C and then raised to 70 to 75°C. Primers anneal to the complementary sequence during the cooling phase and extend the primers with Taq polymerase during the heating phase.

Primer extension time and temperature depend upon the length and concentration of the target sequence and temperature. Primer extensions are usually performed at 72°C (see Figure 12.4C). Estimates for the rate of nucleotide incorporation at 72°C vary from 35 to 100 nucleotides per second, depending upon the buffer, pH, salt concentration, and the nature of the DNA template. An extension time of 1 minute at 72°C is considered sufficient for products up to 2 kb in length.

Denaturation time and temperature affect amplification at several points. The most likely cause for failure of a PCR is incomplete denaturation of the target template and/or the PCR product. Typical denaturation conditions are 95°C for 30 seconds or 97°C for 15 seconds; higher temperatures may be appropriate especially for targets containing a high GC percentage. Incomplete denaturation allows the DNA strand to snap back, reducing the product yield. Denaturation steps that are conducted at too high a temperature and for too long lead to unnecessary loss of enzyme activity.

The optimum number of cycles depends mainly on the starting concentration of the target DNA when other parameters are optimized. Too many cycles can increase the amount and complexity of nonspecific background products (**plateau effect**), and too few cycles can produce low product yield.

Separation

The PCR amplicons produced during the amplification stage have to be separated and individually identified. This is usually achieved using some form of electrophoresis. Early systems used slab gels, where polyacrylamide in hot solution was poured onto a glass plate and allowed to cool. Sample is introduced into wells cut in the gel and separation achieved through application of an electric current across the plate (see Figure 12.10). Polyacrylamide is used because it acts as a molecular sieve in addition to being a support medium for electrophoretic separation.

Better resolution is obtained using capillary column electrophoresis in which polymer is applied as a thin coating to the inside of a capillary column. Sample is injected into the column and driven through it by an electric current as with conventional electrophoresis. Components in the sample are separated according to their electrophoretic mobility and affinity for the polymer coating. They elute as a series of peaks.

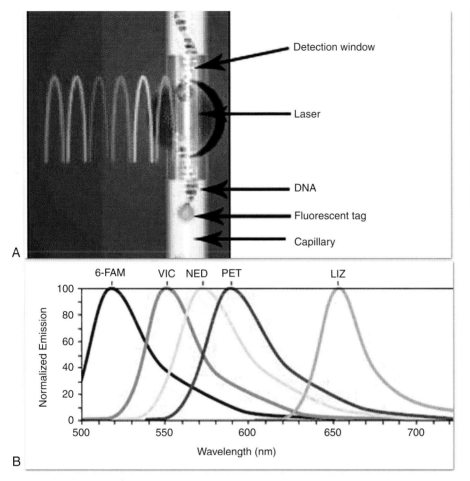

FIGURE 12.11
A. Detection of fluorescent labeled amplicons as they pass through the capillary column. B. Construction of electrophoretogram from the tagged amplicons. The letters "6-FAM." "VIC," "NED," "PET," and "LIZ" are the names of the fluorophore tags on the amplicon primers. Courtesy NFSTC.

Identification of eluted amplicons is achieved by using primers that have been tagged with fluorescent dyes. A laser beam scans the peaks as they near the end of the column and an electrophoretogram is constructed (see Figure 12.11).

POPULATION GENETICS

Basic Principles

GENETICS

Genes are the functional units in chromosomes that contain the nucleotide code for synthesis of specific proteins. The genes are not randomly distributed in nuclear DNA but are found at specific sites (locus) on chromosomes. Normal human tissue cells have 23 pairs of chromosomes (diploid cells). Twenty-two of the pairs are identical in shape and are called *autosomes*. The chromosomes that carry the genes that determine sex are not identical, with the Y, or male, chromosome being smaller than the X, or female, chromosome.

Sperm and egg cells differ from normal tissues in that their chromosomes are single (haploid cells), not paired. Fertilization, when sperm and ovum fuse, results in the embryo having one of each of the 23 chromosome pairs inherited from each parent. **Chromosomes** are therefore the physical units responsible for transmission of inherited characteristics.

The gene at any locus may have two or more variants. The variants are called **alleles**. Where someone inherits the same allele from both parents, either because there are no variant forms or because each parent happened to have contributed the same allele, they are **homozygous** for that allele. When each parent contributes a different allele, the child is **heterozygous**. In some cases heterozygotes will display the same characteristics as one parent. This is because the allele from the other parent is either not active or its expression is masked. The allele make up of the child is called its **genotype** and the observable expression of the genotype is the **phenotype** of the individual. Where only one of the two alleles in a heterozygote is seen in the phenotype, it is said to be a dominant allele and the other is said to be recessive.

BOX 12.3 REDHEADS AND BLONDES

About 4% of northern and western Europeans and their descendants are redheads. Redheads are homozygous for a recessive gene that regulates the production of two forms of the pigment melanin. One, eumelanin, is a dark pigment and the other, phaeomelanin, is red–yellow. The final hair color depends on the ratio of eumelanin to phaeomelanin, which is why redheads can be anything from flame red to auburn. Because the allele is recessive, redheaded parents will have redheaded children. If one parent is homozygous for the dominant form of the gene, then none of the children will be redheaded. True blonds are rare—probably less than 10% of the population. They have hardly any eumelanin or phaeomelanin in their hair, and the natural variations from platinum to strawberry reflect the proportions of the melanins present.

Noncoding regions of DNA are also under genetic control, and some of them display a high degree of heterozygosity. For example, the VNTR system D1S80 has at least 29 alleles.

POPULATION GENETICS

Population genetics is the study of the distribution of and change in allele frequencies under the influence of the four evolutionary forces: natural selection, genetic drift, mutation, and migration. A population is a collection of people or organisms of a particular species living in a geographic area. Historically, humans have tended to consider race as a defining characteristic of populations, but the human genome project has shown that there is greater genetic variability within races than between them. It is perhaps better to consider ethnicity as a measure defining a population.

BOX 12.4   ETHNICITY

Ethnicity is a property of a culture or subculture whose members are readily distinguishable based on traits originating from a common source (e.g., racial, national, linguistic, etc.). Members of an ethnic group are often presumed to be culturally or genetically similar; this is not necessarily true.

Population genetics is important in forensic DNA. Users of test results, whether they be investigators seeking intelligence information, courts weighing evidence, or families dealing with a questioned parentage situation, all want to know how common a DNA profile is.

The number of possible genotypes from a heterozygous locus can be calculated using the formula $k(k + 1)/2$, where k is the number of alleles at a particular locus. The parameter k also represents the expected number of homozygous genotypes, and $k[(k − 1)/2]$ represents the expected number of heterozygous genotypes. Table 12.1 shows how the number of genotypes increases as we go from 2 alleles (e.g., serum haptoglobin as shown in Chapter 11, Figure 11.3) to 4 alleles (e.g., PGM by isoelectric focusing as shown in Chapter 11, Figure 11.2) to the 29 for D1S80.

Table 12.1	Allele Number, Genotypes, and Heterozygosity		
Number of Alleles	Number of Genotypes	Number of Homozygotes	Number of Heterozygotes
2	3	2	1
4	10	4	6
29	435	29	406

However, the number of alleles at a locus is not the only population genetics factor to be considered in its forensic application. The enzyme system ADA shown in Chapter 11, Figure 11.11, is not a very useful one for forensic applications because the ADA-2 variant is found in less than 10% of the population, with more than 90% being type ADA-1. The value of a typing system depends on its ability to distinguish the blood types of random, unrelated individuals.

BOX 12.5   DISCRIMINATING POWER

The ability of a blood grouping system to distinguish between individuals depends on the number of alleles in the system and their individual frequency of occurrence in the population. It can be calculated as the discriminating power (DP) of the system thus: Consider a hypothetical grouping system that has 4 alleles (a, b, c, and d) occurring in 40, 30, 20, and 10% of the population, respectively. The chance that 2 unconnected samples are both "a" is 0.4^2, the chance they are both "b" is 0.3^2, and so on. Therefore the chance that they are both the same type in the hypothetical system is the sum of the chances for each individual allele, or $0.4^2 + 0.3^2 + 0.2^2 + 0.1^2$, or 0.31. The DP of the system is $1 − 0.31$, or 0.69. DNA profiles have DP values greater than 0.99.

Statistical Interpretation

When forensic biologists calculate how common a DNA profile is, they apply some basic statistical rules to information on allele frequencies obtained by sampling populations.

THE HARDY–WEINBERG PRINCIPLE

The first rule is the **Hardy–Weinberg principle**, named after Godfrey Hardy and Wilhelm Weinberg, who first elucidated it. The rule is important because natural selection, genetic drift, mutation, inbreeding, and migration can alter the frequency of alleles in a population. We need to know that the allele frequency data used in calculations are reliable, and that requires that the population is stable. A population that is stable in regard to allele frequencies is said to be in *Hardy–Weinberg equilibrium* (HWE) and can be described mathematically. For example, in a population in HWE for a gene with two alleles, p and q,

$$p^2 + 2\,pq + q^2 = 1$$

The actual frequency of the alleles in the population can be measured by counting, the expected frequencies measured from the equation, and the observed compared with the expected using the Chi square statistical test. If there are no statistical differences between observed and expected, the population is in HWE and the allele frequencies are stable.

Case Study

Familial Searching

A truck being driven on a freeway in the south of England was the subject of vandalism. Two youths threw bricks onto the vehicle from an overpass pedestrian bridge. One smashed through the windscreen and hit the driver on the chest, causing heart failure.

Scientific examination of the first brick provided a DNA profile that was run against the national DNA database, but no match was found.

Analysis of the ethnic markers of the profile indicated the perpetrator was a white male, and details of the crime suggested he was under the age of 35. Believing the killer lived locally, Surrey police carried out an intelligence-led DNA screen, involving 350 people from the surrounding area who volunteered to give samples, but again no match was found.

It was then decided to use familial searching in the hope of pinpointing a suspect by searching the database for any individuals who most closely matched the unknown profile. Other parameters were added by limiting the search to white males, aged under 35, living in the region.

This produced a list of 25 names. The profile on the top of the list matched the profile from the crime scene in 16 out of 20 areas, a very strong match suggesting the person indicated by the database search was a close relative of the killer.

This information led Surrey police directly to Craig Harman. He gave a DNA sample that, when processed, gave a profile that matched the one from the crime scene.

THE PRODUCT RULE

The **product rule** is used to calculate the frequency of a DNA profile that is made up of data from more than one locus. The rule states that if the loci are independent of each other, that is, the alleles at locus 1 are not influenced by the alleles at locus 2, then the frequency data can be combined by multiplying the observed genotype frequencies.

THE COINCIDENCE APPROACH

The product rule can be applied to a DNA profile made up from any number of loci to give the frequency of the combined genotype. The next step is to deal with questions centered around interpretation of the genotype frequency. One way to do this is to use the **coincidence approach**, also referred to as the **random match probability**. Let us assume that a DNA profile is obtained from a bloodstain found on the clothing of the suspect, that the victim has the same combination of alleles, but that the suspect does not. The question posed is what are the chances that the bloodstain came from someone else who has the same combination of alleles by chance. This is the same as saying what is the probability that two profiles selected at random are the same, which is the square of the probability of occurrence of the allele combination. Table 12.2 illustrates the approach using the simple illustration of a three-locus profile.

Table 12.2	Calculation of Combined Genotype Frequency and Random Match Probability for a Three-Locus DNA Profile	
Locus	**Genotype**	**Frequency**
D3S1358	15 (homozygote)	0.0246
vWA	16, 17	0.0529
FGA	19, 23	0.0089

The combined genotype (D3S1358 15; vWA 16, 17; FGA 19, 23) is 0.0246 × 0.0529 × 0.0089 = 0.000011542 or 1 in 86,956 unrelated people. Therefore, the random match probability is $(0.000011542)^2 = 1.3225 \times 10$, or 1 in 7,561,345,936.

THE BAYESIAN APPROACH

The **Bayesian approach** is based on a probability theorem developed by Thomas Bayes whereby the probability of an event in defined circumstances is compared to that if the circumstances did not occur. The probability ratio is called the *likelihood ratio* (LR). In the case of interpretation of DNA evidence, the circumstances compared are the probability of the evidence given that the profile is from the nominated person (the suspect) to that if the profile is not from the suspect. For a simple single bloodstain, this turns out to be the same as the random match probability. The LR approach is more powerful when there are mixed samples to be interpreted, as in the case of a rape with DNA from the victim and more than one assailant.

Note that all of the statistical approaches described as follows are for unrelated persons. Where there is any degree of kinship, for example, due to inbreeding, or when there are possible suspects from within the same family, the statistical analyses are different. However, kinship is being used with DNA database searches to identify suspects.

Innocence or Guilt?

The techniques described previously, along with many others, are applied when the DNA alleles identified in the crime scene sample are the same as those in the blood of the suspect. If they are, then the statistical analysis is used to explore the possibility that the agreement has arisen by chance. Some early DNA cases were tarnished by evidence being presented in a way that suggested that the population data equated to the chance that the accused was guilty. This misleading presentation of evidence became known as the *prosecutor's fallacy.* For example, a scientist might testify that "The chances of finding the matching profiles if this semen (in the crime stain) had originated from a man in the general population other than and unrelated to the defendant is 1 in 5 million." The prosecutor might present this to the jury as "It is 5 million to 1 against that a man other than the defendant left the semen." The first is a valid scientific statement about the chance of finding a random match to the observed alleles. The second is a misleading statement that links the rarity of the profile to the probability that the accused did indeed commit the crime.

One of the most powerful and clear-cut uses of DNA in criminal proceedings is in postconviction testing. For example, the Innocence Project has a data bank of more than 100 cases where convictions based on flawed evidence, poor representation of the defendant, or unfortunate coincidences have been overturned by DNA testing. The success of these cases reflects the fundamental scientific principle of falsification. Falsification, generally attributed to Karl Popper, holds that testing a scientific hypothesis is based on experiments based to disprove it. Results that are concordant with the hypothesis might arise because it is true, or the tests are not capable of finding differences that do exist, or the agreement may have arisen by chance. However, results that find something forbidden by the hypothesis disprove it.

CODIS

Introduction

In 1990, the FBI created the **Combined DNA Index System (CODIS)** program to allow federal, state, and local laboratories to exchange and compare DNA profiles electronically. The CODIS software powers a three-level database system at local, state, and national levels. The national database (NDIS, or National DNA Index System) contains more than 4.5 million profiles.

Successful operation of a database in regard to data entry and interrogation requires standardization of operation. The original DNA databases used RFLP markers, but they now use STRs.

The STR Core Loci

There are 13 core STR loci in the CODIS system. They were selected on the basis of published data that established their suitability for database use. The names reflect the varied historical development: Some are named because of a relationship with a gene; others are named using an agreed convention. For example, vWA is named because it is located by the gene that codes for von Willebrand's factor, a protein involved in the clotting system, and HUMTH01 (or TH01) is associated with the gene for human tyrosine hydroxylase. The naming convention that applies to those whose names begin D is that D indicates a DNA sequence, the following number is the chromosome number on which the sequence is located, S indicates it is a unique DNA segment, and the final numbers are the sequence of identification. Thus, D21S11 is a unique DNA sequence, the 11th to be identified on chromosome 21.

The 13 STR loci selected for use in the Combined DNA Index System are CSF1PO, FGA, TH01, TPOX, vWA, D3S1358, D5S818, D7S820, D8S1179, D13S317, D16S539, D18S51, and D21S11.

OTHER DNA

Mitochondrial

Mitochondria are the site of cellular respiration and capture energy generated by the breakdown of food during the oxidation of simple organic compounds. There can be several hundred mitochondria in a cell, depending on the tissue. They contain their own DNA, which is quite different from that in the nucleus. The DNA inside the mitochondrion is circular in structure and double-stranded.

The mitochondrial genome is maternally inherited; progeny of both males and females inherit the mtDNA from their mother and only the daughter passes on the mtDNA to the next generation.

The structure of the mtDNA molecule is shown in Figure 12.12. The diagram shows the two hypervariable regions, HV1 and HV2, which display variation in their nucleotide sequence and can be used as genetic markers. **Mitochondrial DNA** has a much lower discriminating power compared to the multiplex of the 13 core STR loci because of the manner in which it is inherited. However, the multiple copies of the mt genome mean that it can be easier to analyze in some tissues such as hair. The maternal inheritance makes it easier to obtain reference samples, for example, for use in mass disaster victim identification.

Y Chromosome DNA

As described previously (see section titled "Genetics"), the X and Y chromosomes are responsible for sex determination. This is the only pair in

FIGURE 12.12
Diagram of the mtDNA molecule. The areas at the top of the circular structure marked "Control region or d-loop" contains two sub-regions, "HV1" and "HV2," that display variability in nucleotide sequence and are the target of forensic analyses. From http://en.wikipedia.org/wiki/Image:Mitochondrial_DNA_en.svg

283

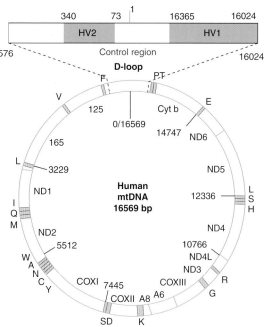

Case Study

William Gregory and the Innocence Project

Two women were attacked in an apartment complex. Both women identified William Gregory as the assailant through a show-up procedure. Gregory lived in the same apartment complex. Forensic evidence consisted of hairs found in the stocking cap worn and left behind by the assailant. The hairs were of Negroid origin, and the victim claimed to not have had any African American visitors in her apartment. Gregory was accused and convicted of rape and burglary of the first victim and of the attempted rape of the second victim. He was sentenced to consecutive sentences of 70 years in prison.

Gregory contacted the Innocence Project after his appeals failed, asserting his innocence. The Project proceeded to locate, preserve, and secure the release of the hair evidence. The hairs were tested using mitochondrial DNA testing, and they excluded Gregory as the source.

When Gregory was released in 2000, he became the first person to be exonerated by mitochondrial testing alone and the first inmate to be exonerated based on DNA testing in Kentucky. He had served 7 years of his sentence.

the nuclear genome where there is an observable physical difference in the two chromosomes. The Y, or male, chromosome, is the result of a massive mutation in which a large part of the X chromosome was lost. Part of the DNA in the resultant chromosome pairs and recombines with X chromosome DNA during meiosis, but part does not. DNA in the nonrecombining part is passed on unchanged from father to son.

In addition to the genes, more than 300 noncoding STR loci have been identified on the **Y chromosome DNA**, not all of them male specific. Somewhere around 16 have been studied and validated for use in forensic casework.

Y-chromosomal DNA is valuable for the specific identification of male markers even in the presence of a considerable excess of female DNA, for identification of semen donors in mixtures, and for disaster victim identification.

SUMMARY

Crick and Watson published the structure of deoxyribonucleic acid (DNA), the molecule that carries an organism's genetic blueprint, in 1953.

The use of DNA in forensic science began in the early 1980s. The case of Colin Pitchfork was the first criminal trial where the perpetrator was identified through DNA profiling. It was the first where there was a mass population screen to narrow the field of possible suspects and the first where DNA was used to exonerate an innocent suspect.

Dr. Ray White, a geneticist, suggested that individualized nongene regions of DNA could be used in parentage testing. Dr. Jeffreys went further and showed how the variability could be used to type blood and body fluids in criminal cases.

The DNA molecule is a double helix, each strand being composed of four bases, or nucleotides: cytosine (C), guanine (G), thymine (T), and adenine (A).

The parts of the DNA molecule discovered by White and developed by Jeffreys for typing body fluids and their stains consist of end-to-end repeats of sequences of bases. These systems are sometimes called variable number tandem repeats (VNTR). The regions in the chromosome where they are located are called minisatellites.

The number of end-to-end repeats of the core units varies between individuals.

Restriction fragment length polymorphism (RFLP) analysis, the earliest form of DNA typing, depended on incubating the DNA extracted from the body fluid with a restriction enzyme to cut it into hundreds of shorter lengths, separating them by size, and identifying the target sequence by adding a probe. This technique is no longer used.

Restriction enzymes, or restriction endonucleases, cut double-stranded DNA into fragments. Because the target sequences are short (4–12 bases), incubating DNA with a restriction enzyme will therefore yield a digest with hundreds of shorter DNA fragments.

The multiple banding results from multilocus probe or repeated single-locus probe development led to the terms DNA fingerprinting and DNA profile being used to describe the results of DNA identity testing.

The polymerase chain reaction (PCR) mimics the way in which the body makes DNA and allows small target regions of DNA to be copied or replicated up to a million-fold. The product is usually referred to as an amplicon.

Short tandem repeat (STR) sequences are VNTR-like regions in the DNA molecule in which the repeated core unit is two to five base pair repeats long (sometimes referred to as a microsatellite). The process is aided by multiplexing, in which eight or more loci are amplified at the same time.

DNA can be purified and removed from blood or body fluid stains, including vaginal swabs, by organic or inorganic extraction.

Quantitative PCR, or qPCR, is the most accurate, precise, and efficient method currently available to quantify DNA. The cycle number at which the product exceeds the background "noise" of the process is directly proportional to the quantity of DNA in the reaction.

The first step in the development of a PCR method is the design of suitable primers. A PCR primer consists of two oligonucleotides of around 18 to 30 bases long that hybridize to complementary strands of the DNA template, and thus identify the region to be copied.

Primer extension time and temperature depend upon the length and concentration of the target sequence and temperature. Denaturation time and temperature affect amplification at several points. The optimum number of cycles depends mainly on the starting concentration of the target DNA when other parameters are optimized.

Genes are the functional units in chromosomes that contain the nucleotide code for synthesis of specific proteins. Genes are found at specific sites (locus) on chromosomes. Normal human tissue cells have 23 pairs of chromosomes (diploid cells). Twenty-two of the pairs are identical in shape and are called *autosomes*. The chromosomes that carry the genes that determine sex are not identical, with the Y, or male, chromosome being smaller than the X, or female, chromosome. Sperm and egg cells differ in normal tissues in that their chromosomes are single (haploid cells), not paired.

The gene at any locus may have two or more variants. The variants are called *alleles.*

The mitochondrial genome is maternally inherited; progeny of both males and females inherit the mtDNA from their mother, and only the daughter passes on the mtDNA to the next generation.

For an allele, phenotypes may be homozygous—the same—or heterozygous—different. Where only one of the two alleles in a heterozygote is seen in the phenotype, it is said to be a dominant allele, and the other is said to be recessive.

The Hardy–Weinberg principle states that a population stable in regard to allele frequencies is at equilibrium (HWE) and can be described mathematically.

The product rule is used to calculate the frequency of a DNA profile that is made up of data from more than one locus. The rule states that if the loci are independent of each other, that is, the alleles at locus 1 are not influenced by the alleles at locus 2, then the frequency data can be combined by multiplying the observed genotype frequencies.

The coincidence approach—or random match probability—looks at the probability that a bloodstain came from someone else who has the same combination of alleles by chance.

The Bayesian approach is based on a probability theorem whereby the probability of an event in defined circumstances is compared to that as if the circumstances did not occur. The circumstances compared are the probability of the evidence given that the profile is from the nominated person (the suspect) to that if the profile is not from the suspect.

The Combined DNA Index System (CODIS) program allows federal, state, and local laboratories to exchange and compare DNA profiles electronically. There are 13 core STR loci in the CODIS system selected on the basis of published data that established their suitability for database use.

DNA in the nonrecombining part of the Y (male) chromosome is passed on unchanged from father to son. Y-chromosomal DNA is valuable for the specific identification of male markers even in the presence of a considerable excess of female DNA.

PROBLEMS

1. Give the word or phrase for the following definitions:
   a. the product of polymerase chain reactions
   b. testing to identify DNA patterns that can be used to determine parentage
   c. the functional units in chromosomes
   d. physical position on a chromosome
   e. blond
   f. maternally inherited DNA
   g. repeating units in a DNA sequence
   h. variations in genes that form the basis for DNA testing
2. What is the difference between homozygous and heterozygous? How is that important?
3. What is a phenotype and how is it important?
4. What is DNA? What is mitochondrial DNA? What is Y chromosome DNA?
5. Describe each of the following techniques:
   a. Gel electrophoresis
   b. Polymerase chain reaction (PCR)
   c. Restriction fragment length polymorphism (RFLP)
6. What is the Combined DNA Index System (CODIS)? Who maintains it? How is it used?
7. What are the ethical concerns for using DNA profiling?
8. What is the product rule?
9. What is the plateau effect?
10. What is the coincidence approach?

287

GLOSSARY

Alleles variations in genes, which form the basis for DNA testing.

Amplicon the product of polymerase chain reactions.

Bayesian approach a statistical approach that assesses the probability of a hypothesis being correct (for example, whether an association is valid) by incorporating the prior probability of the hypothesis and the experimental data supporting the hypothesis.

Blot an experimental technique designed to identify and quantitate DNA by hybridizing to an inert support medium.

Chromosomes structures in the nucleus that contain the genes; normal human tissue cells have 23 pairs of chromosomes (diploid cells). Twenty-two of the pairs are identical in shape and are called *autosomes*. The chromosomes that carry the genes that determine sex are not identical: the Y, or male, chromosome being smaller than the X, or female, chromosome.

Coincidence approach (random match probability) the probability that biological evidence came from someone else who has the same combination of alleles by coincidence.

Combined DNA Index System (CODIS) a computer search engine that allows federal, state, and local laboratories to exchange and compare DNA profiles electronically. There are 13 core STR loci in the CODIS system.

Deoxyribonucleic acid (DNA) the molecule that contains genetic material. The DNA molecule is a double helix composed of four bases, or nucleotides.

DNA profiling testing to identify DNA patterns that can be used to determine parentage or exclude/include individuals as possible sources of biological stains or evidence.

Gel electrophoresis separation and identification of molecules based on their movement through an electrically charged field.

Genes the functional units in chromosomes that contain the nucleotide code for synthesis of specific proteins.

Genotype the allele make up at a locus.

Hardy–Weinberg principle a way to describe allele frequencies mathematically.

Heterozygous having two different alleles at the same locus on homologous chromosomes.

Homozygous having two of the same alleles at the same locus on homologous chromosomes.

Locus physical position on a chromosome.

Mitochondrial DNA maternally inherited DNA.

Phenotype the observable expression of a genotype.

Plateau effect when too many cycles can increase the amount and complexity of nonspecific background products in PCR.

Polymerase chain reaction (PCR) a technique used in DNA profiling allowing small target regions of DNA to be replicated many times, producing an amplicon.

Product rule the product rule is used to calculate the frequency of a DNA profile that is made up of data from more than one locus. The rule states that if the loci are independent of each other, that is, the alleles at locus 1 are not influenced by the alleles at locus 2, then the frequency data can be combined by multiplying the observed genotype frequencies.

Restriction fragment length polymorphism (RFLP) a technique previously used in DNA profiling.

Restriction enzymes a protein isolated from bacteria that recognizes a specific sequence of DNA and cuts the strand at those sites.

Short tandem repeat (STR) sequences regions of the DNA molecule in which the repeated core unit is two to five base pair repeats long, sometimes referred to as a *microsatellite.*

Variable number tandem repeats (VNTR) repeating units in a DNA sequence.

Y chromosome DNA DNA that is paternally inherited; it is valuable for the specific identification of male markers even in the presence of a considerable excess of female DNA.

While bringing someone who knows the victim to view the body is one type of identification, sometimes a body cannot be identified visually. In those cases, clues to a victim's identity can be found among their personal effects.

WALLETS, PURSES, AND BACKPACKS

Wallets, purses, and backpacks can provide a great deal of information about a person. Most people carry at least one form of identification. Many carry credit cards and membership cards. There may be photographs, personally meaningful papers, or even a collection of slips from old fortune cookies. The presence or absence of such items can give clues regarding not just identity but also ownership of the items.

POCKET LITTER

While it does not sound exciting, pocket litter can tell the story of the person from whom it was collected. Receipts and other items with time stamps can be used to create a time line. A specific item—such as a letter or photograph found in a wallet— might help identify a person. In other cases, wallet contents taken together might give a clue to victimology: Book club cards and gym membership identifications could be the clue to where a crime took place or where a victim was selected.

Finding a wallet or purse with a victim can provide presumptive information regarding the identity of a person — a driver's license or credit card. However, a confirmation must still be made. Consider: Just because a purse or wallet is found with a person does not mean it belongs to that person.

What's in your wallet? Most people carry a variety of expired identifications, memberships, and even credit cards.

291

THE MAN WHO NEVER WAS

World War II's most famous and successful intelligence hoax involved the British creation of an identity for a body that was believable enough to persuade the Germans to move troops from the south of Sicily, where the Allied forces successfully invaded in 1943. Lieutenant Commander Ewen Montagu executed the elaborate deception—code-named Operation Mincemeat—and wrote the book *The Man Who Never Was*.

In the plan, the corpse of "Major William Martin," purportedly a Royal Marine courier bearing documents regarding a fictitious Allied assault on Sardinia and Greece, washed up on a Spanish beach. In addition to the intelligence fraud, a wallet with the picture of a fake girlfriend, a crucifix, and a St. Christopher medallion were placed on the body with the hope it would be given a Christian burial in Spain.

The truth behind the corpse's identity is still unknown. In 1997, the Public Record Office in London said the body was that of Glyndwr Michael, a Welsh vagrant who died of pneumonia after attempting suicide by drinking rat poison. A recent documentary suggests the body was that of Tom Martin, a sailor killed when the aircraft carrier Dasher exploded off the Scottish coast.

JEWELRY

Unique and registered jewelry can sometimes be identified. It can also be used to identify a person. Rings, bracelets, medallions, and watches may bear inscriptions that can provide clues to their owners. Lockets and keepsake jewelry can contain pictures or small slips of paper.

CLOTHING AND SHOES

While newly purchased ready-to-wear clothing and shoes of the same brand, model, size, and color may appear alike at first, unique wear patterns emerge after an item is worn. The insoles of some shoes can be particularly good at developing a wear pattern—some are designed to "adapt" to your feet even if the item has been worn only once.

IMPLANTS

Many implants and medical devices have serial numbers that can be traced to the person who received them. Heart valves, knee joints, and breast implants can all be used to help identify a body. Today there is no need for repair or replacement to be the only reason to have an implant. A range of commercially available dental implants exists for the purpose of identifying a person.

FORENSIC ODONTOLOGY

Forensic odontology is forensic dentistry. Teeth can be used in a variety of ways. If a person's dental records are available, the dental work can be matched to a victim. In mass fatalities, teeth may provide DNA for identification. Teeth can also be used to approximate the age of a child. Of course, teeth may also be matched to bite marks.

TATTOOS AND BODY MODIFICATION

Tattoos and body modification are becoming more mainstream. Such body art can be used to help identify a person by the design, type of ink, or even style of the tattoo artist. *Scratch art tattoos*—those not administered professionally—may indicate belonging to a gang or time spent in prison. Even if a tattoo has been partially removed or the victim is burned, that tattoo may be raised from the skin by removing the outer layers of the skin to reveal detail underneath.

DNA FROM PERSONAL EFFECTS

DNA may be sampled from a variety of personal effects. Saliva and DNA can be lifted from drinking glasses or cigarette butts. DNA also may be obtained from hairs left in brushes or—sometimes—from material left on toothbrushes.

If used for identification, it is best that an item was used by only one person. However, advances in mitochondrial DNA and Y chromosome DNA can show relationships even if identification is not possible.

Data storage devices that may be examined for data recovery. Clockwise from top left: External 60 GB data store; Opened internal hard drive; Server rack; Floppy disk; 60 GB data store original by author; other images from everystockphoto.com

Appendix B
Digital Evidence

Crime in the Cornfields

They say there is not much happening around Wichita, Kansas, but the citizens living in the county of Sedgwick didn't see it that way between 1974 and 1991. The area was the locus of a serial killer who became known as the BTK strangler, named for his modus operandi of *blind, torture, kill*. In all, he was responsible for 10 deaths.

A feature of the BTK strangler was the letters that he would write to the police and news outlets, giving details of each killing. The police established a dialog hoping that they could lull the killer into giving away a lead. Sure enough, in 2004 he asked the police if they could trace information

from floppy disks. The police responded that this was not possible—knowing all the time that it was. The strangler then sent them a message on a floppy disk with a Microsoft Word document on it.

Analysis showed that the document had been created by someone called Dennis, with associations to the Lutheran Church. An Internet search for "Dennis + Lutheran Church + Wichita" turned up Dennis Radar.

Careful investigation built up a solid case, and Radar was arrested. He entered a guilty plea at trial and received 10 consecutive life sentences, one for each victim.

295

INTRODUCTION

Digital evidence is information stored or transmitted in binary format that is of potential probative value. Like many fields of forensic examination, the scope of digital evidence examination is very broad. Investigations may cover fraud, e-commerce transactions, Internet communications, identity theft, package tracking, online banking, and Internet searches.

Electronic devices may seem durable, but their data are not. Digital evidence is often quite fragile: It can be damaged, altered, or destroyed if handled improperly. As a consequence, unlike other types of investigation, the original evidence is preserved and the analysis carried out on a copy.

Data in hexadecimal form is just another representation of the data.

CENTRAL QUESTIONS

What can be answered:

- Can the file be accessed?
- Can the file be recovered?

What we cannot answer:

- How can data be recovered from overwritten data storage locations?
- Who performed a specific action at a computer?

What we are learning or researching:

- Can a program automatically reconstruct file fragment data into intelligible files for review?

ANATOMY OF A COMPUTER

Most people are familiar with computers at some level. *Hardware* is the physical equipment needed to run a computer, including the central processing unit, keyboard, monitor, and any storage devices. *Firmware* is a set of instructions or data programmed directly into the circuits of a machine for the purpose of controlling a hard drive or other electronic component. Of course, *software* consists of programs. To better understand the process of digital evidence analysis, it is important to have a basic understanding of computer architecture.

Microprocessor–Central Processing Unit (CPU)

The microprocessor of a personal computer consists of a single integrated circuit, an array of transistors, resistors, and other microelectronic components embedded on a silicon wafer. Each dime-sized piece of silicon may contain several million transistors. The type of CPU in a computer determines how fast it can execute instructions, often measured in floating point operations per second (*flops*). Most computers today can execute millions of instructions per second. (See Figure B.1.)

Hard Disk (HD)

While the microprocessor is excellent for performing calculations, it has almost no capacity for storing information. This job is performed by the hard disk. While not much larger than a floppy disk, a hard disk contains more information and spins faster. This makes it an important component for the forensic examiner. (See Figure B.1.)

FIGURE B.1
Part of a computer circuit board with a processor chip. From Stockxpert.com

Floppy Disk

A floppy disk contains less information than a hard disk. Also unlike the hard disk, the floppy disk can be removed from the computer. The term *floppy* refers to the disk of plastic on which information is magnetically recorded.

Compact Disc (CD)

As a storage media, the popular CD is already becoming obsolete. A compact disc may contain the information of as many as 450 floppy disks.(See Figure B.2.)

Digital Video Disc (DVD)

The larger capacity of DVDs makes them the new trend in media storage; a DVD can hold a minimum of 4.7 gigabytes of data.

Flash Drives

There are several types of external data storage that depend on data being stored on a printed circuit rather than written to the track of a disk. These range from small units about the size of your thumb (and so sometimes called *thumb drives*) with a capacity of 250 MB to a few GB. More recent variants offer extensive external data storage in compact units that interface with the host computer through a USB or FireWire port. (See Figure B.3).

Hard Drive

The hard drive stores and retrieves digital data on a magnetic surface. A *write head*, a special type of antenna, "writes" information to the hard disk by transmitting an electromagnetic flux that changes the polarization of the magnetic media. These changes can be "read" by a *read head* as the changes in the magnetic field are detected by a coil as it passes by. Often these functions are combined into a read–write head. The read–write head floats on a cushion of air nearly in contact but just above the surface of the platter. Because the hard drive is not airtight but requires a narrow range of air pressures in which to operate, it is equipped with a permeable filter that prevents dirt, dust, and other objects from getting between the head and the disk. If the head crashes into the disk, it almost always causes a data loss.

The hard disk is divided into subunits, creating a logical structure for the file operating system to access. The subunits, called *partitions,* are areas of hard disk that can have an independent file system. A *primary partition* serves as a container for itself, while an *extended partition* may contain more than one logical partition. Figure B.4 shows how physical sectors on a hard drive are logically grouped into clusters.

The hard drive is accessed by a bus (*bus bar*), an electrical conductor that serves as a common connection point between two or more electrical circuits. Several types exist.

SMALL COMPUTER SYSTEM INTERFACE (SCSI)

SCSI (pronounced "scuzzy") is a standard interface and command set for the transfer of data between devices on a computer bus. It can be used to connect almost any type of device. (See Figure B.5.)

FIGURE B.2
An optical disk in the loading tray of a PC optical disk drive. CDs and DVDs look the same even though their storage capacity differs. Original image by author.

297

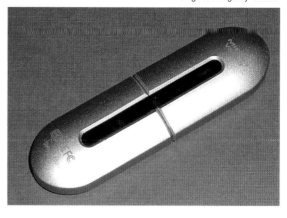

FIGURE B.3
A 250 MB thumb drive. Also known as jump drives, these operate through USB ports and are convenient for data storage and transfer. Original image by author.

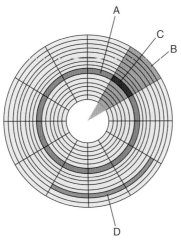

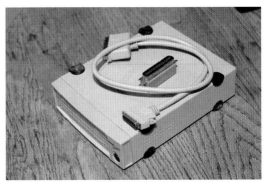

FIGURE B.5
External CD drive with SCSI connector and terminator. Storage devices come in may shapes and sizes. A feature that all external drives share is that they have to have some means of interfacing with the computer in order to transfer data back and forth. Here we have an external CD drive that uses a widely accepted format for the interface, namely the Small Computer System Interface, or SCSI. From http://www.everystockphoto.com/photo.php?imageId=2945111. License http://creativecommons.org/licenses/by/2.5/

FIGURE B.4
Structure of a hard drive disk. The red-colored circle "A" is a track; "B" is a geometric sector; "C" is a track sector; and "D" is a cluster. From http://en.wikipedia.org/wiki/Image:Disk-structure2.svg

FIGURE B.6
FireWire is another interface system, capable of very rapid data transfer. This image shows firewire and USB ports on a laptop computer. From everystockphoto.

FIREWIRE

Developed by Apple Computer, this interface is similar to the IEEE standard 1394. It is commonly used with data storage devices and popular in digital cameras and audio systems. FireWire allows for peer-to-peer communication between devices without having to access the system memory or the CPU. It is faster than a universal serial bus (USB), can supply power (up to 45 watts), and allows for hot swapping. (See Figure B.6.)

UNIVERSAL SERIAL BUS (USB)

The USB system is an asymmetric design in which a hub is used to link multiple devices to a host controller. When a device is added to the hub, the controller loads the driver necessary to operate it. USB is employed in gaming devices and to connect peripherals to computers; however, monitors do not use USB because they require a higher rate of data transfer. As of January 2005, the USB specification is version 2.0.

WRITING TO CDs AND DVDs

A CD is a plastic plate covered with dye, a layer of aluminum, and, finally, the label. As the CD spins, a low-power laser is projected at it. The laser that "reads" the CD looks for light to be reflected from the aluminum surface into an optical sensor. If the light reflects back to the sensor, the reflected light is detected as a 1. If the light is reflected away from the sensor, no light is detected and the machine records a 0. The sensor works with the motor to find the speed at which the laser should fire. To write on a CD requires a slightly higher power laser than that used for a reading laser. The frequency of the laser is such that, when the light shines on the dye, the dye is turned opaque.

A CD-RW uses slightly different technology. A phase shift compound is sandwiched between layers of dielectric materials. The laser writes to the CD-RW by heating that material to its melting point, at which it turns opaque (about 600°C). The material remains opaque as it cools. To make the material translucent again, the material is heated but to a lower temperature (perhaps 200°C). This time, as it cools, it will again allow the beam to reach the surface of the aluminum below. Unlike a hard drive, where space can be made available by labeling it as *free,* a CD-RW must be erased before it can be overwritten.

TYPES OF EVIDENCE

Digital evidence is processed in three categories: computer forensic, digital audio, and digital video examinations.

Computer Forensics

Evidence in computer forensics may take on a wide variety of forms, including computers, hard drives, and storage media. Today storage media can be presented as diskettes, tapes, compact discs (CDs), digital video discs (DVDs), or Zip discs. With the boom in consumer electronics, forensic examiners may also be called upon to investigate cell phones, two-way pagers, cameras, global positioning satellite (GPS) devices, fax machines, thumb drives, and computer gaming equipment. As new technologies emerge, the field must grow to encompass them.

Digital Audio

Digital audio files are most often found on tapes, CDs, DVDs, or drives.

Digital Video

Digital video files are often found on a variety of tape formats, CDs, DVDs, or drives.

Digital evidence has some things in common with questioned documents. Like evidence on paper, digital evidence may be altered or obliterated.

Erasure

Digital evidence that is "erased" is actually just placed in a folder on the computer, which marks it as "erased" by making the space available again. The data may not actually be overwritten for some time. However, the longer the data sit

---

Hot swapping is the ability to remove or replace components of a computer while it is operating. The capability allows users to add or remove peripheral devices such as a keyboard or printer while using the computer without damaging any of the components.

People confuse *hard disk* with *hard drive*. Within the hard drive, there may be multiple disks called *platters*, each with its own read–write head that operates similarly to a phonograph.

What is a *flop*? *Floating point operations per second* are a measure of how fast a computer works based on calculations it can perform per second. A *floating point* is a number representation consisting of a mantissa (M), an exponent (E), and a radix (R). The number represented is M multiplied by R raised to the power of E (M*R^E). For the decimal system, the radix is 10.

in an unallocated sector, the more likely they are to be overwritten or partially overwritten. If the data are partially overwritten, some of the original data may be recovered as a file fragment.

Overwriting

Overwriting is the digital equivalent of obliteration. Sometimes the original data may be able to be partially recovered. Unfortunately, like writing over a document with the same ink used to create it, this is usually a very difficult task.

Wiping the Drive

When done with professional software programs, overwriting can be used to "wipe a drive clean." One way to accomplish this is to write a pattern of data over and over until the disk is full and then declare all the space free.

COLLECTING AND PRESERVING DIGITAL EVIDENCE

While many people think of computers as permanent, the data stored on computers can be as fragile as a tire print in snow. Further, unlike other forms of examination, one of the most important techniques for examining digital evidence—to ensure the evidentiary data are not corrupted—is to work with a copy. The process of collecting and preserving digital evidence is sometimes called *acquisition*.

At the Scene

Once the scene has been properly secured, the investigator may look for evidence. The number and type of computers present should be documented as well as whether or not they are connected by a network. Any removable media must be cataloged, packaged in crush-proof containers, and properly labeled. The investigator must also look for any off-site storage areas or remote computing locations where evidence may be hidden.

For most computers, the best practice is not to shut down the machine but rather to pull the plug and take it to the laboratory. The exception to this type of procedure is business servers, which must be shut down according to their protocols. Hard disks should be parked and padded so that they are not damaged during transport.

The entire computer should be seized, not just a removable hard disk. The internal time–date stamp can provide valuable information.

Data that may be lost if the battery is removed from an electronic device is called *volatile memory*. Depending on the type of device, evidence may be handled differently. Small electronic devices and electronic storage media should be wrapped in bubble wrap or otherwise secured from static electric discharge. The investigator should also ensure that the antenna is off on items such as Blackberries and cellular phones so that the device does not communicate out.

The evidence should be labeled on the outside. All seized materials should be stored in a cool, dry place away from magnetic fields. Any magnet has the potential to cause damage. Moving the magnet around will cause more damage.

301

FIGURE B.7
Sources of digital evidence. Clockwise from top left: Laptop computer (Apple MacBook Pro); Smart phone (iPhone); PDA (HP ipaq). MacBook: http://commons.wikimedia.org/wiki/Image:Apple_MacBook_Pro_2.16GHz-2007-07-22.jpg iPhone: Original image by author; PDA: everystockphoto.

Preserving Digital Evidence

Before the evidence may be submitted for analysis, several additional steps must be taken.

- *Write-block:* To prevent any of the information on the original evidence from being changed, the media will be write-blocked by placing it on a special machine (examination computer) or by linking it through a device that will prevent anything from being written on the evidence.
- *Imaging (copying):* Imaging is the process of making a copy of the evidence. The image becomes a working copy master that is archived and copied for analysis.
- *Archiving:* The working copy is saved to stable media: data tape, hard disk, CD, or DVD. The purpose of the archive is so that the original evidence may be set aside. If the working copy is corrupted, a new working copy can be restored from the archive.

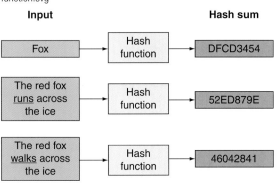

Operating a computer after seizure will overwrite some of the data and may change the date–time stamp information. In some cases, the investigator may also send a "preservation order" to the Internet service provider to obtain e-mail and other information about the account.

AUTHENTICATING DIGITAL EVIDENCE

To ensure that the original data are represented by the working copy, both are compared by an authentication process called *hashing*. The data are examined using a special program that takes in the complete, unique binary pattern of the evidence—trillions of bits!—and summarizes it into an output with a finite number of elements. This output is called the *hash*. The examiner must calculate the hash for the original data and for the copy. They should match. The bigger the hash, the greater the certainty that the original and the copy are the same when compared. If they do match, the copy is considered authenticated for additional work. (See Figure B.8.)

Several commercial programs are available:

- MD5: MD5 has a hash size of 128 bits. It is one of a number of message digest algorithms created by Massachusetts Institute of Technology's Ronald Rivest. As cryptographers exposed weaknesses in MD5, its use was replaced in part by SHA-1.
- SHA-1: Developed by the National Security Agency (NSA) and published by the National Institute of Standards (NIST), SHA (Secure Hash Algorithm) is a family of hash programs. SHA-1 takes longer to calculate than MD5 but has a higher level of accuracy.
- SHA-2: NIST published four variants of SHA, which are collectively called SHA-2. The programs are named after the bit length of their digests: SHA-224, SHA-256, SHA-384, and SHA-512.

Hashing is somewhat analogous to DNA analysis. The question is, how close is the match? An estimate of uncertainty is associated with the use of an algorithm.

ANALYZING DIGITAL EVIDENCE

Once the working copy is authenticated, a variety of techniques may be used to search the evidence. The presumptive test, often called *triage,* is to write-block the original evidence and browse–key word search it to see if it is of potential probative value. The confirmatory tests on the working copy include a detailed or multiple keyword search, browsing, metadata recovery and analysis, file fragment recovery and analysis, and looking at the time line (user logs, system logs).

Techniques that may be used to search the evidence after the working copy is authenticated include the following:

- Browsing: The examiner opens the files and looks at the content.
- Key word search: The examiner queries the drive with key words to identify documents with key words pertinent to the investigation. A running list of the words used will be documented. Because some criminals may use code words, the investigator may also look for numerical data.
- Metadata search: By examining the information about the data files, the *metadata,* investigators can see when the document was created, sent, or received. This may assist in the development of a time line for a crime or establish an alibi.
- Automatic log searches: These files, created by the computer programs as records of activity, show what people are doing on their accounts. For example, while DSL accounts are active all the time, files will be date–time stamped when moved or sent.
- Internal clock search: The setting of the computer's internal clock is also reported as it weights the value of the date–time stamp. The examiner will note the time and time zone to which the computer was set on the day the investigation was performed.

E-mail date–time stamps are set by the servers.

The digital evidence examiner cannot verify that a document was typed by a specific person on a certain day without a witness.

A *clean room* is an enclosure designed to control temperature, magnetic field, and especially dust.

Taken together, the analyses attempt to attribute ownership of the crime via software registration, e-mail accounts used, leads to credit cards, file privileges, user access, and profiles on the computer.

More specialized measures may need to be taken if there are hardware issues associated with digital evidence. Hard disks can be physically destroyed, but attempts can be made to secure whatever data are available. When a hard disk is crashed, the antenna may be sitting in contact with the silicon wafer. The controller card is take off the hard disk and replaced or adjusted until the disk can spin again. For burned disks, after swapping the controller card, the damaged evidence may be taken to a clean room for reconstruction. If a floppy disk has been cut up, the examiner will remove the jacket surrounding it and examine it under a microscope. The examiner will line up the tracks using a magnetic oxide solution, tape the pieces together, rejacket the media, and try to examine it again.

Legal Issues in Searching Electronic Media (Privacy, Search and Seizure)

Searching electronic media is not unlike searching a house. In order to conduct a search on the working copy, the forensic computer examiner needs a warrant for the working copy that sets the scope of the investigation. On a warrant looking for information about drugs, if information about child pornography were discovered, this evidence would require a new warrant. This can be very limiting in certain circumstances. In addition to state and local regulations, a complex set of laws governs electronic media. These include the Electronic Communications Privacy Act of 1986 (ECPA), the Cable Communications Policy Act (CCPA), and the USA Patriot Act of 2001.

Another important law governing digital evidence is the Digital Millennium Copyright Act (DMCA) of 1998. Congress passed this law as part of the copyright act in response to pressure from creative content providers such as the motion picture industry, recording industry, gaming industry, and software publishers. The law has provisions both for violating copyrights and for creating or using technology that will crack protection measures on copyrighted material.

FURTHER READING

Electronic Communications Privacy Act (ECPA). 18 USC 2510 et seq.; 18 USC 2701 et seq.; 18 USC 3121 et seq.

Forensic Examination of Digital Evidence: A Guide for Law Enforcement. Washington, D.C.: U.S. Department Of Justice, Office of Justice Programs, April 2004.

Privacy Protection Act (PPA). 42 USC 2000aa et seq.

Prosecuting Cases That Involve Computers: A Resource for State and Local Prosecutors (CD-ROM), National White Collar Crime Center, 2001.

Searching and Seizing Computers and Obtaining Electronic Evidence in Criminal Investigations. Washington, D.C.: U.S. Department of Justice, Computer Crime and Intellectual Property Section, July 2002.

USA Patriot Act of 2001, Public Law 107-56, amended statutes relevant to computer investigations. Statutes amended include 18 USC 1030; 18 USC 2510 et seq.; 18 USC 2701 et seq.; 18 USC 3121 et seq.; and 47 USC 551.

STEGANOGRAPHY

Steganography comes from the Greek meaning "covered writing." It is the art and science of concealing information. Note the difference between concealing and disguising a message: Writing may be concealed by using lemon juice as ink, while writing may be disguised in a picture. In the realm of digital evidence, this process becomes hiding data in other data. For example, child pornography may be hidden in other pictures, audio files, or written documents.

DISK OR DISC?

When is a *disk* a compact *disc*? The spelling *disk* is most often used and preferred for storage media associated with computers. On the other hand, *disc* is the preferred term for round, flat objects like the ubiquitous optical storage media used for audio, data, and digital video.

BOOBY TRAPS AND MALWARE

Sometimes the investigator must ascertain if the user is aware of a program on a computer. In other cases, booby traps and malware—such as worms and viruses— may be left behind on discs or hard drives to hinder the investigator. These programs may engage in selective wiping of data operating on start-up or shutting down of the computer. To avoid such damage, the examiner will make a copy of the data and attach it to a forensic analysis program. The examiner's machine will be the one running the operating system, so the offender's programs will not be executed.

There are several ways to look for malware. The easiest is to use commercial software to scan a duplicate of the evidence. Because an image file cannot be scanned, the investigator may resort to scanning the findings recovered from it. One way is to look for the digital signature of known viruses as compared to those in a database. Other methods are more heuristic. The examiner must look at the machine-level calls that were made. Write calls to the hard drive are suspect. Because viruses are now increasingly communications programs, the examiner may also look at the computer code of executable programs, opening of computer modem or network connections, or calls to certain ports.

CRASH

In computing, a crash occurs when an application or part of the operating system stops performing its function or stops communicating with other parts of the computer system. Programs that crash may simply stop operating and appear to "freeze." However, if the program is part of the operating system, the entire computer can be affected.

Crime scene reconstruction utilizes scientific methods, visualization techniques, and logic to put physical evidence into the context of the commission of a crime. Technicians try to ascertain what happened and how it happened. While only those present during the crime know the truth, after a crime scene reconstruction, a criminalist should be able to form a theory of the crime that demonstrates the following:

- That a crime occurred or evidence was generated in a manner consistent with the reconstruction
- That a crime likely occurred or evidence likely was generated in a manner consistent with the reconstruction
- That it is unlikely that a crime occurred or evidence was generated in a manner consistent with the reconstruction
- That a crime could not have occurred or evidence could not have been generated in a manner consistent with the reconstruction

TYPES OF RECONSTRUCTION

Reconstruction may be employed to recreate a specific incident such as a traffic accident. Often only a partial reconstruction can be made. For example, it might be easier to reconstruct a vehicular homicide than a barroom brawl because the elements controlled are well understood.

Location is where someone was within the scene. *Position* refers to the actual "attitude" of the body.

Other types of reconstructions examine the plausibility that evidence could be created by the theory of the crime. Could the weapon in question actually have fired under the circumstances? This is sometimes called *functional reconstruction*.

Pattern Evidence

Evidence like fingerprints or shoe impressions can place a person or vehicle at the crime scene. Fingerprints may help identify a victim or perpetrator. Tire impressions may indicate the position, speed, and direction of travel of a vehicle.

Firearms

Reconstruction of the scene of a shooting can provide details about the location and position of both the victim and the perpetrator. Analysts may also be able to determine the sequence and direction of shots, trajectory, and shooting distance. In some cases, the question of whether the wounds could have been self-inflicted can be answered.

Glass

As we learned in Chapter 6, "Physical Evidence," glass can reveal the direction of impact and the sequence of shots or blows.

Blood Spatter

Analysis of blood spatter can help identify the location and position of both the victim and the perpetrator. Blood drops may indicate the direction a victim (the source of the bleeding) or perpetrator (who may be carrying residual blood) moved. Blood spatter also may reveal whether a scene was staged. In some cases, castoff can provide clues to the type of weapon employed and the number of blows that were struck.

Reconstruction of Objects

Reassembly and analysis of objects that have been broken may tell an examiner how an object was shattered. This type of analysis is important in the crime scene analysis of bombing and aircraft that have either exploded or crashed.

PERFORMING RECONSTRUCTION

Reconstruction is best performed at the crime scene under the same conditions as the incident (time of day, weather, etc.). When this is impossible, modeling can be useful. A criminalist should draw on all the available information and evidence from the crime; original crime scene photographs, processing notes, and witness statements must be taken together to get as complete a picture as possible. The evidence can then be placed in the context of the crime for analysis.

Looking at the body of evidence and analysis, the criminalist must form an opinion about how the crime may have taken place — the *hypothesis*. To ensure that the hypothesis is valid, it must then be tested. Tests may be devised to see if it is possible to have created a type of evidence or whether it is reproducible. The criminalist should also be able to evaluate the evidence to see if it supports or contradicts witness statements.

A photograph may not tell the whole story. To reconstruct trajectory, a photograph that provided a location of a bullet hole might not provide any information about the angle of approach, directionality, or depth.

Today some crime scenes are reconstructed using scanning mechanisms interpreted with computer-assisted design (CAD). Range-finding devices can be used to scan a room and create a 3-D model of the crime scene.

Index

Notes: Page numbers followed by *f* refer to figures; page number followed by *t* refer to tables; and *b* refer to boxes.

321